Communications
in Computer and Information Science   342

Tai-hoon Kim   Sabah Mohammed
Carlos Ramos   Jemal Abawajy
Byeong-Ho Kang   Dominik Ślęzak (Eds.)

Computer Applications for Web, Human Computer Interaction, Signal and Image Processing, and Pattern Recognition

International Conferences, SIP, WSE, and ICHCI 2012
Held in Conjunction with GST 2012
Jeju Island, Korea, November 28 – December 2, 2012
Proceedings

 Springer

Volume Editors

Tai-hoon Kim
GVSA and University of Tasmania, Hobart, TAS, Australia
E-mail: taihoonn@hanmail.net

Sabah Mohammed
Lakehead University, Thunder Bay, ON, Canada
E-mail: sabah.mohammed@lakeheadu.ca

Carlos Ramos
GECAD and ISEP, Porto, Portugal
E-mail: csr@dei.isep.ipp.pt

Jemal Abawajy
Deakin University, Waurn Ponds, VIC, Australia
E-mail: jemal.abawajy@deakin.edu.au

Byeong-Ho Kang
University of Tasmania, Hobart, TAS, Australia
E-mail: byeong.kang@utas.edu.au

Dominik Ślęzak
University of Warsaw, Poland
and
Infobright Inc., Toronto, ON, Canada
E-mail: slezak@infobright.com

This work was supported by the Korean Federation of Science and Technology
Societies Grant funded by the Korean Government.

ISSN 1865-0929   e-ISSN 1865-0937
ISBN 978-3-642-35269-0   e-ISBN 978-3-642-35270-6
DOI 10.1007/978-3-642-35270-6
Springer Heidelberg Dordrecht London New York

Library of Congress Control Number: 2012952424

CR Subject Classification (1998): I.4, I.2, H.3-5, I.5, C.2, J.3

Typesetting: Camera-ready by author, data conversion by Scientific Publishing Services, Chennai, India
Printed on acid-free paper

Springer is part of Springer Science+Business Media (www.springer.com)

Foreword

Signal processing, image processing and pattern recognition as well as Web science and engineering and human computer interaction are areas that attract many academic and industry professionals. The goal of the SIP, WSE, and ICHCI conferences is to bring together researchers from academia and industry as well as practitioners to share ideas, problems and solutions relating to this multifaceted field.

We would like to express our gratitude to all of the authors of submitted papers and to all attendees for their contributions and participation.

We acknowledge the great effort of all the Chairs and the members of the Advisory Boards and Program Committees of the above-listed event. Special thanks go to SERSC (Science & Engineering Research Support soCiety) for supporting this conference.

We are grateful in particular to the speakers, who kindly accepted our invitation and, in this way, helped to meet the objectives of the conference: Jack Dongarra, Tao Gong, and Subramaniam Ganesan.

We wish to express our special thanks to Yvette Gelogo for helping to edit this volume.

November 2012

Chairs of SIP 2012
WSE 2012
and ICHCI 2012

Foreword

Preface

We would like to welcome you to the proceedings of the 2012 International Conference on Signal Processing, Image Processing and Pattern Recognition (SIP 2012), the 2012 International Conference on Web Science and Engineering (WSE 2012), and the 2012 International Conference on Human Computer Interaction, which were held during November 28–December 2, 2012, at Jeju Grand Hotel, Jeju, Korea.

SIP 2012, WSE 2012, and ICHCI 2012 provided a chance for academic and industry professionals to discuss recent progress in the related areas. We expect that the conferences and their publications will be a trigger for further related research and technology improvements in this important subject. We would like to acknowledge the great effort of all the Chairs and members of the Program Committee.

We would like to express our gratitude to all of the authors of submitted papers and to all attendees for their contributions and participation.

Once more, we would like to thank all the organizations and individuals who supported this event and helped in the success of SIP 2012, WSE 2012, and ICHCI 2012.

November 2012   Tai-hoon Kim on behalf of the Volume Editors

Organization

General Co-chairs

Sabah Mohammed   Lakehead University, Canada
Carlos Ramos   ISEP-IPP, Portugal
Dominik Slezak   Warsaw University & Infobright, Poland

Program Co-chairs

Haeng-kon Kim   Catholic University of Daegu, Korea
Jemal Abawajy   Deakin University, Australia
Byeong-Ho Kang   University of Tasmania, Australia
Tai-hoon Kim   GVSA and University of Tasmania, Australia

Editorial Committee

Abbad Muneer   Ama International University, Bahrain
Aboul Ella Hassanien   Cairo University, Egypt
Abrahao, Silvia   Polytechnic University of Valencia, Spain
Adamo-villani Nicoletta   Purdue University, USA
Aditya K. Ghose   University of Wollongong, Australia
Adrian Stoica   NASA JPL, USA
Alexander Schill   Dresden University of Technology, Germany
Anant Bhaskar Garg   University of Petroleum and Energy Studies, India
Andre Liem   Norwegian University of Science and Technology, Norway
Andrzej Dzielinski   Warsaw University of Technology, Poland
Andrzej Kasinski   Poznan University of Technology, Poznan, Poland
Andrzej M. Goscinski   Deakin University, Australia
Antonio Dourado   University of Coimbra, Portugal
Barbara Holder   Boeing, USA
Brian Hilburn   CHPR BV Consultant, The Netherlands
Caroline Fossati   Institut Fresnel, France
Chng Eng Siong   Nanyang Technological University, Singapore
Claude Godart   University of Nancy, Lorraine University, France
Coral Calero   University of Castilla-La Mancha, Spain
Debnath Bhattacharyya   Heritage Institute of Technology, India
Dimitris Iakovidis   University of Athens, Greece

Dou Shen   CityGrid Media, USA
Ernesto Exposito   LAAS/CNRS - Groupe Outils et Logiciels
                          pour la Communication, France
Ernesto Pimentel   University of Malaga, Spain
Filip Orsag   BUT, Faculty of Information Technology,
                          Czech Republic
Francesco Masulli   University of Pisa, Italy
Gerard Medioni   USC/IRIS, Los Angeles, USA
Gongzhu Hu   Central Michigan University, USA
Gregory Grefenstette   3DS Exalead, France
Gudela Grote   ETH, Switzerland
Haeng-kon Kim   Catholic University of Daegu, Korea
Han Hao   National Institute of Informatics, Japan
Hideo Kuroda   FPT University, Vietnam
Hong Kook Kim   Gwangju Institute of Science and Technology,
                          Korea
Hong Zhu   Oxford Brookes University, UK
Hsi-Ya Chang (Jerry)   National Center for High Performance
                          Computing, Taiwan
Janusz Kacprzyk   Systems Research Institute, Polish Academy
                          of Sciences, Poland
Javier Garcia-Villalba   Universidad Complutense of Madrid, Spain
Jin Wang   Nanjing University of Information Science and
                          Technology, China
Jocelyn Chanussot   INPG, Grenoble, France
Joonki Paik   Chung-Ang University, Korea
Joseph Ronsin   IETR, Rennes, France
Junzhong Gu   Institute of Computer Applications, ECNU,
                          China
Jurgen Ziegler   University of Duisburg-Essen, Germany
Kenneth Barner   University of Delaware, USA
Kidiyo Kpalma   INSA de Rennes, France
Kirk P. Arnett   Mississippi State University, USA
Kousuke Imamura   Kanazawa University, Japan
Lakshmish Ramaswamy   University of Georgia, USA
Makoto Fujimura   Nagasaki University, Japan
Marie Babel   INSA de Rennes, France
Martin Drahansky   BUT, Faculty of Information Technology,
                          Czech Republic
Mathieu Gineste   Thales Alenia Space, France
Mei-Ling Shyu   University of Miami, USA
Miroslaw Swiercz   Bialystok University of Technology, Poland
Mototaka Suzuki   EPFL Lausanne, Switzerland
Jari Nisula   Airbus, France
Muhammad Khurram Khan   King Saud University, Saudi Arabia

Table of Contents

A Backpropagation Learning System for Content Based Image Retrieval

Aun Irtaza[1], Arfan Jaffar[1,2], and Tae-Sun Choi[2]

[1] National University of Computer & Emerging Sciences, Islamabad, Pakistan
[2] Gwangju Institute of Science and Technology, Korea
aun.irtaza@gmail.com, {arfanjaffar,tschoi}@gist.ac.kr

Abstract. In this paper we have proposed a Neural Network based architecture for content based image retrieval. To enhance the capabilities of proposed technique, an efficient feature extraction method is presented which is based on the concept of in-depth texture analysis. For this we have used wavelet packets and Gabor filters features for repository image representation. To ensure the semantically identical image retrieval, a partial supervised learning based association scheme is presented, which guarantees the retrieval of images in an efficient way. To elaborate the effectiveness of the presented work, the proposed method is compared with several existing CBIR systems, and it is proved that the proposed method has performed better then all of the comparative systems.

Keywords: CBIR, Partial supervised learning, Neural Network based semantic association.

1   Introduction

Content based image retrieval(CBIR) systems [1][2][6] are aimed to search large image repositories based on actual visual contents which are present in the image. Due to the vast applications like architectural design, surveillance systems, data mining etc researchers have shown immense research interests in the area of content based image retrieval in the last decade. But still content based image retrieval is an open problem due to the inherent problems like large image repositories, semantics evaluation and results formulation. Efforts are carried out for determining the ways through which we can assure the retrieval of semantically correct retrieval of images in response of any query from large image repositories.

There are two main reasons due to which CBIR systems are unable to produce good results: (1) first of all they rank the retrieved images on the base of distance or similarity with query image and generate the results, in this regard they do not verify their output. The problem with this approach is that many images may appear as the response images while they are not relevant at all. (2) Secondly they do not consider the neighbors for the finalization of obtained results. So due to this the obtained results are not satisfactory. Keeping the above mentioned points in mind; in this paper we have focused on finding the ways through which such kind of shortcomings can be avoided and performance

T.-h. Kim et al. (Eds.): SIP/WSE/ICHCI 2012, CCIS 342, pp. 1–8, 2012.

of CBIRs can be enhanced. A backpropagation neural network based structure is introduced which is trained on sub repository of images generated from the main image repository. The aim of this training is to insure the retrieval of semantically correct images in response of query images. Based on our experiments we believe that content based image retrieval systems are if incorporated with powerful feature extraction measure and similarity detection way, target images usually contain mostly right results. So if this neighborhood is also utilized for semantic association, right semantic association probability for query images certainly rises. Therefore for powerful feature extraction and strong signature development we have used wavelet packets based method which is fused with Eigen values obtained from Gabor filters. The reason to use wavelet packets for feature extraction is that, with the help of wavelet packets in depth image texture analysis is possible. Details of the system will come in further sections.

Rest of paper is organized as follow. Section 2 provides the technical background required for signature development. Section 3 provides the details about the proposed system. Experimentation and results are discussed in section 4. Finally we concluded in section 5.

2 Signature Development and Similarity Calculation

Images in the image repository are stored in the form of feature vectors. Feature vectors are representation of visual contents present in the image. Efficient retrieval in any CBIR system is strongly dependent on the novelty of feature vectors. This is the reason that we have used hybrid fused features obtained from wavelet packets tree and Eigen values of the Gabor filter. As a first step we have computed the complete Shannon entropy based wavelet packets of the repository images up to the 3rd level. This will result in the form of 64 nodes of wavelet packets tree. But we have considered only those nodes which have the best entropy values. Nodes of the best tree are used for haar based feature generation using the following formula:

$$f_r = \sqrt{\frac{\sum c_{ij}^2}{i * j}}$$

Where f_r is the computed value of the sub image of a wavelet packet tree, C_{ij} is the representation of the intensity value of elements of sub image and i*j is the size of the sub image [7].

Now as a second step of signature development, we take the approximation image of best tree for Gabor analysis. In our implementation we are using only the odd components of Gabor filter to avoid the imaginary values. Filters we used are defined by the following equation: [3]

$$G_o(x, y) = exp(\frac{x_\theta^2 - \gamma^2 y_\theta^2}{\alpha^2})sin(\frac{2\pi x_\theta{}^i}{\lambda}) \tag{1}$$

where

$$x_\theta = x \cos_\theta + y \sin_\theta \tag{2}$$

$$y_\theta = -x\sin_\theta + y\sin_\theta \tag{3}$$

and σ is the standard deviation of the Gaussian function, λ is the wavelength of the harmonic function, θ is the orientation, and γ is the spatial aspect ratio which is left constant at 0.5. The spatial frequency bandwidth is the ratio σ/λ and is held constant and equal to .56. Thus there are two parameters which changes when forming a Gabor filter θ and λ. For obtaining the Gabor response values we are dividing the images into 9x9 non-overlapping regions and Gabor filter is then convolved with above mentioned parameters. After generating the response images we follow the following scheme:

1. Obtain the twelve Gabor based response images after applying the parameters.
2. Obtain the Eigen vector corresponding to every Gabor response image. This will result in the form of twelve Eigen vectors.
3. Take the mean of every Eigen vector.
4. Merge the mean values in one vector.

So after the application of these steps we will have twelve values as Eigen Gabor values against image. Merging these twelve values with wavelet packets feature values will result in the form of corresponding fused hybrid feature vector against any image.

3 Proposed Method

This section starts with the discussion of the general framework which we have introduced in this paper. Then neural network based semantic association of the images is introduced. This is followed by a discussion of the parameter selection and retrieval method.

3.1 Overview of Technique

We perform two main types of retrieval from signature repository for any query image. First type of retrieval is based on its K nearest neighbors; and second type of retrieval is based on its associated semantic class. The reason we have used these two types of retrieval is that in case if our semantic class is matched wrongly; the retrieval system should not put us in a complete blind state where every associated result will be a wrong result. So in such kind of situation semantic type can be compromised with object composition which is present in the query image. The input of the algorithm consists of $R \geq 2$ example images in every semantic class. On these example images we define a neural network structure for every class which is trained on those example images. Then with the help of neural network association for query image and its 'K' neighbors we associate the query image with any semantic class. After semantic association, images from retrieved semantic class are ranked on the base of closeness to the query image. The system also ranked the 'M' closest images on the base of similarity with query image; and as the output system returns these two types of the clusters. In which one will be the most representative one.

3.2   Semantic Association Using Neural Networks

For associating repository images with their actual semantic class; we have generated the sub repository from main image repository having images from 'M' known classes, and every class contains $R \geq 2$ images (R=30 in our implementation). The value of 'R' can vary for every class but ideally it should be same for all classes. On this sub repository we define class specific backpropagation neural networks; which are trained with the concept of one against all classes (OAA) to classify the input images according to their semantic class. For training purposes for a specific class we define training set $\Omega_{tr} = \Omega_{pos}\Omega_{neg}$ where Ω_{pos} means those images which belong from that class for which network is defined and are labeled with '1'; and Ω_{neg} means all other images in the sub repository which do not belong from that specific class and are labeled with '0'. In this way we define training sets for all classes and train backpropagation neural networks upon them with one hidden layer having 20 neurons. All repository images will be tested against all trained neural networks and on the base of decision function and association rules we will associate them with their specific semantic class.

Due to the object composition present in the images many images may tend to belong from more than one semantic class. So in this case it is possible that decision function may associate them with undesired class; so it is required that the process of association should be further enhanced. This is the reason that for the finalization of semantic class for any input image we do consider its top 'K' (K=5 in our implementation) neighbors as well. These top neighbors are tested on neural networks and based on decision function their semantic class will be detected as well. When semantic classes for input image and top neighbors will be declared, we finalize the semantic class for the input image based on rules which are neural network output dependent. For input image and top neighbors we have used the following decision function to associate them with their semantic class: $F(x, y1, y2... yM) = arg\ max_{i=1,,M}\ (yi)$ Where 'yi' represents the output of 'M' neural networks in the form of obtained association factors. Through the above decision function we will associate the input image and its neighbors with the semantic classes. After this we define following rules to finalize the class of input image:

If $\left(count(\arg\max_{=1,...,M}\ (yi\,query) = 1\right) = 1$

and $count(\arg\min_{=1,...,M}\ (yi\,query) = 0) = M - 1)$

Than

Final class $= F(x_{query}, yi)$

Else

$F(x, f1, f2,...,fk+1) = max\ i=1,...,k+1\ (count(\sum fi))$

Than

Final class $= F(x_{query}, fi)$

Where f1 is the semantic class of input image and f2 to fk+1 are the semantic classes of top 'k' neighbors obtained through decision function. So with the help of max associations we will finalize the class for any input image. As our decision is neighbor dependent therefore the probability of right semantic association automatically increases. The process of semantic association will be applied to all repository images and the results of association will be stored in a file on disk. So by this way we will prepare a database of semantic associations that will be further utilized to generate the system output against query images.

3.3 Content Based Image Retrieval

It is possible that in some particular situation our semantic association system may associate the query image with wrong class. So there should be a mechanism through which such kind of situation can be avoided. So to achieve this goal, the system returns us two representative images one is representing the retrieved semantic class; and other is representing the set of images which are supposed to have the same object composition as that of the query image. The benefit of this approach is that our system will never stuck in a blind situation where every retrieved result is a wrong result. The top matched image from the set of 'K' nearest neighbors will represent the set of images suppose to have the same object composition. While any image from the sub repository of the obtained semantic class will be returned to represent the similarity class. User will have the option to see both sets of images. Both set of images will have equal images. The difference is that in case of right association our semantic set will have many more accurate results than that of the nearest neighbor set. In this case images will belong from the same class and will have the same object composition as well. While in case of nearest neighbors returned images may belong from several classes, and many of them will have right object composition and some of them won't have this.

4 Experiment and Results

To eleborate the performance of proposed system, we have compared it with several existing CBIR systems. Further sub-sections contains the details of experiments we have performed.

4.1 Query Examples

We have implemented the proposed method on COREL image database which is a general purpose image database. The database has 1000 images belonging from 10 semantic classes namely Africa, Beach, Buildings, Buses, Dinosaurs, Elephants, Flowers, Horses, Mountains, and Food. Each class has 100 images size. As a first step for the implementation of proposed technique we have converted the image database into gray-scale image database, This preprocessing is required to generate the signatures of any repository image in a cost effective

Fig. 1. Image retrieval results for class Horses, Africa, and Beach. 1st image in every group is the query image and all other images in that group are retrieved results

way. So as a back-end process we convert images into gray-scale images and to display the results we display the color versions of the retrieved images. Each image in the database is tested against the trained neural networks and their semantic class is determined. We store the results of retrieval in a file which serve for us the association database or the semantic class specific cluster. Benefit of this scheme is that this process will be done only once on the database images and after that whenever any query image will come only the class of that image will be needed to determine and results for that specific class will be returned as a cluster. Overall class association accuracy is determined by following formula:

$$ClassAccuracy = \frac{Total\ right\ class\ retrievals}{Total\ class\ images} x100$$

Table 1. Comparison of average precision obtained by proposed method with other standard retrieval systems [[1], [2], [5], [4]]

Class	Proposed Method	Simplicity [1]	CLUE [2]	CTCHIRS [5]	Motif Coocurance [4]
Africa	69%	48%	49%	68%	45%
Beach	60%	32%	37%	54%	39%
Buildings	56%	35%	37%	56%	37%
Buses	89%	36%	64%	88%	74%
Dinasours	96%	95%	95%	99%	91%
Elephants	64%	38%	29%	65%	30%
Flowers	97%	42%	73%	89%	85%
Horses	66%	72%	70%	80%	57%
Mountains	57%	35%	28%	52%	29%
Food	86%	38%	78%	59%	37%
Average	**74%**	**47%**	**54%**	**72%**	**52%**

To elaborate the performance of proposed system we have randomly selected three images belonging to three different semantic classes (as query images) namely Horses, Africa, and Elephants; and then displayed the results. The results of top 20 retrievals against any query image are shown in figure 1. The quantitative analysis of the proposed method suggests that, quality of the system is very good. We have shown the results of top 20 matched images in response of random query images. The response of the system can be observed from the number of correct matched images presented in figure 1. In case of horse query top 20 images are all from same class. For Africa query 18 out of 20 images are from Africa class; and for Elephant query top 19 images are from elephant class. Hence on the base of retrieval accuracy we can say proposed method is quite efficient in terms of accuracy.

4.2   Systematic Comparison Analysis

To elaborate the power of proposed technique it is compared with SIMPLICITY [1], CLUE [2], CTCHIRS [5], and Jhanwar's motif co-occurrence systems [4]. The reason we have used these systems for the comparison is that results of these techniques are based on the same COREL subset database having ten semantic classes as described earlier. So it can give the clear comparison. Table 1 describes the class wise comparison of the proposed system with comparative systems. Results show that proposed system has performed better than all other systems in terms of overall accuracy.

5   Conclusion

The paper has introduced an image retrieval system, which is based on the concept of semantic class association through trained neural networks. For an efficient image retrieval system, it is necessary that it must focus on three main things. One is to uniquely represent the thumb impact of repository images which is the image signature; secondly to measure the similarity with other repository images it must have an efficient similarity calculation way; and lastly it must be able to retrieve the image results which are semantically similar to the query image. So in this paper we have focused on these three key issues. Wavelet packets based signature development is introduced which are fused with Eigen Gabor values; this makes a wonderful combination for signature development that it guarantees retrieval in an efficient way. For similarity calculation, Pearson correlation based similarity calculation is introduced; and for efficient retrieval, neural networks based technique is introduced; according to which semantic association occurs in a more systematic way. The results of the proposed method are compared with several standard retrieval systems.

Acknowledgments. This work (2012-0005542) was supported by Midcareer Researcher Program through NRF grant funded by the MEST.

References

1. Wang, J.Z., Li, J., Wiederhold, G.: SIMPLIcity: Semantics-Sensitive Integrated Matching for Picture Libraries. IEEE Transactions on Pattern Analysis and Machine Intelligence 09 (2001)
2. Chen, Y., Wang, J.Z., Krovetz, R.: CLUE: Cluster-Based Retrieval of Images by Unsupervised Learning. IEEE Transactions on Image Processing 14 (2005)
3. Lama, M., Disney, T., et al.: Content based image retrieval for pulmonary computed tomography nodule images. In: SPIE Medical Imaging Conference, San Diego (2007)
4. Lin, C.-H., Chen, R.-T., Chan, Y.-K.: A smart content-based image retrieval system based on color and texture feature. Elsevier Journal on Image and Vision Computing 27, 658–665 (2009)
5. Jhanwar, N., Chaudhurib, S., Seetharamanc, G., Zavidovique, B.: Content based image retrieval using motif co-occurrence matrix. Image and Vision Computing 22, 1211–1220 (2004)
6. da Silva, A.T., Falcão, A.X., Magalhães, L.P.: Active learning paradigms for CBIR systems based on optimum-path forest classification. Elsevier Journal of Patren Recogonition 44, 2971–2978 (2011)
7. Gnaneswera Rao, N., Vijaya Kumar, V., Vinkata Karishna, V.: Texture based image indexing and retrieval. IJCSNS International Journal of Computer Science and Network Security 09 (2009)

Full-Search Free
Intra Prediction Algorithm
for Real-Time H.264/AVC Decoder

Tarek Elarabi and Magdy Bayoumi

The Center for Advanced Computer Studies,
University of Louisiana at Lafayette, LA USA
http://www.cacs.louisiana.edu

Abstract. The standard H.264/AVC Intra frame encoding process has several data dependent and computational intensive coding methodologies that limit the overall encoding speed. It causes not only a high degree of computational complexity but also an unacceptable delay especially for the real-time video applications. In this article, high throughput Full-Search Free (FSF) Intra mode selection and direction prediction algorithm is proposed based on DCT properties and spatial activity analysis. It significantly reduces the computational complexity and the processing run-time required for the H.264/AVC Intra frame prediction process. The empirical results using standard benchmark frames showed that the proposed FSF Intra prediction algorithm not only significantly reduces the computational complexity but also speeds up the Intra prediction operation with a factor of x2.2 at a slight PSNR degradation of less than 1.8% When compared with the Intra prediction algorithm currently used in the H.264/AVC standard software JM 18.2 while keeping the same bit rate.

Keywords: Video, H.264/AVC, Intra Prediction, Mode Selection and Direction Prediction.

1   Introduction

The video coding standard recommendation of ITU-T, H.264/ AVC, is jointly developed and approved by ISO/IEC [1]. It employs many new coding tools to achieve better coding performance compared to previous standards [2]. Also, H.264/AVC provides enhanced video compression performance while preserving quality degradation cost to a minimum [3]. In addition, it has a very high network adaption flexibility when using error prone networks like mobile channels where bit errors are common for UMTS, GSM and LTE or when using the Internet where packet loss occurs over cable modems or DSL. All these privileges are achieved at the cost of additional computational complexity of the video coding algorithms which is almost 10 times more complex than the MPEG-4 Advanced Simple Profile [1]. The Intra prediction is an important part of H.264/AVC,

T.-h. Kim et al. (Eds.): SIP/WSE/ICHCI 2012, CCIS 342, pp. 9–16, 2012.

which makes full use of the images' spatial correlation for raising the compression ratio. It also plays an important role on enhancing the encoder's overall performance. The Intra prediction process encodes every Macro Block (MB) using previous encoded neighboring MBs' samples within the same frame. Its coding performance is comparable to that of JPEG2000 [4]. Therefore, H.264/AVC Intra frame encoding is suitable for both image and video compression. Moreover, the performance of H.264/AVC Intra frame encoding is depending on its computation intensive coding tools such as multiple modes Intra prediction, Lagrangian-based mode selection and entropy coding algorithms [3]. However, its high computational complexity makes it impractical to interactive real-time video applications.

A very interesting work was introduced by Liu et al. They proposed a mode skipping rule of Intra prediction mode decision in the H.264/AVC encoder. The idea is based on an experimental analysis results, which show that DCT energy has a strong correlation with the Intra prediction modes of H.264/AVC [5]. Yoo et al. proposed an Intra decision method based on a spatial activity analysis for the DCT coefficients [6]. Lin et al. have proposed several H.264 intra frame encoders. However, in their work in [7], they eliminated the plane mode prediction to speed up the encoding process Also they proposed an enhanced cost function to compensate video quality and a three steps heuristic Intra prediction algorithm. The algorithm skips to predict the modes that have a lower probability to be the best mode. In this article, we propose a fast yet precise Intra mode decision and prediction direction. The proposed algorithm selects the MB mode then predicts the reconstruction direction in a completely full search free technique. The rest of this paper is organized as follows: in Section 2, we introduce our proposed Full Search Free (FSF) Intra prediction algorithm. Then, we present the experimental results in Section 3. Finally, we conclude our work objectives and results in Section 4.

2   The FSF Intra Prediction Algorithm

Our proposed Full-Search Free (FSF) Intra prediction algorithm is based on empirical observations, characteristics of DCT coefficients and other well known image processing properties. By default, our proposed FSF Intra prediction algorithm processes the Intra video frame (I-Frame) in MB units of size 16x16 samples. As follows, the algorithm is composed of two phases: The first phase only concerns with deciding the Intra prediction mode. In other words, it decides the operational MB size, either 16x16 or 4x4 MB mode. Depending on the MB smoothness, the FSF algorithm either selects the reconstruction direction for the whole 16x16 MB as one unit, or it divides the 16x16 MB into its sixteen non overlapped 4x4 sub-MBs then decides the best reconstruction direction for each of sub-MB independently. The FSF mode selection process builds its decision based on our optimized version of the smoothness factor for the 16x16 MB that was introduced in [5]. Furthermore, if the optimized smoothness factor indicates a smooth enough MB, then the mode decision is the 16x16 mode.

Otherwise, the mode decision is the 4x4 mode. In contrast with the algorithm in [5], the FSF mode decision process is using only the DC coefficients from DCT samples to calculate the smoothness factor (S) as illustrated in (1) and (2).

$$E_{avg} = \left\{ \sum_{m=0}^{3} DC_m \right\} \div 4 \qquad (1)$$

$$S = \sum_{m=0}^{3} |DC_m - E_{avg}| \qquad (2)$$

where DC_m is the DCT's DC sample of the mth MB, E_{avg} is the average estimated energy for the four 16x16 MBs: the current MB (0), the top MB (1), the top/left MB (2) and the MB directly to the left (3). Finally, S is our optimized smoothness factor for the current 16x16 MB [8]. Successively, the process is initiated and completed in the DCT domain of the H.264/AVC decoder. Also, the DCT coefficients are used directly after the H.264/AVC inverse quantization process (Q^{-1}) is completed and before the inverse transformation process (T^{-1}) is initiated.

Afterwards, the second phase of the FSF algorithm is depending on the output decision of the FSF mode selection phase for the current MB. And, it only concerns with deciding the Intra direction prediction. In this phase of the FSF Intra prediction algorithm, the reconstruction direction candidates are chosen for the Intra prediction mode that has been decided by the FSF Intra mode decision phase. In case of the current Intra Luma mode is the 16x16 mode, the FSF algorithm calculates the non-homogeneity factor for the four Luma 16x16 direction candidates: Vertical (V), Horizontal (H), Plane (P) and DC. Then, it uses the resulting non-homogeneity values to nominate one reconstruction direction for the current 16x16 MB, which is the direction that results the least non-homogeneity value. In other words, the algorithm chooses the direction that introduces the highest homogeneity. If the MB is homogeneous in a specific direction, this implies that the objective MB, in the examined frame, is extended through the neighboring MBs at the same directions. Accordingly, the samples' values of the examined MB can be precisely predicted from such neighboring MBs at the direction that achieves the highest homogeneity. Also, the non-homogeneity factors calculation process is inherited from the Intra prediction algorithm in [5], but with two significant enhancements. The first enhancement is that the FSF algorithm uses only the DC coefficient out of the four adjacent MBs' DCT samples to calculate the current MB energy. The FSF is totally excluding the AC coefficients from the calculations as shown in (1) and (2). Hence, our experimental results, using the standard video benchmark frames, indicate that the AC coefficients have a negligible effect on the direction decision. consequently, excluding the AC coefficients from our calculations dramatically reduces the Intra prediction over all computational complexity. On the other hand, the second enhancement is in computing the non-homogeneity factor for the plane (P) direction as shown in (6). The following set of equations, (3),

(4) and (5), illustrates the non-homogeneity factors' calculations for each of the 16x16 MB Intra reconstruction direction candidates:

$$H_{dc} = S \div 2 \qquad (3)$$

$$H_v = |DC_0 - DC_2| + |DC_1 - DC_3| \qquad (4)$$

$$H_h = |DC_0 - DC_1| + |DC_2 - DC_3| \qquad (5)$$

$$H_p = |DC_0 - DC_3| + |DC_1 - DC_2| \qquad (6)$$

After calculating the non-homogeneity factors for each of the 16x16 MB reconstruction direction candidates, the direction decision would be the direction that achieves the minimum non-homogeneity factor. In this stage, The FSF algorithm nominates only one reconstruction direction for the Intra 16x16 mode without the need to any Rate Distortion Operations (RDO). In contrast, the H.264/AVC standard Intra direction prediction for the Luma 16x16 mode executes one RDO for each of the four direction prediction candidates. Accordingly, the FSF eliminates all the required RDO computations form the Intra Luma 16x16 mode, which effectively reduces the computational complexity of the over all Intra prediction process. On the other hand, in case of the Intra Luma mode is decided to be the 4x4 mode, the direction prediction process in the FSF algorithm computes the edge orientation factor as in (7). In fact, we have adopted the edge orientation technique introduced in [6]. However, we have significantly optimized the process of calculating the edge orientation as discussed in [8].

$$\theta = arctan \left\langle \{ \sum_{m=0}^{3} Eng_{top}(m)/Eng_{left}(m) \}/4 \right\rangle \qquad (7)$$

$$Eng_{top}(m) = \sum_{i=0, j=1}^{j=15, j=j+1} |DCT_m(i,j)| \qquad (8)$$

$$Eng_{left}(m) = \sum_{i=1, j=0}^{i=15, i=i+1} |DCT_m(i,j)| \qquad (9)$$

First, the angle (θ) is estimated from the DCT coefficients of the current 16x16 MB and its neighboring 16x16 MBs: top, top/left and left. The process of calculating the angle (θ) is modelled in (7). Also, the energy of the top and the left of the four mentioned MBs are calculated as in (8) and (9). Based on the resulting angle value, the Luma 4x4 MB direction candidates are chosen from Table 1. Obviously, the direction candidate that achieves the minimum RD value is chosen as the reconstruction direction for the current examined 4x4 MB. Clearly, the FSF algorithm nominates only four direction candidates for each of the sixteen 4x4 sub MB. Accordingly, each 4x4 sub-MB will need only four RDO computations to decide the reconstruction direction. In contrast, the standard H.264/AVC Intra 4x4 Luma mode calculates the RDO for each of the nine direction prediction candidates. Indeed, the FSF Intra prediction algorithm cuts down the required

Table 1. Intra 4x4 Direction Prediction Candidates

Candidate group	Luma 4x4 Candidates
1 (60 to 90) or (-90 to -60)	0, 2, 5, 7
2 (-30 to 30)	1, 2, 6, 8
3 (30 to 60) or (-60 to -30)	0, 1, 2, 3

number of RDOs from nine in the standard Intra Luma 4x4 mode to only four RDOs, which significantly reduces the computational complexity of the over all Intra prediction process. By deciding the 4x4 direction prediction, the FSF Intra prediction algorithm has efficiently concluded the Intra mode selection and reconstruction direction prediction for Luma component of the current MB. On the other hand, the Chroma Intra prediction has only one mode in the H.264/AVC baseline profile. Moreover, the proposed FSF algorithm predicts the reconstruction direction for both Chroma components of the current 16x16 MB without performing any additional computations. Our proposed algorithm only checks if the current Luma 16x16 direction prediction is the DC reconstruction direction. Then, the current MB Chroma reconstruction direction will be the DC direction. Otherwise, the Chroma reconstruction direction candidates for the current MB are the DC direction and the reconstruction direction of the current Luma 16x16 MB. All in all, the flowchart in Figure 1 summarizes our proposed FSF Intra prediction algorithm.

3   The FSF Software Implementation

For evaluation purpose, the proposed FSF Intra prediction algorithm and both Kim's algorithm in [5] and Yoo's algorithm in [6] have been implemented using C++ and integrated in the H.264/AVC reference software (JM 18.2). The system platform is Intel Core 2 Due 2.4 GHz CPU, 4GB 1067 MHz DDR3 RAM and Mac OS X (Lion 10.7.2). Furthermore, a comparison have been constructed in respect of the Intra prediction time, bit-rate and PSNR. Also, we compared between the proposed FSF Intra prediction algorithm, the Intra prediction technique currently used in the standard H.264/AVC (JM 18.2) and both of the enhanced Intra prediction techniques that have been introduced in [5] and [6], which we call in the scope of this article Kim's algorithm and Yoo's algorithm, respectively. Then, using a benchmark of ten different standard benchmark frames, all the implemented algorithms have been repeatedly tested with different QP values of 28, 32, 36 and 40. The empirical results show that our proposed FSF Intra prediction algorithm reduces the Intra prediction run-time by 56% compared to Intra prediction time taken by the standard Intra prediction algorithm in H.264/AVC (JM 18.2). On the other hand, the FSF is offering almost the same bit-rate as the standard H.264/AVC. Yet, the cost was a little drop in the PSNR by a factor of 1.8% (or 0.72 dB in average)less than the PSNR that is achieved by the standard H.264/AVC Intra prediction algorithm.

Furthermore, both Kim's and Yoo's algorithms introduce some enhancements in the Intra prediction run-time with proportionally higher reduction in the

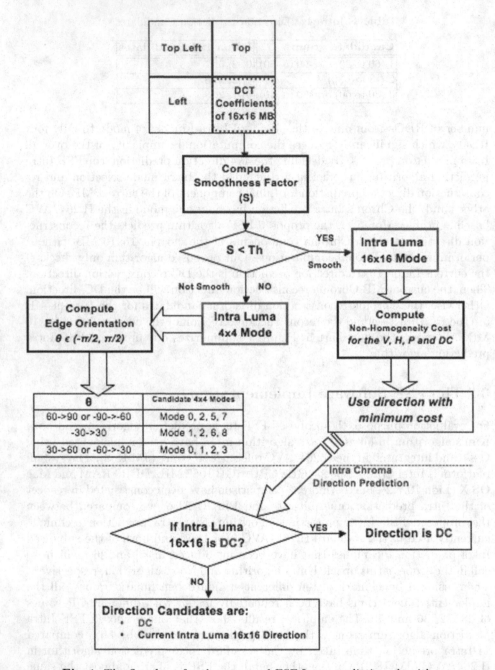

Fig. 1. The flowchart for the proposed FSF Intra prediction algorithm

PSNR. Also, the FSF Intra prediction algorithm achieves in average 35.29% and 39.73% reduction in the Intra prediction run-time comparing to both Kim's and Yoo's Intra prediction techniques, respectively. In addition, it shows an

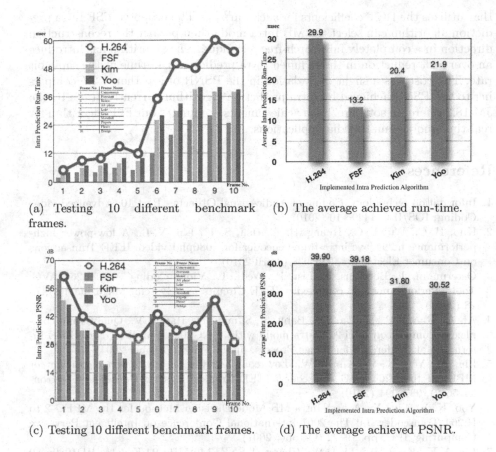

(a) Testing 10 different benchmark frames.

(b) The average achieved run-time.

(c) Testing 10 different benchmark frames.

(d) The average achieved PSNR.

Fig. 2. The run-time and the PSNR achieved by the FSF Intra Prediction Algorithm

improvement in the PSNR by 18.84% and 22.10%, in average, more than the PSNR introduced by Kim's algorithm and Yoo's algorithm, respectively. Figure 2(d) and Figure 2(b) illustrate all the previously mentioned average run-time and average PSNR comparisons, respectively. In addition, Figure 2(c) and Figure 2(a) show the PSNR cost and the Intra prediction run-time that have been achieved by testing all the implemented algorithms on all of the tested standard benchmark frames, which is composed of ten standard frames of different sizes and textures.

4 Conclusion

The Intra mode decision and direction prediction dramatically increases the complexity of the H.264/AVC Encoder. The DCT coefficients in H.264/AVC Encoder can be used for significantly speed up the Intra frame prediction process. We presented a fast yet precise Intra mode decision and direction prediction that utilizes the DCT coefficients for such purpose. The proposed FSF Intra prediction algorithm can select the MB Intra mode then predict the reconstruction direction in a completely full search-free technique. The algorithm has introduce an over 65% reduction in the required Intra prediction run-time at the same bit rate. The cost was a slight degradation in the PSNR of less than 1.2% comparing to the PSNR achieved by Intra prediction algorithm currently in use by the JM 18.2 reference software. Such achievements nominates our FSF algorithm for real-time mobile multimedia applications.

References

1. Information technology, Coding of Audio-visual Objects - Part 10: Advanced video Coding, IOS/IEC 14496-10 (2010)
2. Kuo, H.-C., Wu, L.-C., Huang, H.-T., Hsu, S.-T., Lin, Y.-L.: A low-power high-performance h.264/avc intra-frame encoder for 1080phd video. IEEE Transactions on Consumer Electronics, 925–938 (April 2010)
3. Ostermann, J., Bormans, J., List, P., Wedi, T.: Video Coding with H.264/AVC: Tools, Performance and complexity. IEEE Circuits and Systems Magazine 4(1), 7–28 (2004)
4. Al, A., Rao, B.P., Kudva, S.S., Babu, S., Suman, D., Rao, A.V.: Quality and complexity comparison of H.264 intra mode with JPEG2000 and JPEG. In: IEEE International Conference for Image Process, pp. 525–528 (October 2004)
5. Liu, X., Yoo, K.-Y., Kim, S.W.: Low complexity intra prediction algorithm for MPEG-2 to H.264/AVC transcoder. IEEE Transactions on Consumer Electronics 56(2), 987–994 (2010)
6. Yoo, K.-Y., Liu, X.: A Fast Intra MB Mode Decision Method for the MPEG-2 to H.264 Transcoder. In: The 2007 International Conference on Intelligent Pervasive Computing, IPC, pp. 19–22 (October 2007)
7. Lin, Y.K., Ku, C.W., Li, D.W., Chang, T.S.: A 140-MHz 94 K gates HD1080p 30 frames/s intra-only profile H.264 encoder. IEEE Transactions on Circuits System Video Technology 19, 432–436 (2009)
8. Elarabi, T., Ragab, A., Mahmoud, H., Bayoumi, M.: High Speed Intra Mode and Direction Prediction for MPEG-2 to H.264/AVC Real-time Transcoder. In: IEEE Workshop for Signal Processing Systems (SiPS 2011), pp. 78–83 (October 2011)

Image Enhancement Using a Modified Histogram Equalization

M.M. Naushad Ali and M. Abdullah-Al-Wadud

Industrial and Management Engineering Department
Hankuk University of Foreign Studies, REPUBLIC of KOREA
naushad_iut@yahoo.com, wadud@hufs.ac.kr

Abstract. Image enhancement algorithms based on Histogram equalization (HE) often fall short to maintain the image quality after enhancement due to quantum jump in the cumulative distribution function (CDF) in the histogram. Moreover, some detail parts appear to be washed out after enhancement. To solve this problem, we propose an algorithm, which enhance the image details parts separately and combine it with the enhanced image using a weighted function. This gives a way to control the enhancement of the details improving the quality of the image. Experiments show that the proposed method performs well as compared to the existing enhancement algorithms.

Keywords: Contrast Enhancement, detail enhancement, histogram equalization, weighted sum.

1   Introduction

Image contrast enhancement is a typical problem in the field of image processing and computer vision. It is broadly used in many image processing applications such as object recognition, medical image processing and as a preprocessing step in video processing applications [15-17]. Image enhancement means the improvement of the quality of image using different types of techniques. These modifications may include contrast enhancement, color enhancement, edge enhancement and so on.

Histogram Equalization (HE) [1] technique is very popular for image Enhancement due to its simplicity and good performance in almost all types of images. It is performed by remapping the intensity levels of an image based on the probability density function (PDF) of the input intensities. However, this method fails to enhance an image when there is a quantum jump in the cumulative distribution function (CDF). Local HE (LHE) algorithm has the capability to remove the local brightness problem [2]. However, LHE suffers from amplified noise, and the result often looks unnatural due to over-enhancement. Global Histogram Equalization (GHE) transforms the histograms using the complete information of the input image [1, 18]. However, this method fails to adjust the local brightness textures of the input image. Another approach is to focus on the improvement of the HE by partitioning method and equalize separately. Bi-Histogram Equalization (BHE) divides the histogram into two parts depending on the mean of the histogram [3, 4]. After the bright preserving

T.-h. Kim et al. (Eds.): SIP/WSE/ICHCI 2012, CCIS 342, pp. 17–24, 2012.

bi-histogram equalization (BBHE) method [12] some algorithms were proposed based on partitioning the histogram into two or more parts. The Dualistic Sub-Image HE (DSIHE) method uses input histogram median [5]. Chen and Ramli propose the Minimum Mean Brightness Error Bi-HE (MMBEBHE) in [6], an extension of the BBHE method for maintaining the optimal mean brightness [7]. Recursive Mean-Separate HE (RMSHE) is another upgrading of BBHE, which equalize the every new histograms based on the recursive mean [8]. In this method histogram is partitioned into r partitions. However, finding r is a difficult task as the larger value of r may not maintain the enhancement.

The majority of the HE techniques only use global information for enhancement without taking care of the local information. S.-H. Yun *et al.* [9] proposed a method of image enhancement to overcome the problem of quantum jump in the CDF using the local and global information. However, if the image intensity is very low then this method may fail to perform acceptable enhancement as the edges of the image become blurred and the overall image quality decreases. Moreover, this method suffers from losing small details and texture information.

In this paper, we propose an image enhancement algorithm which generates the detail parts of an image from the luminance Image. Then these are also enhanced separately. In the final step we combine the enhanced image and the enhanced details using a weighted function to yield a desired enhancement.

The rest of the paper is organized as follows. The proposed framework and the detail description of the proposed algorithm are described in Section 2. Section 3 shows the experimental results and Section 4 concludes this paper.

2   Proposed Algorithm

2.1   Framework

HE-based methods mainly focus on the global contrast of an image while the local contrast or details in the image are given low priority during enhancement. To solve this problem we extract the details from the original image. Fig.1 shows the block diagram of the proposed method. At first we obtain the luminance component I from an RGB image and apply a 5x5 Gaussian filter to obtain the smooth image S. Then subtracting the smoothed image from the original luminance, we obtain the detail image D as shown in Fig.2. D is enhanced using a detail gain function and I is enhanced using a contrast enhancement based on HE. After that a weighted sum is used to combine these two. Color is restored in the final step similar to [10] and [11] to reflect the enhanced luminance image on color channels.

2.2   Description of the Proposed Algorithm

In HE- based methods, the output is sometimes over enhanced and some information is lost in some area where there is a quantum jump occurs in the CDF. To suppress this effect, a boosting algorithm is used to boost the histogram of the image I.

Before applying the boosting algorithm, we smooth the histogram of I using a Gaussian filter. This Gaussian filter smoothes the histogram otherwise many local minima would have been boosted. After boosting is done the histogram is clipped slantwise and then the luminance mapping function is generated using HE technique. To enhance the detail image D we modify the details using an adaptive gain function and noise reduction function.

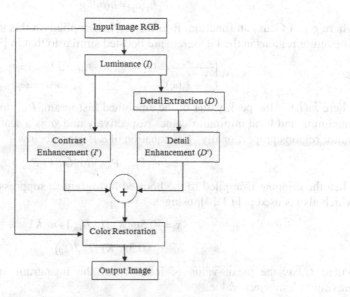

Fig. 1. Block Diagram of the proposed method

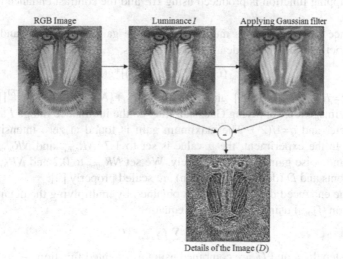

Fig. 2. An example of extracting the details of an image

Here we explain the processes in detail. In the first step we generate the histogram of I using

$$h(a_j)= n_j \tag{1}$$

where a_j is the jth intensity level and n_j is the number of pixels having intensity level a_j. Then this histogram is smoothed using a Gaussian filter using

$$h_g(a_j)= h(a_j)*g \tag{2}$$

where g is a Gaussian function. Boosting is then applied on this smoothed histogram. The minor regions in the histogram are boosted similar to that in [9] using.

$$h_b(a_j)= \begin{cases} \frac{h_g a_j - P_{min}}{(P_{max}-P_{min})} (m(K) - P_{min})\alpha + P_{min}, & if\ h_b(a_j) > P_{min} \\ h_g(a_j), & otherwise \end{cases} \tag{3}$$

where $m(K)$ is the peak value of the smoothed histogram, P_{max} and P_{min} are the local maximum and local minimum values respectively and α is a scale factor to boost the minor regions proportionally. The equation of α is given below

$$\alpha=log(P_{max}-P_{min})/log(m(k)-P_{min}) \tag{4}$$

Then the clipping is applied to the boosted histogram to suppress the quantum jump, which also is used in [13-14], using

$$x_1= -0.5m(K).[I_{mn}/I_{md}]+m(K) \tag{5}$$

$$x_2= 0.5m(K).[I_{mn}/I_{md}] \tag{6}$$

where I_{mn} is the mean value of intensity of the histogram and I_{md} is half of maximum luminance value.

The residual after clipping is distributed to the whole histogram bins uniformly. Then the mapping function is produced using HE and the contrast enhanced image (I') is generated.

To enhance the details, D is multiplied with the gain function (f_g) and the noise reduction function (f_n) [9]. The detail gain function is

$$f_{detail}(i,j) = [f_g(i,j).f_n(i,j)]*g(i,j) \tag{7}$$

where $f_g(i,j)=1/\{q.[I_s(i,j)+1.0]^p\}$ and $f_n(i,j)=NR_{offset}+\{NR_{band}/[1+e^{-(D(i,j)-E)}]\}$ where I_s is smoothed image after applying Gaussian filter to the luminance image I and p is the gain parameter and $q=1/(2^p)$. The maximum gain is found at zero intensity and the value is 2^p. In the experiment, the p value is set to 1.7. NR_{offset} and NR_{band} are noise gain offset and noise gain band respectively. We set NR_{offset} to 0.2 and NR_{band} to 1.0 in the experiments and D (detail) and E (gain) are scaled properly [9].

Finally the enhanced detail image D' is obtained by multiplying the details with the detail function (f_{detail}) using the following equation

$$D'(i,j)= \sum f_{details} . D(i,j) \tag{8}$$

In the final step the I' and D' are combined using a weighted function

$$I''(i,j) = w \times I'(i,j)+ (1-w) \times D'(i,j) \tag{9}$$

where $I''(i,j)$ is the final enhanced image and w is a weighted function. The value of w may vary from 0.0 to 1.0. The effect of w plays an essential role in the enhancement. If we keep decreasing w then the detail part gets more emphasis.

3   Experimental Result

We have compared our algorithm with the HE method and the algorithm proposed by S.-H. Yun *et al.* [9]. We have used different values of w to see the optimum result in the enhanced image.

In Fig. 3(a) the original image has very low brightness and contrast. Histogram equalization has over enhanced the image and the originality is not maintained. Moreover, the wrinkles in the right hand are not visible. In the method, proposed by S.-H. Yun *et al.* [9] the originality is preserved. However, the wrinkles in the right hand are not prominent, and the overall image has lost some details. In the proposed method the image is enhanced keeping the originality of the image and also the wrinkles in the hands are clearly visible. In Fig. 4(a) the original image is also very low in contrast. In the HE method the grass in field in the bottom right corner has become dark and also the image has lost its originality. In Fig.4(c) the image is enhanced but the field and the trees have lost some details. In the proposed method the image is enhanced keeping the originality of the image and the details are more prominent. In Fig. 5(a) the original image contains some cloud, mountain and trees. Using the HE method the cloud is over enhanced and the trees in the bottom right corner have become dark. In the method of S.-H. Yun *et al.* the image is enhanced but the trees in the upper portion of the image have lost some details. In the outcome of the proposed method the details of the image are more evident and the image is well enhanced.

(a) Original Image   (b) HE Image

Fig. 3. Enhancement done by different methods

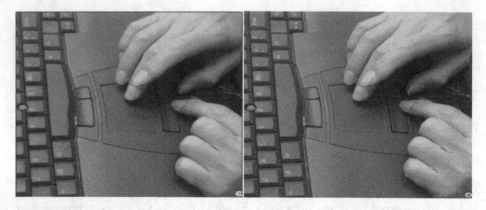

(c) Method proposed by S.-H. Yun *et al.*   (d) Proposed Method

Fig. 3. (*continued*)

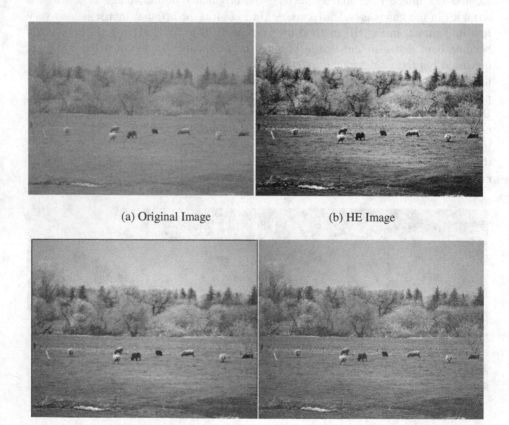

(a) Original Image   (b) HE Image

(c) Method proposed by S.-H. Yun *et al.*   (d) Proposed Method

Fig. 4. The outcomes of applying different enhancement methods

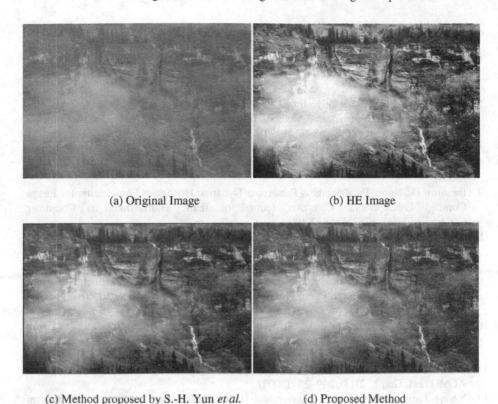

(a) Original Image   (b) HE Image

(c) Method proposed by S.-H. Yun *et al.*   (d) Proposed Method

Fig. 5. Another set of experimental results of applying different enhancement methods

4   Conclusion

In this paper we have proposed a robust method for image enhancement using a modified version of Histogram Equalization combining the enhanced intensity with the separately enhanced detail of the image. The proposed method can produce natural- look image with enhanced sharpness and without losing the little details.

Acknowledgement. This research was supported by Basic Science Research Program through the National Research Foundation (NRF) of Korea funded by the Ministry of Education, Science and Technology (2012-0007801).

References

1. Gonzalez, C., Woods, E.: Digital Image Processing. Addison-Wesley (1992)
2. Zhu, H., Chan, F.H.Y., Lam, F.K.: Image Contrast Enhancement by Constrained Local Histogram Equalization. Computer Vision and Image Understanding 73(2), 281–290 (1999)

3. Kim, T.: Contrast Enhancement Using Brightness Preserving Bihistogram Equalization. Computer Journal of IEEE Transactions on Consumer Electronics 43(1), 1–8 (1997)
4. Sengee, N., Choi, K.: Brightness Preserving Weight Clustering Histogram Equalization. Computer Journal of IEEE Transactions on Consumer Electronics 54(3), 1329–1337 (2008)
5. Wang, Y., Chen, Q., Zhang, B.: Image Enhancement Based on Equal Area Dualistic Sub-Image Histogram Equalization Method. Computer Journal of IEEE Transactions on Consumer Electronics 45(1), 68–75 (1999)
6. Chen, D., Ramli, R.: Preserving Brightness in Histogram Equalization Based Contrast Enhancement Techniques. Computer Journal of Digital Signal Processing 14(5), 413–428 (2004)
7. Ibrahim, H., Kong, P.: Brightness Preserving Dynamic Histogram Equalization for Image Contrast Enhancement. Computer Journal of IEEE Transactions on Consumer Electronics 53(4), 1752–1758 (2007)
8. Chen, D., Ramli, R.: Contrast Enhancement Using Recursive Mean-Separate Histogram Equalization for Scalable Brightness Preservation. Computer Journal of IEEE Transactions Consumer Electronics 49(4), 1301–1309 (2003)
9. Yun, S.-H., Kim, J.H.: Image Enhancement using a Fusion Framework of Histogram Equalization and Laplacian Pyramid. IEEE Transactions on Consumer Electronics 56(4) (November 2010)
10. Baek, Y.M., Kim, H.J., Lee, J.A., Oh, S.G., Kim, W.Y.: Color Image Enhancement Using the Laplacian Pyramid. In: Zhuang, Y.-t., Yang, S.-Q., Rui, Y., He, Q. (eds.) PCM 2006. LNCS, vol. 4261, pp. 760–769. Springer, Heidelberg (2006)
11. Fattal, R., Lischinski, D., Werman, M.: Gradient domain high dynamic range compression. ACM Trans. Graph. 21(3), 249–256 (2002)
12. Yeong-Taeg, K.: Contrast enhancement using brightness preserving bihistogram equalization. IEEE Trans. Consum. Electron. 43(1), 1–8 (1997)
13. Pizer, S.M., Amburn, E.P., Austin, J.D., Cromartie, R., Geselowitz, A., et al.: Adaptive Histogram Equalization and Its Variations. Computer Vision Graphics and Image Processing 39(3), 355–368 (1987)
14. Yang, S., Oh, J.H., Park, Y.: Contrast enhancement using histogram equalization with bin underflow and bin overflow. In: Proceedings of the 2003 International Conference on Image Processing, vol. 1, pp. 881–884 (2003)
15. Pizer, M.: The Medical Image Display and Analysis Group at the University of North Carolina: Reminiscences and Philosophy. Computer Journal of IEEE Transactions on Medical Image 22(1), 2–10 (2003)
16. Torre, A., Peinado, M., Segura, C., Perez-Cordoba, L., Benitez, C., Rubio, J.: Histogram Equalization of Speech Representation for Robust Speech Recognition. Computer Journal of IEEE Transaction on Speech Audio Processions 13(3), 355–366 (2005)
17. Wahab, A., Chin, H., Tan, C.: Novel Approach to Automated Fingerprint Recognition. In: Proceedings Vision, Image and Signal Processing, pp. 160–166 (1998)
18. Sengee, N., Choi, K.: Brightness Preserving Weight Clustering Histogram Equalization. Computer Journal of IEEE Transactions on Consumer Electronics 54(3), 1329–1337 (2008)

Spectro-Temporal Features for Howling Frequency Detection

Jae-Won Lee[1] and Seung Ho Choi[2,*]

[1] Graduate School of NID Fusion Technology
Seoul National University of Science and Technology, Seoul 139-743, Korea
[2] Department of Electronic and IT Media Engineering
Seoul National University of Science and Technology, Seoul 139-743, Korea
shchoi@seoultech.ac.kr

Abstract. The howling varies depending on the room environment and it is difficult to predict the howling. In this research work, we develop spectro-temporal features for howling frequency detection. For the detection of howling frequency, several techniques have been developed such as least mean square method. The proposed approach is based on statistical properties of temporal power spectra, which requires less computational complexity than conventional methods. The proposed method is experimentally shown to be suitable for applications in sound systems.

Keywords: Howling frequency detection, Spectro-temporal feature, Acoustic feedback circuit.

1 Introduction

Howling is generated in audio amplifier when an acoustic feedback circuit (AFC) [1, 2] diverges by positive feedback [3]. The howling varies depending on the overall environment such as the positions of microphones and loudspeakers, room shape and arrangement, the position and movement of talker, room temperature [1]. Therefore, it is difficult to predict the howling. Furthermore, it is hard to distinguish original and howling signals before recognizing howling sound.

To suppress howling, gain or frequency control methods have been developed, which uses equalizer [4], frequency shifter [5] and notch filters [6, 7]. For the detection of howling frequency, several techniques have been developed such as least mean square (LMS) method [8]. Recently, notch filters have been employed, which suppress howling by reducing the gain at a specific frequency [6, 7]. However, these filters must accurately detect the howling frequency and require a large amount of operations [8].

In this paper, we develop spectro-temporal features for the detection of howling frequency based on statistical properties of temporal power spectra. The remainder of this paper is organized as follows. Howling phenomena are summarized in Section 2.

---

* Corresponding author.

T.-h. Kim et al. (Eds.): SIP/WSE/ICHCI 2012, CCIS 342, pp. 25–30, 2012.
© Springer-Verlag Berlin Heidelberg 2012

The proposed spectro-temporal features are described in Sections 3. Experimental results are illustrated in Section 4. Finally, conclusions are given in Section 5.

2   Howling Phenomena

The AFC can easily diverge due to a positive feedback circuit. The microphone input signal $x(t)$ is amplified by gain g and then the loudspeaker output signal $y_0(t)$ is generated as shown in Fig. 1(a) [1]. The $y_0(t)$ makes the multiple reflection signals $\{y_i(t)\}$ that are summed to the feedback signal $y(t) = \sum_{i=1}^{n} \alpha_i y_0(t - \tau_i)$, where α_i is the attenuation factor of indoor wall and τ_i is delay time [1]. These signals are again entered to the microphone.

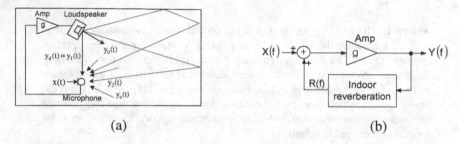

(a)   (b)

Fig. 1. Howling model. (a) AFC in the indoor reflection environment, (b) AFC model.

The AFC model is shown as Fig. 1(b) and the transfer function can be represented as

$$H(f) = \frac{Y(f)}{X(f)} = \frac{g}{1 - gR(f)} \; , \tag{1}$$

where $R(f)$ is room impulse response (RIR). The frequencies at $\angle H(f) = 2\pi m$ become potential howling frequencies, where m is an integer [1]. In indoor conditions, magnitude response is changed according to the RIR. Fig. 2 shows an example of frequency response of an AFC.

3   Proposed Howling Detection Method

We examined the temporal variation of power spectra, $V(f) = |X_{curr}(f)|^2 - |X_{prev}(f)|^2$, where $X_{curr}(f)$ and $X_{prev}(f)$ are FFT spectra of the current and previous analysis frame, respectively. As can be seen in Fig. 3, the $V(f)$ can be seen as random samples in stable condition, whereas the $V(f)$ is close to 0 at around a specific frequency of 1 kHz in howling condition.

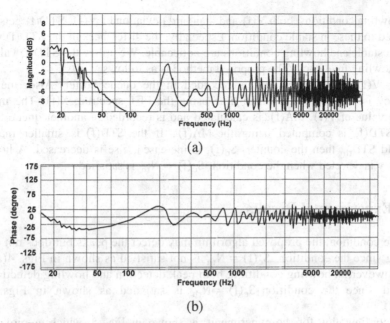

Fig. 2. Example of AFC. (a) Frequency response, (b) phase response.

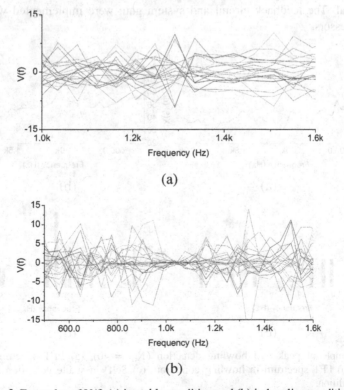

Fig. 3. Examples of V(f) (a) in stable condition and (b) in howling condition

In howling conditions, both V(f) and standard deviation of V(f), STD(f) gets small compared to those in stable condition. Especially, the differences in the STD(f) values between stable and howling conditions are noticeable. We utilize the STD(f) values to detect howling frequency. The proposed method is as follows.

First, V(f) is calculated and is recorded in the queue buffer. Also, the peak frequency is detected at the same time using the FFT spectrum X(f). The moving average value of V(f), MA(f), is calculated and is recorded in another queue buffer. Then, STD(f) is computed using the MA(f). If the STD(f) is smaller than the threshold STD_{th}, then the counter, $S_c(f)$, is increased, else is decreased. A howling frequency is detected when the condition $S_c(f) = N_{th}$ is satisfied.

4   Experimental Results

In stable condition, the proposed algorithm may detect the peaks but does not detect howling since the condition $S_c(f) = N_{th}$ is not satisfied as shown in Figs. 4(a) and 4(c). However, in howling condition, both peak detection and howling detection are occurred since the condition $S_c(f) = N_{th}$ is satisfied as shown in Figs. 4(b) and 4(d).

The configuration for the experiments is shown in Fig. 5, which employed the electric reverberator to generate the indoor sound. The signal block provided a music sound signal. The feedback circuit and system gain were implemented with digital signal processors.

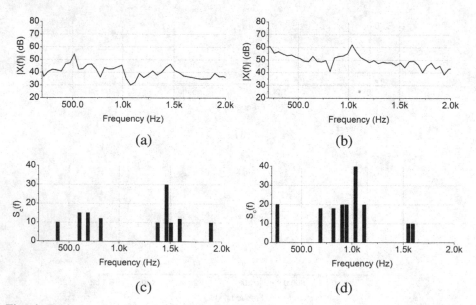

Fig. 4. Example of peak and howling detection (N_{th} = 40). (a) FFT spectrum in stable condition, (b) FFT spectrum in howling condition, (c) Sc(f) in stable condition (d) Sc(f) in howling condition.

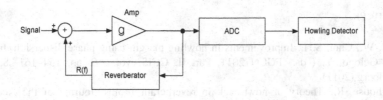

Fig. 5. Configuration for the experiments

Fig. 6 shows the experimental results with the reverberation time of 0.7 sec. We can notice that the proposed method successfully detect the howling at two positions.

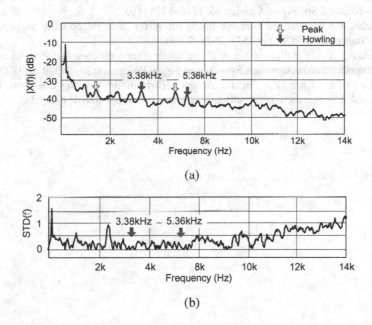

Fig. 6. Example of howling detection (at 3.38 kHz and 5.36 kHz) with the reverberation time of 0.7 sec. (a) FFT spectrum, (b) STD(f)

5   Conclusion

In this paper, we developed spectro-temporal features for howling frequency detection based on statistical properties of temporal variation in power spectra. The proposed method was experimentally shown to be suitable for howling detection in reverberant sound systems.

Acknowledgments. This work was supported by Seoul National University of Science and Technology.

References

1. Lee, J.-W., Choi, S.H.: Improvements in howling margin using phase dispersion. In: Kim, T.-h., Gelogo, Y. (eds.) FGCN 2011, Part II. CCIS, vol. 266, pp. 154–161. Springer, Heidelberg (2011)
2. Waterhouse, R.: Theory of howl-back in reverberant rooms. Journal of the Acoustical Society of America (Letters to the Editor) 37, 921 (1965)
3. Lindberg, E.: The Barkhausen criterion (observation). In: Proc. the 18th IEEE Workshop on Nonlinear Dynamics of Electronics System, Dresden, Germany, pp. 15–18 (2010)
4. Kuto, S.M., Gan, W.S., Shau, F.: Design and synthesis of the audio equalizers. In: IEEE 7th International Conference on Signal Processing, pp. 579–582 (2004)
5. Schroeder, M.R.: Improvement of acoustic feedback stability by frequency shifting. Journal of the Acoustical Society of America 36, 1718–1724 (1932)
6. Gil-Cacho, P.: Regularized adaptive notch filters for acoustic howling suppression. In: Proceedings of EUSIPCO, pp. 2574–2578 (2009)
7. Nehorai, A.: A minimal parameter adaptive notch filter with constrained poles and zeros. IEEE Transactions on Acoustics, Speech, and Signal Processing 33, 983–996 (1995)
8. Wei, J., Du, L., Chan, Z., Yin, F.: A new algorithm for howling detection. In: IEEE International Symposium on Circuits and Systems, vol. 4, pp. 409–411 (2003)

Imperceptibility Improvement of Image Watermarking Using Variance Selection

Xun Jin and JongWeon Kim[*]

Dept. of Copyright Protection, Sangmyung University, Seoul, Korea
jinxun0110@gmail.com
jwkim@smu.ac.kr

Abstract. In this paper, we propose a method of complex region selection for digital images using variance selection. In order to improve the imperceptibility of the watermarked image, our method selects blocks based on their variance. The watermark embedding process operates in the discrete fractional random transform and discrete cosine transform domains. The watermark is embedded into the selected blocks, which are transformed into the frequency domain. For security, visual cryptography is used to encode the watermark. The watermark extraction process is the reverse of the embedding process. The experimental results show that the proposed block selection method significantly improves imperceptibility over a randomly chosen block, and that the watermarking algorithm is robust against common attacks.

Keywords: Variance Selection, Visual Cryptography, Discrete Fractional Random Transform, Discrete Cosine Transform.

1   Introduction

As the rapid transmission of digital content through the internet has become easier, protecting the copyright of digital content has developed into a serious problem. A lot of digital content, including text, images, audio, and video, can easily be modified by unauthorized users. In response, digital watermarking techniques, which provide copyright protection by hiding copyright information in the digital content, have been developed[1-5].

In the case of image content, digital image watermarking is widely used, and the watermark is imperceptible. Most image watermarking techniques operate in the spatial domain or the frequency domain. There are several frequency domains, such as the discrete cosine transform(DCT) domain, the discrete fourier transform(DFT) domain, the discrete wavelet transform(DWT) domain, and the discrete fractional Fourier transform(DFRFT) domain.

A watermarking algorithm based on the discrete fractional random transform (DFRNT) has been reported, and this algorithm exploits the inherent randomness of the transform itself[6]. To improve the imperceptibility of the watermarked image, we

---

[*] Corresponding author.

T.-h. Kim et al. (Eds.): SIP/WSE/ICHCI 2012, CCIS 342, pp. 31–38, 2012.

select complex regions in which to embed the watermark. In order to select these complex regions, we compute the variance of each region and choose those with highest values.

2   Basic Theories

In this section, we briefly review some basic theories about variance selection, visual cryptography, and DFRNT.

2.1   Variance Selection

The variance is a measure of the spread of a set of numbers. A lower variance indicates that the data points are close to the average, whereas a higher variance implies that the data points are spread out over a large range of values. The standard deviation is a measure of the variation from the mean. and is defined as:

$$S_N = \sqrt{\frac{1}{N}\sum_{i=1}^{N}\left(x_i - \overline{x}\right)^2}. \tag{1}$$

The variance is the square of the standard deviation, and can thus be written as:

$$\sigma^2 = \frac{1}{N}\sum_{i=1}^{N}\left(x_i - \overline{x}\right)^2. \tag{2}$$

In the case of image contents, the variance is related to the image components. High variance implies that the image block is comprised of complex components, and vice versa.

2.2   Visual Cryptography

Visual cryptography was introduced by Naor and Shamir in 1995 [7]. Their method decomposes an image I_O into two images, I_1 and I_2. For the security of I_O, its information is encoded into I_1 and I_2. The human visual system cannot recognize I_O from I_1 or I_2. To obtain the information in I_O, I_1 and I_2 must be overlapped, allowing the encoded information to be recognized directly by the human visual system.

Each pixel in the original image is represented by at least one subpixel in each of the n transparencies (or shares) generated. Each share is comprised of collections of m black and white subpixels, where each collection represents a particular original pixel [7-9]. The human visual system can perceive small variations from simple images but finds it difficult to catch variations in complex images.

A digital image copyright protection scheme based on visual cryptography was proposed by Hwang [9], and Zaghloul et al.[10] improved Hwang's method to give a visual cryptography watermarking algorithm. Their algorithm employs visual cryptography to ensure the security of the image content.

It has been reported that a DFRNT can essentially be derived from the DFRFT [11]. Its randomness is generated by a random matrix. The overall process is quite similar to that which obtains the transform matrix of the DFRFT.

3   Proposed Watermarking Scheme

The proposed watermarking scheme is made up of variance selection, visual cryptography, DCT, and DFRNT. The variance selection is used to select the blocks(regions) for watermarking. In this paper, the watermark is a QR code that is decomposed into a random number(RN) generated by the random seed β and verification information(VF) using visual cryptography. To encode the watermark, the VF is embedded into the DCT coefficients of the DFRNTed blocks, which are selected from the host image based on their variance. For the same random number β, a change in the value of the fractional order α produces an entirely different transformed image, and can make the watermark undetectable.

3.1   Variance Selection

To calculate the variance of a block, the mean of the block is computed first. Then subtract the mean from each pixel of the block and square the result. The variance is the average of those squared differences. The proposed algorithm for selecting complex blocks based on the values of their variance is as follows.

Step 1: Calculate the variance of each block.
Step 2: Arrange the variance of n blocks in descending order.
Step 3: Select the m blocks with the highest variance to embed the watermark, and store the positions of these blocks.

3.2   Generation of Verification Information

The proposed algorithm encodes the watermark using visual cryptography. The encoded watermark VF is generated by RN and the QR code that expresses the watermark information. Fig. 1 shows the visual cryptography of QR code. The VF generation process is as follows.

Step 1: Generate RN composed of 0s and 1s with seed β_2.
Step 2: If $RN_i = QR_i$, then assign $VF_i = 1$.
Step 3: If $RN_i \neq QR_i$, then assign $VF_i = 0$. The VF is then generated from the RN and QR code.

QR code   Random numbers   Verification information

Fig. 1. Visual cryptography of QR code

3.3   Watermark Embedding Process

The proposed algorithm embeds the VF into DCT coefficients of DFRNTed blocks. The blocks are selected from the original image based on variance selection, and do not overlap. The embedding process is as follows.

Step 1: Select blocks with the highest variance and store their positions.
Step 2: Transform the selected blocks to the DFRNT domain with the fractional order α and the random seed β_1.
Step 3: Transform the DFRNTed blocks to the DCT domain.
Step 4: Generate random numbers RN with seed β_2.
Step 5: Generate verification information VF form the QR code and RN.
Step 6: Quantize the DCT coefficients.
Step 7: Embed VF into DCT coefficients.

Fig. 2 shows the embedding process above.

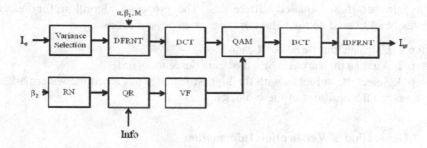

Fig. 2. Watermark embedding process

3.4   Watermark Extraction Process

The extraction process is the reverse of the embedding process, and is described as follows.

Step 1: Select blocks using their stored positions.
Step 2: Transform the selected blocks to the DFRNT domain with the fractional order α and the random seed β_1.
Step 3: Transform blocks to the DCT domain.
Step 4: Quantize the DCT coefficients to extract VF.
Step 5: Generate RN with seed β_2.
Step 6: Extract the watermark from VF and RN.

Fig. 3 depicts the extraction process, described above.

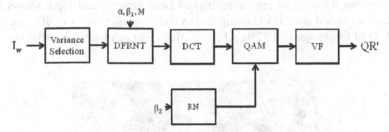

Fig. 3. Watermark extraction process

4 Performance Evaluation

We evaluated the proposed watermarking scheme using the 512×512 cover images "Lena," "Baboon," "Girl," "Goldhill," "Airplane," and "Milk." The watermark QR code is a 25×25 image.

Fig.4 shows the (black) blocks chosen using variance selection and random selection. The size of each block is 8×8, and the minimum value of the variance is 255.32.

Fig. 4. Variance selection(left) and random selection(right)

Fig.5 shows the variance of four 32×32 blocks from the image "Lena." A higher variance means that the block is more complex.

Variance = 124.94   Variance = 433.55   Variance = 1149.17   Variance = 3692.03

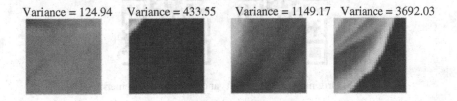

Fig. 5. Variance of four blocks from "Lena"

Fig.6 shows the original and watermarked Lena images, and Fig.8 shows the QR watermark extracted after JPEG compression with a quality factor of 70. The bit error rate(BER) of this image is 0.32%, which is equivalent to two pixels error(those in the circles).

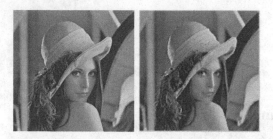

Fig. 6. Original image(left) and watermarked image(right)

Fig.7 shows the watermarked image obtained using variance selection and that given by random block selection.

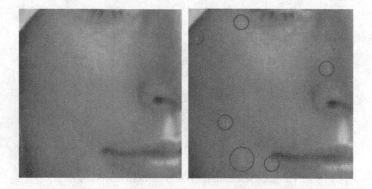

Fig. 7. Variance selection(left) and random selection(right)

Fig. 8. Original watermark(left) and extracted watermark(right)

Table 1 shows the BER and peak signal-to-noise ratio (PSNR) under different attacks on the Lena image. The algorithm recovers the QR code to within 8% under these attacks. QR codes have an in-built error correction capability(ECC). The 25×25 QR code can incorporate 272 bits with an ECC level of L(about 7%), and 224, 176, and 128bits when the levels are M(=15%), Q(=25%), and H(=30%), respectively. For example, if the algorithm recovers the QR code with a 15% BER, 224bits of watermark information can be extracted.

Table 1. BERs and PSNR for various attack types(Lena)

Attack	BER	PSNR
JPEG(80%)	0	37.80
JPEG(60%)	0.8	36.27
JPEG(40%)	5.12	35.15
JPEG(30%)	6.40	34.35
Gaussian(0.001)	3.04	29.78
Salt & Pepper(0.01)	1.60	25.30
Cropping(10%)	0.48	16.78
Rotation(45)	7.52	15.06

Fig.9 shows the BERs for different QFs of JPEG compression and several attacks, such as Gaussian noise, Salt&Pepper noise, cropping, and rotation by 10°, 30°, and 45°. The BERs decrease as the QF increases, which means that the proposed watermarking scheme is robust to JPEG compression. The results demonstrate that the proposed algorithm is robust to frequency attacks because of the use of DCT and DFRNT.

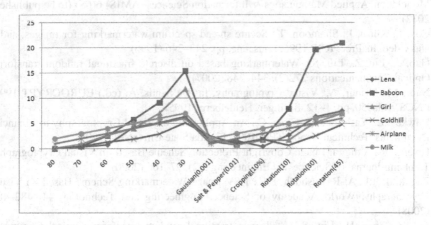

Fig. 9. BER of JPEG compression and various attacks

5   Conclusions

In this paper, we proposed a digital image watermarking scheme using variance selection, visual cryptography, DFRNT, and DCT. The proposed method selects complex blocks based on their variance and transforms them to the DFRNT and DCT domains. Verification information that is encoded by the watermark image is then embedded into the DCT coefficient. The experimental results indicate that the proposed algorithm improves the quality of the watermarked image over random block selection, and maintains a better degree of imperceptibility.

We evaluated the performance of the proposed method by examining the BER under a variety of attacks. Our method showed an improve capacity and robustness under compression and noise attacks. The results demonstrate that the proposed method is robust against JPEG compression and attacks.

Acknowledgments. This research project was supported by the Ministry of Culture, Sports and Tourism(MCST) and the Korea Copyright Commission in 2011.

References

1. Kim, J., Kim, N., Lee, D., Park, S., Lee, S.: Watermarking two dimensional data object identifier for authenticated distribution of digital multimedia contents. Signal Processing: Image Communication 25, 559–576 (2010)
2. Li, D., Kim, J.: Secure Image Forensic Marking Algorithm using 2D Barcode and Off-axis Hologram in DWT-DFRNT Domain. Applied Mathematics & Information Sciences (AMIS) 6(2S), 513–520 (2012)
3. Cox, I.J., Kilian, J., Leighton, T., Shamoon, T.: Secure Spread Spectrum Watermarking for Multimedia. IEEE Transactions on Image Processing 6(12), 1673–1687 (1997)
4. Nah, J., Kim, J., Kim, J.: Video Forensic Marking Algorithm Using Peak Position Modulation. Applied Mathematics & Information Sciences (AMIS) 6(6S) (to be published, 2012)
5. Cox, I., Kilian, J., Shamoon, T.: Secure spread spectrum watermarking for images, audio and video. In: Proc. ICIP 1996, Lausanne, pp. 243–246 (1996)
6. Guo, J., Liu, Z., Liu, S.: Watermarking based on discrete fractional random transform. Optical Communications 272(2), 344–348 (2007)
7. Naor, M., Shamir, A.: Visual Cryptography. In: De Santis, A. (ed.) EUROCRYPT 1994. LNCS, vol. 950, pp. 1–12. Springer, Heidelberg (1995)
8. Hawkes, L., Yasinsac, A., Cline, C.: An Application of Visual Cryptography to Financial Documents. Technical Report TR001001, Florida State University (2000)
9. Hwang, R.: A digital Image Copyright Protection Scheme Based on Visual Cryptography. Tambang Journal of Science and Engineering 3(2), 97–106 (2000)
10. Zaghloul, R.I., Al-Rawashdeh, E.F.: HSV Image Watermarking Scheme Based on Visual Cryptography. World Academy of Science, Engineering and Technology 44, 482–485 (2008)
11. Liu, Z., Zhao, H., Liu, S.: A discrete fractional random transform. Optical Communications 255(4-6), 357–365 (2005)

A Digital Watermarking Scheme Using Hologram Quantization

Ruichen Jin and Jongweon Kim[*]

Department of Copyright Protection, Sangmyung University, Seoul, Korea
kimyejin0602@gmail.com
jwkim@smu.ac.kr

Abstract. In this paper, we propose a digital watermarking scheme that uses hologram quantization to spread the watermark information and analyze the cover image detail. The watermark is a hologram generated using a QR code and quantization based on the cover image. This hologram is transformed by a discrete fractional random transform with a random seed β to make the watermark. The generated watermark can then be embedded into the subband of the discrete wavelet transform (DWT). The proposed scheme includes encryption techniques for security, and is robust because the watermark is inserted in the DWT. When conventional methods are used to watermark an image, the invisibility is poor in the boundary region, but using the proposed method reduces the bit error rate to just 0–0.45%.

Keywords: Hologram, Quantization, Discrete Fractional Random Transform, Discrete Wavelet Transform, QR code.

1   Introduction

Recently, due to the development of network technologies and the widespread use of personal computers as multimedia systems, the problem of illegal distribution has become a social issue. However, the unauthorized copying and distribution of digital content presents a serious threat to the rights of content owners in a number of industries. Furthermore, people's awareness of copyright has increased dramatically, to prevent this phenomenon, copyright protection technologies are required. As a result, watermarking techniques have been proposed for copyright protection and the authentication of digital media [1-4].

There are several schemes to hide information as a watermark. Takai and Mifune used an optical hologram technology as a watermarking embedding method [5]. The holograms were generated from watermark information, and overwritten on the original images using a Fourier transform to facilitate their embedding. A watermarking algorithm based on a discrete fractional random transform (DFRNT) has been reported [6]; this algorithm exploits the inherent randomness of the transform itself. Generally, intrinsic randomness improves the watermark's robustness against attacks.

---

[*] Corresponding author.

T.-h. Kim et al. (Eds.): SIP/WSE/ICHCI 2012, CCIS 342, pp. 39–46, 2012.

2   Hologram Quantization and DFRNT

There are numerous images of arbitrary size on the internet. As image-capture devices improve, we are increasingly able to obtain mega-size images. These have a different characteristic that has different frequency energy for each other when the image is split into a grid, requiring the analysis of each part in the frequency domain. For instance, some parts have lots of high-frequency energy around the edges, and some parts have mostly low-frequency energy. Thus, we can form a quantization table by analyzing the energy, and use this to multiply the generated hologram.

Holograms employ a technique that allows the light scattered from an object to be recorded and later reconstructed, so that when an imaging system is placed in the reconstructed beam, an image of the object will be seen even when the object is no longer present. The image changes with the position and orientation of the viewing system in exactly the same way as if the object were still present, thus making the image appear three-dimensional. The hologram recoding itself is not an image; it consists of an apparently random structure of varying intensity, density, or profile [7]. Holograms were first proposed by Gabor in 1948 [8], and coherent light interference holograms, which use two separate off-axis holograms, were released by Leith and Upatnieks in 1962 [9].

The object wave and reference wave equation using Fourier holograms is as follows:

$$U_H(\xi,\eta) = I(\xi,\eta)^* R(\xi,\eta) + I(\xi,\eta)R(\xi,\eta)^* \tag{1}$$

To restore the information representing the complex amplitude of the wave in Eq. (1), we use the following expression,   :

$$U_R(\xi,\eta) = R(\xi,\eta)\exp\{-j\frac{2\pi}{\lambda_2 f}(\xi x_r{}' + \eta y_r{}')\} \tag{2}$$

Fig. 1. Hologram generation of a QR code

In this paper, we use a QR code for the watermark information. QR codes consist of black modules (square dots) arranged in a square pattern on a white background. They have become popular in a range of environments because of their fast readability and high data capacity.

Figure 1 shows the QR code and its holographic image.

Using hologram quantization, we can restore the QR code. If a hologram (128×128) is generated using a QR code, then the range of the value which average of wavelet coefficient is (-9, 9). According to observations, a minimal portion of values approach the extremes of this range, whereas 98.5% of them are located in (-5, 5). We can appoint a threshold range so that values outside the range are changed to the closest value in the quantization threshold range. For example, if the quantization threshold range is [-3, 3], and the generated hologram has a value of -8.03; then this value is changed to -3. Following quantization, the hologram values are distributed as in Figure 2-(b).

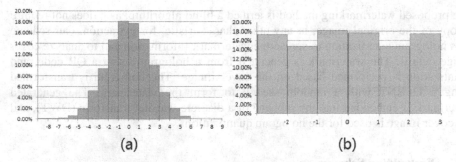

(a)   (b)

Fig. 2. Histograms of hologram values before and after quantization

A quantization table is formed using a random integer matrix of values from 0 to 10 (Fig. 3). Each 32×32 block of the changed hologram is matched to the relevant integer in the quantization table, and is then multiplied by this value.

1	10	10	1
2	5	3	10
4	2	7	0
9	2	7	7

Fig. 3. Quantization table based on a random integer matrix

We can recover the QR code with a 0% bit error rate (BER) when the range of the hologram quantization is limited to [-3, 3] (Fig. 4).

Fig. 4. Original QR code (left) and QR code recovered from the quantized hologram (right)

Recently, it has been established that a DFRNT can be formulated from a discrete fractional Fourier transform (DFRFT) [10]. The randomness is generated by a random matrix. The overall process is quite similar to that by which the transform matrix of the DFRFT is obtained. The DFRNT can be defined by a diagonal, symmetric random matrix, and is linear, unitary, index-additive and energy conserving. However, its kernel transform matrix is random, and this affords high security in information security applications such as digital watermarking.

3   Proposed Watermarking Scheme

The proposed watermarking method is termed a blind algorithm, as it does not require a copy of the original image, or any other characteristic, for extraction. Our scheme uses hologram quantization to spread the watermark information and to analyze cover image details. The watermark is generated from a hologram using a QR code, and quantization is performed based on the cover image. The hologram is transformed using a DFRNT with a random seed β to form the watermark. The generated watermark is embedded into the subband of a discrete wavelet transform (DWT), and the cover image is used for the hologram quantization.

3.1   Embedding Scheme

Step 1: Transform the QR code using a DFRNT with seed β, and generate the hologram. (Figure 5 shows the process of the embedding scheme.)

Step 2: Transform the cover image using a two-depth DWT, and apply the transform to LL1, but also the subband which LH1, HL1 in the 2nd DWT.

Step 3: Calculate the average of the HH2 subbands' (128×128) energy for each 32×32 block. Form a quantization table based on the (4×4) matrix of average energy, and replace the insertion strength corresponding to this average value.

Step 4: Generate the hologram quantization block based on the quantization table.

Step 5: Add the hologram quantization block and the matrix of the LL1-HH2, LH1-LH2, and HL1-LH2 subbands.

Step 6: *Transform them by Inverse DFRNT with seed β.*

Step 7: Transform them by two-depth Inverse DWT.

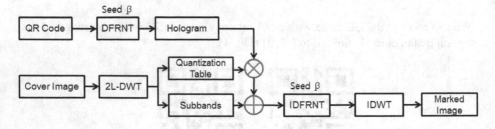

Fig. 5. Watermark embedding process

3.2   Extraction Scheme

The extraction process is the reverse of the embedding procedure, and uses the same seed β in the DFRNT. (Figure 5 shows the process of the extraction scheme.)

Step 1: Transform the marked image using a two-depth DWT, and select the subbands that will incorporate information.

Step 2: Add the subbands to obtain the new matrix.

Step 3: Transform them by DFRNT with seed β.

Step 4: Restore them with ReHologram, and extract the QR code.

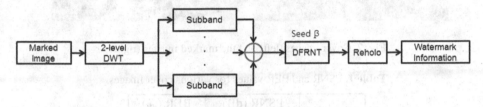

Fig. 6. Watermark extraction process

4   Experimental Evaluation

The performance of the proposed watermarking scheme was measured using the several cover images with a 512×512 image size. The size of the QR code was 21×21.

The watermark's invisibility is generally measured using the peak signal-to-noise ratio (PSNR) and the mean squared error (MSE):

$$PSNR = 20\log_{10}(255/MSE) \tag{3}$$

$$MSE = \sqrt{\frac{1}{MN}\sum_{x=1}^{M}\sum_{y=1}^{N}[f^{\omega}(x,y) - f(x,y)]^2} \, , \tag{4}$$

where M and N represent the width and height. Fig. 7 shows the cover images and marked images, and Table 1 lists the PSNRs and BERs corresponding to the cover images. Although the PSNR value is less than 40 dB, the watermark is invisible if the cover image has mainly high-frequency components. In the case of the Baboon image, although it has many high-frequency components and a PSNR of about 33 dB, it exhibits good invisibility. Thus, controlling the insertion strength in our watermarking scheme by analyzing the frequency components in detail is an effective strategy.

Fig. 7. Cover images (left) and the marked images (right)

Table 1. PSNR and BER values for various cover images

	PSNR (dB)	BER (%)
Lena	40.42	0
Baboon	33.39	0.45
Plane	39.33	0
Pepper	39.28	0.23

The proposed method was robust to several types of attack (Fig. 8). In the case of Gaussian noise and Salt & Pepper noise, our experiments showed that the BERs remained stable. In contrast, the BER increases with a decreasing JPEG quality factor (QF); when the QF is 40, the BER is as high as 14.51%. However, QR codes have the capability to recover data from code degradation of up to 30%. Thus, we can recover all information without error.

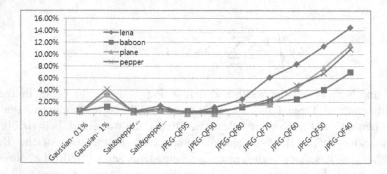

Fig. 8. BER corresponding to various attacks

It is difficult to analyze the variation of frequency components in portions of mega-size images. The proposed method is particularly suitable for the image shown in

Fig. 9. Conventional methods struggle to watermark this image, as the invisibility is not good in the boundary regions indicated. Using the proposed method, we obtain a BER of 0–0.45%.

Fig. 9. Marked mega-size image

Fig. 10 shows an enlargement of box 'a' in Fig. 9. As we can see, Fig. 10-(b) is messier than Fig. 10-(a), and conspicuous close to the boundary. Comparing the circled areas, we can see the difference more clearly. Thus, there are positive effects to using hologram quantization.

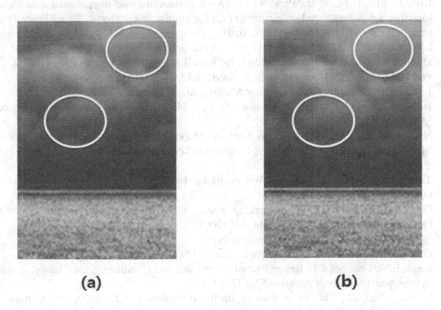

(a)   **(b)**

Fig. 10. Comparison of marked images (a) with and (b) without using hologram quantization

5   Conclusion

In this paper, we proposed a digital watermarking scheme using hologram quantization to spread the watermark information and analyze the cover image detail. We used a DFRNT with the random seed β to form the watermark, which was then embedded into the subband of the DWT.

To evaluate the performance of the proposed method, watermark information was embedded in the wavelet-transformed domain. Performance evaluations were conducted using hologram quantization to control the embedding strength by analyzing the frequency components of the image. Our results showed that the proposed method gives improvements in robustness under compression and noise attacks.

In conclusion, we have determined that hologram quantization is an effective watermarking method that does not interfere in the frequency characteristics of an image.

Acknowledgements. This research project was supported by the Ministry of Culture, Sports and Tourism (MCST) and by the Korea Copyright Commission in 2011.

References

1. Kim, J., Kim, N., Lee, D., Park, S., Lee, S.: Watermarking two dimensional data object identifier for authenticated distribution of digital multimedia contents. Signal Processing: Image Communication 25, 559–576 (2010)
2. Lee, Y., Kim, J.: Robust Blind Watermarking Scheme for Digital Images Based on Discrete Fractional Random Transform. In: Kim, T.-h., Gelogo, Y. (eds.) MulGraB 2011, Part II. CCIS, vol. 263, pp. 139–145. Springer, Heidelberg (2011)
3. Li, D., Kim, J.: Secure Image Forensic Marking Algorithm using 2D Barcode and Off-axis Hologram in DWT-DFRNT Domain. Applied Mathematics & Information Sciences (AMIS) 6(2S), 513–520 (2012)
4. Nah, J., Kim, J., Kim, J.: Video Forensic Marking Algorithm Using Peak Position Modulation. Applied Mathematics & Information Sciences (AMIS) 6(6S) (to be published, 2012)
5. Takai, N., Mifune, Y.: Digital Watermarking by a holographic technique. Applied Optics 41(5), 865–873 (2002)
6. Guo, J., Liu, Z., Liu, S.: Watermarking based on discrete fractional random transform. Optical Communications 272(2), 344–348 (2007)
7. Wikipedia, http://www.wikipedia.org
8. Gabor, D.: A New Microscope Principle. Nature 161, 777 (1948)
9. Leith, E.N., Upatnieks, J.: Reconstructed Wavefronts and Communication Theory. Journal of the Optical Society of America 52, 1377 (1962)
10. Liu, Z., Zhao, H., Liu, S.: A discrete fractional random transform. Optical Communications 255(4-6), 357–365 (2005)

Development of Information System to Control the Increasing Prevalence of Diabetic Patients

Seong-Ran Lee

Department of Medical Information, Kongju National University, 56 Gongjudaehak-ro,
Kongju, Chungnam, 314-701, South Korea
lsr2626@naver.com

Abstract. This paper is focused on the development of information system to control the increasing prevalence of diabetic patients. The subjects of this paper were 114 patients who had been visited a general hospital which located in urban area. The validity of the developed information system was estimated using intervention method that measured action-oriented, relevant, and effect of time elapsed between groups. The present research showed that health practice behavior in diabetic patients can be increased to 61.5-87.2% by information system. This paper showed that information system could help diabetic patients in providing effective practice of their health behavior.

Keywords: Development, Information system, Diabetic Patient, Prevalence.

1 Introduction

Diabetes mellitus is one of most common disease in the world. Diabetes mellitus has approached to us as a social epidemic in Korea[1]. The prevalence of diabetes mellitus in Korea has increased five to six-fold from 1.5% to 7-9% during the past 30 years. This increasing rate is remarkably high in comparison with those of developed countries. In addition, diabetic complication is very common in diabetic patients. For example, a total of 70.5% among new patients who were started with renal replacement therapy over the last 20 years[1],[2]. The age-sex adjusted mortality rate of diabetic patients was about three-fold higher than those of general population. As a result, medical cost of diabetes mellitus covered by the national health insurance corporation was 3.2 trillion won and accounted for 19.2% of all medical costs[3],[4]. On the other hand, the rate of awareness and treatment in diabetic patients has improved from 2000 to 2010[5]. Therefore, the comprehensive and integrated information system including public approach is urgently needed to control the increasing prevalence of diabetes mellitus and its related desirable outcomes.

However, we don't have any national program at all about it[6].[7]. In order to solve the urgent problem, we should look for the practical plans. There were few studies to deal with effect of information system for the prevention diabetic patients until present in Korea. To overcome this situation, this paper developed effective information system to prevent the incidence of diabetic patients. And then this paper

T.-h. Kim et al. (Eds.): SIP/WSE/ICHCI 2012, CCIS 342, pp. 47–54, 2012.

sought to apply the effect of it on the change of practice behavior of subjects for occurrence prevention of diabetic mellitus using information system.

Therefore, this paper was performed the series of information intervention for control the increasing prevalence of diabetic patients. On the other hand, the follow-up survey was conducted at the end of this trial to compare the change before and after information intervention for health promotion behavior between the two groups. Thus, this paper is designed to develop the short-term information system for the prevention of diabetes mellitus and ultimately to analyze the adoption effect through its application. The development of the research field of diabetic patient-related outcomes in information system will make it possible to conduct better quality studies in the future.

2   Materials and Methods

2.1   Development of Information System

This paper is to develop information system by making use of intervention method. This first of the development is to identify a problem through need-assessment of the participants[Fig.1]. And then it carries out the procedures of conducting problem analysis and sets a goal of the information system. When all of the above are done properly, the system planning is to be implemented. Second step is to identify the functional elements of successful models and gather the information about this. Information system which will be reflected in health promotion behavior is designed as part of information gathering and synthesis. In the third step, an experimental stage, where preliminary program is to be applied in the field has been implemented. In the final step, in order to evaluate the program durability, follow-up test has been done for three months after termination of the program.

2.2   Study Materials

Study participants were 114 patients who were diagnosed with diabetes mellitus at least 6 months ago by internal medicine of a general hospital in urban area. The data were collected by interview and self-administered questionnaire from February 8 through March 8, 2012.

For this, quasi-experimental groups which are equivalent control groups have been implemented. The experimental group of 57 patients which was assigned as group with information intervention, while the control group of 57 patients was assigned as group with no information intervention. To conduct the intervention, large and small group education, e-mail, telephone counseling and so on were performed. The two groups are compared to know the difference of changes which affects health promotion behavior. In order to evaluate the program durability, follow-up test has been done for three months after termination of the program.

2.3   Study Methods

General characteristics of study subjects was measured by percentage and number. The pairwise t-test was done to compare the before and after intervention effect of health practice rate of diabetes mellitus. This was conducted to observe some significant differences between the two groups before and after the intervention program.

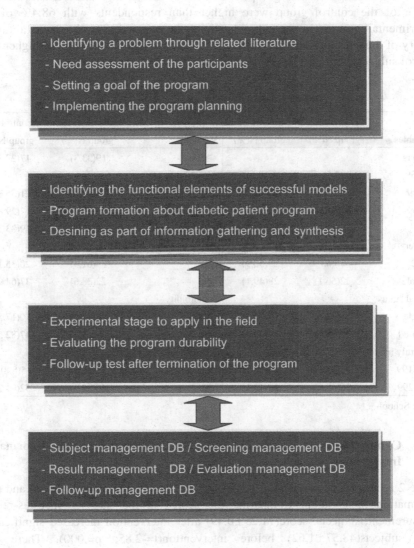

- Identifying a problem through related literature
- Need assessment of the participants
- Setting a goal of the program
- Implementing the program planning

- Identifying the functional elements of successful models
- Program formation about diabetic patient program
- Desining as part of information gathering and synthesis

- Experimental stage to apply in the field
- Evaluating the program durability
- Follow-up test after termination of the program

- Subject management DB / Screening management DB
- Result management   DB / Evaluation management DB
- Follow-up management DB

Fig. 1. Information System Structure for Health Promotion Behavior of Diabetic Patients

3   Results

3.1   Basic Information of Study Subjects

Table 1 presents basic information of study subjects. Comparing the proportion in the gender, male with 50.9% of the control group showed more than male with 43.9% of the experimental group. In a marital status, married respondents with 73.7% of the control group were higher than respondents with 68.4% of the experimental group. On the other hand, about respondents who have a family history of diabetes mellitus, the experimental group with 61.4% showed higher than control subjects with 35.1%.

Table 1. Basic Information of Study Subjects

Variables	Experimental group N(%)	Control group N(%)	Variables	Experimental group N(%)	Control group N(%)
Age/yrs.			≥300	19(33.3)	17(29.8)
☐ ≤39	4(7.0)	6(10.5)	Education level		
40-49	13(22.8)	10(17.5)	Under middle s.†	18(31.6)	21(36.8)
50-59	19(33.3)	17(29.8)	High school s.	23(40.4)	17(29.8)
≥60	21(36.8)	24(42.1)	Over college	16(28.1)	19(33.3)
Gender			Family history		
Male	25(43.9)	29(50.9)	Yes	35(61.4)	20(35.1)
Female	32(56.1)	28(49.1)	No	22(38.6)	37(64.9)
Marital status			Comorbidity		
Single	18(31.6)	15(26.3)	Yes	18(31.6)	10(17.5)
Married	39(68.4)	42(73.7)	No	39(68.4)	47(82.5)
Monthly income			Complication		
≤199	12(21.1)	16(28.1)	Yes	11(19.3)	5(8.8)
200-299	26(45.6)	24(42.1)	No	46(80.7)	52(91.2)

† S : School

3.2   Comparison of Health Practice of Before and After Information Intervention

Table 2 represents comparison of health practice of diabetic patients before and after information intervention. Comparing the scores in the diabetes mellitus-related measurement, subjects' score(71.25±0.49) after intervention increased significantly than subjects(48.57±1.62) before intervention(t=-2.85, p=.000). There was significantly high difference in the diet control after information intervention(t=-2.69. p=.007).

Table 2-A. Comparison of Health Practice of Before and After Information Intervention

Items /intervention	Before Mean±S.D	After Mean±S.D	t	P
DM measurement†	48.57±1.62	71.25±0.49	-2.85	.000
B.W control ‡	52.91±0.37	61.74±1.57	-3.74	.065
Complication	49.65±1.22	60.55±0.30	-0.02	.004
BP measurement¶	45.10±0.42	53.83±0.63	-1.62	.210
Exercise	55.67±0.17	67.18±0.62	-0.82	.029
Medication	64.52±0.63	59.30±0.44	0.17	.586

† DM : Diabetes mellitus   ‡B. W : Body weight   ¶ BP : Blood pressure

Table 2-B. Comparison of Health Practice of Before and After Information Intervention

Items /information	Before Mean±S.D	After Mean±S.D	t	p
Diet control	58.72±1.69	65.42±0.49	-2.69	.007
Knowledge of diabetes mellitus	42.73±1.28	67.02±1.81	-2.40	.002
Health care	57.41±0.26	64.72±0.81	-0.03	.038
Smoking	45.52±0.67	41.28±0.47	1.79	.759
Alcohol	48.37±0.29	42.61±0.52	0.26	.521

3.3   Change of Health Promotion Behavior Before and After Intervention

Fig. 2 presents the change of health promotion behavior in diabetic patients before and after information intervention. According to the health promotion behavior, after

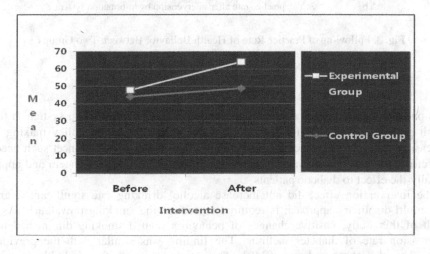

Fig. 2. Change of Health Promotion Behavior Before and After Intervention

the intervention, the mean scores of the experimental group showed increase after intervention than control group.

3.4   Follow-Up of Practice Rate of Heath Behavior between Two Groups

Fig. 3 compare the follow-up of practice rate of health behavior between two groups The follow-up survey was estimated to be higher in the experimental group, regardless of the time elapsed of 20 days after the information intervention. However, the intervention effect was estimated to decrease more rapidly with time elapsed of 60 days after intervention in the experimental group as compared to the control group.

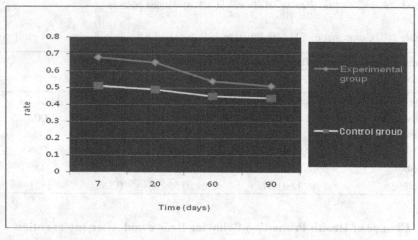

*Slope = $\frac{\triangle Y}{\triangle X}$ Where $\triangle X$: time interval

$\triangle Y$: variation of intervention effect by information system

*Ratio = $\frac{\triangle Ya}{\triangle Yb}$ Where $\triangle Yb$: practice rate before intervension by information system

$\triangle Ya$: practice rate after intervension by information system

Fig. 3. Follow-up of Practice Rate of Health Behavior Between Two Groups

4   Discussion

This paper is focused mainly on the intervention effect of information system in the health promotion behavior for diabetic patients. Recently, health policy making is increasing based on evidence. Information system was developed to meet such need. Therefore, the paper is to evaluate the development of information system and apply actually the effect to diabetic patients.

The intervention effect did not increase alcohol drinking rate significantly, and then multi-displinary approach is required to reduce the smoking prevalence. As a result of this study, positive changes of behaviors related smoking diminished the progression rate of diabetes mellitus. The finding was similar with the previous studies on the chronic disease[8],[9]. This study suggests that individuals with diabetes mellitus should be targeted for specific health behavioral intervention to prevent the progression of diabetes mellitus. Based on the results obtained by the study, it is anticipated that this paper may be used as basic data for developing and intervening health promotion behavior for the chronic disease patients. However, the result shows that in order to maintain non-smoking of diabetic patients, various and long-term smoking cessation program is more successful than single and short-term program. The results of this paper, after receiving intervention, there were significant changes for the diet control than before intervention in the mean score of diet control. The finding was consistent with the result of earlier research[10]. Therefore, it needs to perform systematic diet management. There is a need for a separate program to be implemented on the groups who characterize having lower levels of health knowledge and health promotion behavior.

The present research showed that practice rate of the health behavior can be increased 61.5-87.2% by information system, which is similar to data reported in the previous studies[11],[12]. However, it should be noted that the intervention effect by information system is not maintained for a long period of time. Accordingly, in order to maintain the intervention effect by information system, it is very important to determine adequate intervention period and perform various programs in consideration of their circumstances. The present work elucidated throughout the statistical analysis how effectively the synthetic and systematic education contributes to health promotion behavior for the prevention of diabetes mellitus. The future work should focus on the study of the intervention effect as a classification of patient throughout more prolonged research based on a larger data base.

Until the present, the limitation of diabetic patients lies in that there in nothing put into action despite the increase of knowledge. The result of this study would be the enhancement of practice behavior for the prevention of diabetes mellitus. Thus, this paper indicated that the implemented systematic intervention showed significant positive effects on the life of subjects and health behavior. The quality of life in the experimental group has been enhanced as time passes by compared to control group, showed that it is an effective program for the prevention of diabetes mellitus. This information intervention has been developed by complementing and revising preliminary program. Therefore, the information program for diabetic patients implemented by intervention research is quite meaningful in that it is evidence-based program development which will contribute in replicating the intention under field conditions for diabetic patients.

Diabetic patients who had moderate exercise level and who were under diet care had better quality of life. Current practice of exercise in diabetic patients were obtained through intervention of information system. Therefore, adequate health practice behavior in diabetic patients will improve their quality of life in accordance with proper information program. The development about information system is so essential to the diabetic patients. For successful performance of this study, this paper had tried to provide various information to enhance the practice rate of health behavior in diabetic patients using information system. So, there were many changes which improve the quality of life in diabetic patients using information system. This study showed that information system could help diabetic patients in providing effective practice of their health behavior.

5   Conclusion

This paper developed information system to control the increasing prevalence of diabetic patients and applied it to subjects. The developed information system focuses on health practice rate before and after intervention to identify health promotion behavior by information system in diabetic patients. As a result of the research, this paper found that the health promotion behavior in diabetic patients were many increased compared to the previous status and the patients positively perceived on information system. Moreover, this paper showed that using information system as health practice tool was a good way to enhance the practice rate of health behavior in diabetic patients.

The information system for health promotion can be applied to any hospital which has health promotion center. Also, this system can be extended to inpatient or outpatient departments. With integration of information system, the effective management of chronic disease patients would also be possible.

References

1. Statistics Korea, Annual Report on the Cause of Death Statistics, pp. 13–15 (2011)
2. Ministry of Health and Welfare, Annual Report of Cancer Registry Programmes, pp. 23–24 (2011)
3. American Cancer Society, The American Cancer Society Guidelines for the Cancer Related Checkup. Cancer, 42–43 (2003)
4. Preis, S.R.: Trends in Cardiovascular disease Risk Factors in Individuals with and without Diabetes Mellitus in the Gramingham Heart Study. Circulation, 123–126 (2008)
5. Rimm, E.B.: Prospective Study of Cigarette Smoking, Alcohol Use and the Risk of Diabetes in Men. British Medical Journal, 316–321 (2007)
6. Suarez., L., Lloyd, L., Weiss, N., Rainbolt, T., Pulley, L.V.: Effect of Social Networks on Cancer-Screening Behavior of Older Mexican-American Women. Journal of the National Cancer Institute 86, 776–778 (2004)
7. Moran, W.P., Nelson, K., Wofford, J.I., Velez, R.: Computer-Generated Physician and Patient Reminder Tools to Improve Population Adherence to Selected Preventive Services. J. Fam. Pract. 5, 534–536 (2002)
8. Omstein, S.M., Garr, D.R., Jenkins, R.G., Rust, P.F., Amon, A.: Computer-Generated Physician and Patient Reminder Tools to Improve Population Adherence to Selected Preventive Services. J. Fam. Pract. 32, 83–85 (2008)
9. Jefferson, I.G., Smith, M.A., Baum, J.D., Litzelman, D.K., Dittus, R.S., Miller, M.E., Tiene, W.M.: Requiring Physicians to Respond to Computerized Reminders Improves Their Compliance with Preventive Care Protocols. J. Gen. Intern. Med. 8, 315–316 (2003)
10. Santiago, J.V.: Clinical Report: Intensive Management of Insulin Dependent Diabetes: Risks, Benefits and Unanswered Questions. J. Clin. Endocrinol. Metab. 81, 102–105 (2009)
11. Nicolucci, A.: A Comprehensive Assessment of the Avoidability of Long-Term Complication of Diabetes. A Case-Control Study SID-AMD Italian Study Group for the Implementation of the St. Vincet Declaration. Diabetes Care 21, 812–816 (2006)

Digital Watermarking Robust to Geometric Distortions

Jihah Nah[1] and Jongweon Kim[2,*]

[1] Digital Copyright Protection Research Institute, Sangmyung University, Korea
[2] Department of Copyright Protection, Sangmyung University, Korea
jihah.nah@gmail.com
jwkim@smu.ac.kr

Abstract. In this paper, we propose a digital watermarking scheme that is robust against geometric distortions. The proposed method uses image moment normalization and a correlation peak position modulation (CPPM) to recover geometric distortions. This mechanism is invariant to affine transform attacks and suitable for public watermarking applications, where the original image is not available for watermark extraction. In addition, CPPM ensures that there is sufficient capacity to hide specific information. We verify the robustness of our approach to rotation, scaling, and Gaussian noise attacks. The watermark can be detected with zero BER, because disadvantages disappear when CPPM is combined with image moment normalization—only the advantages of the two methods remain.

Keywords: Image moment normalization, Correlation peak position modulation, Image watermarking, Spread spectrum, Geometric attacks.

1 Introduction

Rapid advances in digital multimedia and network technology have made it possible for people to easily access and distribute multimedia content. Digital watermarking is considered a useful technology for copyright protection and the authentication of digital media [1]. Although significant progress has been made in the watermarking of digital images, many challenging problems remain in practical applications [2], [3]. Many existing watermarking algorithms can be ineffective against geometric attacks, such as rotation, scaling, translation, shearing, or a change of aspect ratio [4-6]. Such attacks can destroy the synchronization required for watermark extraction and, as a result, the original image cannot be extracted.

In the literature, several approaches for handling geometric attacks have been proposed. Various watermarking techniques have used the Fourier–Mellin transform (FMT) [7], [8], discrete Fourier transform (DFT) [9], and image moment normalization [10], [11]. In [7], Ruanaidh and Pun dealt with rotation, scaling, and translation attacks using the invariant properties of FMT. This approach was somewhat difficult to implement. Lin et al. [8] embedded the watermark in a

---

* Corresponding author.

T.-h. Kim et al. (Eds.): SIP/WSE/ICHCI 2012, CCIS 342, pp. 55–62, 2012.
© Springer-Verlag Berlin Heidelberg 2012

one-dimensional signal obtained by projecting the FMT image onto the log-radius axis. However, this method can embed only one bit of information.

Pereira and Pun [9] used a pilot signal to estimate the affine geometry of attacks in the image, embedding the watermark in the DFT domain. Their approach requires the detection of both the synchronization pattern and the watermark. If a common pilot signal is used for different watermarked images, the signal may be susceptible to collusion-type detection [12].

In [10], [11], a watermark scheme that used block-based watermarking and moment normalization mechanisms to recover geometrical distortions was proposed. In this approach, only one bit of information per block is inserted via the watermark.

In this paper, we propose a robust watermarking scheme using image moment normalization and correlation peak position modulation (CPPM). The proposed watermarking scheme is robust to general affine geometric attacks, and can acquire sufficient capacity via the CPPM.

The rest of this paper is organized as follows. Section 2 describes the proposed watermarking based on image moment normalization, as well as the embedding and extraction processes. In Section 3, we evaluate the performance of the algorithm and analyze our experimental results, before presenting some conclusions in Section 4.

2   Proposed Watermarking Method

The proposed watermarking method uses a moment normalized image and CPPM for both watermark embedding and detection. Fig. 1 depicts a block diagram of the proposed image watermarking scheme.

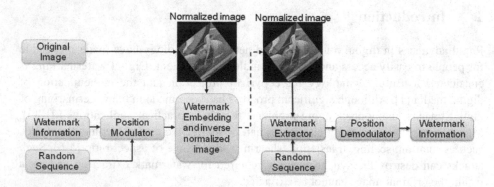

Fig. 1. Block diagram of watermark embedding and extraction process

2.1   Image Moment Normalization

The normalized image is invariant to any affine distortions, and can be obtained from a geometric transformation procedure.

Image Moments. Let $f(x, y)$ denote a digital image of size $M \times N$. Its *geometric moments* and *central moments* can be respectively defined as:

$$m_{pq} = \sum_{x=0}^{M-1} \sum_{y=0}^{N-1} x^p y^q f(x, y), \tag{1}$$

and

$$\mu_{pq} = \sum_{x=0}^{M-1} \sum_{y=0}^{N-1} (x - \bar{x})^p (y - \bar{y})^q f(x, y), \tag{2}$$

where $p, q = 0, 1, 2, \ldots$ and:

$$\bar{x} = \frac{m_{10}}{m_{00}}, \quad \bar{y} = \frac{m_{01}}{m_{00}}. \tag{3}$$

An image $g(x, y)$ is said to be an affine transform of $f(x, y)$ if there is a matrix $\mathbf{A} = \begin{pmatrix} a_{11} & a_{12} \\ a_{21} & a_{22} \end{pmatrix}$ and vector $\mathbf{d} = \begin{pmatrix} d_1 \\ d_2 \end{pmatrix}$ such that $g(x, y) = f(x_a, y_a)$, where

$$\begin{pmatrix} x_a \\ y_a \end{pmatrix} = \mathbf{A} \cdot \begin{pmatrix} x \\ y \end{pmatrix} - \mathbf{d}. \tag{4}$$

Image Normalization. For a given image $f(x, y)$, the normalization procedure consists of the following steps:

1. Center the image $f(x, y)$; this is achieved by setting $\mathbf{A} = \begin{pmatrix} 1 & 0 \\ 0 & 1 \end{pmatrix}$ and the vector $\mathbf{d} = \begin{pmatrix} d_1 \\ d_2 \end{pmatrix}$ in (4), with:

$$d_1 = \frac{m_{10}}{m_{00}}, \quad d_2 = \frac{m_{01}}{m_{00}}, \tag{5}$$

where m_{10}, m_{01}, and m_{00} are the moments of $f(x, y)$ defined in (1). This step achieves translation invariance. Let $f_1(x, y)$ denote the resulting centered image.

2. Apply a shearing transform to $f_1(x, y)$ in the x direction with matrix $\mathbf{A}_x = \begin{pmatrix} 1 & \beta \\ 0 & 1 \end{pmatrix}$ so that the resulting image, denoted by $f_2(x, y) \cdot \mathbf{A}_x[f_1(x, y)]$, achieves $\mu_{30}^{(2)} = 0$, where the superscript is used to denote $f_2(x, y)$.

3. Apply a shearing transform to $f_2(x,y)$ in the y direction with matrix $\mathbf{A}_y = \begin{pmatrix} 1 & 0 \\ \gamma & 1 \end{pmatrix}$ so that the resulting image, denoted by $f_3(x,y) \cdot \mathbf{A}_y [f_2(x,y)]$, achieves $\mu_{11}^{(3)} = 0$.

4. Scale $f_3(x,y)$ in both the x and y directions with $\mathbf{A}_s = \begin{pmatrix} \alpha & 0 \\ 0 & \delta \end{pmatrix}$ so that the resulting image, denoted by $f_4(x,y) \cdot \mathbf{A}_s [f_3(x,y)]$, achieves: i) a prescribed standard size, and ii) $\mu_{50}^{(4)} > 0$ and $\mu_{05}^{(4)} > 0$.

The final image $f_4(x,y)$ is the normalized image on which the subsequent watermark embedding or extraction is performed. Equation (4) points to the fact that a general affine transform attack can be decomposed into a translation, shearing in both the x and y directions, and scaling in both the x and y directions. The four steps in the normalization procedure are designed to eliminate each of these distortion components. Step 1 eliminates the translation part of the affine attack by setting the center of the normalized image at the density center of the affine-attacked image. Steps 2 and 3 eliminate shearing in the x and y directions by forcing $\mu_{30}^{(2)} = 0$ and $\mu_{11}^{(3)} = 0$. Finally, step 4 eliminates scaling distortion by forcing the normalized image to be a standard size.

Using this method, there is very little information that can be embedded into the cover image. Image moment normalization is robust to geometric attacks, but has the disadvantage that only a limited amount of information can be embedded.

2.2   Watermarking Algorithm

The image normalization procedure yields a normalized image that is invariant to any affine geometric transforms. It is on this normalized image that we perform watermark embedding and detection. In this paper, we propose an improved CPPM watermarking scheme [13], which is robust against common signal processing attacks and has abundant information capacity.

CPPM can provide more robustness than traditional spread spectrum techniques, because it has a longer sequence length for the same image, and different users are apt to have different image correlation peak positions. This is due to each user having a different piece of information, each of which is loaded at a different position in the image [13], [14].

The quality of digital content, and the detection performance of embedded information, can be ensured by using long sequences as watermarks, as shown by (6) and (7). In other words, CPPM achieves superior robustness to other schemes for the same amount of information, because the length of the watermark sequence can be maximized. For example, when 16 bits of information are embedded in a 256 × 256 image, CPPM has a longer sequence, with a watermark block size of 256 × 256, than spread spectrum watermarking methods, which have a block size of 64 × 64.

CPPM is introduced to ensure appropriate payloads and robustness. The existence of a spread spectrum sequence can generally be identified using correlation. CPPM inserts the position of a correlation peak as embedded information. The basic equation can be written as:

$$\rho_{I_w w}(u, v) = \iint I_w(x, y) w(x + u, y + v) dx dy \tag{6}$$

where $I_w(x,y)$ is a marked image and w is a watermark generated by a pseudo-random number sequence. The variables u and v represent the amount of shift in the 2D coordinate system.

The peak position, representing the embedded information, is then given by:

$$p = u + v \times width = B_n 2^n + B_{n-1} 2^{n-1} + \cdots + B_1 2^1 + B_0 \tag{7}$$

where B_n represents the nth bit.

The message is modulated to the peak position using (6) and (7). The information capacity per watermark block can be maximized because the position of the correlation peak is shifted according to the embedded information. Figure 2 shows the shift process for the correlation peak.

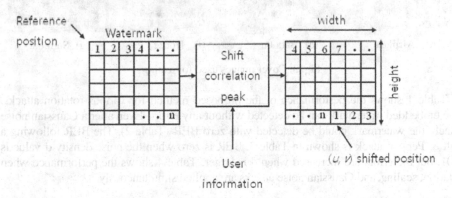

Fig. 2. Shift process for a correlation peak

CPPM is able to embed a lot of information, but is weak against geometric attacks. However, this disadvantage disappears when CPPM is combined with image moment normalization—only the advantages of the two methods remain.

3   Experiments

We conducted a series of experiments to evaluate the performance of the robust watermarking scheme. The proposed algorithm was evaluated using six image samples. The performance evaluation was conducted by observing the bit error rate (BER) according to various rotation angles, scaling, and noise. The number of watermark bits was 60 for a 512×512 sized image, and a watermark block of 128×128 was used. In our experiments, we used seven different color cover images, shown in gray-scale in Fig. 3. The watermarked images were distorted by a variety of geometric and common signal processing attacks. The BER, defined as the ratio between the number of incorrectly decoded bits and the total number of embedded bits, was then computed and averaged over all the test images.

(a) Lena   (b) Milk   (c) Peppers

(d) Airplane   (e) Baboon   (f) House   (g) Sailboat

Fig. 3. Cover images used for testing

Table 1 shows the performance of the proposed method for various rotation attacks. The embedded watermark can be detected without any errors. Even after a Gaussian noise attack, the watermark could be detected with zero BER (Table 2). The BER following a Salt & Pepper attack is shown in Table 3. BER is zero when the noise density d value is 0.01, but the errors are increased when d is larger. Table 4 shows the performance when rotation, scaling, and Gaussian noise attacks are applied simultaneously.

Table 1. BER after various rotation attacks

Test image	PSNR after WM (dB)	BER after rotation (%)					
		0°	10°	30°	45°	60°	90°
Lena	38.28	0	0	0	0	0	0
Milk	40.73	0	0	0	0	0	0
Pepper	38.76	0	0	0	0	0	0
Airplane	38.61	0	0	0	0	0	0
Baboon	32.35	0	0	0	0	0	0
House	36.55	0	0	0	0	0	0
Sailboat	35.79	0	0	0	0	0	0

Table 2. BER after Gaussian noise attack

Test image	BER (%)			Test image	BER (%)		
	20 dBW	25 dBW	30 dBW		20 dBW	25 dBW	30 dBW
Lena	0	0	0	Baboon	0	33.3	33.3
Milk	0	0	0	House	0	0	33.3
Pepper	0	0	0	Sailboat	0	0	0
Airplane	0	0	0				

Table 3. BER after Salt & Pepper attack

Test image	BER (%)		Test image	BER (%)	
	d = 0.01	d = 0.02		d = 0.01	d = 0.02
Lena	0	0	Baboon	0	46.7
Milk	0	33.3	House	0	0
Pepper	0	53.3	Sailboat	0	0
Airplane	0	53.3			

Table 4. BER after rotation, scaling, and Gaussian noise attacks

Test image	BER (%)
	0 with 35 ° rotation, 30 dBW WGN = 0.01, 350 × 350 scaling
	0 with 10 ° rotation, 30 dBW WGN = 0.01, 256 × 256 scaling
	0 with 35 ° rotation, 30 dBW WGN = 0.01, 350 × 350 scaling
	0 with 10 ° rotation, 30 dBW WGN = 0.01, 256 × 256 scaling

4   Conclusion

We have demonstrated that the proposed method of combining image moment normalization and CPPM can provide robustness and sufficient information capacity. Our method is robust to general affine geometric transformation attacks, a result of both embedding and extracting the watermark message using the normalized images.

We verified the robustness of our approach using rotation, scaling, and Gaussian noise attacks. The majority of the attacks studied led to a zero BER in the extracted image.

Acknowledgments. This research project was supported by the Ministry of Culture, Sports and Tourism (MCST) and the Korea Copyright Commission in 2011.

References

1. Hartung, F., Kutter, M.: Multimedia watermarking techniques. Proc. IEEE 87, 1079–1107 (1999)
2. Kim, J., Kim, N., Lee, D., Park, S., Lee, S.: Watermarking two dimensional data object identifier for authenticated distribution of digital multimedia contents. Signal Processing: Image Communication 25, 559–576 (2010)
3. Li, D., Kim, J.: Secure Image Forensic Marking Algorithm using 2D Barcode and Off-axis Hologram in DWT-DFRNT Domain. Applied Mathematics & Information Sciences (AMIS) 6, 513–520 (2012)
4. Petitcolas, F.A.P., Anderson, R.J., Kuhn, M.G.: Attacks on Copyright Marking Systems. In: Aucsmith, D. (ed.) IH 1998. LNCS, vol. 1525, p. 218. Springer, Heidelberg (1998)
5. Kutter, M., Petitcolas, F.A.P.: A fair benchmark for image watermarking systems. In: Electronic Imaging 1999, Security and Watermarking of Multimedia Contents, San Jose, CA, vol. 3657 (January 1999)
6. Cox, I.J., Linnartz, J.P.M.G.: Public watermarks and resistance to tampering. In: IEEE International Conference on Image Processing, vol. 3 (1997)
7. Ruanaidh, J.O., Pun, T.: Rotation, scale and translation invariant spread spectrum digital image watermarking. Signal Processing 66(III), 303–317 (1998)
8. Lin, C.Y., Wu, M., Bloom, J.A., Cox, I.J., Miller, M., Lui, Y.M.: Rotation, scale and translation resilient public watermarking for images. IEEE Trans. on Image Processing 9(6), 767–782 (2001)
9. Pereira, S., Pun, T.: Robust template matching for affine resistant image watermarks. IEEE Trans. on Image Processing 9(6), 1123–1129 (2000)
10. Dong, P., Brankov, J.G., Galatsanos, N.P., Yang, Y., Davoine, F.: Digital Watermarking Robust to Geometric Distortions. IEEE Transactions on Image Processing 14(12), 2140–2150 (2005)
11. Lu, C.-S.: Towards robust image watermarking: combining content-dependent key, moment normalization, and side-informed embedding. Signal Processing: Image Communication 20, 129–150 (2005)
12. Cox, I.J., Miler, M.L., Bloom, J.A.: Digital Watermarking. Morgan Kaufmann (2001)
13. Nah, J., Kim, J., Kim, J.: Video Forensic Marking Algorithm Using Peak Position Modulation. Applied Mathematics & Information Sciences (AMIS) 6(3S) (to be published, 2012)
14. Nah, J., Kim, J., Kim, J.: Image Watermarking for Identification Forgery Prevention. Journal of the Korea Contents Association 11(12) (2011)

On a New Enhancement of Speech Signal Using Non-uniform Sampling and Post Filter

Seonggeon Bae, Hyungwoo Park, and Myungjin Bae[*]

Information and Telecommunication Department,
Soongsil University, 1-1 Sangdo 5 dong DongJak-Ku,
Seoul, 156-743, Republic of Korea
sgbae123@empal.com, park.hyungwoo@gmail.com,
mjbae@ssu.ac.kr

Abstract. To enhance speech signal by reducing the redundancy within samples that resulted from uniform sampling method like PCM, non-uniform sampling or non-redundant-sample coding methods can be considered. However, it is well known that when conventional non-uniform sampling methods are applied directly to speech signal, the required amount of data in the computation is comparable to or more than that of uniform sampling method. To overcome this problem, a new non-uniform sampling method is proposed, in which non-uniform sampling is applied to the speech signal after using the low pass filter and the remain signals are compensated by the rectified signals with various harmonics frequencies.

Keywords: Non-uniform sampling, Quantization, Peak and valley.

1 Introduction

Speech encoding method for storing or transmitting in signal processing can largely be classified into waveform coding method, source coding method, hybrid encoding method, etc., and to maintain intelligibility and naturalness, waveform coding method is mainly used. This coding process is the method of storing and synthesizing after removing repeated, unnecessary remaining components, and The waveform coding methods until now have been researched as PCM, ADM, DPCM, ADPCM, etc. However, it has the disadvantage that large amount of memory is required due to enormous quantity of data. Main point of speech coding is to process it by considering, especially, transmission and compression rate of data, speech quality of playback, and processing velocity among the information transmitted. In general, unnecessary remaining component which is existed in the voiced signal is known to be derived from relatively high correlation between samples. Therefore, to reduce data quantity or transmission rate for storing or transmission of speech, the remaining ingredient which is existed in the uniform sampling, i.e., the sample which has high correlation between samples and gives lesser influence from the viewpoint of recognition shall be removed.

---

[*] Corresponding author.

T.-h. Kim et al. (Eds.): SIP/WSE/ICHCI 2012, CCIS 342, pp. 63–69, 2012.
© Springer-Verlag Berlin Heidelberg 2012

In general, for speech signal, problem can be generated for the recognition when voice is reconstructed in accordance with the characteristic of input signal for speech signal. Therefore, to maintain intelligibility and naturalness of speech, work to improve speech shall be carried out. Due to the improvement of calculation time of computing, various calculation methods have been presented. One of these methods is the waveform method in which improvement work is performed at time domain, and it is known to be excellent in terms of intelligibility and naturalness characteristic. In addition, there is the frequency method which is the parameter method to have improvement by detecting characteristic frame of speech, and this has the disadvantage that calculation quantity is too much to be applied to various speech. It is the hybrid method which is made by taking advantages of waveform and frequency method, and improvements have been made for this owing to the development of computing. In this study, to use this hybrid method, the method with non-uniform sampling in speech signal obtained from time domain will be used. Especially, in the case of voiced signal, as it is concentrated in the voiced signal with large amplitude, the improvement method which is searching and using peak and valley which are characteristics of voiced signal for synthesizing to emphasize linearity is to be presented. At chapter II, existing method which is to search recognizable characteristic of voiced signal, and at chapter III, signal method to use the proposed non-uniform sampling method will be described, and at chapter IV, conclusion and study direction in the future will be presented.

2   Existing Method

According to the study which considers recognizable characteristic of voice signal, it can be understood that in the case of the signal made by differentiating and clipping original voice wave from the recognition test of Licklider and Pollack, almost no deterioration is generated when comparing to 99% of recognition level of original signal as its value of recognition level is 97%. The coding method to use peak and valley of sound by utilizing this characteristic has been presented, and this has been used by considering the recognizable aspect. Therefore, this recognizable aspect of voice signal will be affected by the peak and valley which are appeared in the standardization and quantization. By utilizing this characteristic, numerous applications for synthesizing or coding section are possible, and especially for jamming environment, great support have been conducted for searching important factors of recognition signal by re-constituting filter and considering characteristics of peak and valley. As shown in the figures, the first one shows typical characteristics of peak and valley, and the second one displays properties of peak and valley. Final figure indicates influences which appear from clipping of sound and overload.

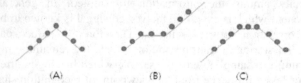

(A)   (B)   (C)

Fig. 1. Quantization influence signal
(a) Typical peak (b) Peak, valley simultaneously (c) Overload

In these 1 cases, as the last one is appeared by the influence for overload, it can give the most influence to the recognizable characteristic of sound. In here, overload is the phenomenon which is appeared in the clipping environment of sound, and great influence will be affected to the recognizable section when deteriorated signal is re-constituted at this section. Therefore, in this study, the improvement method applying to clipping signal will be used by considering only the section which is generated by the influence of overload and by using this kind of important recognition signal.

Waveform reconstruction is performed by using cosine interpolation method based on such parameters as the magnitudes and the intervals of the peak and the valley. The reconstructed waveform, $S_k(n)$, obtained by cosine interpolation method is represented as follows;

$$S_k(n) = [\frac{M(k-1) - M(k)}{2} \cos(\frac{\pi n}{I(k)})$$
$$+ \frac{M(k-1) + M(k)}{2}], \qquad 1 \leq n \leq I(k) \tag{1}$$

where, $M(.)$ is the magnitude of non-uniformly sampled data and $I(.)$ is the interval of them.

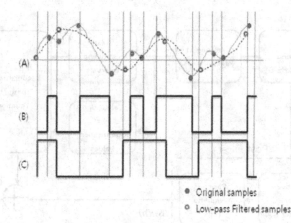

Fig. 2. Examples of non-uniform coding (A) peaks and valleys (B) original nonuniform coding (C) nonuniform coding using Low pass filter signal

3   Proposed Method

To the speech production mechanism, since higher frequency band is related to the sound produced from the constriction structure than from the resonance structure, the 3rd and upper formants have broad bandwidths. Moreover, from the viewpoint of speech Perception, higher frequency band components are not significant, while the 1st and the 2nd formants are indispensible to reconstruct the high-intelligible speech.

Therefore, the samples related to the frequency band higher than the 2nd formant are Considered as redundant information in the speech perception.

The 1st and the 2nd formant frequencies of most phonemes of speech are less than 2.5 kHz. Also, the formants higher than this cut-off frequency have quite broad bandwidths. Therefore, non-uniform sampling can be only applied to the signal component of the original waveform less than 2.5 kHz without terrible loss of intelligibility. Since the low-pass filtered signal is smoother than the original one, fewer number of the peak and the valley sample are obtained when non-uniform sampling is performed on it. This makes it possible to achieve high compression ratio. Fig. 3 shows the encoding and the decoding block diagram of the method proposed in this paper. In this block diagram, $S(n)$ is speech signal digitized uniformly by A/D converter and sampler, and $S_{LP}(n)$ is the law-pass filtered signal at 2.67 kHz as cutoff frequency. The conventional non-uniform sampling as like (1) equation is applied to this low-pass filtered signal and such parameters as the magnitudes, $M(.)$ and the intervals, $I(.)$, of the peak and the valley points are Quantized by the scalar quantizer to interval I, and gain, M. At the same time, LPFed speech component $S_{LP}(n)$, is reconstructed by the inverse quantizer, the non-uniform sampling, and the cosine Interpolation technique. Also, to improve high frequencies the harmonic signals, $S_H(n)$, using the post filter as the positive clipping and the weighted filter is obtained.

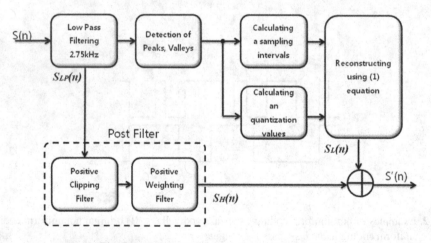

Fig. 3. A speech coding scheme using post filter

Major components of the residual signal consist of the 3rd and upper formants of speech. Generally, the magnitude spectrums of the higher formants have a more bandwidth than that of 1st or 2nd formant and the positions of the formants are assigned to a little important information to speech intelligibility. To preserve the naturalness of speech by the 3rd and upper formants, pseudo random Gaussian noise is added to the waveform reconstructed roughly with the nonuniform sampling parameters. Generally, since the characteristic of the residual signal between the original and the reconstructed low-band waveform is rather a pseudo colored than a white noise, we can roughly approximate the residual signal to one of eight colored Gaussian noise.

$$S_L(n) = y_k(n) \tag{2}$$

$$S_H(n) = 0.7*|S_{LP}(n)| \tag{3}$$

$$S'(n) = S_L(n) + S_H(n) \tag{4}$$

where N is the frame size. The encode procedure can much reduce the data rate to achieve higher compression ratio than that of the conventional non-uniform sampling even in the noisy environment and also get a good quality of speech by reconstructed harmonics signal.

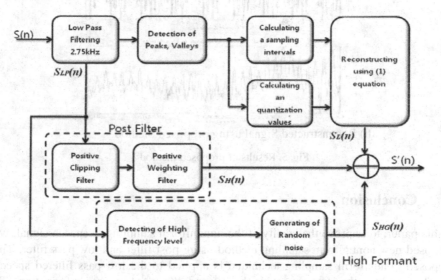

Fig. 4. A new speech coding scheme proposed in this paper

$$S_{HG}(n) = Gaussian \left[\frac{1}{N}\sum_{N=0}^{\infty}(S(n+N) - S_{LP}(n+N))\right] \tag{5}$$

$$S'(n) = S_L(n) + S_H(n) + S_{HG}(n) \tag{6}$$

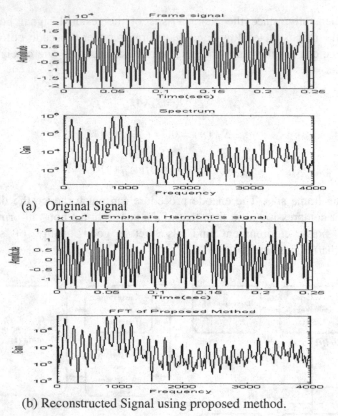

(a) Original Signal

(b) Reconstructed Signal using proposed method.

Fig. 5. Results of proposed method

4   Conclusion

In this paper, to improve the quality of the nonuniform sampling in speech signal, we proposed new nonuniform sampling method using post filter and low pass filter. The proposed nonuniform sampling technique is applied to the low-pass filtered speech signal to reduce the data rate with the 1st and the 2nd formants information. To preserve the naturalness, the high frequency components are compensated by adding the post filter using rectified signal.

References

1. Sohn, J., Kim, N.S., Sung, W.: A statistical model-based voice activity detector. IEEE Signal Processing Lett. 6(1), 1–3 (1999)
2. Accardi, A.J., Cox, R.V.: A modular approach to speech enhancement with an application to speech coding. J. Acout. Soc. Am. 10(3), 1245 (2001)

3. Jeong, C.-J., Bae, M.-J.: Analysis regarding vocalizations of teuroteu singers, The institute of electronics engineers of Korea, Summer scholarship contest of 2009, pp. 1090–1091 (2009)
4. Bae, M.J., Lee, S.H.: Digital Voice Signal Analysis, ch. 3, p. 6. Books Publishing Dong Young (1998)
5. Gazor, S., Zhang, W.: A soft voice activity detector based on a Laplacian-Gaussian model. IEEE Trans. Speech Audio Processing 11(5), 498–505 (2003)
6. Agarwal, T., Kabal, P.: Pre-processing of noisy speech for voice coders. In: Proc. IEEE Workshop on Speech Coding, Tsukaba, Japan, pp. 169–171 (October 2002)

Correlation Analysis between N18 Acupuncture Point and Liver Function Using Bio Signals Analysis Technologies

Bong-Hyun Kim[1], Min-Kyoung Ka[2], Dong-Uk Cho[3], and Sang-Young Oh[4]

[1] Department of Computer Engineering, Kyungnam University, Korea
[2] Department of Computer Engineering, Chungbuk National University, Korea
[3] Department of Electronic Communications, Chungbuk Provincial University, Korea
[4] Department of Business Administration, Youngdong University, Korea
`hyun1004@kyungnam.ac.kr, {kplus,ducho}@cpu.ac.kr,`
`culture@yd.ac.kr`

Abstract. As indicators of life quality, early stage medical examination and health care before diseases occur have recently shown great improvement. From this point of view, hand acupuncture, as an alternative medicine to reflect these movements of preventative medicine and health care, is widely used in these days. Therefore, in this paper, we measured the change of bio signals parameters related to liver by stimulating N18 acupuncture point on hand, and then we investigated that possible improvements of liver function is happened or not. For this, we collected image and voice samples related to liver function before and after stimulating the N18 acupuncture point, and we performed experiments by applying image and voice signal processing technologies.

Keywords: N18 Acupuncture Point, Liver Function, Bio Signals Analysis, Third Formant Frequency Bandwidth, Left Cheek Skin Color Analysis, Lab System.

1 Introduction

In recent years, it is gradually increasing interest about health care and welfare of modern people according to change in social environment. In particular, it has been very much concern about the social health care system that a prevention of disease through early diagnosis. Reflecting the situation of the times, the government's national policy in the field of health services is focused on the future medical technology and industry development of the next generation. Such a preventive medicine for healthy life, the health services industry is concentrated on the research and investment in the nation as well as in the world. The main role of these changes in medical fields is alternative medicine[1]. There exists a variety of medical fields that alternative medicine forms medical system as the center human and natural. In these situations, fewer side effects, the field of hand acupuncture is getting a lot of interests from modern man. Hand acupuncture is a part of alternative medicine which each points are related to whole organs and body shown as the following fig. 1.[2][3].

T.-h. Kim et al. (Eds.): SIP/WSE/ICHCI 2012, CCIS 342, pp. 70–76, 2012.
© Springer-Verlag Berlin Heidelberg 2012

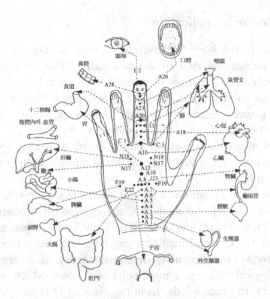

Fig. 1. Correspondence diagram of hand and human body

Therefore, in this paper, we performed experiments to analyze image and voice biometric signals which is based on the facial image and voice of N18 acupuncture point related to liver before and after stimulation. For these experiments, we measured the face color from left cheek region by image analysis which reflects the physiological signals associated with the liver. For this, the Lab color system is adopted and b value is measured which means the degree of blue color. In addition, we measured the third formant frequency bandwidth which is to extract velar sounds such as the "ga kka ka geu kkeu keu" and that sounds mean the liver function associated with physiological signals in the voice[4][5][6].

Finally, we performed the evaluation about the improvement degree of liver function according to stimulate an acupuncture point related to liver by measuring and comparing the change values b color of left cheek region in face image and the third formant frequency bandwidth from voice signal.

2 Research Methods and Procedures

Firstly, in this paper, we performed a study to extract interrelationship the third formant frequency bandwidth which obtains the elements of voice signal analysis. Also, color analysis of left cheek in facial area is accomplished according to stimulate the N18 acupuncture point which related to the liver. For this experiment, we collected ordinary facial image and voice before stimulation the liver-related acupuncture point with healthy 20s male without liver diseases.

2.1   Theory of Research Application

As the largest organ in the body, the weight of liver is about 1 ~ 1.5kg which is approximately the size of the sum of the two palms. The liver is involved in all functions of our body. The function of normal liver must be supplied a sufficient oxygen and nutrients in hepatocytes to the blood circulation in the liver. If we continue to have a protein deficiency or starvation, we are reduced to liver protein degradation and efficacy of enzyme degradation. Typical function of liver is metabolism, alcohol metabolism, detoxification, creation of bile, blood coagulation, and antibody production, liver is variously indicated aspects of illness as the backbone of the internal organs[7].

Oriental medicine is the evolution of natural medicine which is based on Yin-Yang five parameters theory of Oriental medicine, at the same time, observing the natural philosophy of the Orient is a review of the Yin-Yang and five parameters theory and research. In addition, the Oriental medicine can be thought as a kind of hypothetical academic philosophy[5]. In particular, diagnosis theory of liver-related region is focused on physiological changes, shape, color and voice which are based on Yin Yang five parameters. In other words, from the view of Oriental medicine, liver can check disease the degree of blue color in the left cheek of the face image and sound is Gak-sound of pentatonic, phonic velar sounds corresponding to the pronunciation of molar. Pronunciation of molar belongs to "ㄱ(giyeok), ㅋ(kieuk), ㄲ(ssang giyeok)" pronunciation. So, when you occur problems the ambiguity of these sound, the liver function is damaged from several liver diseases[8].

Table 1. Five Parameters Table

Separation	Mok(wood)	Wha(fire)	To(soil)	Geum(iron)	Su(water)
Five viscera	Liver	Cardiac	Spleen	Lung	Kidney
Five color	Blue	Red	Yellow	White	Black
Sounds	ㄱ,ㅋ	ㄴ,ㄷ,ㄹ,ㅌ	ㅇ,ㅎ	ㅅ,ㅈ,ㅊ	ㅁ,ㅂ,ㅍ
Pronunciation	Velar sound	Lingual sound	Guttural sound	Dental sound	Labial sound
Five sounds	Gak	Chi	Goong	Sang	Woo

2.2   Analysis Method of Image Signals

For analysis the image signals, we collect before and after values to stimulate liver-related acupuncture point. For this, we extract facial left cheek area which liver-related area in ocular inspection of Oriental medicine. Extracted left cheek is to apply the Lab color system to analyze liver-related color value such as blue, we compared and analyzed of b color value change. Environment for the collection of face images input is under constant lighting, constant distance, place of Canon's EOS-400D and f1.4/50mm a lens. The camera's condition is to set ISO 200, exposure is priority mode of aperture, aperture is about 1.4 reflective exposure metering in the state opened up to the appropriate exposure values[9].

In addition, the color representation of the input images are used RGB for image processing and analysis process. However, ocular inspection theory of Oriental medicine is based on the face for a particular area of color differences through the associated organs abnormalities to determine observing a person's shape and color for human five viscera corresponding to the blue, red, yellow, white and black respectively which requires the analysis for efficient digital color system. In this paper, for representation and analysis of five colors, efficient face image analysis of device-independent color, we used CIE Lab color system which is easy to get the acquisition reproduction in color [10][11].

2.3 Analysis Method of Voice Signals

For voice signal analysis, we measure voice the before and after value such as the third frequency bandwidth to stimulate hand acupuncture point which liver-related velar sounds in auscultation theory of Oriental medicine. In the vocal tract like cavity to vibrate inside the human body, the end voice (vocal cords, tongue, teeth, lips), etc. by the final sound is generated when the air have passed the vocal tract. A resonance of vocal tract is formant and its generated waveform is called formant frequency[12].

The formant frequency can be extracted by using LPC of voice signals. LPC can be predicted a linear combination with output signal of the current and the input signal of the past. This is showing good performance accuracy and computational speed, its associated with a voice production model can be expressed fewer parameters with features of voice. In other words, the voice of a certain interval divided by the N piece voice samples s(1), ..., s (N) of one point in the voice signals (n), a constant section M (M <N) piece of one sample are divided by the signals (n-1), ..., s(nM) which can be expressed by the following formula:

$$s(n) = \sum_{i=1}^{M} a_i s(n-i) + e(n) \quad M+1 \leq n \leq N \tag{1}$$

$$s(n) = \sum_{i=1}^{M} a_i s(n-i) + e(n) \quad M+1 \leq n \leq N \tag{2}$$

The above formula (1) and (2), s(n) is the voice signal, a_i are the prediction coefficients, M is prediction degree and e(n) means prediction error. In this paper, we can be extracted all candidates of formant frequency and bandwidth to compute A(z), root of inverse filter obtain formant frequency values using value of LPC, bandwidth B and F complex about z of complex roots means z-periodicity in the plane T from s-plane to z-plane for change[13].

$$F = (\frac{f_s}{2\pi}) \tan^{-1} [\frac{I_m(z)}{R_e(z)}] \tag{3}$$

$$B = -(\frac{f_s}{\pi}) \ln|z| \tag{4}$$

In this paper, we performed a study to extract interrelationship the third formant frequency bandwidth and an elements of voice signal analysis. Also, color analysis of left cheek in facial area according to stimulate liver-related region N18 acupuncture point is accomplished.

3   Experimental Results and Observations

3.1   Analysis of Image Signals and Result of an Experiment

Firstly, we extracted left cheek area which is the liver-related region. Also, from the facial input image, we collected the before and after a stimulation value in acupuncture point which is related to liver. In the left cheek area, we extracted the Lab color system value such as b color value and we carried out comparison and analysis before and after stimulation. Figure 2 is shown program screen to measure extraction of left cheek area and b color values by applying Lab color system.

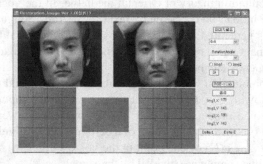

Fig. 2. Left Cheek Color Analysis of M01

By the experimental results such as the following the table 2, measured b color values of left cheek area showed a lower value of b the 86.7% of subjects in facial left cheek area after stimulation than before stimulation liver-related hand acupuncture point. From these results, according to the stimulation associated with the liver-related hand acupuncture point, we can be analyzed that the b color values is decreased which is the evidence of liver function improving status.

Table 2. Experimental Results(Image Signal)

Left cheek b value	Before stimulation	After stimulation	Deviation
M01	18.80	17.89	-0.91
M02	16.09	14.50	-1.59
M03	12.42	10.39	-2.03
M04	16.74	15.15	-1.59
M05	18.98	18.38	-0.60
M06	20.70	19.43	-1.27
M07	19.81	15.54	-4.27

Table 2. (*continued*)

M08	14.45	9.91	-4.54
M09	15.65	15.72	+0.07
M10	16.92	11.17	-5.75
M11	17.42	18.82	+1.40
M12	21.08	18.85	-2.23
M13	18.63	18.06	-0.57
M14	14.92	14.37	-0.55
M15	18.37	17.20	-1.17

3.2   Analysis of Voice Signals and Result of an Experiment

Firstly, we carried out comparison and analysis to measure the third formant frequency bandwidth liver-related voice signal. For this, we collected voice signal and analysis has done from the collected before and after hand acupuncture stimulation associated with voice input related to liver function. Table 3 is shown measurements and the deviation of the third formant frequency bandwidth between the hand acupuncture stimulation on the N18 region before and after respectively. As we can see from the experimental results, the third formant frequency bandwidth after the acupuncture stimulation than before stimulation is decreased 93.3% subjects in joining the experiment. From these results, decreasing value of the third formant frequency bandwidth is to improve liver function according to stimulating the liver-related hand acupuncture associated with the point.

Table 3. Experimental Results(Voice Signal)

3 Formant frequency bandwidth	Before stimulation	After stimulation	Deviation
M01	962.203	680.141	-282.062
M02	796.607	548.940	-247.667
M03	661.506	506.730	-154.776
M04	578.385	168.819	-409.566
M05	546.460	384.624	-161.836
M06	485.998	412.485	-73.513
M07	845.605	487.442	-358.163
M08	1024.745	836.145	-188.600
M09	596.042	552.741	-43.301
M10	846.485	748.143	-98.342
M11	684.259	725.058	+40.799
M12	805.937	671.682	-134.255
M13	729.681	689.350	-40.331
M14	548.392	348.058	-200.334
M15	472.390	395.825	-76.565

From these results, we showed clearly that decreasing values reflects the improvement the liver function than before stimulation the acupuncture point.

4   Conclusion

In this paper, a variety of alternative medicine and the body's internal organs which interrelated acupuncture point distributed in the palm of our hands with acupuncture to prevent and treat disease based on the theory applied to biological signal analysis techniques to analyze the correlation liver function was carried out. The experimental results are shown that stimulating the acupuncture points related to liver based on ocular inspection in Oriental medicine theory is effective to improve the liver function by the liver-related facial image region analysis and voice analysis. In particular, the blue value of left cheek area, the 86.7% of the subjects after stimulation is lower than before stimulation. In addition, the third formant frequency bandwidth of a liver-related 93.3% of the subjects in the experiments is lower than before stimulation.

In other words, we concluded that the acupuncture stimulation through N18 acupuncture point improves liver function and state that the application of image and voice analysis have proved the parameters. As a result, we verified that reflex point acupuncture stimulation improves the liver activity and liver function clearly.

References

1. Maeng, H.Y., et al.: Introduction to Complementary & Alternative Medicine. Hanol Pub. (2010)
2. Yoo, T.W.: Hand Acupuncture. Korea Hand Acupuncture Pub. (2008)
3. Yoo, T.W.: Life Hand Acupuncture of Dr. Tae-Woo Yoo. Taeung Pub. (1998)
4. Shin, D.W.: Dong-uibogam, pp. 108–143. Field Pub. (1999)
5. Choi, H.J.: Hwangjenaegyeong-Somun. Freedom Mungo Pub. (2004)
6. Sung, H.J.: A Study on Dong-uibogam. Korea Institute of Science and Technology Information Journal 13(1), 253–268 (2000)
7. Marieb, E.N., Mallatt, J., Wilhelm, P.B.: Human Anatomy. Gyechuk Culture Pub. (2010)
8. Ikeda, M.: Hwangjenaegyeong-Nangyeong. Cheonghong Pub. (2002)
9. Jeong, H.G.: Digital Camera Technology. Future Com Pub. (2001)
10. Cho, D.U., et al.: Application of Skin Color Analysis about Digital Color System for Oriental Medicine Observing a Person's Shape and Color Implementation. Korea Information and Communications Society Journal 33(2) (2008)
11. Kim, Y.S., et al.: Understanding of Color. Iljin Pub. (2007)
12. Welling, L., Ney, H.: Formant Estimation for Speech Recognition. IEEE Trans. on Speech and Audio Processing 06, 1063–1076 (1998)
13. Wakita, H.: Direct Estimation of the vocal Track shape by Inverse Filtering of Acoustic Speech waveforms. IEEE Trans. A&E 50(02), 637–655 (1971)

A Research on the Investment Pattern between Real-Estate and Stock Market in South Korea: Using the Granger-causality Test[*]

Yeonjoon Kim[1] and Yong-Kyu Yi[2,**]

[1] Department of International Trade & Commerce, Kyungsung University,
309, Suyeong-ro(Daeyeon-dong), Nam-gu, Busan 608-736, Rep. of Korea
yeonjoonkim@ks.ac.kr
[2] School of Architecture, Jeju National University, D116 College of Engineering
4th building 102 Jejudaehakno, Jeju-si, 690-756, South Korea
ykyi@jejunu.ac.kr

Abstract. We live in a rapidly changed society. In 2008, we experience economic difficulties because of the sub-prime mortgage crisis starting from the U.S. At that time, world's stock prices and real-estate's prices have been plummeted. When investors decide that stock market is very volatile and dangerous to invest, they change their pattern of investment toward real-estate market that is a safer one. This paper investigates whether stock markets are related to real-estate market. Results of correlation test show that housing price of Jeju has a negative correlation with apartment price of Seoul and stock price of Korea. And, there is a negative correlation between housing price in Korea and Jeju. And, results of the Granger-causality test show that apartment price affects to housing price in case of Busan.

Keywords: The Granger-causality test, Real-estate, Urban area, Rural area, Stock price.

1   Introduction

In 2008, we experience economic difficulties because of the subprime mortgage crisis in the U.S. At that time, world's stock prices and real-estate prices are being plummeted. During those times, investors worry about their targets of investment, that is, where they should invest their money. Generally, we know that investors invest their money to a safer market guaranteeing high profits. When investors decide that stock market is a very volatile and dangerous to invest their money, they change their target of investment to real-estate market. We generally know that investors make their portfolio of investment to invest their money in search for better profits. When our economy is solid enough, we invest more our money to real-estates, stocks, gold,

---

[*] This paper is supported by Kyungsung University Research Grants in 2012. All errors are ours.
[**] Corresponding author.

T.-h. Kim et al. (Eds.): SIP/WSE/ICHCI 2012, CCIS 342, pp. 77–84, 2012.
© Springer-Verlag Berlin Heidelberg 2012

and etc. In 2008, investors make reduce their amounts of investment due to uncertainty. However, investors gradually invest their money to real-estate, stock, and etc. again in 2009 with economic recovery. With this, stock prices have recovered and real-estate prices also have been recovered. When investors increase their investment to stock markets, price of stock will be increased and investors, *relatively*, will decrease their investment to real-estate. This is our assumption to test and we would like to prove this assumption using the Granger-causality test.

There are a bunch of papers that deal with the topic regarding prices of real-estate and macroeconomic variables. Lee's (2008) paper researches on the housing prices and macroeconomic variables using data of South Korea. He uses the structural vector auto regressive (SVAR) model to investigate the relationship. He finds that interest rates affect to the housing price. Additionally, he digs out that housing price affects to consumption, output, and prices. Chang and Sim's (2007) paper investigates on the REITs[1] with respect to real-estates and stocks. Results of their paper show that real-estate markets affect to the REITs. Their research uses the multi-factor model. Son (2010) investigates on multi-relationship regarding monetary policy, housing prices, and the other economic variables. They use database of South Korea from 1991 to 2008 in their testing the model. Chang and Sim's (2007) paper shows stock market does not affect to the REITs. They use the multi-factor model. However, changes in real-estate market affect to the REITs with positive sign using the multi-factor model. Chung et al.'s (2011) paper studies markets' analysis of housing purchase and lease using the Granger-causality analysis. They concentrate on housing markets of Busan area using the factors in supply and demand. Chung et al. (2011) prove that changes in non-manufacturing sector affects to a lease market. Namely, non-manufacturing sector Granger-causes a lease market. Per Jang et al.'s (2010) paper, we understand that there is a relationship between demand of investment and housing markets with low interest rates. Jang et al.'s (2010) paper investigates that stock market and real-estate market have a different dynamic relationship because of regional characteristics of real-estate market. This regional characteristic of real-estate market can control the demand of investment.

Per Shin et al.'s (2005) research, stock market as a method of investment affects to motivation of asset investment in demand of housing. And this can affect to housing prices. Per Park's (2007) research, liquid money flows in stock and real-estate market because of the low interest rate. This low interest rate creates benefits with the differences in interest rates. He points out that stock market and real-estate market have a substituting relation and co-movement relation between assets.

With these previous researches, this paper investigates whether there is a relationship between stock market and real-estate market in the perspective of investment pattern. And this paper investigates whether there is a relationship with regard to housing prices between local region in South Korea, especially for Busan and Jeju. The reason why we choose Busan in our study is because Busan is an urban center in South Korea. And, the reason why we choose Jeju is because Jeju is a non-urban center in South Korea. Some scientists insist that there is a relationship between stock market and real-estate market. However, the other scientists insist that there is

---

[1] The REITs means real estate investment trusts.

no distinct proof between the two markets. This paper investigates whether stock markets are related to the real-estate market. Economic fluctuation is directly related to restructuring of portfolio in investment. This paper extends the ideas of previous researches to verify when investors understand that stock markets are not stable enough then; they tend to change their targets in investment to the real-estate. We use time series analysis with the Granger-causality test for this test. These are the contribution of this paper that is different from the previous researches. One more contribution of this paper is that this paper uses the Granger-causality test with 'urban and rural data of South Korea' and 'stock prices of South Korea' to investigate the relationship between real-estate market and stock market.

Chapter 2 explains methodologies and models, chapter 3 explains test results, and chapter 4 concludes this paper.

2   Methodologies and Models

This paper uses the Granger-causality methodology. In our model, this paper investigates the relationship between real-estate prices and stock prices. For this research, we use housing related data from Kookmin Bank in South Korea. This paper uses housing-related price index data from January of 1993 to July of 2011. Namely, we use Housing Purchase Price Composite indices. We define that June of 2011 is 100 for this indices. Let's explain about variables that this paper uses. Here, HPT means Housing Purchase Price Composite indices of all regions in South Korea. HPS means Housing Purchase Price Composite indices of Seoul. HPB means Housing Purchase Price Composite indices of Busan. HPJ means Housing Purchase Price Composite indices of Jeju. For Apartment Purchasing Price Index, we define that June of 2011 is 100. HPAT means Apartment Purchasing Price Index of all regions in South Korea. HPAS means Apartment Purchasing Price Index of Seoul. HPAB means Apartment Purchasing Price Index of Busan. HPAJ means Apartment Purchasing Price Index of Jeju.

For data of stock prices, we use the data from the bank of Korea between January of 1993 and July 2011. We use transactions in securities and stock price from the Korea Composite Stock Price Index (KOSPI). And, this data is an annual or monthly averaged one. And, it is an original data.

When we test whether one factor affects to the other factor, we use 'correlation test' and 'the Granger-causality test.' Let's explain this with factor A and B. Limitation of correlation test is that we can find that factor A can affect to factor B or factor B affect to factor A, but we cannot find exact direction of the causality test. A methodology that overcomes this limitation is the Granger-causality relation. We can tell the causality relation with the direction of the test. This paper uses the Granger-causality methodology in proving whether there is any relationship between stock prices and real-estate price in South Korea.

Clive Granger publishes "Investigating causal relations by econometric models: cross spectral methods" at the *Econometrica* in 1969. At that time, Dr. Granger would like to find the relation between two factors using econometric tools. His idea is that a certain result of causation cannot come before the phenomenon of the reason. Namely, 'results' could not come before 'causes'. Hamilton (1994) studies that when we put factor Y in side of the information set if there is no change in expecting factor X, Y cannot Granger-cause X. The Granger-causality test shows that when we estimate time series Y we can estimate Y more precisely when we use factor X and factor Y together instead of just estimating time lag variables of factor Y except factor X.

Let's assume that there are two factors, factor X and factor Y in our world. With factor X and factor Y, we can construct many models like a vector auto-regressive (VAR) model using an estimation of simple ordinary least square (OLS). We create error terms, $u(t)$ with $u(1)$ and $u(2)$. There is a possibility that $u1$ and $u2$ are correlated with each other, however we assume in our model that there is no correlation between $u1$ and $u2$.

$$Y(t) = \alpha Y(t\text{-}1) + \beta X(t\text{-}1) + u(t) \tag{1}$$

$$X(t) = \gamma Y(t\text{-}1) + \delta X(t\text{-}1) + u(t) \tag{2}$$

Table 1 shows data description that we use for this test. In table 1, '*std*' means standard deviation. '*ske*' means skewedness. '*kur*' means kurtosis. '*jb*' means Jarque-Bera results, '*prob*' means probability. '*obs*' means number of observation. '*sto*' means stock price. We do log-transformation for the data we use to do the test.

Table 1. Data Descriptions

	mean	*std*	*ske*	*kur*	*jb*	*prob*	*obs*
hpt	4.45	0.09	-0.17	2.59	3.66	0.00	95
hps	4.46	0.14	-0.37	1.38	12.56	0.00	95
hpb	4.37	0.06	1.95	6.21	101.47	0.00	95
hpj	4.54	0.05	1.63	5.34	63.90	0.00	95
hpat	4.43	0.10	-0.32	1.60	9.33	0.00	95
hpas	4.47	0.15	-0.51	1.49	13.18	0.00	95
hpab	4.27	0.10	1.98	6.09	100.36	0.00	95
hpaj	4.44	0.06	1.48	4.08	39.81	0.00	95
sto	7.20	0.30	-0.43	2.04	6.56	0.03	95

Data of skewedness like HPT, HPS, HPAT, HPAS, and STO shows minus value. It means that the tail on the left-hand side of the probability density function (PDF) is longer than the right-hand side and the bulk of the values (median) lie to the right-hand of the mean. On the other hand, data of skewedness like HPB, HPJ, HPAB, and HPAJ shows positive value. It means tail on the right-hand side of the PDF is longer than the left-hand side and the bulk of the values, such as median, lie to the left-hand of the mean. KUR means kurtosis. If the absolute value of KUR is three, then we can say that it is normally distributed. When KUR is less than three, it shows that it is not steep. All the variables that we use show that it is not steep because they are less than three with absolute value. JB means the Jarque-Bera statistics if sample for test comes from the normal distribution without knowing mean and variance. Regarding the Jarque-Bera statistics, we assume null hypothesis that time series does not follow normal distribution. When the Jarque-Bera statistics is greater than alpha=0.05, we cannot reject the null hypothesis. All the test statistics in our model show that test statistics do not follow normal distribution.

Table 2. Correlation Test

	hpt	hps	hpb	hpj	hpat	hpas	hpab	spaj	Sto
hpt	1								
hps	0.98	1							
hpb	0.53	0.40	1						
hpj	-0.30	-0.39	0.46	1					
hpat	0.99	0.97	0.52	-0.34	1				
hpas	0.97	0.99	0.33	-0.46	0.97	1			
hpab	0.63	0.50	0.98	0.32	0.62	0.44	1		
hpaj	0.76	0.67	0.92	0.17	0.75	0.61	0.96	1	
sto	0.83	0.80	0.49	-0.32	0.86	0.81	0.59	0.69	1

Table 2 shows test result of correlation test between the variables that we discuss. We see that there is a high relationship between Housing Purchase Price Composite indices of all regions in South Korea and Apartment Purchasing Price Index of all regions in South Korea. There is a high correlation between Housing Purchase Price Composite indices of all regions in South Korea and Apartment Purchasing Price Index of Seoul. There is a negative correlation between Housing Purchase Price Composite indices of all regions in South Korea and Housing Purchase Price Composite indices of Jeju. Housing Purchase Price Composite indices of Seoul has a high correlation with Apartment Purchasing Price Index of all regions in South Korea and Apartment Purchasing Price Index of Seoul. Housing Purchase Price Composite indices of Seoul has a negative correlation with Housing Purchase Price Composite indices of Jeju. Housing Purchase Price Composite indices of Busan has a high correlation with Apartment Purchasing Price Index of Busan and Apartment Purchasing Price Index of Jeju. Housing Purchase Price Composite indices of Jeju has a negative correlation with Apartment Purchasing Price Index of all regions in South Korea, Apartment Purchasing Price Index of Seoul, and stock price of South Korea. Apartment Purchasing Price Index of all regions in South Korea has a high correlation with Apartment Purchasing Price Index of Seoul. Apartment Purchasing Price Index of Busan has a high correlation with Apartment Purchasing Price Index of Jeju.

Let's explain about variables that this paper uses. HPT means Housing Purchase Price Composite indices of all regions in South Korea. HPS means Housing Purchase Price Composite indices of Seoul. HPB means Housing Purchase Price Composite indices of Busan. HPJ means Housing Purchase Price Composite indices of Jeju. For Apartment Purchasing Price Index, we define that June of 2011 is 100. HPAT means Apartment Purchasing Price Index of all regions in South Korea. HPAS means Apartment Purchasing Price Index of Seoul. HPAB means Apartment Purchasing Price Index of Busan. HPAJ means Apartment Purchasing Price Index of Jeju.

3   Test Results

This paper does the Granger-causality test. To do the Granger-causality test, this paper does log-transformation of the variables that we use. Additionally, this paper does the Unit Root Test. To do the Unit Root test, this paper uses the augmented dickey-fuller (ADF) test. Test results of the ADF test show that level variables have a unit root. In this case, to remove the unit root, we make differentiation for the variables that this paper uses. To do the Granger-causality test, we need to find the optimal lag. By inserting the optimal lag in the *Eviews 7* program, we do the Granger-causality test. To find out the optimal lag, we use the akaike information criterion (AIC). After the AIC, we find that the optimal lag for our variables is two. Table 3 shows statistics of the Granger-causality test's results. Test results show that Apartment Purchasing Price Index of Busan affects to Apartment Purchasing Price Index of Jeju. Housing Purchase Price Composite indices of Busan affects to Apartment Purchasing Price Index of Busan. Housing Purchase Price Composite indices of Busan affects to Apartment Purchasing Price Index of Jeju. Housing Purchase Price Composite indices of all regions in South Korea affects to Apartment Purchasing Price Index of Jeju. Test results of the Granger-causality test show that it is hard to say that there is a relationship between stock market and real- estate market. The reason why the relationship of substitution between stock market and real-estate market has been disappeared is because there exits regional bias. And, additionally, economic downturn and decreasing merit for housing market are the other reasons why the relationship has been disappeared. Because of these reasons, demand for investment itself has been disappeared.

Table 3. Results of the Granger-causality Test

	F-statistics	*Prob.*		*F-statistics*	*Prob.*
HPAJ→HPAB	0.56	0.35	HPB→HPAS	1.81	0.16
HPAB→HPAJ	7.03	0.00**	HPAS→HPB	1.45	0.23
HPAS→HPAB	1.04	0.12	HPS→HPAS	2.68	0.07
HPAB→HPAS	1.48	0.23	HPAS→HPS	1.43	0.24
HPAT→HPAB	2.26	0.11	HPT→HPAS	0.62	0.54
HPAB→HPAT	0.06	0.93	HPAS→HPT	1.06	0.35
HPB→HPAB	3.31	0.04*	STOCK→HPAS	0.37	0.68
HPAB→HPB	1.55	0.21	HPAS→STOCK	0.37	0.68
HPS→HPAB	1.01	0.36	HPB→HPAT	1.01	0.36
HPAB→HPS	1.32	0.27	HPAT→HPB	1.97	0.14
HPT→HPAB	1.90	0.15	HPS→HPAT	0.92	0.40
HPAB→HPT	0.009	0.99	HPAT→HPS	1.67	0.19
STOCK→HPA	1.03	0.35	HPT→HPAT	1.56	0.21
HPAB→STOCK	0.08	0.91	HPAT→HPT	2.10	0.12
HPAS→HPAJ	1.47	0.23	STOCK→HPAT	0.62	0.53
HPAJ→HPAS	1.96	0.14	HPAT→STOCK	0.41	0.66
HPAT→HPAJ	2.84	0.06	HPS→HPB	1.23	0.29
HPAJ→HPAT	0.18	0.83	HPB→HPS	1.77	0.17
HPB→HPAJ	9.04	0.00**	HPT→HPB	1.59	0.20
HPAJ→HPB	0.20	0.81	HPB→HPT	2.05	0.13
HPS→HPAJ	1.09	0.33	STOCK→HPB	0.45	0.63
HPAJ→HPS	1.58	0.21	HPB→STOCK	0.47	0.62
HPT→HPAJ	3.11	0.04*	HPS→HPT	1.25	0.28
STOCK→HPA	0.29	0.74	STOCK→HPS	0.32	0.72

Table 3. (*continued*)

HPAJ→STOCK	0.22	0.79	HPS→STOCK	0.59	0.55
HPAT→HPAS	0.68	0.50	STOCK→HPT	0.55	0.57
HPAS→HPAT	0.53	0.58	HPT→STOCK	0.76	0.46

Note: '*' means that it is significant at 5% and '**' means that it is significant at 10%

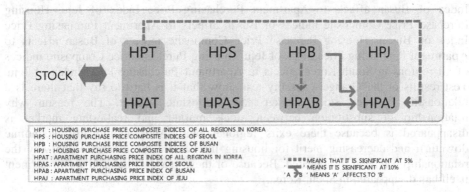

HPT : HOUSING PURCHASE PRICE COMPOSITE INDICES OF ALL REGIONS IN KOREA
HPS : HOUSING PURCHASE PRICE COMPOSITE INDICES OF SEOUL
HPB : HOUSING PURCHASE PRICE COMPOSITE INDICES OF BUSAN
HPJ : HOUSING PURCHASE PRICE COMPOSITE INDICES OF JEJU
HPAT : APARTMENT PURCHASING PRICE INDEX OF ALL REGIONS IN KOREA
HPAS : APARTMENT PURCHASING PRICE INDEX OF SEOUL
HPAB : APARTMENT PURCHASING PRICE INDEX OF BUSAN
HPAJ : APARTMENT PURCHASING PRICE INDEX OF JEJU

' ▪▪▪▪ MEANS THAT IT IS SIGNIFICANT AT 5%
' ⬛ ' MEANS IT IS SIGNIFICANT AT 10%
'A ⮕ B ' MEANS 'A' AFFECTS TO 'B'

Fig. 1. Test Results of the Granger-causality test

4   Concluding Remarks

We live in a very rapidly changed society. In 2008, we experience economic difficulties because of sub-prime mortgage crisis in the U.S. At that time, world's stock prices and real-estate price have been plummeted. During those times, investors worry about their targets of investment. Generally, we know that investors invest their money to a safe market with high profits. When investors decide that stock market is very volatile and dangerous to invest their money, they change their investing target to real-estate market. This paper investigates whether stock markets are related to real-estate market. This paper uses the Granger-causality test in investigating the relationship. This paper uses data from Kookmin bank database. Test results of correlation test shows like following: interestingly, there is a negative correlation between Housing Purchase Price Composite indices of all regions in South Korea and Housing Purchase Price Composite indices of Jeju. We see that there is a high relationship between Housing Purchase Price Composite indices of all regions in South Korea and Apartment Purchasing Price Index of all regions in South Korea. There is a high correlation between Housing Purchase Price Composite indices of all regions in South Korea and Apartment Purchasing Price Index of Seoul. Housing Purchase Price Composite indices of Seoul has a high correlation with Apartment Purchasing Price Index of all regions in South Korea and Apartment Purchasing Price Index of Seoul. Housing Purchase Price Composite indices of Seoul has a negative correlation with Housing Purchase Price Composite indices of Jeju. Housing Purchase Price Composite indices of Busan has a high correlation with Apartment Purchasing Price Index of Busan and Apartment Purchasing Price Index of Jeju. Housing Purchase Price Composite indices of Jeju has a negative correlation with Apartment

Purchasing Price Index of all regions in South Korea, Apartment Purchasing Price Index of Seoul, and stock price of South Korea. Apartment Purchasing Price Index of all regions in South Korea has a high correlation with Apartment Purchasing Price Index of Seoul. Apartment Purchasing Price Index of Busan has a high correlation with Apartment Purchasing Price Index of Jeju.

Test results of the Granger-causality test show that Apartment Purchasing Price Index of Busan affects to Apartment Purchasing Price Index of Jeju. Housing Purchase Price Composite indices of Busan affects to Apartment Purchasing Price Index of Busan. Housing Purchase Price Composite indices of Busan affects to Apartment Purchasing Price Index of Jeju. Housing Purchase Price Composite indices of all regions in South Korea affects to Apartment Purchasing Price Index of Jeju. Test results of the Granger-causality test show that it is hard to say that there is a relationship between stock market and real-estate market. The reason why relationship of substitution between stock market and real-estate market is disappeared is because there exits regional bias. And, additionally, economic downturn and decreasing merit for housing market are the other reasons why the relationship has been disappeared. Because of these reasons, demand for investment itself has disappeared in South Korea.

References

1. Chang, B., Sim, S.-H.: Does Korean REITs Act Like Real Estate or Stock? Housing Studies Review 15(2), 31–52 (2007)
2. Chung, K.S., Kim, S.W., Lee, S.Y.: Markets analysis of housing purchase and lease using the Granger-causality Analysis: Concentrating on housing markets of Busan area using supply and demand. Journal of Policy Analysis and Assessment 21(2), 179–198 (2011)
3. Darrat, A.: Are Exports and Engine of Growth? Another Look at the Evidence. Applied Economics, 277–283 (February 1987)
4. Engle, R.F., Granger, C.W.J.: Co-Integration and Error-Correction: Representation, Estimation and Testing. Econometrica, 251–276 (March 1987)
5. Ghartey, E.: Casual Relationship between Export and Economic Growth: Some Empirical Evidence in Taiwan, Japan and the US. Applied Economics, 1145–1152 (September 1993)
6. Granger, C.W.J., Newbold, P.: Spurious Regressions in Econometrics. Journal of Econometrics, 111–120 (July 1974)
7. Hamilton, J.D.: Time Series Analysis. Princeton University Press, Princeton (1994)
8. Jang, S., Lee, S., Kim, J.: An Analysis of the relationship between the Stock price and the Real Estate Price. Journal of the Architectural Institute of Korea 26(3), 177–184 (2010)
9. Johansen, S., Juselius, K.: Maximum Likelihood Estimation and Inference on Cointegration – With Applications to the Demand for Money. Oxford Bulletin of Economics and Statistics, 169–210 (May 1990)
10. Lee, Y.-S.: Housing Price and Microeconomy in Korea:SVAR Analysis. Journal of the Korea Real Estate Analysts Association 14(3), 129–147 (2008)
11. Park, J.: A Research on the Correlation of interest rates, apartment price, and stock prices using the VECM. Dong-A University, Ph.D. Dissertation (2007)
12. Shin, H., Son, J., Kim, J.: Analyzing Dynamics of Korean Housing Market Using Causal Look Structures. Korea Construction Management Society 6(3), 144–155 (2005)
13. Son, J.C.: Dynamic Analysis of Correlations among Monetary Policy, Real and Financial Variables and Housing Prices. Gyeong Je Hak Yon Gu 58(2), 179–219 (2010)

Characteristic of AZO/SiCO Film by X-Ray Diffraction Pattern and X-Ray Photoelectron Spectroscopy

Teresa Oh

Semiconductor Engineering, 36 Naeduckdong Sangdangku, Cheongju South Korea
teresa@Springer.com

Abstract. Effect of polarity in SiCO film as gate insulator for AZO-TFT was researched. The aluminum doped ziinc oxide films were deposited on SiOC/p-Si wafer by a RF magnetron sputtering system. Polarity in SiCO film with increasing the oxygen gas flow rates changed, and SiCO film lowering polarity was observed the chemical shift in the binding energy such as Si 2p and C 1s, because of lowering the polarity due to chemical reactions between CH group and OH group as the opposite polar sites by high plasma energy. Oxidation of Si atoms will lead to a chemical shift to move higher binding energy in O 1s spectra, due to the additional potential modulation with the Si nanocrystallites by a long range Coulombic interaction of oxygen ions. The chemical shift after AZO deposition on SiCO film made was attributed to defects owing to the Vo and Zni and the valence band in AZO at interfaces between AZO and SiCO films. AZO grown on SiCO film including polar sites showed high on current in transfer characteristic of TFT because of increase of the trap charge owing to the defects.

Keywords: AZO, XRD pattern, O 1s, C 1s, Zn 2p, sputter, polarity.

1 Introduction

Transparent semiconducting ZnO with a wide and direct bandgap of about 3.4eV has found many applications in different field such as transparent conductive contacts, thin film gas sensors, varistors, solar cells, luminescent materials or displays. To realize high performance ZnO-based devices, it is essential not only the formation of high quality metal electrodes but also substrate materials for ZnO. In view of ohmic contacts to n-ZnO, it is difficult to make Schottky contacts to n-ZnO, because of a high donor concentration at the surface region of n-ZnO involving native defects such as oxygen vacancies and zinc interstitials. For Schottky, several noble metal schemes such as Au, Ag, Pd and Al have been investigated. Or to obtain effective Schottky contacts on n-ZnO, surface treatments using the solutions of HCl, HNO_3 and by the oxygen-based plasmas of O_2, and N2O have been performed. Kim et al, researched the electrical behavior of the Pt contacts to n-ZnO (000-1) surface, and suggested the electric characteristic of ZnO depending on the surface treatment conditions. In comparison with undoped ZnO, Al-doped ZnO films have lower resistivity and better stability [11-16]. Al doped ZnO (AZO) films have attractive much attention because

T.-h. Kim et al. (Eds.): SIP/WSE/ICHCI 2012, CCIS 342, pp. 85–89, 2012.
© Springer-Verlag Berlin Heidelberg 2012

of their comparative high optical transmittance and low electrical resistivity with respect to other TCOs widely used such as Tin-doped Indium Oxide (ITO) films []. In this works to realize low temperature process, AZO was prepared on SiOC/p-Si by RF magnetron sputter. SiOC film, which can be replaced with SiO_2 film as a gate-insulator, was also by RF magnetron sputter. From the results of XPS and XRD, it was observed the influence of properties of SiOC film to achieve high mobility performance of AZO.

2   Experimental Method

The SiOC film was prepared by RF magnetron sputtering with a 2 in. diameter ceramic target (SiO:C, 97%:3% wt.) targets supplied by LTS Research Laboratories, Inc., U.S.A. The flow rate of the oxygen (99.9999%) was controlled by mass flow controller (MFC) from 5~30 sccm for 20 min, and the sputtering RF power was 250W. The substrate temperature was kept constant at room temperature. AZO film on SiOC/Si was prepared at room temperature. The AZO targets (99.99% purity) were supplied by LTS Research Laboratories, Inc., U.S.A. AZO thin film was deposited on p-type Si wafers by RF magnetron sputter at a pressure of 0.01 Torr in argon atmosphere. The target to substrate distance was kept at 100 mm and the base pressure was 4.5×10^{-5} Pa and the working pressure of the chamber with argon gas was $1.2~1.4 \times 10^{-3}$ Torr. The flow rate of the argon (99.9999%) was controlled by mass flow controller (MFC) with 30 sccm for 5 min, and the sputtering RF power was 300W. To investigate the chemical and the structural properties of the AZO film on SiOC film, the chemical analyses were performed using X-ray photoelectron spectroscopy (ESCALAB 210) and X-ray diffraction pattern (XDS 2000), which was at Center for research facilities, Chungbuk University, Cheongju, South Korea.

3   Results and Discussions

In order to evaluate the effect of chemical properties of the substrate on the AZO electrical properties, SiOC films were prepared with various O_2 gas flow rates of 10 sccm to 30 sccm by using RF sputtering at the room temperature, and AZO film was deposited on SiOC substrate by using RF sputtering. Figure 1 is the X-ray photoelectron spectra of AZO/SiCO film with O_2 gas flow rate of 10 sccm to 30 sccm. Concerning the possible influence of SiCO film with polarity to the characteristic of substrate for the growth of AZO film, SiCO film of amorphous structure due to the low polarity would lead to an increase of the crystallinity of AZO film that would affect the electrical properties of the film.

There were much difference in O 1s spectra between AZO/SiCO film and SiCO film, but no change in C 1s spectra between them. The chemical shift of O 1s spectra originated from the existence of trap charges and interface traps due to the oxygen vacancy in AZO film, therefore the intensity of O 1s spectra in AZO on SiCO film

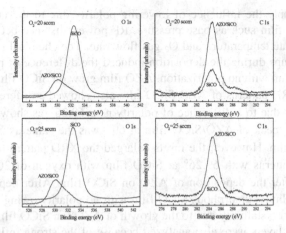

Fig. 1. Analysis of the O 1s and C 1s electron orbital spectra between SiCO thin films with various O_2 gas flow rates and AZO grown on SiCO film

decreased in comparison with that of SiCO film. The chemical shift could be attributed to electron transitions between point defects, such as Vo and Zni and the valence band in AZO. On the other hand, C 1s spectra increased and did not change the peak position after AZO growth on SiCO film, because the increase of crystallinity owing to the increase of thickness.

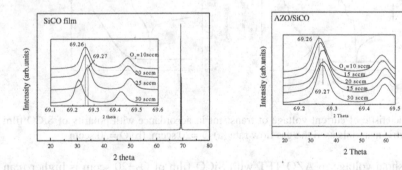

Fig. 2. XRD diffraction patterns with strong peaks at 69.25° and 69.45°, (a) SiCO films with peaks at 69.26°nd 69.27°in accordance with various gas flow rates at room temperature, (b) AZO film grown on SiCO film with strong intensity at 69.26° and 69.27°

Figure 2 is the XRD diffraction patterns of the SiOC thin films grown at the room temperature by RF magnetron sputtering. These spectra revealed strong preferred peaks at 69.25° and 69.45°. The inset was observed the chemical shift in the location of the measured diffraction peaks with increasing the oxygen gas flow rates. There was a difference about 0.02° between samples of 20 sccm and 25 sccm near 69.26° in Fig. 2(a). Besides, XRD pattern of sample with O_2=30 sccm moved to lower degree.

These results imply the influence of lowering polarity due to the conditions of the growth of SiCO film such as base pressure, RF power, distance between target and substrate, substrate temperature and O_2 gas flow rate. The chemical reaction between OH and CH groups during the deposition induced the difference of polarity in SiCO film and SiCO film with no polarization. AZO film grew on SiCO film as a gate insulator, and the XRD patterns of AZO/SiCO film also showed a difference about 0.01° between samples due to a difference of polarity near 69.26° as shown in the inset of Fig. 2(b). Strong peak of AZO/SiCO film at 69° was the same as XRD patterns of previous SiCO film. However, the insets enlarged the XRD pattern near 69° showed that the XRD patterns with 69.26° at SiCO film with oxygen of 20 sccm move to higher 69.27° after the deposition of AZO on SiCO film. After deposition of AZO film with crystallinity, amorphous SiCO film with no polarity owing to oxygen of 20 sccm changed to crystallinity due to the growth of AZO fon SiCO film. The electrical properties of the layers were also analyzed because of the strong influence that AZO growth depends on the properties of SiCO film with polarity. The device was manufactured for TFT and SiCO film was used as gate insulator. The transfer characteristic of AZO TFT on SiCO film deposited as a function of O_2 gas flow rates at the drain to source voltage is observed in Fig. 3.

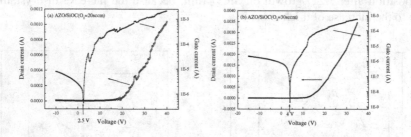

Fig. 3. Characteristic of current-voltage of transistor in accordance with polarity of SiCO film as gate dielectric materials used the gas flow rate (a) O_2=20 sccm, (b) O_2=30 sccm

The threshold voltage in AZO TFT with SiCO film of O_2=20 sccm is higher than that of AZO film with SiCO film O_2=30 sccm. Because SiCO film with the low dielectric constant and low capacitance due to the low polarization as a gate insulator suppressed the conductance in TFT. However, SiCO gate dielectric materials with polarity due to the gas flow rate O_2=30 sccm showed higher transfer curve and low threshold voltage, because of interface charge trap owing to the polar sites in SiCO film. TFT with SiCO gate insulator deposited with the gas flow rate O_2=30 sccm showed conductive behavior because the conduction path flow through the interface layer, where it was formed near the gate insulator. Moreover, the threshold voltage shift also originated from the charge trap within gate insulator and interface charge trap. The Vth of AZO TFT of O_2=20 sccm in compared with that of O_2= 30 sccm was positively shifted by about 5 V. TFT with SiCO gate insulator with lower polarity (O_2= 20 sccm) was observed 2.5 gate-source voltage when the gate current was zero, but that with (O_2= 30 sccm) was 4.0 V because the polar group in SiCO film leads to improvement in the electron transport properties. However, the meaning of this result can be explained as that SiCO film with no polarity is more stable than SiCO film with polar sites. The stability of TFT is related to the sub threshold voltage. The gate current characteristic of Ig-Vg curve is related to the sub-threshold voltage swing, TFT with SiCO gate insulator with lower polarity (O_2= 20 sccm) was observed lower sub threshold voltage.

4   Conclusions

The effect of polarization at low-k SiCO film as gate insulator for AZO TFT was researched. SiOC film was deposited by rf magnetron sputter using oxygen gas flow rates of 10~30 sccm, and the AZO was also prepared with argon gas flows by rf magnetron sputter for low temperature process. AZO film would lead to an existence of high present of defects at the interface between the AZO and SiCO film, which was formed by high polarization. The threshold voltage was observed when charges are trapped within gate insulator and at the interface between two layers. These defects and trap charges induced to increase the transfer characteristic of AZO TFT. However, TFT with SiCO as gate insulator materials of no polarity showed low on current and better stability than others with polar sites. It was observed the chemical shift at low polarity SiCO film deposited with increasing the oxygen gas flow rate from XPS and XRD analysis. There are the existence of trap charges due to many defects in AZO grown on SiCO film with polarity, so the transfer characteristic was improved.

References

1. Fan, Z., Wang, D., Chang, P.C., Tseng, W.Y., Lu, J.G.: Applied Physics Letters 85, 5923–5925 (2004)
2. Park, J.S., Maeng, W.J., Kim, H.S., Park, J.S.: Review of recent developments in amorphous oxide semiconductor thin film transistor devices. Thin Solid Films 520, 1679–1693 (2012)
3. Hosono, H.: Journal of Non-Cryatalline Solids 352, 851–858 (2006)
4. Chun, Y.S., Chang, S., Lee, S.Y.: Microelectronic Engineering 88, 1590–1593 (2011)
5. Cho, Y.J., Shin, J.H., Bobade, S.M., Kim, Y.B., Choi, D.K.: Thin Solid Films 517, 4115–4118 (2009)
6. Kim, S.H., Kim, H.K., Seong, T.Y.: Applied Physics Letters 86, 022101 (2005)
7. Park, T.E., Kim, D.C., Kong, B.H., Cho, H.K.: Journal of the Korean Physical Society 45, S697–S700 (2004)
8. Fernandez, S., Martinez-Steele, A., Gandia, J.J., Naranjo, F.B.: Thin Solid Films 517, 3152–3156 (2009)
9. Mazumder, K., Moriyama, R., Watanabe, D., Kimura, C., Aoki, H., Sugino, T.: Jpn. J. Appl. Phys. 46, 2006 (2007)
10. Oh, T., Kim, C.H.: IEEE Trans. Plasma Science 38, 1598–1602 (2010)

Swirling Flow in Tubes with Sudden Expansion by Using 3D Particle Image Velocimetry Technique

Tae-Hyun Chang[1,*] and Chang-Hoan Lee[2]

[1] RESEAT, Korean Institute of Science and Technology Information, DaeJeon South Korea,
changtae@reseat.re.kr
[2] Korean Institute of Science and Technology Information, DaeJeon, South Korea
cheree1@kisti.re.kr

Abstract. The effect of swirling on the flow characteristics of tubes with sudden expansion is experimentally examined by 3D particle image velocimetry technique to determine velocity profiles. The swirling flow of water in sudden 1:2 axisymmetric expansion has been previously studied within a horizontal round tube. A tangential slot is used as a swirl generator for swirling flow, whereas a honey comb is used for flow without swirling. Three velocities with swirling flows are compared along the test section at Re=14800, and the streamline in the recirculation zone is described.

Keywords: PIV, Swirling flow, Sudden expansion, tube flow.

1   Introduction

Swirling flows in circular and rectangular tubes have received increased research attention. The characteristics of turbulent swirling flows are extensively studied because of the technological and scientific importance of these flows. Swirling flows improve heat transfer in tube flows because of the effect of the streamline curvature associated with the tangential velocity component.

Nuttall(1) performed an experimental work in a vertical circular tube using guide vanes to produce swirling flow at Re = 3 x 104. Reverse water flow occurs in the center of the pipe for specific rates of swirling and discharge. As the swirling intensity increases, the axial velocity at the center of the test tube becomes negative. However, a positive axial velocity is observed at a high swirling intensity near the tube wall.

Binnie et al. (2) conducted experimental studies on test sections with different diameters. They examined the pressure and velocity distributions inside a convergent nozzle that discharges water downward under pressure. A volute for swirling flow was used in the test section. Results show two large departures from inviscid flow because of permanganate injection into the nozzle with a hyperdermic tube inserted through pressure tapping.

In another work of Binnie (3), a Perspex tube with an internal diameter of 2 in and a wall thickness of 0.25 in was used. A volute was utilized to generate swirling flow,

---

* Corresponding author.

T.-h. Kim et al. (Eds.): SIP/WSE/ICHCI 2012, CCIS 342, pp. 90–95, 2012.

which was adjusted by supply valves, inside the test tube. A notable vortex collapse occurred when the pressure head was about 9 ft.

Talbot (4) made one of the first attempts in this field in 1954, when he considered the decay of a rotationally symmetric steady swirling imposed by Poiseuille flow in a circular pipe. He used a linearization technique to solve the equations of motion by considering laminar conditions only. A further attempt to analyze the effect of swirling on laminar flow in pipes was made by Sparrow et al. (5) in 1984. The studies of Talbot and Sparrow both included the effects of mass transfer, with the former adopting a boundary layer integral method and the latter using perturbation techniques.

Max et al. (6) examined the effect of swirling on the flow characteristics in a chamber with sudden axisymmetric expansion in the ratio of 2.5. Particle image velocimetry (PIV) was used to capture the instantaneous flow field with a guider vane at Re=10000, in which the swirl number was varied from 0 to 0.65. Their results showed that increasing the swirl number up to 0.65 causes the flow to reverse at the centerline because of vortex breakdown.

By contrast, swirling flow in a pipe with sudden expansion has relatively not been examined well. This field includes a wall-bounded recirculation region adjacent to the face of the expansion. Therefore, this study aims to characterize the turbulent flow that passes on a pipe with axisymmetric sudden expansion and to determine the effect of the resulting swirl with 3D PIV technique.

2   Experimental Rig

The swirling flow of water through sudden 1:2 axisymmetric expansion was experimentally studied in a horizontal round tube. The measurements of this flow were performed with the 3D PIV system. The test section was manufactured from a round Perspex tube with an inner diameter of 50 mm, a wall thickness of 5 mm, and a length of 1.2 m. The swirl generator is a tangential slot that consists of two cylinders with the following dimensions: an outer chamber with an outside diameter of 100 mm, a length of 150 mm, and a wall thickness of 5 mm (Fig. 1). A square box was installed to avoid the reflective effects of the circular tube on the results. This box recovered the reflected light waves from the visualized section of the flow.

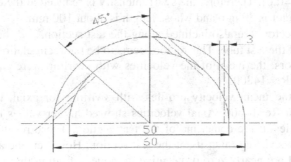

Fig. 1. Schematic of the swirl generator

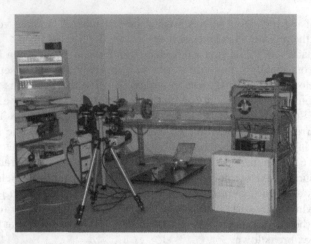

Fig. 2. The experimental apparatus with the PIV system

Fig. 2 shows the experimental equipment used with the 3D PIV system. Stereoscopic PIV technique was utilized for most isothermal flow velocity measurements. Laser (2W) was employed to measure velocities, and two charge-coupled device cameras were installed perpendicular to the visualized section of the flow.

3   Result and Discussion

This study aimed to introduce different velocity profiles to the expansion region with swirling and non-swirling flows. It also aimed to verify the recirculation zone of the swirling flow along the test section.

Fig. 3 shows the velocity vectors with swirling in a horizontal tube with sudden expansion at Re=14800. Weak velocity vectors are found near the entry of the test tube. These weak vectors can be attributed to the swirling intensity that decreases as the length of the test tube increases. Therefore, the velocity vectors show positive values. However, the negative value at the entry of the test section is associated with strong swirling (s=0.6). Therefore, the swirl intensity is reduced at the entrance of the tube, whose diameter is 30 mm and whose length is about 100 mm.

The velocity vectors are also inclined along the test section, and they increase toward the center of the test tube. This region seems to be the recirculation area.

From these vectors, the mean of the velocities with swirling were calculated along the test section at Re=14800.

Fig. 4 shows the mean velocity profiles with swirling for axial, tangential, and radial velocities at Re=14800. Axial velocities showed higher values than tangential and radial velocities at the centerline of the test section. These results can be attributed to the weak swirling intensity at the test section. However, the axial velocities near the tube wall are nearly zero or negative in value, a finding that is related to the recirculation area.

The axial velocities are compared along the test section with swirling at Re=14800 (Fig. 5). The axial velocities show low or negative values at the entry point. However, they increase with an increase in the length of the test tube. This result is attributed to the weak swirling intensity.

Fig. 6 shows the streamlines along the test section with swirling flow at Re=14800. The figure clearly illustrates the recirculation zone and the reattachment point. The reattachment length with swirling has a value of ~8.0 at Re=14800. The length of the recirculation point decreases with an increase in swirling intensity and Re number.

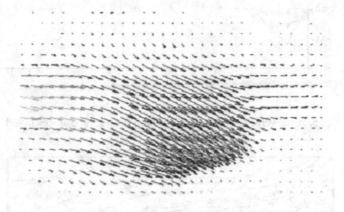

Fig. 3. Velocity vectors with swirling at Re=14800

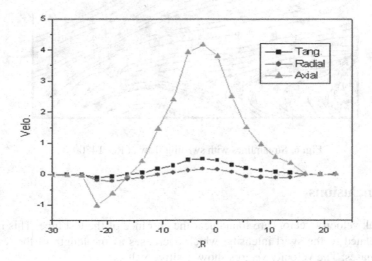

Fig. 4. Mean velocities with swirling at Re=14800

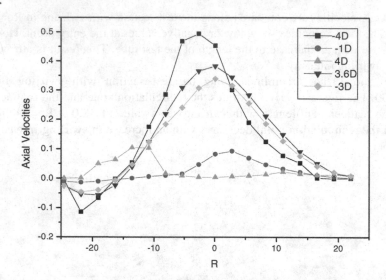

Fig. 5. Axial velocities with swirling along the test tube at Re=14800

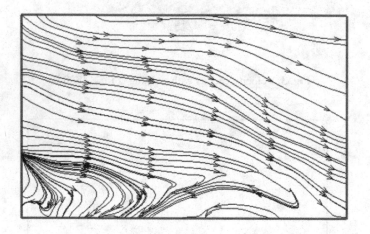

Fig. 6. Streamlines with swirling flow at Re=14800

4   Conclusions

1. Weak velocity vectors are found near the entrance of the test tube. This finding is related to the swirl intensity, which decreases as the length of the test tube increases. The velocity vectors show positive values.
2. Axial velocities have higher values at the centerline of the test section than the tangential and radial velocities. These results are attributed to the weak swirl

intensity at the test section. However, the axial velocities near the tube wall are nearly zero or negative in value, a finding that is related to the recirculation area.

3. The length of the recirculation point with swirling is about 8.0 at Re=14800. The length decreases as the swirl intensity and the Re number increase.

Acknowledgments. This study was supported financially by the Ministry of Education, Science and Technology and the Korean Institute of Science and Technology Information.

References

1. Nuttall, J.B.: Axial flow in a vortex. Nature 172(4378), 582–583 (1953)
2. Binnie, A.M., Teare, J.D.: Experiments on the flow of swirling water through a pressure nozzle and open trumpet. Quart J. of Mech. and Applied Math. X(Pt. 3), 78–89 (1957)
3. Binne, A.M.: Experiments on the swirling flow of water in a vertical pipe and a bend. AIAA Journal, 452–465 (1962)
4. Talbot, L.: Laminar swirling pipe. J. of Applied Mechanics 21, 1–7 (1954)
5. Sparrow, E.M., Chaboki, A.: Swirl-Affected turbulent fluid flow and Heat Transfer in a circular Tube. ASME Trans., J. of Heat Transfer 106, 766–773 (1984)
6. Mak, H., Balahani, S.: Near field characteristics of swirling flow past a sudden expansion. Chemical Engineering Science 62, 6726–6746 (2007)
7. Chang, S.W., Yang, T.L.: Forced convective flow and heat transfer of upward concurrent air-water slug flow in vertical plain and swirl tubes. Experimental Thermal and Fluid Science 33, 1087–1099 (2009)
8. Doh, D.H., Hwang, T.G., Saga, T.: 3D-PTV measurements of the wake of a sphere. Measurement Science and Technology 15, 1059–1066 (2004)
9. Kimura, I., Takamori, T., Inoue, T.: Image Processing Instrumentation of Flow by using Correlation Technique. Journal of Flow Visualization and Image Processing 22(6), 105–108 (1986)

Visual Communication Methods of Computer-Generated Images for Making Television Graphics System

Hyun Hahm[1] and Keun-Wang Lee[2,*]

[1] Dept. of Broadcasting & Digital Media, Chungwoon University
[2] Dept.of Multimedia Science, Chungwoon University
San 29, Namjang-ri, Hongseong, Chungnam, 350-701, South Korea
{poparts,kwlee}@chungwoon.ac.kr

Abstract. A computer-generated image for making TV graphics system is very important role of communication methods of storytelling in terms of programs to use many genres. In TV production system where to use a variety of methods of computer-generated images such as titling, subtitle, three dimensions of graphic images, etc. Recently, it may become a major part of making TV program elements not only produced an information, but also recognized as images as a whole. Because it is become a major part of communication methods of storytelling in TV programs. Nevertheless, it taken as part of TV programs makes system into a variety of genres in Korea. Therefore, this paper shows how computer-generated graphic system get into TV programs as a visual communication methods, and figure it out the various from of visual contribution to storytelling of TV programs.

Keywords: Visual Communication, Visual Character, Computer-generated Images, Sub-title, Moving Images.

1 Introduction

Television making system has been rapidly changed in a decades of years. It mostly affected by digital technology as grew up in terms of many different aspect of environment in broadcasting industry. Where you are watching Television programs, it may find out the visualization of picture images given information not only picture image itself, but also graphic images of visual character, sub-titling and graphics. The principle of making visual character and graphic images are effectively using Television production system, therefore, it has become breakthroughs in simple Character generators of information to important role of storytelling of Television programs.

In Korea, the visualization of making computer-generated images such as titling, sub-title, three-dimensional graphic images are rapidly produced in Television program, especially variety programs. The graphic tool in Television program becomes a part of story, or as a whole. The audiences are that it recognized the

---

* Corresponding author.

T.-h. Kim et al. (Eds.): SIP/WSE/ICHCI 2012, CCIS 342, pp. 96–101, 2012.

characteristics of program content of storytelling. It makes audience to understand what Television programs given them to variety of picture images with a different aspect of information elements.

The elements of Television graphics system used the number of thing. For example, it used simply works that form of lettering taken such as printed imaged from character generator invented the early times. The system was very simple to use that runs on insert the lettering. It contains simple color to use over background of color, or picture images. In case of sub-title, it aim to keep titling information to a minimum, particularly if it is combined with detailed background [1]; however, when digital non-linear editing system invented, it has changed a big differ from in the past. For example, non-linear editing system was given not only manufacture the images unrestricted but also, integration of work as a whole.

All these considered, this paper propose how computer-generated images making system provided TV programs in terms of tools of frame works. And, how it can be use sending information of storytelling of TV programs. To do this paper, I assume that computer-generated images are effect into target audience as well as, give decorative and powerful information tools ever before.

2   Related Works

Computer-generated images which are graphic system have become an important role of communication method in TV industry. It also defined the different aspect of figures that given a variety of field to study called text image of graphic, visual character, sub-title, TV character, typography, etc. Many researchers are defined the phenomenon of computer-generated images from their field of works in order to figures that how it possibly works throughout the viewers. To understand how computer-generated images affect to viewer in terms of sending a variety of information. And, it also has increased the high rate to use in TV programs as a hybrid method of visual communication.

Even though some scholars are defined the different aspect of computer-generated images, they focus on information methods of storytelling in terms of variety of TV genres. The case of study defends as perceptive of object that should consider is legibility as communication method of computer-generated system. Moreover, Many scholars are defined the aspect of use frame works such as font size and style, space between lines which are must be legible.

Haley (1999) argues that one of the most important features that make the letter legible and easy to recognize is the character shape [2]. Al-Harkan and Ramadan (2005) also defined that configuration and recognition rate are the main two elements should be considers in terms of making digital typeface design [3]. And, Lee (2008) suggested that TV visual characters help the drawing the audience's attention and pay a positive role in making various types of program appeal their unique characteristics and themes to the audience [4].

Therefore, Many researchers focus on the visual method of computer-generate system is an important role of frame works. It mostly focuses on legible to create the image text itself. Which are essential for viewer to understand and effects to have information through ought the variety of graphic images.

3   Characteristics of Computer-Generated Image System

To do understand how Korean character's design affect readability in terms of the basic reading process such as character units, configuration, recognition of those element that affected by design of visual characters. It is also very important features that must make the legible and recognize many different aspects of characters. There are many different shape of design, or layout of character produces in frame area especially the size of fonts, the width of columns, the number of lines in picture area of frame within safety area, etc. In other worlds, visual character must realize that the most important role of sending an information throughout the viewers.

A consist of visual characters are complex units with image and text that help the viewers, therefore, good visual character must to help viewer's comprehension of the visual images with many different types of text. The aspect of visual character has been rapidly changed as digital technology develops as mention before. In order to creates the visual character with TV program also essential to become use as well as common types of process in Korea. However, the ratio of frame works is very important to create the visual characters because it requires with equal balance with both picture images and visual characters must fit into safe title area.

In contrast, the characteristic of visual character to use computer-generated system frequently fit into all safe title area. For example, visual character's position has been changed linear area to non-area as digital technology systems develop. The early period of time when using visual character fit into the top, middle, and lower position of frame of works. However, when non-linear editing system developed to use TV industry, visual character fit into all space of frame to use with not only text, but also sign of iconography as representation methods.

3.1   Functional Sub-title Model

One of the most important and mostly used visual characters called functional sub-titles in order to send simple information of TV program. For example, TV news often to used in terms of a variety of information that position at lower column in frame of safe title area. The functional sub-title also used in sports program, TV commercial, music program, and others. Which are early invented in computer-generated system base on linear environment that still to use in TV production system.

3.2   Emphasis of Sub-title Model

Visual character uses on emphasis of scene of TV program in order to make the complements of storytelling. For example, interview program often to use when interviewer point out the main answer for the question, inadequate of conversation, insufficient of audio level, etc. However, it has been changed the form and style to use visual character which emphasis of TV programs especially talk-show program in Korea. The position of visual character replaced from linear area to non-linear area of frame works which non-linear editing system given a variety of method of expression of sub-titles. Furthermore, it emphasis not only expression of feeling with situation of guest of program but also, it creates and produces a pleasant atmosphere of studio of guest of people.

3.3   Creation of Sub-titles Model

Visual character uses as form of creation of sub-titles by director and producer. It is very popular and spread into reality show program in Korea. Recently, Korean reality show program often to use a variety of icon of subject rather than text of sub-title in the past. For example, using a variety of icon of sign with text given the viewers right to understand with a contents of story of program using a variety of graphic materials. It occur the enjoyment of fun, guidance of laughing by idea of director and producer, however, it has also negative aspect of opinion that has interfered with original contents of storytelling.

4   Evaluation of Contents

Visual character using by computer-generated system of TV program has three types of case that evaluate of contents as follows:

First, Fig. 1 shows the case of TV news and home-shopping program used by functional sub-title as visual character [5]. The composition of frame works used visual character placed in lower column both images with text. The placement of lover column with visual character uses as a writing space and given easy to read information of storytelling. Furthermore, home-shopping program using the number of information such as code number of product, phone number, cost, information of size and quantity, etc, therefore, it is very unique to express of number of information using by functional visual character.

Classification	Contents		
Features' Subtitles			
Screen Configuration	Picture-in-picture	A lower column	A lower column
Representation	Image and text	Text information	Text information

Fig. 1. The case of TV news and home-shopping program used by functional sub-title as visual character

Second, Fig. 2 shows visual character of emphasis of sub-title using by graphic image with text [5]. The comparison between Fig. 1 and Fig. 2, it looks quite similar Two of them; however, they are little differ from each others. Fig. 1 use original image with text, but Fig. 2 use the mutual form of graphic images with text. It mostly uses a variety of effect of colors and sound in order to express the situation of TV studio to the viewers. And, it is also often to use a symbol of icon rather than text because is very useful to express toward of viewers given a reality situation.

Classification	Contents		
Features' Subtitles			
Screen Configuration	A upper and lower column	Full screen	Middle
Representation	Icon and text	Icon and text	Icon

Fig. 2. Visual character of emphasis of sub-title using by graphic image with text

Third, Fig. 3 shows visual character of creation method of director and producer's ideology of storytelling [5]. One of the most important aspect of creation to use visual characters are not only use a variety of graphic and icon but also, it has position at non-linear area to express as whole. As mention above the sentence that given more understanding of storytelling, and also boundary between picture images and visual character's position has broken. This means on air area and safe title area both mutually use of frame works. Moreover, the creation of visual character is very important role of storytelling with viewer's satisfaction of pleasures.

Classification	Contents		
Features' Subtitles			
Screen Configuration	A lower column	The center of person	A upper column
Representation	Icon and text	The expression of feelings of person	The expression of atmosphere

Fig. 3. The case of creation on sub-titles

5   Conclusion

This study was conducted to analysis the visual communication method of visual character based on computer-generate system to use TV programs in Korea. Visual Character includes sub-title, graphic images with icon, special effect of graphic images, etc. The visual character become one of the most important elements of storytelling of TV program in order to send information and it become a part of images as a whole. And, the composition of visual characters to make the process of TV program into viewer.

This study classified that Korean TV program use a variety of visual character ever before. The importance value of using visual character is functional sub-title, emphasis of sub-title, and creation of sub-title produced by director. In particular, Fig. 3 shows big improvement of visual character that major part of using computer-generated system into TV program in Korea. It also contributed to new expression of visual character with digital technology as grew up. The various form of visual character shows director's own idea that express toward of viewers.

All these considered, the visual communication method of visual character has been rapidly changed by digital technology development and based on writing system. Which computer-generate system contribute on digital making system into TV programs. Furthermore, digital technology effects on making TV production system but also, affected on the ideology of thought. Future work need to figure not only analysis of content of TV program, but also focus on viewer's behavior of watching TV program with a variety of visual characters.

References

1. Millerson, G.: The Technique of Television Production, 5th edn., p. 349. Focal Press An imprint of Butterworth-Heinemann Ltd., Linacre House (1990)
2. Haley, A.: Online type tips: how the pros create web typography. Step-By-Step Graphics 15(2), 26–29 (1999); Al-Harkan, I.M., Ramadan, M.Z.: Effects of Pixel Shape and Color, and Matrix Pixel Density of Arabic Digital Typeface on Characters' Legibility. International Journal of Industrial Ergonomics 35, 653 (2005)
3. Al-Harkan, I.M., Ramadan, M.Z.: Above of all, p. 653
4. Lee, M.-J.: A Study on the Practical Applications and Expression of Visual Characters in TV Program. Journal of Communication Design 27, 27 (2008)
5. Hahm, H., Bolter, J.D.: Writing Space in the Configuration of the Visual Representation of the Subtitle. Journal of Moving Image Technology Association of Korea 13, 39–42 (2007)

Imperceptibility Metric for DWT Domain Digital Image Watermarking

Youngseok Lee[1] and Jongweon Kim[2,*]

[1] Dept. of Electronic Engineering, Chungwoon University,
San 29, Namjang-Ri, Hongsung-Kun, Hongsung-Eup, Chungnam, 350-701, Korea
[2] Dept. of Copyright Protection, Sangmyung University,
7, Hongji-dong, Jongno-gu, Seoul 110-743, Korea
yslee@chungwoon.ac.kr, jwkim@smu.ac.kr

Abstract. The human visual system is very complicate and able to handle a voluminous amount of visual information. It is composed of a receiver with a pre-processing stage, the eye and the retina, a transmission channel, the optic nerve, and a processing engine, the visual cortex. Though one has attempted to understand and model the human visual system process a stimulus is progressed through its huge neural network has not well known because of our lack of knowledge about brain behavior. As well known, the discrete wavelet transform is widely used in signal processing applications such as signal analysis, de-noising, compression etc. It has also played a key role in the field of digital image and/or audio watermarking. A general metric to measure perceptible transparency is peak signal to signal ratio which is the ratio between the maximum possible power of a signal and the power of error that affects the fidelity of its representation. But peak signal to noise ratio does not consider the characteristics of human visual system. In this paper we proposed new metric to measure the invisibility of discrete wavelet transform domain watermarked image based on human visual system using 2- dimensional contrast sensitivity function. The proposed metric was applied to a spread spectrum image watermarking scheme in discrete wavelet transform domain and evaluated by the Minkowski pooling. The experimental results were compared with peak signal to noise ratio.

Keywords: Imperceptibility metric, Digital image watermarking, DWT domain, Human visual system, Contrast sensitivity function.

1   Introduction

The rapid expansion of the internet media technologies in the last few decades has greatly increased of the production and distribution of digital media-based contents. These developments also have lead undesirable results such as the illegal and unauthorized manipulation of multimedia products. Protection of the ownership of digital products while allowing a full utilization of the Internet resources becomes an urgent issue [1, 2, 3].

---

* Corresponding author.

T.-h. Kim et al. (Eds.): SIP/WSE/ICHCI 2012, CCIS 342, pp. 102–109, 2012.

One way to solve this problem is the digital watermarking. Digital watermarking is defined as a technique of embedding the securable message called watermark into digital multimedia by preserving perceptual quality of watermarked data. The watermark can later be detected or extracted for purpose of owner or author identification and integrity verification of tested data. There are three basic requirements of digital watermarks: perceptual transparency, robustness to wanted and unwanted attacks, and capacity. These conditions are in conflict with each other. For example if we try to increasing the embedding strength of watermark to improve its robustness we face with a severe problem related to perceptual transparency and also if we want to get very good perceptual transparency we have to decrease the embedding strength of the watermark and so the embedded watermark will not be robust to attacks and signal processing.

General metric to measure perceptible transparency is PSNR (peak signal to signal ratio) which is the ratio between the maximum possible power of a signal and the power of error that affects the fidelity of its representation. But PSNR does not consider the characteristics of human visual system (HVS).

In this paper we proposed new metric to measure the invisibility of discrete wavelet transform (DWT) domain watermarked image based on HVS using 2- dimensional contrast sensitivity function (CFS). The proposed metric was applied to a spread spectrum image watermarking scheme and evaluated by the Minkowski pooling. The experimental results were compared with PSNR.

2   Proposition of New Metric DWT Domain Watermarking

2.1   Contrast Sensitivity Function of Human Visual System

The HVS is very complicate and able to handle a voluminous amount of visual information. To be brief, it is composed of a receiver with a pre-processing stage, the eye and the retina, a transmission channel, the optic nerve, and a processing engine, the visual cortex. Though one has attempted to understand and model the HVS behavior, the process a stimulus is progressed through its huge neural network has not well known because of our lack of knowledge about brain behavior. In physiological experiment [6], the CSF was proposed by Mannos and Sakrison, expresses contrast sensitivity, i.e. the reciprocal of the just visible contrast, as a function of spatial frequency f. $Lmax$ and $Lmin$ being respectively the maximal and minimal luminance value of the grating, Michelson's contrast C and the $CSF(f)$ are defined by:

$$C = \frac{Lmax - Lmin}{Lmax + Lmin} \tag{1}$$

and

$$CSF(f) = C_0 (1 + C_1 f) exp(\alpha \cdot f)^{\beta} \tag{2}$$

where C_0, C_1, α and β depend on parameters such as mean luminance, temporal frequency and orientation and were evaluated as 0.05, 0.28, -0.114 and 1.1 respectively by Mannos and Sakrison [6]. And also they found that HVS is a sort of bandpass filter bank with high gain in low frequencies.

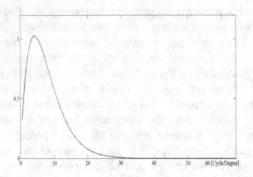

Fig. 1. Contrast sensitivity function of human visual system

Fig. 1 shows the normalized 1-dimensional CSF function with high values between 5-10 cycle/degree. A 2- dimensional version can be easily obtained by replacing f with radial frequency, $\sqrt{u^2+v^2}$, where u and v are the horizontal and vertical frequencies. Fig. 2 shows the 2- dimensional contrast sensitivity function. Magnitude of the function decays rapidly. Red indicates high value and blue low.

Fig. 2. 2D contrast sensitivity function

2.2   Proposition of New Metric

As well known, the DWT is widely used in signal processing applications such as signal analysis, de-noising, compression etc. It has also played a key role in the field of digital image and/or audio watermarking [7, 8].

In typical watermarking applications of DWT for an image a hidden message modulated by pseudorandom noise is embedded into an HL or an LH subband to be robust against various attacks such as compression, filtering, noising etc. And the performance of an applied watermarking scheme is evaluated by the robustness and the quality of watermarked cover object. The former is to measure the resistance against various signal processing and geometric attacks and the latter, the invisibility of a hidden message in the watermarked image [9]. The metric of invisibility of the applied watermarking scheme has widely used peak signal to noise ratio (PSNR) because of simplicity, though it is not consider the characteristics of HVS but justly calculate power of error with respect to the original image [10].

Considering the visible contrast of HVS, in this paper, we proposed a new metric of invisibility for DWT domain watermarking scheme. As showing in Fig. 3, the proposed metric applied the spatial frequency characteristics of the CSF.

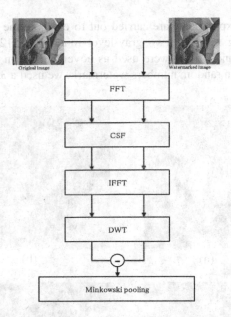

Fig. 3. Proposed imperceptibility metric for DWT domain digital image watermarking

At first, considering the HVS, two images, an original and a watermarked image are transformed to Fourier domain and then weighted to the 2- dimensional SCF to generate distortion by HVS. In this process, a hidden message in the watermarked image is also distorted whether the invisibility of the hidden message enhances or not.

Then two images are inverse transformed to the spatial domain and applied to DWT to measure difference error of two images at the watermark- embedded subbands. To analyze error term, we used the Minkowski pooling in (3). The generalized Minkowski summation in case of $P \neq Q$, provides additional flexibility for adjusting the response of individual parameters to changes in perceived quality. As a special case, (3) reduces to the mean absolute error (MAE) when $P = Q = 1$, and the mean squared error (MSE) if $Q = 2$. Finally if $P = Q = 2$, the Minkowski summation is equivalent to the root- MSE (RMSE). As Q increases, more emphasis will be put at the image regions of high distortions.

$$\text{Mink}(P,Q) \quad \left[\frac{1}{N}\sum_{i=1}^{N}|e_i|^Q\right]^{\frac{1}{P}} \tag{3}$$

where N is the number of pixels in the image, and e_i the absolute difference value at the i-th spatial location in difference value of   two images.

3   Experimental Results

In this section, some experiments are carried out to evaluate the performance of the proposed watermarking scheme. Two gray-level images of 512×512 pixels, *Lena, Baboon, Living room* and *Pirate*, were used as cover images in Fig. 4. Rather than using a pseudo-Gaussian random numbers watermark, we used a 32×32 binary image.

(a)   (b)

(c)   (d)

Fig. 4. Original images to test the new metric
(a) Lena (b) Baboon (c) Living room and (d) Pirate

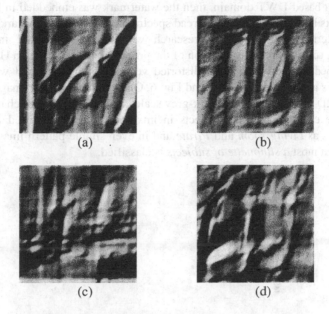

(a)   (b)

(c)   (d)

Fig. 5. Distorted versions of the original images by 2D- CSF of HVS

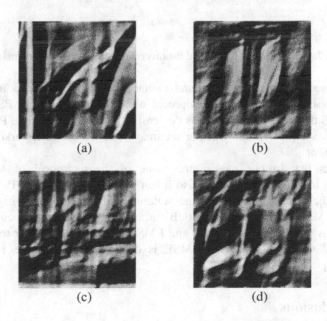

(a)   (b)

(c)   (d)

Fig. 6. Distorted versions of the watermarked images by 2D- CSF of HVS (PSNR, 40dB)

D4 wavelet based-DWT domain, then the watermark was embedded in LH and HL subbands of its DWT domain using spread spectrum processing watermarking scheme which is referred in [9]. In our research we are not interested in the used watermarking scheme but the validation of the proposed metric based on HVS.

As described in Section 2.2, the distorted versions of original and watermarked images images are showing in Fig 5 and Fig. 6. One can observe that images in Fig. 5 distorted by 2D- CSF of HVS are dark-grey scales and bandpass filter characteristics. And also one can observe that subjects in image cannot be classified in complex pattern images as *Living room* and *Pirate* and in even simple pattern images as *Lena* and *Baboon*, at most *a silhouette of subjects* is classified.

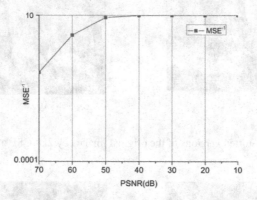

Fig. 7. Comparison of PSNR and the inverse of MSE for the *pirate* image

In HVS-based MSE analysis, we found a notable observation at the point of PSNR, 40dB. Fig. 7 shows the curve of reciprocal of MSE corresponding PSNR. When PSNR is 40dB the reciprocal of MSE is decreasing as PSNR increasing. PSNR, 40dB has known to a critical point whether an image quality of watermarked image is *acceptable or not*.

This means that in our metric, the value of the reciprocal of MSE, 10 is corresponding to PSNR, 40dB. And also it can be analyzed that the HVS with CSF can instinct the difference between the watermarked and original image over the reciprocal of MSE or under PSNR, 40dB. In analysis of our experiment, we could lead the results that HVS-based MAE and RMSE are reciprocal linear to PSNR and the reciprocal value of HVS-based MSE is decreasing from value 10 which is corresponding to PSNR, 40dB.

4   Conclusions

In this paper we proposed the imperceptibility metrics for wavelet transform domain watermarking scheme. The proposed metrics are MAE, MSE and RMSE for the distorted versions by CSF of HVS. In experimental results, we compared our metric with PSNR that is a general metric to measure the quality of image. Then we concluded that HVS-based metrics, MAE and RMSE are reciprocal linear to PSNR and that HVS-based MSE is decreasing MSE is decreasing from value 10.0 which is corresponding to PSNR, 40dB. In the inverse of MSE, MSE^{-1} we found that it has similar characteristics to the HVS. In JND test we concluded that the HVS cannot perceive the watermark embedded in high complex- patterned images under 10.0, MSE^{-1} while it can perceive the watermark embedded in low- complex patterned images over 10.0, MSE^{-1}.

We restricted the research boundary to integer P and Q at the Minkowski pooling and wavelet transform-based watermarking scheme in this paper. But it is extensible to a rational number P and Q, and another candidate of transform domain. So as further study, we focus on the Minkowski pooling with rational numbers P and Q to find a metric to come close the HVS with CSF.

Acknowledgments. This research project was supported by Ministry of Culture, Sports and Tourism(MCST) and from Korea Copyright Commission in 2011.

References

1. Kim, J.W., Kim, N.G., Lee, D.W., Park, S.B., Lee, S.W.: Watermarking two dimensional data object identifier for authenticated distribution of digital multimedia contents. Signal Processing: Image Communication 25, 559–576 (2010)
2. Nah, J.H., Kim, J.W.: Video Forensic Marking Algorithm using Peak Position Modulation. AMIS 6(6S) (2012)
3. Li, D., Kim, J.W.: Secure Image Forensic Marking Algorithm using 2D Barcode and Off-axis Hologram in DWT-DFRNT Domain. AMIS 6(2S), 513S–520S (2012)
4. Dugad, R., Ratakonda, K., Ahuja, N.: A new wavelet-based scheme for watermarking Images. In: Proceedings of the IEEE International Conference on Image Processing. IEEE Press, Chicago (1998)
5. Barni, M., Podilchuk, C.I., Bartolini, F., Delp, E.J.: Watermark embedding: Hiding a signal within a cover image. IEEE Communications Magazine 39(8), 102–108 (2001)
6. Eskicioglu, A.M., Delp, E.J.: An overview of multimedia content protection in consumer electronics devices. Signal Processing: Image Communication 16(7), 618–699 (2001)
7. Jayant, N.J., Johnston, J., Safranek, R.: Signal Compression Based on Models of Human Perception. Proceedings of the IEEE 81, 1385–1422 (1993)
8. Stein, C.S., Watson, A.B., Hitchner, L.E.: Psychophysical Rating of Image Compression Techniques. In: Proceedings of the SPIE, vol. 1077, pp. 198–208. SPIE Press (1989)
9. Watson, A.B., Taylor, M., Brothwick, R.: Image Quality and Entropy Masking. In: Proceedings of SPIE, vol. 3016, pp. 358–371. SPIE Press (1998)
10. Eckert, M.P., Chakraborty, D.P.: Video Display Quality Measurements for PACS. In: Proceedings of the SPIE, vol. 2431, pp. 328–340 (1989)

An Ant Colony Optimization Algorithm Based Image Classification Method for Content-Based Image Retrieval in Cloud Computing Environment

Kwang-Kyu Seo

Dept. of Management Engineering, Sangmyung University
Sangmyungdae-gil 31, Dongnam-gu, Chonan, Chungnam 330-720, Korea
kwangkyu@smu.ac.kr

Abstract. Feature selection and feature extraction are the most important steps in classification problems. Feature selection is commonly used to reduce dimensionality of datasets with tens or hundreds of thousands of features which would be impossible to process further. One of the problems in which feature selection is essential is content-based image classification problems. This paper presents a novel method for image classification method based on an ant colony optimization algorithm which can significantly improve the classification performance for content-based image retrieval in cloud computing environment. Ant colony optimization algorithm is inspired by observation on real ants in their search for the shortest paths to food sources. The proposed algorithm is easily implemented and because of use of a simple classifier in that, its computational complexity is very low. We compared the previous algorithm with the proposed algorithm in terms of image classification performance. As a result, the proposed algorithm showed higher performance in terms of accuracy.

Keywords: Feature selection, Ant colony optimization algorithm, Image classification, Content-based image retrieval, Cloud Computing.

1 Introduction

As the need for effective multimedia information services is significant, the study on image classification and retrieval methods has become considerably important in various areas such as entertainment, education, digital libraries, and medical image retrieval, etc. Content-based image retrieval (CBIR) techniques are becoming increasingly important in multimedia information systems in order to store, manage, and retrieve image data to perform assigned task and make intelligent decisions. CBIR uses an automatic indexing scheme where implicit properties of an image can be included in the query to reduce search time for retrieval from a large database.

Cloud computing is provided by service providers and consumed by service consumers. Since computing resources are located in service providers' side, service consumers have relatively little burden to manage computing resources, surely which brings various advantages of cloud service to service consumers such as the reduction

T.-h. Kim et al. (Eds.): SIP/WSE/ICHCI 2012, CCIS 342, pp. 110–117, 2012.

of manpower and cost to manage computing resources and the increasing of scalability. The CBIR is good suitable to cloud computing environment, so the proposed image classification method for CBIR is provided by cloud service. This paper focus on developing image classification algorithm based on ACO.

Features like color, texture, shape, spatial relationship among entities of an image and also their combination are generally being used for the computation of multi-dimensional feature vector. The features such as color, texture and shape are known as primitive features. Images have always been an essential and effective medium for presenting visual data. With advances in today's computer technologies, it is not surprising that in many applications, much of the data is images. There have been considerable researches done on CBIR using artificial intelligence techniques [1-3].

Feature selection (FS) is a commonly used step in machine learning, especially when dealing with a high dimensional space of features. The objective of feature selection is to simplify a dataset by reducing its dimensionality and identifying relevant underlying features without sacrificing predictive accuracy. By doing that, it also reduces redundancy in the information provided by the selected features. In real world problems FS is a must due to the abundance of noisy, irrelevant or misleading features. Feature selection is extensive and it spreads throughout many fields, including text categorization, data mining, pattern recognition and signal processing [4].

Several AI approaches are applied to the feature selection problems. Among these methods which are proposed for FS, population-based optimization algorithm such as genetic algorithm (GA)-based method and ant colony optimization (ACO)-based method have attracted a lot of attention. These methods attempt to achieve better solutions by application of knowledge from previous iterations.

In this paper, we apply the ACO algorithm based algorithm for content-based image classification in cloud computing environment. To the best of our knowledge, it is the first paper to apply an ACO-based technique to the problem of feature selection in content-based image classification. In this paper a new modified ACO-based feature selection algorithm has been introduced. The classifier performance and the length of selected feature subset are adopted as heuristic information for ACO.

2   Research Background

2.1   Ant Colony Optimization (ACO) Algorithm

In the early 1990s, ant colony optimization was introduced by Dorigo and colleagues as a novel nature-inspired meta-heuristic for the solution of hard combinatorial optimization problems. ACO belongs to the class of meta-heuristics, which includes approximate algorithms used to obtain good enough solutions to hard CO problems in a reasonable amount of computation time. The inspiring source of ACO is the foraging behavior of real ants [5].

The first ACO algorithm developed was the ant system (AS) [6], and since then several improvement of the AS have been devised [7]. The ACO algorithm is based on a computational paradigm inspired by real ant colonies and the way they function.

The underlying idea was to use several constructive computational agents (simulating real ants). A dynamic memory structure incorporating information on the effectiveness of previous choices based on the obtained results, guides the construction process of each agent. The behavior of each single agent is therefore inspired by the behavior of real ants [8].

The paradigm is based on the observation made by ethnologists about the medium used by ants to communicate information regarding shortest paths to food by means of pheromone trails. A moving ant lays some pheromone on the ground, thus making a path by a trail of this substance. While an isolated ant moves practically at random, exploration, an ant encountering a previously laid trail can detect it and decide with high probability to follow it, exploitation, and consequently reinforces the trail with its own pheromone. What emerges is a form of autocatalytic process through which the more the ants follow a trail, the more attractive that trail becomes to be followed. The process is thus characterized by a positive feedback loop, during which the probability of choosing a path increases with the number of ants that previously chose the same path. The mechanism above is the inspiration for the algorithms of the ACO family [9].

2.2   Image Features

In this paper, color and texture information are used to represent image features. Color is the dominant component of human perceptions. We used color features to represent images. We used an RGB (Red, Green and Blue) color model and an HSV (Hue, Saturation and Value) color model. The RGB color model is used for many image retrieval systems. For global image representation and fast search, RGB color histograms of the image, which are quantized into 16 bins per R, G, and B coordinates, are extracted. For local information, the image is divided into rectangular regions. The HSV model is closely correlated to human color perception. A set of HSV joint histograms are extracted from each rectangular region, and dominant hue, saturation, and value are used as features in that region.

RGB Color Model: A histogram is a widely used form of representing an image, which has rotational and translational invariance. A suitable normalization can also provide scale invariance. In this study, we used an RGB color histogram to represent global information about an image.

HSV Color Model: We used HSV color model for representing color because this model is closely related to human visual perception. Color quantization is useful for reducing the calculation cost. Furthermore, it provides better performance in image classification because it can eliminate the detailed color components that can be considered noises. The human visual system is more sensitive to hue than saturation and value so that hue should be quantized finer than saturation and value. In the experiments, we uniformly quantized HSV space into 18 bins for hue (each bin consisting of a range of 20 degree), 3 bins for saturation and 3 bins for value for lower resolution [3].

Texture Feature: Texture analysis is an important and useful area of study in computer vision. Most natural images include textures. Scenes containing pictures of wood, grass, etc. can be easily classified based on the texture rather than color or shape. Therefore, it may be useful to extract texture features for image clustering. Like as color feature, we include a texture feature extracted from localized image region. The co-occurrence matrix is a two-dimensional histogram which estimates the pair-wise statistics of gray level. The $(i, j)^{th}$ element of the co-occurrence matrix represents the estimated probability that gray level i co-occurs with gray level j at a specified displacement d and angle θ. By choosing the values of d and θ, a separate co-occurrence matrix is obtained. From each co-occurrence matrix a number of textural features can be extracted. For image clustering, we used entropy, which is mostly used in many applications [3].

3   The Proposed Image Classification Method Based on ACO

Typically an image classification system consists of several essential parts including feature extraction and feature selection. After preprocessing of images, feature extraction is used to transform the input image into a feature set (feature vector). Feature selection is applied to the feature set to reduce the dimensionality of it. This process is shown in Fig. 1. ACO is used to explore the space of all subsets of given feature set. The performance of selected feature subsets is measured by invoking an evaluation function with the corresponding reduced feature space and measuring the specified classification result. The best feature subset found is then output as the recommended set of features to be used in the actual design of the classification system.

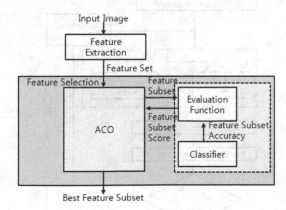

Fig. 1. Block diagram of proposed feature selection algorithm based on ACO

The main steps of proposed feature selection algorithm are shown in Fig. 2 and as follows:

1. Initialization
- Determine the population of ants.
- Set the intensity of pheromone trial associated with any feature.
- Determine the maximum of allowed iterations.
2. Solution generation and evaluation of ants
- Assign any ant randomly to one feature and visiting features, each ant builds solutions completely. In this step, the evaluation criterion is mean square error (MSE) of the classifier. If an ant is not able to decrease the MSE of the classifier in ten successive steps, it will finish its work and exit.
3. Evaluation of the selected subsets
- Sort selected subsets according to classifier performance and their length. Then, select the best subset.
4. Check the stop criterion
- Exit, if the number of iterations is more than the maximum allowed iteration, otherwise continues.
5. Pheromone updating
- Decrease pheromone concentrations of nodes then, all ants deposit the quantity of pheromone on graph. Finally, allow the best ant to deposit additional pheromone on nodes.
6. Generation of new ants
- In this step previous ants are removed and new ants are generated.
7. Go to 2 and continue

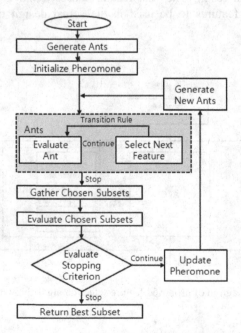

Fig. 2. Flowchart of the FS algorithm based on ACO

The time complexity of proposed algorithm is $O(Imn)$, where I is the number of iterations, m the number of ants, and n the number of original features. In the worst case, each ant selects all the features. As the heuristic is evaluated after each feature is added to the candidate subset, this will result in n evaluations per ant. After the first iteration in this algorithm, mn evaluations will have been performed. After I iterations, the heuristic will be evaluated Imn times.

4   Experimental Results

In order to evaluate the proposed algorithm, all experiments were performed on a Pentium IV with 512Mb of main memory and 100Gb of storage. All programs were implemented in Visual C++. We collected 1000 images, most with dimensions of 192 × 128 pixels. These were collected from public sources and represent natural scenes such as animals, plants and airplanes. The 1,000 images can be divided into 10 categories, each with 250 images, which are; elephant, airplane, horse, lion, dolphin, polar bear, rose, sunset, tiger and eagle. Fig. 3 shows images used in the experiments.

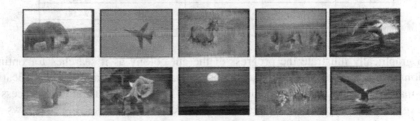

Fig. 3. Images from the selected 10 categories used in the experiments

We used support vector machine (SVM) classifier with RBF kernel function to discriminate images. In various SVM kernel functions, an RBF kernel function is very useful for solving problems in which linear separation is impossible. An SVM model with good performance must reduce generalization errors. In this paper, we used k-fold cross-validation to obtain the best parameters for reducing generalization errors. 80% of data is used for learning, and the remaining 20% of data is used for validation. In this experiment, we used a 5-fold cross validation method to obtain a generalized result.

Retrieval effectiveness can be defined in terms of precision (π). The precision function is in eq. (2).

$$\pi_i = \frac{TP_i}{TP_i + FP_i} \tag{2}$$

where TP_i is the number of test documents correctly classified under ith category (c_i), FP_i is the number of test documents incorrectly classified under c_i.

To show the utility of proposed ACO-based algorithm we compare proposed algorithm with GA based algorithm. Various values were tested for the parameters of proposed algorithm. The results show that the highest performance is achieved by setting the parameters. Analyzing the precision shown in Table 1, we see that on average, the ACO-based algorithm obtained a higher accuracy value than the GA-based algorithm.

Table 1. Image classification precision by GA based and ACO based methods

Image category	GA based algorithm		ACO-based algorithm	
	Training(%)	Validation(%)	Training(%)	Validation(%)
Horse	95.50	94.00	97.50	96.00
Rose	93.00	92.00	95.00	92.00
Polar bear	96.00	92.00	98.00	94.00
Sunset	98.00	96.00	99.00	96.00
Eagle	96.00	94.00	98.00	96.00
Dolphin	97.00	96.00	98.00	96.00
Airplane	96.50	90.00	97.50	92.00
Tiger	94.00	90.00	96.00	92.00
Elephant	94.00	94.00	96.00	94.00
Eagle	95.50	92.00	96.50	94.00
Average	95.55	93.00	97.15	94.20

To graphically illustrate the progress of the ant colony as it searches for optimal solutions, we take percent features as the horizontal coordinate and the classification performance measure as the vertical coordinate. This should illustrate the process of improvement of the best ant as the number of features increase. Fig. 4 shows the classification measure for each of the feature selection algorithms as we change the number of selected features. The results show that as the percentage of selected features exceeds 12%, the ACO-based algorithm outperforms GA-based algorithm.

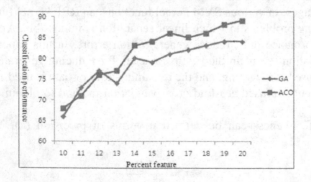

Fig. 4. Comparison of image categories of GA and ACO algorithms

From the result and figure, we can see that, compared with GA, ACO is quicker in locating the optimal solution. ACO has powerful exploration ability: it is a gradual searching process that approaches optimal solutions. The running time of ACO is affected more by the problem dimension (feature numbers), and the size of data.

For some datasets with more features, after finding a sub-optimal solution, the GA cannot find a better one. However, ACO can search in the feature space until the optimal solution is found. The GA is affected greatly by the number of features.

5   Conclusion

In this paper, we proposed a new optimal feature selection technique based on ant colony optimization (ACO) to improve the performance of image classification for CBIR. We compare its performance with the GA-based feature selection algorithm in image categorization. Experimental results demonstrate competitive performance. The computational results indicated that proposed algorithm outperforms GA-based algorithm since it achieved better performance with the lower number of features. Eventually, ACO has the ability to converge quickly; it has a strong search capability in the problem space and can efficiently find minimal feature subset.

In future, we investigate a relevance feedback approach based on the proposed ACO-based method, in order to capture a user's visual perception. In addition, we intend to investigate the performance of proposed feature selection algorithm by taking advantage of using more complex classifiers in that. Another research direction will involve experiments with other kinds of datasets. Finally, we plan to combine proposed feature selection algorithm with other population-based feature selection algorithms.

Acknowledgement. This research was supported by the KCC, Korea, under the CPRC support program supervised by the KCA (KCA-2012-1194100004-110010100).

References

1. Fournier, J., Cord, M., Philipp-Foliguet, S.: Back-propagation Algorithm for Relevance Feedback in Image retrieval. In: IEEE ICIP 2001, vol. 1, pp. 686–689 (2001)
2. Koskela, M., Laaksonen, J., Oja, E.: Use of Image Subset Features in Image Retrieval with Self-Organizing Maps. In: Enser, P.G.B., Kompatsiaris, Y., O'Connor, N.E., Smeaton, A., Smeulders, A.W.M. (eds.) CIVR 2004. LNCS, vol. 3115, pp. 508–516. Springer, Heidelberg (2004)
3. Park, S.S., Seo, K.K., Jang, D.S.: Expert system based on artificial neural networks for content-based image retrieval. Expert Systems with Applications 29(3), 589–597 (2005)
4. Jensen, R.: Combining rough and fuzzy sets for feature selection, Ph.D. dissertation, School of Information, Edinburgh University (2005)
5. Dorigo, M., Blum, C.: Ant colony optimization theory: A survey. Theoretical Computer Science 344(2-3), 243–278 (2005)
6. Dorigo, M.: Optimization, learning and natural algorithms, Ph.D. dissertation, Dipartimento di Electtronica, Politecnico di Milano, Italy (2005)
7. Dorigo, M., Maniezzo, V., Colorni, A.: Ant system: Optimization by a colony of cooperating agents. IEEE Transaction on Systems, Man, and Cybernetics-Part B 26(1), 29–41 (1996)
8. Montemanni, R., Gambardella, L.M., Rizzoli, A.E., Donati, A.V.: A new algorithm for a dynamic vehicle routing problem based on ant colony system, Istituto Dalle Molle Di Studi Sull Intelligenza Artificiale, Technical Report IDSIA-23-02 (2002)
9. Bonabeau, E., Dorigo, M., Theraulaz, G.: Swarm intelligence: From natural to artificial systems. Oxford University Press, New York (1999)

2D AR(1,1) Analysis of Blurring Image by Empirical Mode Decomposition

Myungwoo Nam[1] and Youngseok Lee[2]

[1] Department of Electronic CAD, Hyejeon College,
Daehak-Gil 25, Hongsung, Chungnam, 350-702, Korea
[2] Department of Electronic Engineering, Chungwoon University,
Daehak-Gil 25, Hongsung, Chungnam, 350-701, Korea
`mwnam@hj.ac.kr, yslee@chungwoon.ac.kr`

Abstract. In this paper we propose the method that can estimate the relative degree of blurring from images. 2 dimensional(2D) autoregressive(AR) model and empirical mode decomposition are used for estimating blurring parameter to represent the degree of blurring in the method. In experimental results, we found that the relative degree of blurring in image is represented by the estimated AR coefficient of residue of empirical mode decomposition result and also maximum auto-correlation value of the residue in empirical mode decomposition results is proportional to the degree of blurring. As a result, we show that the proposed method can parameterizes blurring image by AR coefficient.

Keywords: 2D AR model, empirical mode decomposition, blurring image.

1 Introduction

One of interesting area in the image processing is the restoration of blurred image. Blurring image is an unfocused or contaminated image by noise [1]. The outline of objects in the blurring image is seen dim and edgeless.

The human visual system (HVS) perceives a blurring image and the brain system estimates outline of objects in the image. Human can estimate the relative degree of blurring from image perceived by the HVS. The relative degree of blurring means a measure that can discriminate the difference between blurring images.

In this paper we propose the method that can estimate the relative degree of blurring from images. In the method, 2 dimensional(2D) autoregressive(AR) model and empirical mode decomposition are used for estimating blurring parameter to represent the degree of blurring. Especially in case of image that has high correlation property with adjacent pixel, our method is much effective. The proposed method is applies to burring images that are contaminated by Asian dust.

In experimental results, we found that the degree of blurring in image is proportional to the estimated AR coefficient of residue of empirical mode decomposition results and also maximum auto-correlation value of residue is proportional to the degree of blurring. This result implies that the blurring image by Asian dust is parameterized by coefficient of 2D AR(1,1) model.

T.-h. Kim et al. (Eds.): SIP/WSE/ICHCI 2012, CCIS 342, pp. 118–125, 2012.

2   EMD and 2D AR Model

2.1   Empirical Mode Decomposition

Empirical mode decomposition (EMD), originally developed by Huang et al [5], is a data driven signal processing algorithm that has been established to be able to perfectly analyze nonlinear and nonstationary data by obtaining local features and time-frequency distribution of the data. The first step of this method decomposes signal into characteristic intrinsic mode functions (IMFs), while the second step finds the time frequency distribution of the signal from each IMF by utilizing the concepts of Hilbert transform and instantaneous frequency. The complete process is also known as Hilbert-Huang transform (HHT). This decomposition technique has also been extended to analyzing two dimensional images, which is known as bidimensional EMD (BEMD), image EMD (IEMD), 2DEMD and so on [2].

The required properties of IMFs are archived by empirical iteration process in EMD. The same algorithm applies for BEMD as well, where extrema detection and interpolation are carried out using 2D versions of the corresponding 1-D methods. Let the original image be denoted as I, a BIMF as F. and the residue as R. In the decomposition process i-th BIMF S_i is obtained from its source image F_i, where S_i is a residue image obtained as $S_i=S_{i-1}-F_{i-1}$ and $S_1=I$. It requires one or more iterations to obtain F_i, where the intermediate temporary state of BIMF (ITSBIMF) in j-th iteration can be denoted as F_{Tj}. With the definition of the variables, the steps of the BEMD process can be summarized as follows [3].

The BIMFs and the residue of an image together can be named as bidimensional empirical mode components (BEMCs). Except for the truncation error of the digital computer, the summation of all BEMCs returns the original image back as given by

$$\sum C = \sum_{i=1}^{k+1} C_i, \quad C_0 = I \tag{1}$$

where C_i is i-th BEMC and K is the total number of IMFs excluding the residue.

2.2   Parameter Estimation by 2D Autoregressive Model

We assume image as as a 2D random field $\{x[n,m], (n,m) \in \mathcal{Z}^2 \}$. We define a total order on the discrete lattice as follows

$$(i, j) \leftrightarrow (s,t), i \leq s \text{ and } j \leq t. \tag{2}$$

The 2D AR (p_1, p_2) model is defined for the $N_1 \times N_2$ image $I = \{x[n,m] : 0 \leq n \leq N_1-1, 0 \leq m \leq N_2-1\}$ by the following difference equation

$$x[m, n] + \sum_{i=0}^{p_1} \sum_{j=0}^{p_2} a_{ij} x[m - i, n - j] = w[m, n] \tag{3}$$

where $\{w[n,m]\}$ is a white noise field with variance σ^2, and the coefficients $\{a_{ij}\}$ is the parameter of the model [5].

From (3), the image $\{x[n,m]\}$ can be viewed as the output of the linear time-invariant causal system $H(z_1, z_2)$ excited by a white noise input, where

$$H(z) = \frac{1}{A(z_1, z_2)} = \frac{1}{\sum_{i=0}^{p_1} \sum_{j=0}^{p_2} a_{ij} z_1^{-i} z_2^{-j}} \tag{4}$$

with $a_{00}=1$.

Assume first that the noise sequence $\{w[n,m]\}$ were known. Then the problem of estimating the parameters in the AR model (3) would be a simple input-output system parameter estimation problem, which could be solved by several methods, the simplest of which is the least-squares (LS) method. In the LS method, (2) is expressed as

$$x[n,m] + \varphi^t[n,m]\theta = w[n,m] \tag{5}$$

where

$$\varphi^t[n,m] = [x[n,m-1], \cdots\cdots, x[n-p_1, m-p_2]], \tag{6}$$

and

$$\theta = [a_{01}, \cdots\cdots, a_{p_1 p_2}]^t. \tag{7}$$

The parameter estimator, $\hat{\theta}$ is expressed as

$$\hat{\theta} = -(\Phi^t \Phi)^{-1} \Phi \Phi^t X \tag{8}$$

where

$$\Phi = \begin{pmatrix} x[L+1,1] & \cdots & x[L+1-p_1, & M+1-p_2] \\ x[L+2,1] & \cdots & x[L+2-p_1, & M+1-p_2] \\ \vdots & \ddots & & \vdots \\ x[N_1-1, N_2-2] & \cdots & x[N_1-1-p_1, & N_2-1-p_2] \end{pmatrix} \tag{9}$$

Therefore, we can estimate $\{w[n,m]\}$ by first estimating the AR parameters $\{a_{ij}\}$ and next obtaining $\{w[n,m]\}$ by filtering $\{x[n,m]\}$ as in (2). Since we cannot estimate an infinite number of (independent) parameters from a finite number of samples, we approximate the finite AR model by one of finite orders, (p_1, p_2). The parameters in the truncated AR model can be estimated by using a 2D extension of the Yule-Walker equations [6].

3   Experimental Results

To experiment the proposed method, we prepared blurring images in Figure 1 which are blurred by Asian dust. Asian dust is commonly called 'yellow sand' in China, Korea, and Japan in their languages of Huang Sha, Hwang Sa, and Kosa. It is a well-known phenomenon during the spring season in East Asia. In fact, Asian dust has been a matter of meteorological concern in East Asia. The optical properties of Asian dust have been studied using ground-based instruments such as ladar, a sun photometer, sky radiometer, and an optical particle counter (OPC) in the last two decades [7].

Original photos prepared at first were 1024×768 24bit colored images, we pre-processed them to 256×256, 24bit colored and 256×256, 8bit gray-scaled images for image processing without blurring characteristics. Figure 1 (a), (b) and (c) are pre-processed weak, medium and severe blurring colored images and Figure 1 (d), (e) and (f) are corresponding gray-scaled images One can observe that the silhouette of skyscraper in Figure 1 is blurred by effect of Asian dust.

(a) Asian dust image with light tone

(b) Asian dust image with medium tone

(c) Asian dust image with medium tone

(d) Gray scale version of image (a)

Fig. 1. Photos of Asian dust to experiment with color and gray scale

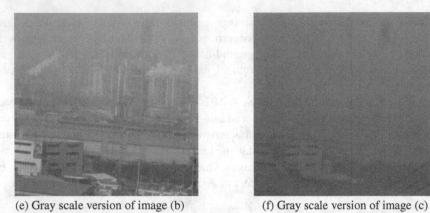

(e) Gray scale version of image (b)   (f) Gray scale version of image (c)

Fig. 1. (*continued*)

In order to analyze the blurring images, we applied 4-level EMD to gray-scaled images as in Figure 2, 3 and 4. IMF1s in EMD results show the silhouette of original images which are the same effect as high pass filter or edge detector. As Asian dust being increasing, IMF1s are more burring in the figures. IMF2s and IMF3s in the figures have very similar pattern to each other, which is estimated that frequency components in IMF2 and IMF3 of EMD results are common. From the result of EMD, an interesting region is Residues of EMD. One can observe that the intensity of residue images is varying to the degree of Asian dust.

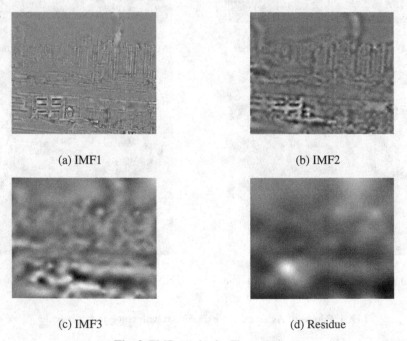

(a) IMF1   (b) IMF2

(c) IMF3   (d) Residue

Fig. 2. EMD results for Figure 1(d)

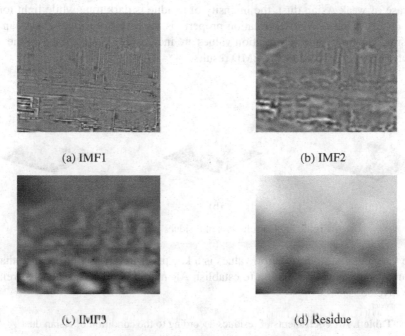

(a) IMF1   (b) IMF2

(c) IMF3   (d) Residue

Fig. 3. EMD results for Figure 1(e)

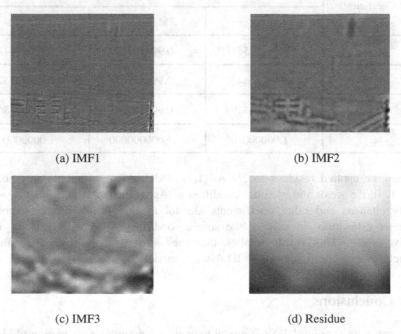

(a) IMF1   (b) IMF2

(c) IMF3   (d) Residue

Fig. 4. EMD results for Figure 1(f)

In case of weak Asian dust, the intensity of residue is dark tone while light tone in severe case. And also Auto-correlation property is varying to residue. As Asian dust increasing Maximum auto-correlation values are increasing. Figure 5 shows the auto-correlation results of residues by EMD results.

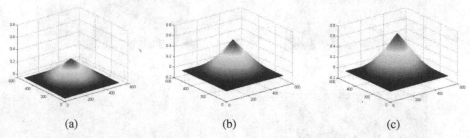

(a)   (b)   (c)

Fig. 5. 2D Correlations of residues of EMD results

The varying of auto-correlation values is a key point in AR model because that the solution of Yule-Walker equation to establish AR model is related to auto-correlation and its inverse.

Table 1. AR coefficients of residues according to the condition of Asian dust

AR Coefficients	Condition of Asian dust		
	Weak	Medium	Severe
a_{11}	-0.997135831	-0.996569672	0.99644141
a_{12}	-0.996754451	-0.996539712	-0.996437327
a_{21}	0.993896198	0.993121655	0.992891863
a_{22}	1.000000000	1.000000000	1.000000000

When we applied residues to 2D AR(1,1) model, AR coefficients are shown in Table 1. In the weak and medium condition of Asian dust, AR coefficients, a_{11} are slightly changed and other coefficients are not meaningful in the view point of parameter estimation. In case of the severe condition, AR coefficients, a_{11} is not negative value. This result implies that the blurred image by Asian dust is parameterized by coefficient a_{11} of 2D AR(1,1) model.

4   Conclusions

In this paper we proposed 2D AR model to apply for parameter estimation of blurring image. The proposed method was applied to residue in EMD domain of images blurred by Asian dust. In experimental results, we found that the degree of blurring in image is proportional to the estimated AR coefficient, a_{11} of residue of EMD result and also maximum auto-correlation value of residue is proportional to the degree of blurring. This result implies that the blurring image by Asian dust is parameterized by coefficient a_{11} of 2D AR(1,1) model.

Acknowledgements. The authors want to thank Prof. Heekwan Lee from the Department of Civil and Environmental Engineering, University of Incheon, Korea for providing the Asian dust images.

References

1. Wong, W.H., Hu, X., Chen, C.T.: Image Restoration using Gibbs Priors: Boundary Modeling, Treatment of Blurring, and Selection of Hyper Parameter. IEEE Transactions on Pattern Analysis and Machine Intelligence 13, 413–425 (1991)
2. Nunes, J.C., Bouaoune, Y., Delechelle, E., Niang, O., Bunel, P.: Image analysis by bidimensionalempirical mode decomposition. Image and Vision Computing 21, 1019–1032 (2003)
3. Sharif, M.A., Bhuiyan, Reza, R., Adhami, R., Khan, J.F.: Fast and Adaptive Bidimensional Empirical Mode Decomposition Using Order-Statistics Filter Based Envelope Estimation. EURASIP Journal on Advances in Signal Processing, 1–18 (2008)
4. Bi, N., Sun, Q., Huang, H., Yang, Z., Huang, J.: Robust Image Watermarking Based on Multiband Wavelets and EMD. IEEE Trans. on Image Processing, 1956–1966 (2007)
5. Alacam, B., Yazici, B., Bilgutay, N., Forsberg, F., Piccoli, C.: Breast tissue characterization using FARMA modeling of ultrasonic RF echo. Ultrasound in Medicine and Biology 30(10), 1397–1407 (2004)
6. Wei, L., Yang, Y., Nishikawa, R.M., Jiang, Y.: A study on several machine-learning methods for classification of malignant and benign clustered microcalcifications. IEEE Transactions on Medical Imaging 24(3), 371–380 (2005)
7. Arao, K., Ishizaka, Y.: Volume and mass of yellow sand dust in the air over Japan as estimated from atmospheric turbidity. J. Meteorology Society of Japan 64, 79–94 (1986)

Domain-Specific Marker Recognition Method to Improve Marker Efficiency and Reusability

Sungmo Jung and Seoksoo Kim[*]

Department of Multimedia, Hannam University, 306-791 Daejeon, Korea
sungmoj@gmail.com, sskim0123@naver.com

Abstract. Studies on Augmented Reality (AR) have recently received attention. However, the marker-based AR may detect markers of similar patterns as the same markers and the markers can be overlapped. To solve this problem, this paper suggests a method of domain-specific marker recognition, which can increase marker efficiency and reusability.

Keywords: Augmented reality, Marker recognition, Reference marker detection, Focal point.

1 Introduction

Augmented Reality (AR) [1] refers to a virtual world which can provide a sense of reality in interactions with users, where images of real world and virtual objects are generated by computer, and it is almost a lower level of virtual reality rather than a virtual reality realizing a complete immersion environment. It is a computer graphic technology field that provides the image with information such as characters and graphic objects in real life to enhance users' understanding of the situation of moving objects in 3D space. The computer graphic technology is also called mixed reality, and it could be based on a marker or not [2].

In the marker-based AR technology [3], the direction of a camera is decided using markers on the plane. On the white plane there are black squares and various patterns [4]. The existing marker based AR technology can only load a designated object in one marker and actually has to add another marker to load other objects. However, the marker-based AR technology may detect markers of similar patterns as the same markers and the markers can be overlapped.

To solve this problem, this paper suggests a method of domain-specific marker recognition, which can increase marker efficiency and reusability.

2 Method of the Existing Marker-Based AR Technology

In the marker-based AR technology, the direction of a camera is decided using markers on the plane. On the white plane there are black squares and various patterns using a method of template matching [5].

---

[*] Corresponding author.

T.-h. Kim et al. (Eds.): SIP/WSE/ICHCI 2012, CCIS 342, pp. 126–132, 2012.

A general expression for a template matching algorithm is shown in Formula (1).

$$SS(x,y) = \sum_{i=0}^{K-1}\sum_{j=0}^{K-1} f\{s(x+i,y+j),T(i,j)\} \tag{1}$$

CC(Correlation Coefficient) [6] and SAD(Sum of Absolute Difference) [7] are methods of finding correlation for template matching. For CC formula f is multiplication in Formula (1) as in the case of Formula (2). For SAD formula f is subtraction and the absolute value in Formula (1) as in the case of Formula (3) [8].

$$SS_{CC}(x,y) = \sum_{i=0}^{K-1}\sum_{j=0}^{K-1} f\{s(x+i,y+j)\cdot T(i,j)\} \tag{2}$$

$$SS_{SAD}(x,y) = \sum_{i=0}^{K-1}\sum_{j=0}^{K-1} f\{s(x+i,y+j) - T(i,j)\} \tag{3}$$

However, both methods require a great amount of computation and a large amount of time if applied to data with great bit depth.

Therefore, this paper suggests a method of domain-specific marker recognition that requires a little amount of computation and a small amount of time, which can increase efficiency and reusability.

3   Suggested Method: Domain-Specific Marker Recognition

3.1   Confirmation of Non-overlapping Area, Based on Marker's Focal Point

A circle's area should be divided every 45 degrees when calculating the area from the marker's focal point in a square. The process of creating a circle with the discriminant is shown Fig. 1 $d = F(x+1, \frac{y-1}{2})$, for $F(x,y) = b^2\cdot x^2 + a^2\cdot y^2 - a^2\cdot b^2$.

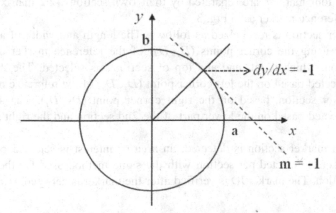

Fig. 1. Structure to create a circle

If d value is less than 0, $(x+1, y)$ and greater than 0, $(x+1, y-1)$ will be selected. If d_{old} is less than 0, it is $d_{new} = F(x + 2, y) = d_{old} + b^2\{2(x + 1) + 1\}$ and if d_{old} is greater than 0, it is $d_{new} = F\left(x + 2, \frac{y-3}{2}\right) = d_{old} + |b^2\{2(x + 1) + 1\} - a^2\{2(y - 1)\}|$ for the update of the discriminant to be calculated on the marker's focal point coordinate.

As the independent variables of x are between 0 and -1 of the slope, for an interval of independent variables in y, the roles are just changed in the numerical formulas calculating independent variables in x. The process of creating a circle's area based on the marker's focal point is shown Fig. 2. In case four markers that are located on screen are designated as non-overlapping area, the applicable area is not interfered.

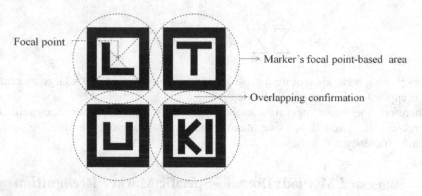

Fig. 2. Creation of the marker's focal point area and Overlapping confirmation by designating the created area as non-overlapping area

3.2   Singling Out of A Reference Marker and Sub Markers

After Fig. 2, four markers are separated by their own sections (2·2 matrix) to single out one of reference marker as in Fig. 3.

The marker section is recognized as follows. The length and width of a marker is measured by using the corner points (D_1~D_4) of the reference marker and then a marker section, which is left end and top of sections, is selected. The 2nd marker section is selected based on the left corner point (D_1, D_4) of the reference marker and the 3rd marker section, based on the right corner point (D_2, D_1). The 4th marker section is selected based on the lower part of the 2nd section and the right side of the 3rd section.

After each marker section is detected, an area of interest is selected per section. Then, a marker is detected per section with the same method used for the reference marker detection. The marker ID is verified after the marker is detected.

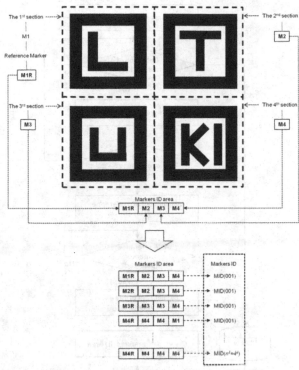

Fig. 3. Process of four sections and singling out of a reference marker and Conversion from markers' ID area to marker ID

3.3   Process of Marker Detection

Upon completion of singling out of a reference marker, a marker ID area is created based on the coordinates of the corner points $(D_1{\sim}D_4)$ in order to recognize a sub marker. In the marker ID area a sub marker is detected by applying the method used for recognizing and matching the reference marker. Fig. 4 shows the flow of marker detection process suggested in this paper.

After a sub marker is detected, a marker ID area is created. Then, an object is augmented by contents warping.

3.4   Simulation: Creation of Marker's ID Area

In order to verify markers' ID area(MIDA), one-dimension markers ID should be created as shown in Fig. 3. To do this, markers' ID, detected by marker sections (2·2 matrix), is applied to the area in sequence.

The marker ID (MID) is verified by using the created MIDA. And contents corresponding to the markers' ID area are confirmed. Also, contents warping are done by creating a coordinated conversion matrix based on the coordinates of the corner points of the reference marker, calculating a difference caused by warping, and correcting the error.

A general expression to create MID (n^4) is shown Formula (4).

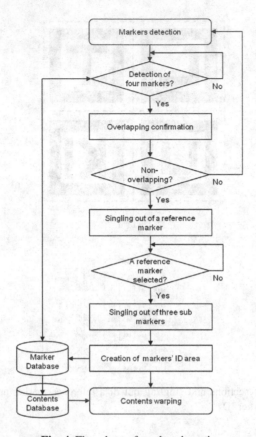

Fig. 4. Flowchart of marker detection

$$MID(n^4) = \sum_0^{n-1} MIDA \begin{pmatrix} D_{n_1} & D_{n_2} \\ D_{n_3} & D_{n_4} \end{pmatrix} \tag{4}$$

Fig. 5 shows the implementation of suggested method in this paper.

Fig. 5. Implementation of domain-specific marker recognition method

4   Comparative Analysis

The domain-specific marker recognition method suggested in this paper, recognizes the marker section separated into four sections in the form of the 2·2 matrix in which four markers are applied to each sections and objects of 44 can be augmented.

The following table compares suggested domain-specific marker recognition method with existing one marker-based recognition method.

Table 1. Comparison of suggested method with the existing marker-based AR technology

Classification	Existing method	Suggested method
Number of markers for 4^4 expression	256	4
Number of cases for expression using only 4 markers	4	256
Marker detection time	71ms	192ms
Number of database	1	1

5   Conclusion

In this paper, domain-specific marker recognition method has been suggested to improve marker efficiency and reusability without creating a multitude of markers.

The main contribution of this paper is to single out a reference marker, to separate markers' sections, and to recognize sub markers.

Domain-specific marker recognition method in this paper could augment a large number of objects with a limited number of markers and no similar patterns, which solves the problem of overlapped detection of markers. However, domain-specific marker recognition method has the limitation that only marker-based AR can be used.

For further studies, we have to research on an algorithm which reduces more the marker detection time.

Acknowledgements. This work (Grants No.00044953-2) was supported by Business for Cooperative R&D between Industry, Academy, and Research Institute funded Korea Small and Medium Business Administration in 2011.

References

1. Azuma, R., Baillot, Y., Behringer, R., Feiner, S., Julier, S., MacIntyre, B.: Recent advances in augmented reality. IEEE Computer Graphics and Applications 21(6), 34–47 (2001)
2. Ziaei, Z., Hahto, A., Mattila, J., Siuko, M., Semeraro, L.: Real-time markerless Augmented Reality for Remote Handling system in bad viewing conditions. Fusion Engineering and Design, 2033–2038 (2011)

3. Kato, H., Billinghurst, M.: Marker tracking and hmd calibration for a video-based augmented reality conferencing system. In: 2nd IEEE and ACM International Workshop on Augmented Reality Proceedings, pp. 85–94 (1999)
4. Lee, Y.J., Lee, G.H.: Augmented Reality Game Interface using Effective Face Detection Algorithm. International Journal of Smart Home 5(4), 77–87 (2011)
5. Lewis, J.P.: Fast template matching. Vision Interface 95, 120–123 (1995)
6. Lin, L.I.: A concordance correlation coefficient to evaluate reproducibility. Biometrics 45(1), 255–268 (1989)
7. Sun, K.: Adaptive step-size motion estimation based on statistical sum of absolute differences. U.S. Patent 6,014,181, January 11 (2000)
8. Fu, X.P., Liao, S.L.: A Fast Template Matching Algorithm Based on Wavelet Coefficient Projection Transform. Applied Mechanics and Materials 48, 21–24 (2011)

The Study on Surround Sound Production beyond the Stereo Techniques

Yoemun Yun and Taesun Cho

Dept. of Applied Music, Chungwoon University
San 29, Namjang-ri, Hongseong, Chungnam, 350-701, South Korea
{hippie740,entheos}@chungwoon.ac.kr

Abstract. In the music recording industry, 5.1 surround sound productions have already become popular throughout the world, and music engineers have developed more advanced and complicated recording techniques for improved sound. This paper introduces the newly developed and integrated 5.1 surround recording techniques, which many engineers have proved effective over many years, and demonstrate some of the techniques used in specific venues under different situations and with various types of instrumentation. This paper consists of two different parts: Part 1 is about general stereo recording techniques and its developments and Part 2 is about specific concepts of 5.1 microphone techniques, such as the Sony/Philips and Fukada Tree microphone techniques used in 5.1 surround sound productions by combining and adapting from the best of the stereo techniques.

Keywords: Blumlein, A/B/C, Decca Tree, Fukada Tree, Sony/Philips.

1   Introduction

The most distinguishing feature of multi-channel in the application to stereo microphone techniques is the addition of surround channels. The reason for this is that in some of the systems, a center microphone channel is already present, such as with spaced omnis, ABC as mentioned below or Decca Tree, and it is no stretch to provide a separate channel and loudspeaker to a microphone already in use. In other methods, it is simple to derive a center channel. Surround channels must have a signal derived from microphone positions that may not have been used in the past.

Since stereo microphones were introduced in the 1930s, they have been designed to create stereo images based on the intensity differences, for example XY, generated between the two microphones. However, it has somewhat constricted width and has a tendency to sound dry because stereo microphone technique's intensity differences mostly use cardioid pattern microphones.

The other spaced microphone techniques such as spaced omni, A/B and A/B/C, can capture and reproduce both the intensity and time of arrival signals, but this technique has problems with a lack of articulation across the stereophonic image and some ambiguity in the center imaging [1].

Therefore, music engineers and producers often get a strong demand for location accuracy from listeners for both of these reasons which are image articulation and

T.-h. Kim et al. (Eds.): SIP/WSE/ICHCI 2012, CCIS 342, pp. 133–140, 2012.
© Springer-Verlag Berlin Heidelberg 2012

envelopment by the sound track. So, the solution to these problems is to combine and adapt from the best of the stereo technique to the surround techniques.

2   Experiment 1

2.1   Session 1 (Violin with Piano)

Three stereo techniques plus spot miking –
A/B/C – Schoeps MK 2 omni directional capsule <flat response>
ORTF – Schoeps MK 6 cardioids
Blumlein – Neumann SM69 figure-8's
Spot mics –
2 AKG c414's for piano
Neumann K140 for violin

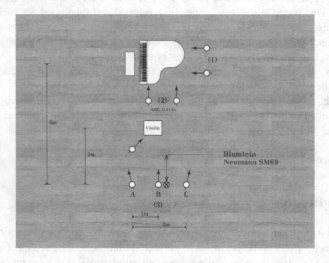

Fig. 1. Microphone placement for stereo

2.2   Analysis

Blumlein
With one figure-8 pointed left, the other pointed right, and the microphone (Neumann SM 69 which is multi-stereo microphone) pickups located very close to one another, sources from various locations around combined microphones are recorded, not with timing differences because those have been essentially eliminated by the close spacing, but with level differences. A source located on the axis of the left facing figure-8 is recorded at full level by it, but with practically no direct sound pickup in the right-facing figure-8 [2]. For a source located on a center axis in between left and right, each microphone picks up the sound at a level that is a few dB down from pickup along its axis.

In this session, the stereo separation sounded quite wide, but the overall sound was a bit thinner compared to other techniques. Usually, this system makes no distinction between the front and back of the microphone set, and thus it might have to be placed closer than other coincident types; in addition it may expose the recording to defects in the recording space acoustics.

Generally speaking, the biggest attraction of the Blumlein is the crisp and accurate phantom imaging from sources; it has a natural blend of ambient sound from the rear. Some cancellation of ambience sometimes happened, especially when I panned hard left and right or put both signals in the same position, which is equivalent to mono. The same result can happen if there is a lot of reverberant sound picked up from the side or rear. Disadvantages with Blumlein can occur because of the large out of phase region, and in the size of the rear pickup, that is not desirable in all cases if it is left right reversed, which results in sound from the right side showing up in the left channel because of reverberation.

A/B/C
In terms of the A/B/C technique here, the time delay between the signals of the two or three microphones of up to about 1ms, or less depending on the venue, causes a similar time delay at the two loud speakers. This leads to phantom sound (so-called phantom image) sources which are located on the base line away from the center during playback signals [3]. The distance from the source to the microphones in this session is about 4 meters, no delay causes the phantom sound source to be centered because these microphone techniques' differences at the microphones are caused by differing path lengths from the sound sources to the microphones.) The stereo sound image in these techniques has an impressive spaciousness.

Decca Tree and A/B/C, in the category of spaced omni techniques use omni directional polar patterns because these two techniques are usually used for a larger sound source, such as an orchestra, to make rich ambient sound especially for the low-end[4]. Omni directional microphones are pressure-responding microphones with frequency response that extends to the lowest audible frequencies, whereas all pressure-gradient microphones, all directional microphones have a pressure-gradient component, and roll off the lowest frequencies.

Therefore, spaced omni recordings in session 1 contain the deepest bass response compared to other stereo microphone techniques. So, this technique must take into consideration the venue in terms of reverberation and the noise in the recording space. Compared to other stereo techniques that I tried in the session, spaced microphones offer a greater sense of spaciousness than the other types. Also, when good imaging of source location in this technique is not as good as with other types, one can spread the angles of the outer microphones from the center microphone for a better stereo image.

3   Experiment 2

3.1   Session (Small Chamber Orchestra)

Set-up #1:
Sony/Philips with 2 DPA 4003s and 3 Schoeps MK2s <All Omni-directional>

Set-up #2:
Fukada with 2 Neumann KM140s, 2 Sennheiser MHK 800s, and 1 Schoeps MK4
<All cardioids>

Shared microphones –
DPA 4011 on soloist
ES with 2 DPA 4011 on the stage
Boundary microphones: Neumann 184.

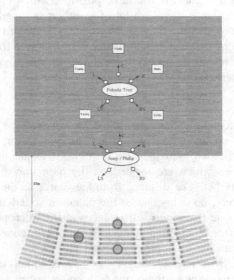

Fig. 2. Microphone placement for surround

3.2   Analysis

Fukada Tree

Like the Sony/Philip surround microphone technique, the advantage of omni
microphones is in the classical music recording industry, which recently uses it as the
main microphone in many cases of stereo recordings because it can represent rich
reverberation in halls. But, if surround microphones are added to this stereo method
for surround recording, too much reverberation components can produce sounds such
that the environment is too enhanced. Everyone knows that usually the reverberation
component has spatial information of the hall which is perceived as natural by the
audience, thus the total sound levels in both stereo and surround recordings
procedures must be equal. Recording reverberation components with an omni
microphone can result in the reproduction of rich reverberation. However, if the
microphone picks up delayed direct sound components as well, because of time delay
in the hall, rear sounds can become unnatural and the sound positioning in the front
can be broken.

Fukada Tree is based on a Decca Tree but instead of using omni microphones, it mainly uses cardioids. The reason for this is to reduce the amount of reverberant sound pick up by the front microphones [5][6]. Originally, there are omni outriggers to emphasize between front and rear channel sound, but in the recording sessions, it's not used in order to compare the sound easily to Sony/Philips technique, and others, which is typically panned between Left, Left Surround and Right, Right Surround, in an attempt to increase the width of orchestral pickup and to integrate front and rear elements. The rear microphones are also cardioids and are typically located at approximately the critical distance of the spaced concerned (where the direct and reverberant components are equal).

They are sometimes spaced further back than the front microphones by nearly 2 meters, although the dimensions of the tree can be varied according to the situation, distance, and the size of the orchestra, for example, variations are known that have the rear microphones quite close to the front ones. The spacing between the microphones more closely fulfils requirements for the correlated microphone signals needed to create spaciousness, depending on the critical distance of the space in which they are used. The front imaging of such an array would be pretty much similar to that of an ordinary Decca Tree.

Based on the original Fukada Tree, Schoeps MK4 (Center), two Neumann KM140s (Left and Right) and two Sennheiser MHK 800s (Left and Right Surround). The shape of the tree was a bit different depending on the hall's acoustic characteristics, while the distance of each microphone was changed conforming to the orchestra's size. However, it must be made sure that the horizontal angles of microphones were aligned in order to pick up the orchestra's sounds. A few things that I considered were that no microphone pointed directly at a source, distance of each microphone from the sound source did not exceed more than 5 meters, and all microphones in the array could pick up all sources and active sound field for strong reflection.

The expectations have mostly been verified: Width and depth are somewhat impaired by the cardioid-pattern microphone. Also, reverberation and low-end are not sufficient, so additional reverb is required. However, the clarity and localization is significantly better than other techniques. While it does provide a very stable front image, this technique does not provide fullness of ambient sound, smooth bass sound and harmonization with other sources.

Sony/Philips Surround Technique
Compared to the use of the 5 cardioid microphone technique by Fukada Tree, this is one of the most popular surround microphone techniques using 5 omnis, the so-called Sony/Philips surround technique.

The Sony/Philips surround technique configuration has been developed for 5.1 surround recording of a large ensemble in a venue and this gives very nice bass sound and smooth front channel images with well-harmonized rear sound images[7 – 8]. The purpose of this technique is to gain a natural impression of the acoustic space in halls. Because this technique uses 5 omni directional microphones, even though this technique does not represent very accurate sound in terms of phase and surround image compared to Fukada Tree, however, it produces a very warm, heavy result with a very large sweet spot, and a great sense of reproduction of acoustics.

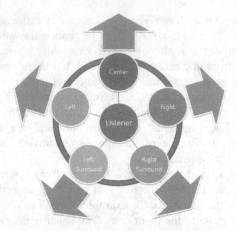

Fig. 3. Sound image of Fukada Tree

The setup of this technique was developed and refined using the ITU, International Telecommunication Union, Standard for loudspeaker configuration, which represents angles of incidence of 30 between center and each of left and right, and 110 - 120 between center and each rear speaker, with all loudspeakers set at equal distance from the listening position [9]. The ITU configuration is used for bigger forms of instrumentation, such as orchestral recording, but it can be used for smaller ensembles as well. Imagine the size of the Session and rather than the typical Decca Tree setup like Fukada Tree, this technique uses a combination of a Left and Right pair of microphones with a third center microphone on a separate stand, so that I can adjust the center microphone position. The center microphone was placed a bit deeper into the stage than the typical distance of the Decca Tree. Like Fukada Tree, the consideration of setting up the Sony/Philips technique was the same that any microphone,—except it did not point directly at a source, the distance of each microphone did not exceed more than 5 meters, and all microphones in the array could pick up all sources and active sound field for strong reflection. The use of omni directional as opposed to cardioid microphones allows the full frequency range in front channels and configuration to be placed very close to the ensemble. The excellent sound color and reproduction that is unique to omni microphones.

This represents front channels with great dynamic response and clarity (but not as much as Fukada Tree does) in the session, combined with a good direction of reverberant balance. Like Decca Tree, omni microphones also yield greater low frequency response (warmth). The use of spaced microphones generates time of arrival differences between the five channels, which enhance the overall sense of envelopment for the listener. Therefore, the width of the array should be adjusted to meet the size of the ensemble, and as the Left and Right microphones are moved further apart, the level of the center channel should be increased accordingly. As the center microphone is moved farther into the ensemble, the center channel level should be lowered accordingly in order to preserve depth of image.

Except the hiss noise and low frequency muddy sound, the five omni microphones configuration utilizes very warm and low frequency correlation that is offset by the natural time delay which relates to the distance from the front Left and Right to the Left Surround and Right Surround.

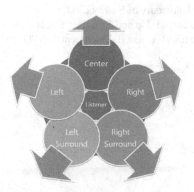

Fig. 4. Sound image of Sony/Philips

4   Conclusion

Based on the results of the two different recording tests in this paper, 5.1 channel surround sound is almost always superior to stereo, however surround sound techniques still have problems, when engineers and producers create an inaccurate acoustic analysis, distance and height of the microphones from the sources in tracking session. I did not use artificial reverberation for clear results, however reverberation is recommended for some techniques, especially for Fukada Tree.

The Sony/Philips technique is recommended for full-size orchestra recording with two ambient microphones. Both the Fukada and Sony/Philips techniques have lack of sound images from rear channel speakers compared to the front channels. In those cases, other ambient microphone techniques are recommended.

5.1 surround sound production is not perfect because it does not represent all possibilities of sound reflections from the source, such as vertical sound images. NHK developed new surround monitoring systems which are 22.2 multi-channel surround, 9 channels for upper layer, 10 channels for middle layers, 3 channels for lower channel and 2 channels for LEF. So, creating three-dimensional techniques are needed to provide perfect sound images. In this case, multi surround channel microphone techniques are necessary to be developed in further work.

References

1. Eargle, J.: Handbook of Recording Engineering, 4th edn. Springer (2005)
2. Clifford, M.: Modern Audio Technology. A Handbook for Technicians and Engineers. Prentice Hall (1992)

3. Owsinski, B.: Recording Engineer's Handbook. Mix Books (2006)
4. White, G.D.: The Audio Dictionary, 2nd edn. University of Washington Press (1991)
5. Surround Sound - System Fukada Tree (NHK) (2005),
   http://www.nhk.or.jp/digital/en/technique/02.html
6. Berg, J., Rumsey, F.: Validity of Selected Spatial Attributes in the Evaluation of 5-channel Microphone Techniques, University of Surrey (2002)
7. Holman, T.: 5.1 Surround Sound: Up and Running. Focal Press (2000)
8. Masataka, N.: AES Technical Council Document ESTD1001.0.01-05. AES convention paper (2002)
9. AES 112th Convention, Munich, Germany (2002)

Resistance Mentality in the Lyrics of Popular Music- Focus on Kim Min-ki's 1st Album

Woo-il Joung[1,*] and Tae-Seon Cho[2]

[1] Dept. of Practical Music,Kookje College,
(Jangan-dong)56, Janganut-gil, Pyeongtaek-si, Gyeonggi-do(459-070), South Korea
garam051@naver.com
[2] Dept. of Applied Music, Chungwoon University
San29, Namjang-ri, Hongseong, Chungnam, 350-701, SouthKorea
22019686@daum.net

Abstract. This essay bases on the semiological analysis on the lyrics of the 70's folk songs. For the analysis, it is essential to understand the contemporary social phenomenon. At the time, everything, from hair to ladies' skirts, was controlled by the military regime. It is not difficult to deduce that culture was another victim of it. I study about the youth's mind in the contemporary society and how the lyrics of the songs represented their mind.

Keywords: Folk song, Lyric, Popular Music.

1   Introduction

There is no argument in that the Korean War had laid the foundation for Korean popular music. During the war, serving in the United States Forces Korea (8th United States Army) was one of the Korea's highest paying jobs, and it was no exception for the musicians. American culture, the leading civilization in the meantime, could naturally flow into Korea through the USFK and as a result, the American music started a trend among the youth After the war, as the quality of life got better, people's goal in life changed from pure 'survival' to a happy life that involved 'culture', which undoubtedly helped popular music to grow. Subsequently, generation gap between parents and children grew bigger and bigger which led to differentiation in culture. As transition in main consumers in the society happened from parents to children, the media focuses on the youth as target consumers accordingly.

While war-torn society was healing itself steadily, the movement of the youth was noticeably different from that of parents. The hippie culture that was predominant in the 60's was beyond understandable to the older generations. Older generation that could understand long hair, loose jeans, miniskirts, beer-drinking culture and folk guitar was nonexistence and at the same time, the younger generation couldn't understand hard-working, success-hungry older generation. Therefore for the younger

---

* Corresponding author.

T.-h. Kim et al. (Eds.): SIP/WSE/ICHCI 2012, CCIS 342, pp. 141–148, 2012.
© Springer-Verlag Berlin Heidelberg 2012

generation, the older generation and the contemporary politics were in the center of their criticism. Some expressed it in a direct manner, demonstration, some in a rather indirect manner, music.

Here, I analyze how their resistance is immersed in the lyrics and discuss how it reflects or satirize the contemporary society.

2   Aim

After the war, Koreans certainly did live in a dark age. President Park and Jeon's military regime gave us the fruit called economic growth, but the fruit had bitterness too. It is well known that a massive sacrifice had been made for the fruit. Especially during Park's presidency, Korean popular music was given a scarlet letter, namely 'banned songs', while Jeon eliminated rooting grounds for the true musicians by conducting3S(Sex, Sports, Screen) policy. Consequently, the aim is to clarify how resistance mentality immersed into the lyrics of Korean popular music of 60's to 80's, and why they had to be banned by reflecting the periodic characteristics in the reasoning. Furthermore, it is also to clarify the structure of signification in the leader of resistance mentality, Folk, by analyzing hidden meanings with semiological background while reflecting resistive and periodic characteristics in the analysis.

3   Theoretical Background

3.1   Folk music of Korea

In 1945, the US conducted atomic bombs against cities of Hiroshima and Nagasaki, resulting in surrender of Japan which consequently led to the end of Japanese forced occupation in Korea. However, as the Korean War broke out in 1950, Korea was forced back to the chaos of War. President Truman of the US gave the dispatch order to the marine troops and air force to Korea two days after the break out, General MacArthur on the 30th, succeeding in the Battle of Incheon on September 15th. Even after the end of war, the American troops prolonged their stay in Korea, establishing bases of operation in Seoul and its outskirts. In order to relieve the American troops, a number of stars such as Marilyn Monroe, Elvis Presley and Nat Cole King visited Korea. However, despite the effort, it was impossible to meet the demand with the limited number of American stars, so the Korean singers were introduced to the table. The American culture in the 60's along with the Hippie culture had become the popular culture among the youth born in the post-war baby boom generation. Folk guitar, one of the symbols of Hippie culture, was easy to carry, easy to play and easy to compose with. Not surprisingly, it was also easy to form communities with it. Within the communities, people created their own language and music. It was the beginning of Korean Folk music and resistance music.

4   Research Methods

4.1   Lyrics Analysis

A song has a literary structure that consists of an abstract element and non-abstract element. Therefore, instrumental music has an apparent downfall in terms of popularity compared to a song. Hence it was unavoidable for the musicians to introduce solutions in order to appeal to the public, and one of them was by giving meanings to the lyrics.

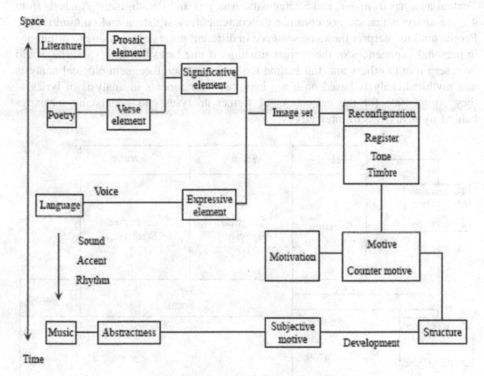

Melodic : universality, direction set for emotion
Rhythm : part relationship, union and diversity
Harmonic : harmoney of universe and parts, background atmosphere

Fig. 1. The relationship between literature and music [5]

As shown in figure 1, a song is composed of literature (a spatial concept), language (a temporal concept) and music. It is expressed by extracting an image from a prosaic element of literature, or a verse element of poetry, which is then recreated with melody, rhythm and harmony.

4.2   Syntagmatic Analysis and Paradigmatic Analysis

Syntagmatic Analysis is the analysis in which the surface structure (syntax) of the text is examined by analyzing consequences of events that compose narrative structure.

On the other hand, Paradigmatic Analysis is the analysis in which the paradigms of the text are examined by finding encoded patterns of oppositions that create meanings. In other words, a group of paradigmatic signs in a meaningful order is syntagmatic structure. [4] A paradigmatic structure combines with other paradigmatic structures to form a syntagmatic structure.

4.3   SemiologicalMyth Analysis

Textual analysis from 4.1, and Syntagmatic Analysis and Paradigmatic Analysis from 4.2 are analyses that do not consider the contemporary situation and cultural aspect. People tend to interpret the same sentence in different points of view due to difference in personal experiences or the current situation. If one lacks the ability, he/she would be insensitive to others and fall behind the society. Therefore, semiological analysis and mythical analysis based on it are important components in analysis of lyrics as they compensate for the drawbacks of former analyses and understand meanings behind signs in terms of interactivity.

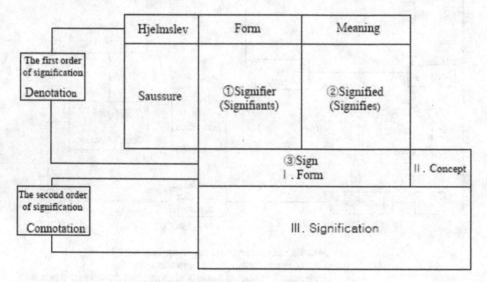

Fig. 2. Barthes's model of signification

As Figure 2 shows, Roland Barthes divided Signification into 2 levels, the first order of signification being Denotation and the second being Connotation. The sign produced in Denotation becomes a signifier as it becomes a single form in Connotation. The signifier subsequently interacts with another concept which corresponds to a signified, to produce context. The correlation between signifier and signified produced by the 2-level signification is called a sign in the myth, and the sign is called signification. The signification emerges from the 2-level signification, and it is when the myth is created. [3]

As mentioned, Barthes used semiology in order to interpret language, and denotation and connotation in order to deduct the effective context. Here, I apply semiological interpretation to deduct connoted meanings in the lyrics.

5   Results

The banned songs in the 60's to 70's, the era of military regime, are the subjects of analysis. The results are the reasons behind why they had to be banned in the contemporary society. The songs analyzed for the case-study are from Kim Min-ki's first album was the icon of resistance movement.

Kim's first album, titled Kim Min-ki, was released in 1971, and songs that raised a huge issue in the society are selected for the analysis. The alphabet and the number in the brackets refer to LP side and track number respectively.

5.1   A Child That Grows Flowers (A-5)

The major reason behind ban on Kim's first album is this song. Kim sang this song a year after the album release in 1971 at the freshmen welcome party held in Seoul University, and considered resistive by the government. As a result, the entire stock of albums was scraped, along with the master tape.

Lyrics	Analysis
Motive 1	
A child that grows hibiscus	Hibiscus = Korea, flower bed, child = people of Korea
Waters the flower bed early morning	Water = hope
As days pass, the flower withers	Withers = persecution, military regime
And so the child sobbed on the flower bed	flower bed = lives of the masses, sobbing child = the oppressed masses
Motive 2	
Flower withered and fell to ground	Fell to ground = no hope
The flower growing child fell ill too	Fell ill = persecution by the military regime
Who ruined the child's flower bed	Who = military regime
Who would grow the flower again	Who = the masses, flower = freedom
Motive 3 (repeating motive)	
Flower bed full of hibiscus	Hibiscus, flower bed = base of freedom
Like poor child's hand	Poor child = the grass root hoping for freedom

Fig. 3. Motive analyze of 'A Child That Grows Flowers'

Firstly, hibiscus is very symbolic. Hibiscus is the national flower of Korea and flower bed symbolizes people. As polysemy, hibiscus has diverse significations, as shown in figure 4. Therefore, it is apparent that the song was a resistance song to the government, democratic activists' song to the youth.

Sign		Meaning
hibiscus	→	Nation
Watering hibiscus bed	→	Hopeful, free nation
Withered hibiscus	→	Nation that lost freedom
Fallen withered hibiscus	→	People lose freedom and hope

Fig. 4. Meaning structure of hibiscus

5.2   Morning Dew (B-2)

Some believe that Morning Dew was the spark that started resistance culture in Korea. In 1975, the military conducted 'the 9th President's emergency measure' which initiated censorship on culture, especially on popular music. The standards applied on the censorship were unreasonable. For example, the government censored Han Dae-soo's 'Give Me Water' for allegedly reminding water torture that was performed in the Agency for National Security Planning, Yang Hee-eun's 'Impossible Love' forallegedly promoting nihilism, Shin Joong-hyun's 'Beauty' for having 'vulgar lyrics', Bae ho's

Lyrics	Analysis
Motive 1	
After a long night	Long night = grim present situation
There formed on every leaf	Leaf = the masses
A dew that is more beautiful than a pearl	Pearl = everything in the world, morning dew = hope
Motive 2	
When sorrow in my mind	Sorrow = sorrow like you lost a country
forms drop by drop	Pierces the heart
I climb up a morning hill to learn a little smile.	Morning hill = imaginary utopia, hopeful place, little smile = hope in the future
Motive 3	
The red Sun rises over the grave	The Sun = desire for freedom, grave = military regime
The burning heat is a trial for me	Heat = persecution by the military regime
I now leave for the wilderness	Wilderness = fight
Sorrow left behind, I now leave	Sings freedom by fighting

Fig. 5. Motive analyze of 'Morning Dew'

'Goodbye at midnight' for promoting meetings after curfew, and the most ridiculous of all, Shim Soo-jong's 'Soon-ja's Autumn' for having the name 'Soon-ja' which was the name of the First Lady. Regardless of the legitimacy, they all had a reason, but 'Morning Dew'. It was banned without a reason. Apparently, the song had a major impact, significant enough to shake the government, on the society.

Kim mentioned in a number of broadcasting media that the song wasn't composed with the resistance mentality in mind. However, he was a student in Seoul University, and the military regime was in power. Even if his words are true, he might have wanted to imply resistance unconsciously. Strolling outside at dawn, unable to sleep from fear, he might have found the dews on the leaves like the sorrow in his mind. Nevertheless, perhaps he wanted to find hope. Perhaps he wanted to gather all the hopes of others to start a fight.

6   Conclusion

In the days of Japanese forced occupation, 1927, JeonSoo-lin and Wang Pyung made a song 'Hwang-sung-yet-ter' (meaning old castle ruins). It was recorded by VICTOR record company and made an unprecedented hit. Stimulating sentiments of the Koreans, it has been said that no one could sing this song without tears. As a respond, the Japanese government tortured the composer and banned the song, which marked as the first ban on a song in the history of Korea.

Lately, Yang Hee-eun made an appearance in a TV show and mentioned 'Morning Dew'. She said that before it got banned by President Park's military regime, it received an award for a 'propaganda song' by President Park's government. In 1996 Seo Tai-ji's 'Sidaeyugam' was banned because the lyrics were considered to be too pessimistic and therefore potentially dangerous for people's mind. As a result, the song lost its lyrics and was included in the album as an instrumental only. However, due to fan's persistent protest, Korea Media Rating Board renounced the pre-release-review and adopted the post-release-review instead. Not long ago, Ministry of Gender Equality and Family had banned songs that included cigarette or alcohol in the lyrics.

There always was censorship on lyrics regardless of time. However, the problem is that the censoring criteria are ambiguous. Songs in the 60's and 70's were resistance for survival and freedom. They had to defeat the military regime and enlighten the masses. In other words, it was a meaningful resistance. Meanwhile, the government banned a lot of songs with their self-righteous standards and scraped them off the streets.

The contemporary social atmosphere and lyrics have a deep correlation. Especially the lyrics from Kim Min-ki's first album not only gathered the youth in one, but also made them sing on the streets, and proved that their voice was significant. It was the voice that the current Hook Song infested music industry can never make. Of course, it is not to say that resistance music is the only true music. However, we still have issues that we ought to resist, and ignoring the matter is probably not the approach that an intellectual should have. I believe that if every musician did what they could within their ability as a musician, Korean music industry would grow balanced in the future.

References

1. Kim, J.-Y.: Music of Resistance in Era of Ideology. Munyaemadang (1995)
2. Chang-Nam: Understanding Popular Culture. Hanyuel Academy (1998)
3. Kim, C.-S., et al.: Development of Contemporary Semiology. Seoul University Publishing Department (1998)
4. Baek, S.-K.: Popular Music and Enjoyment of its SemiologicalInterpretion. Communication Books (2004)
5. Seok, J.-H.: Research into Songs that Emerged from University Towns –Based on Movement Songs of 1980's, Sukmyung Woman's University, Postgraduate Doctorate Essay for Education (1991)
6. Lim, J.-M.: Rock, the Chord of Youth. Book House (2003)

A Study on the Defect Analysis of Image Plate
by Accumulated Radiation Dose

Eun Mi An, Seok Hwan Bae, and Yong Gwon Kim

Department of Radiological Science in Konyang University,
Daejeon, Korea
shbae@konyang.ac.kr

Abstract. This study was aimed to analyze the degree of image plate defect by
the accumulated radiation dose, and find out the effect IP defect on the image
quality. For the test, the subject was irradiated by 0times, 5,000times(about
3Gy), 10,000times(about 6Gy), and 20,000times(about 11Gy). Whenever there
was the 500th increase in irradiation, the Line pair value was obtained by
scanning resolution chart with a measuring tool, Modulation Transfer
Function(MTF), and to find out the degree of image plate defect, Scanning
Electron Microscope(SEM) was conducted. As a result of study, there was
reduction in resolution with the increase of the accumulated radiation dose.
When the accumulated dose was more than 6.2Gy, the value of Line pair was
decreased less than 2~2.5 lp/mm that is a distinguishable measure with the
unaided eye at a minimum. Therefore, when the accumulated dose was more
than 6.2Gy, image plate is replaced with a new one.

Keywords: Accumulated Radiation Dose, Image plate, Defect, Resolution.

1   Introduction

Recently, digital equipment, such as Computed Radiography(CR) and Digital
Radiography(DR), has been much supplied and being used in hospitals, beyond an
analogue method, a type of Film-screen. According to the present condition of
medical equipment by types published by Health Insurance Review & Assessment
Service, the number of CR and DR was 426 and 280 respectively in Dec, 2006.
However, according to the present condition of medical equipment by types on the
second quarter in 2011, there were 3,251 CRs and 1,241 DRs, which showed a rapid
rate of increase of 663.2% in CR, and 343.2% in DR, compared with 2006. The
reason that CR and DR increase rapidly is that they enhance the efficiency with a fast
flow of image information using Network and Picture Archiving and Communication
System(PACS), compared with Film-screen System.

CR and DR, digital radiation equipment, which are rapidly increasing in use like
this, show the difference in the methods to obtain the image. In the case of DR
method, it uses a flat-type detector instead of films and can directly obtain digital
image. However, in the case of CR, it uses Image Plate(IP) where photostimulable
phosphor is coated, instead of the film of the existing Film-screen System. In specific,

T.-h. Kim et al. (Eds.): SIP/WSE/ICHCI 2012, CCIS 342, pp. 149–157, 2012.

irradiate x rays on IP, latent image is formed on IP. At this time, scan laser beam on IP, and X-ray information stored in IP shines. Collect the light with a condenser, send it to a photo-multiplier tube, change it into electric signal and amplify it. The image is obtained by changing the amplified analogue signal into digital one in Analog/Digital converter, and the information in IP is reused through the process of Erase.

The use of IP in CR is also increasing in proportion to the rapid rate of increase of CR. Although IP was known to be used up to the maximum 20,000 times, it was considered that as the accumulated radiation dose as well as the number of scanning increased, there would happen defect in IP, which would cause the quality of image to degrade.

This study was aimed to analyze the degree of IP defect by the accumulated radiation dose among the several causes of the image quality degradation, measure the resolution using Modulation Transfer Function(MTF) and resolution chart, identify whether IP defect by the accumulated radiation dose affects the quality of image with the Scanning Electron Microscope(SEM) scan, and study the proper replacement time through the quantitative image quality evaluation of IP.

2   The Subject and Method of Study

2.1   Framework of Study

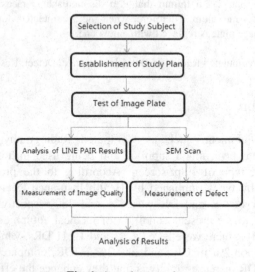

Fig. 1. A study procedure

2.2   The Subject and Method of Study

As an IP, four IPs(Flexible Phosphor screen GP2 10×12 inch) of K company were used in this study, as a X-ray generator, Progen 650R of Listem and KXO-15R of Toshiba which passed the test standard under the separate tables 1 in Rules of

Diagnosis Radiation Equipment Safety Management, and as Reader, DirectView Vita CR of K was used. As a measuring instrument, Piranha 657 model of RTI was used. To measure the image quality, Line pair chart, resolution chart, was used, and to measure MTF, tungsten plate(2.0mm(thickness), 100mm(width), 75mm(length)) and lead plate(2mm (thickness)) were used(Fig. 2).

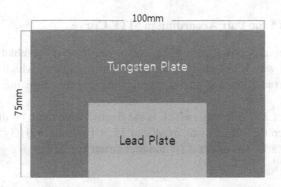

Fig. 2. A MTF measurement test tool

For test, the distance between X-ray radiation aperture and the surface of IP was set 100cm, and while measuring MTF, it was done 150cm according to the manual. The center of X-ray radiation field was set to correspond to that of IP, and the conditions were made 72kV, 320mA, and 16mAs, which were Skull AP conditions. X-ray irradiation by IPs was conducted 0 times for IP-1, 5,000 times for IP-2, 10,000 times for IP-3, and 20,000 times for IP-4.

To evaluate the image quality, whenever there was the 500th and 501st increase in irradiation, respectively, image was obtained using Line pair chart and MTF tool. The value of Line pair chart was read by referring to 2 specialists of Radiology and 5 radiological technologists, and its average value was used. To derive MTF curve from the image obtained using MTF tool, Image J program and the Excel program of Microsoft, Inc were used. In specific, project the image obtained using MTF tool in Image J program, and then to obtain Edge Spread Function(ESF), read Plot Profile by drawing lines on the part of tungsten plate several times. Save all of them with Excel program, differentiate the saved values, and obtain Line Spread Function(LSF). And after making it as an Excel file, and take Imaginary number absolute value function(IMABS), function of getting the absolute value of a complex number, into the saved data. Obtain Maximum value among the values from by taking IMABS function, and obtain MTF value by dividing the values from IMABS by Maximum value(2).

$$MTF(f) = |Fourier\ Transform\,|\,LSF(x)]\,|\,| \ . \tag{1}$$

$$Fourier\ Transform\ \ f(x) = \frac{1}{2\pi}\int_{-\infty}^{\infty}F(k)e^{ikx}dk \tag{2}$$

To identify the degree of IP defect, Cold Type FE-SEM, S-4800 model of HITACHI, was used. The part of IP to be scanned was cut and put into the liquid nitrogen. And then its protective coat was removed, and phosphor layer was scanned.

3   Results

3.1   Results of Line Pair According to MTF Curve

The Line pair value derived from MTF curve, an objective evaluation method, was 3.27 lp/mm, and was 1.95 lp/mm in the 20,000th irradiation, which indicated that as the number of irradiation and the accumulated radiation dose increased, Line pair value decreased.

In the region of 2~2.5 lp/mm, which is the degree which can be discerned with the unaided eye, when the subject was irradiated 15,501st times(8.04Gy), Line pair value was 2.08 lp/mm, and was under 2 lp/mm thereafter(Fig. 3, 4).

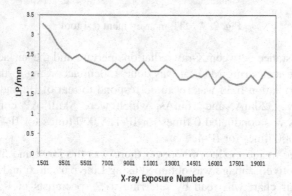

Fig. 3. Line pair obtained according to MTF

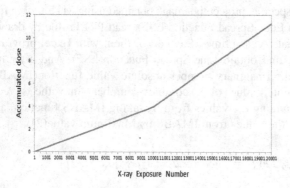

Fig. 4. The relation between X-ray Exposure Number and Accumulated dose

3.2   Results of Line Pair According to Resolution Chart

In the subjective evaluation method, Line pair value by resolution chart was 3.35 lp/mm at first, and Line pair in the 20,000th times was 1.25 lp/mm.

In the region of 2~2.5 lp/mm, which is the degree which can be discerned with the unaided eye, when the subject was irradiated the 13001st(6.20Gy) times, Line pair value was 2 lp/mm, and it was under 2 lp/mm thereafter(Fig. 4, 5).

Although there was no big change in Line Pair value at first, as the number of irradiation increased, the value showed a gradual decrease as a whole, which was similar to the results that appeared in Line Pair according to MTF curve, which indicated that as the accumulated irradiation dose increased, Line Pair value dropped(Fig. 4. 5).

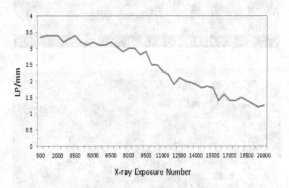

Fig. 5. Line pair obtained according to Resolution chart

3.3   Results According to SEM Scan

As a result of SEM Scan to find out the defect of the phosphor layer of IP irradiated by 0 times, 5,000 times(about 3Gy), 10,000 times(about 6Gy), and 20,000 times(about 11Gy), there was a slight change due to the accumulated irradiation dose in the image, however, a distinct change couldn't be identified(Fig. 6)

(a)

Fig. 6. SEM images of Phosphor layer exposed by X-ray in (a) 0 times, (b) 5,000 times, (c) 10,000 times and (d) 20,000 times

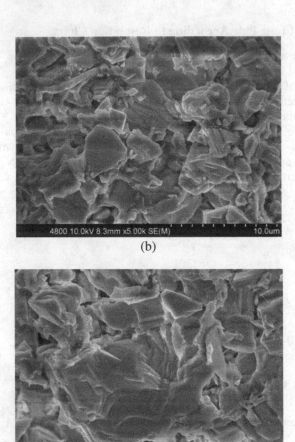

(b)

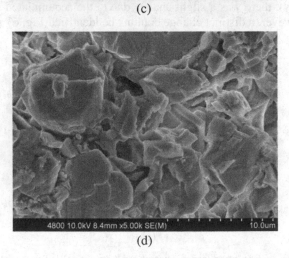

(c)

(d)

Fig. 6. (*continued*)

4   Consideration

This study was aimed to analyze the degree of IP defect by the accumulated radiation dose among the several causes of the image quality degradation, measure the resolution using Modulation Transfer Function(MTF) and resolution chart, identify whether IP defect by the accumulated radiation dose affects the quality of image with the Scanning Electron Microscope(SEM) scan, and study the proper replacement time of IP.

The IP of K company was used. To identify the change in the image quality according to the increase in the accumulated dose with scan conditions of 72kV, 320mA, and 16mAs, Line pair chart was observed by the specialists of Radiology and radiological technologists through the monitor for reading through PACS, and to identify the degree of IP defect, SEM Scan was conducted(Fig 6).

In the "Study on Quantitative Evaluation of Image Quality of Imaging Plate Depending on Number of X-ray Exposures" by Lee Jong Woong, when the number of X-ray Exposures was more than 20,000 times in using the added filtration(21 mmAI), it was indicated that IP was inappropriate to be used for clinics, however, in this study, the value was less than 2 lp/mm when it was after 13,000 times(6.20Gy) and after 15,501 times(8.04Gy), which was different in replacement time slightly from the result of Lee Jong Woong. That's because, it is considered, the IPs used in the test were manufactured by other companies, the internal structure of CR Reader was different, and there was difference in exposure technique. In the study of "Defect Analysis of Phospher(Ba, Sr) FBr : Eu by X-ray Irradiation" by Jung-Ki Shin, et al, the result was that if even the small X-ray irradiation energy was continuously exposed, the defect of the sample got large due to the increase in fatigue and the sensitivity dropped with the occurrence of the defect. In this study, Line pair value decreased according to the accumulated radiation dose, however, as there was a slight defect of IP when it was scanned with SEM, it is considered that the image quality degradation was brought about by the crack due to the increase in the fatigue of phosphor which happened with a repetitive work of IP Reader as well as the accumulated radiation dose.

In " Imaging Characteristics of Computed Radiography Systems" by Jiyoung Jung, et el, the result was that IP could be reused by 8,000 ~ 10,000 times. However, in this study, the result was that it could be reused by 13,001~15501 times and by the accumulated radiation dose 6.20 ~ 8.04Gy. Therefore, there was a slight difference in the replacement time of IP.

There are several things which bring about the image quality degradation of IP, such as scan conditions, the difference in CR work, and the structural characteristics of every manufacturer as well as the accumulated radiation dose, which should be considered in combination.

5   Conclusion

This study was aimed to analyze the degree of IP defect by the accumulated radiation dose and find out the effect of IP defect on the image quality. The test was conducted by irradiating the subject by 0 times, 5,000 times(about 3Gy), 10,000 times(about 6Gy), and 20,000 times(about 11Gy) using the IP of K company. Whenever there was the 500th increase in irradiation, the Line pair value of subjective, objective methods was obtained by scanning the resolution chart with a measuring tool, Modulation Transfer Function(MTF), and to find out the degree of IP defection, it was scanned with Scanning Electron Microscope(SEM).

As a result of study, in the resultant value of Line pair derived from MTF curve, when the subject was irradiated by 5,000 times(about 3Gy), 10,000 times(about 6Gy), and 20,000 times(about 11Gy), Line pair value decreased in all of them with the increase in the accumulated radiation dose, and the result of Line pair by resolution chart showed a similar trend to that of MTF as well. In SEM Scan, there was a slight difference in the particles of fluorescent substance by the accumulated radiation dose, however, there was no distinct difference in defect. The reason is that 40 images in total were obtained through IP Reader whenever the number of scanning increased by 500 times, and there was a work course where image information remembered by exposing it from IP Reader to natrium lamp was erased and reused in repetition, which could bring about IP fatigue. However, it seemed to have affected the degradation of image efficiency a little. As a result of analyzing the effect of the accumulated radiation dose on the image quality through the test, on the basis of the scope of 2~2.5 line pair/mm, threshold frequency, which can be distinguished with the unaided eye, when the subject was irradiated by 13000th ~ 15500th times, the image quality degraded, being less than 2 1p/mm. That is, it was certified that the image quality degraded from when the accumulated radiation dose was more than about 6.2~8.04Gy.

Therefore, when the accumulated dose became more than 6.2~8.04Gy, IP must be replaced with new one.

References

1. Woong, L.J.: Study on Quantitative Evaluation of Image Quality of Imaging Plate Depending on Number of X-ray Exposures. The Graduate School of Bio-Medical Science, Korea University (2010)
2. Shin, J.-K., Lee, C.-Y., Bae, S.H., Kim, J.-H., Kwon, J.-H.: Defect Analysis of Phospher (Ba, Sr) FBr: Eu by X-ray Irradiation. Korea Journal of Materials Research 18(8) (2008)
3. Lee, C.Y., Bae, S.H., Kim, J.H., Kwon, J.H.: Defect Analysis of Gd_2O_2S:Tb Using Coincidence Doppler Broadening Positron Annihilation Spectroscopy. Korea Journal of Materials Research 16(7) (2006)
4. Kim, C.-B., Lee, Y.-S., Kim, Y.-K.: Comparison of the Modulation Transfer Function of Several Image Plate. Journal of Radiological Science and Technology 27(3) (2004)
5. Korean Statistical Information Service, http://kosis.kr
6. Kwonn, D.-M.: Analog & Digital · PACS Medical imaging informatics, pp. 329–398. Daihaks Publishing Company (2008)
7. Ko, S.-K.: Medical Radiation Equipment, pp. 279–295. Daihaks Publishing Company (2010)

8. Jung, J., Park, H.-S., Cho, H.-M., Lee, C.-L., Nam, S., Lee, Y.-J., Kim, H.-J.: Imaging Characteristics of Computed Radiography Systems. Korean Journal of Medical Physics 19(1) (2008)
9. Miyahara, J.: Science and Technology of Japan 26, 28 (1985)
10. Sonoda, M., Takano, M., Miyahara, J., Kato, H.: Radiology 148, 833 (1983)
11. Barnes, G.T., Hendrick, R.E.: Radiographics 14, 129 (1994)
12. Greer, P.B., van Doorn, T.: Med. Phys. 27, 2048 (2000)

Mobile Applications Software Testing Methodology

Haeng-Kon Kim

School of Information Technology, Catholic University of Daegu, Korea
hangkon@cu.ac.kr

Abstract. Today's Mobile Applications deliver complex functionality on platforms that have limited resources for computing. Yet, unlike the PC-based environment, the Mobile environment comprises a number of devices with diverse hardware and software configurations and communication intricacies. This diversity in mobile computing environments presents unique challenges in mobile application development, quality assurance, and deployment, requiring unique testing strategies. Many enterprise applications that were deployed as desktop/web applications are now being ported to Mobile devices.

In this paper, we have constructed the Mobile Applications Quality Assurance Tool(MAQAT) by integrating tools and prototype systems that we built for program analysis and testing for mobile applications software. MAQAS provides a architecture of program analysis and testing for mobile, and supports many program-analysis-based techniques, including automated mobile applications software inspection, software visualization, testing coverage analysis, performance evaluation, concurrent program debugging, software measurement, etc. The paper briefly describes the overall architecture of MAQAS, and introduces the implementation of its tools and components.

Keywords: Mobile applications testing, Mobile applications quality assurance, Software testing tools and methodology.

1 Introduction

Mobile applications, although they have limited computing resources, are often built to be as agile and reliable as PC-based applications. In order to meet the challenge, mobile application testing has evolved as a separate stream of independent testing. The goal of Mobile Application testing is not to find errors. Perhaps your developer has actually done a great job and did not make any mistakes. Instead, our goal in mobile application testing should be to understand the quality of your offering. Does it work? Does it function as you thought of? Will it meet the needs of end customers so that they are delighted and come back to your app again and again?

These applications are empowering workforces across various functions, especially that in sales, supply chain, field support, and on the shop floor. Here's checklist to help you with Mobile Application Testing:

- Understand network landscape and device landscape before testing.
- Conducting mobile application testing in uncontrolled real-world environment.

T.-h. Kim et al. (Eds.): SIP/WSE/ICHCI 2012, CCIS 342, pp. 158–166, 2012.
© Springer-Verlag Berlin Heidelberg 2012

- Select right automation testing tool for the success of mobile application testing program. That could be: a) One tool should support all desired platforms b) The tool should support testing for various screen types, resolutions and input mechanism c) the tool should be connected to the external system to carry out end-to-end testing.

- Use Weighted Device Platform Matrix method to identify the most critical hardware/platform combination to test. This will be very useful especially when hardware/platform combinations are high and time to test is low.

- Check the end-to-end functional flow in all possible platforms at least once.

- Conduct performance testing, UI testing and compatibility testing using actual devices. Even though these tests can be done using emulators, testing with actual device is recommended.

- Measure performance only in realistic conditions of wireless traffic and maximum user load.

In addition to actual device-based testing, emulators should be included as an integral part of the mobile application testing program. Enterprise applications require special testing techniques. Partnering with third-party vendors who are operating an independent testing practice can be a viable option to manage the expertise, scalability, and quality assurance requirements for mobile application delivery. At Organic, our goal is to stay on the cutting edge of emerging platforms by launching new and diverse applications. We have this goal in mind when developing mobile web applications. We utilize some of the same styles of programming used for the developing of web applications.

Mobile applications software inspection, testing and debugging are important and expensive parts of the software development process. Much research has been done for the automated techniques and tools to reduce their cost. With the increase of the tools, we find that there is a lack of a platform, which provides the infrastructure to facilitate develop and examine new techniques of mobile program analysis and testing. And the basic requirements of the platform focus on automated software analysis, software inspection, combination test case generation, testing analysis, and software measurement. Mobile program analysis is the foundation of automated software engineering tasks, such as automated software inspection and structural testing. It is necessary to build a series of program analysis tools to construct a platform, on which researchers can extend the original components or integrate new techniques. The platform should provide sufficient information and empirical data to facilitate the development of program-analysis-based techniques and tools. We construct the Mobile Applications are Quality Assurance Tool (MAQAT), which has three basic requirements:

- The system should be an extensible platform for extending the existing components and integrating new techniques and tools. The tools of MAQAT should provide stable interfaces to communicate with each other, so that the modification in one component may not impact others. To minimize the complexity of interactions between tools is also helpful to develop a new tool.
- MAQAT should share the common modules as many as possible. The system should have a common front end to produce the basic information of the program.

Some advance analysis engines are designed to provide further analysis results for the application tools. This requirement may help to avoid redundant codes and reduce the cost of the maintenance.

- MAQAT should have the ability to collaborate in different activities of mobile program analysis and testing. It means that the software engineers can use MAQAT in many quality assurance activities. And it is important to pass some useful information smoothly from one tool to another.

2   Related Works

The first page of the manuscript should have a concise title limited to about 15 words and the names of all authors, complete mailing address for correspondence, telephone, fax numbers and email address. Please indicate with an asterisk (*) the author to whom correspondence regarding the manuscript should be directed.

2.1   Mobile Applications Software Testing Methodology

We also follow the same testing methodology employed for web development testing when testing our mobile applications.

- **Test Strategy** is a high level document that defines "Testing Approach" to achieve testing objectives. The Test Strategy document is a static document meaning that it is not frequently updated. Components of the document include Approach, Risks, Contingencies & Recommendations, Testing Responsibility Matrix, Defect Management Process and Resource requirements (schedule, tools, roles & responsibilities).

- **Performance Test Plan** specifies how performance testing will proceed from a business perspective and technical perspective. At a minimum, a performance testing plan addresses Dependencies and baseline assumptions, Pre-performance testing actions, Performance testing approach and Performance testing activities.

- **Test Design Specification** outlines, defines and details the approach taken to perform mobile application testing. The objective is to identify user flows and annotations, features to be tested, test scenarios, acceptance and release criteria.

- **Test Cases** are derived from Test Scenarios and are identified in the Test Design Specification. They are a set of test actions, test data/user input data, execution conditions, and expected results developed to verify successful and acceptable implementation of the application requirements.

- **Test Case Execution Summary Report** provides information uncovered by the tests and is accomplished by the testing type. The report is used to relay the overall status of Test Execution on an iteration-by-iteration basis.

2.2   Mobile Applications Software Testing Tools

The dynamic mobile program-based analysis often requires the ability to collect runtime information of programs, which includes execution paths, consumed time, sequences of synchronization events, etc. The mobile testing analysis tools use a mobile source code instrumentation to insert probes that can record the mobile programs' dynamic behaviors at runtime. The instrumentation provides a set of APIs and hooks, so that its behavior is programmable. We can order the instrumentation to bind program constructs with specific probes, without changing its implementation. While scanning the abstract syntax tree, the instrumentation inserts probes around the corresponding program constructs, and writes the tree out as source for compilation and execution. The dynamic behaviors of the annotated program are recorded in the runtime information database during the running period.

The test coverage evaluation tool accesses the runtime information database to obtain the execution tracks of the program. Based on these tracks and the program structure, the tool generates reporters about function coverage, statement coverage, and branch coverage. The result is useful to evaluate the testing sufficiency. The performance evaluation tool analyzes the runtime data of program entities to generate reports about the consumed time of functions and statements, and their time percentages during the running period. These reports are valuable to evaluate the performance of a module, and find out the bottleneck of the system performance. It scans the runtime information database to find the execution sequence of synchronization events in the program. Then it utilizes the source code instrumentation to insert new probes into the original program. These probes can force the annotated program to execute in the same sequence of synchronization events. The tool is very helpful in concurrent program debugging.

The runtime information database stores the runtime information of the program dynamic behaviors. We also defined some database access routines to facilitate other tools to access it. The database and the source code instrumentations provide a platform for other dynamic program-based techniques and tools, such as regression test case selection and structural test case generation.

3   Design of Mobile Applications Quality Assurance Tool

3.1   Design Guidelines

MAQAT is designed to analyze and test mobile programs, specially java and c. It contains a common front end and four tool sets: source code analysis tool set, test case generation tool set, testing analysis tool set, and software measurement tool set. Figure 1 shows the architecture of MAQAT. The front end is the foundation of MAQAT, which parses the source codes and stores the analysis results in the common information database. It also provides some advanced analysis engines for specific requirements. Most application tools obtain their data from the common information database and the advanced analysis engines As shown in Figure 1, MAQAT's front end consists of three components: a source code parser, a common information database, and a series of advanced analysis engines. The parser parses the source codes, builds the abstract syntax trees, and stores the results into the common information database. The advance analysis engines access the common information database to produce more complex results, which can be stored back to the common information database. The front end is the core of MAQAT, which provides data for other tools. Based on the common information database, we can build new tools for advanced program analysis and automated testing. The source code analysis tool set is composed of a code style checker, a static defect detector, and a software visualization tool. The code style checker inspects the abstract syntax tree according to a set of code style guidelines, and picks up codes written in bad styles. The static defect detector detects the data corruption and structural defects that lead to abnormal action through static dependence analysis. The software visualization tool can produce the visualization documents for the concurrent programs, which contains several kinds of graphs to represent the communication among concurrent tasks.

Based on the information provided by the common information database and the advanced analysis engines, we build tools to detect bad code-style and program defects. The *code style checker* produces the code-style inspection reporters to mark the codes written in bad code-style. With the increase of the mobile software scale, it is hard to ensure the readability and understandability of all the codes. The code style checker is an efficient tool that helps program developers to comply with the coding standards. The code style checker scans the abstract syntax tree to check each token with strict lexical rules, and examine the program structure with strict syntax and structure rules. Since it is a prototype tool focusing on the code structure and style, it utilizes little information of the program dependence, and cannot detect the defects related to the control flow and data flow. Compared with the code style checker, the *static defect detector* depends on the control-flow and data-flow information to detect program defects. The tool can detect five kinds of defects, including memory leak, dead pointer reference, NULL pointer reference, bad memory release, and uninitialized variable.

The static defect detector first constructs the program's abstract representation based on the PDGs and type information in the common information database. It adopts a control-flow-intensive strategy to perform the alias analysis, and store the results in the abstract representation. Then, it analyzes each function according to the topological structure of the call graph. The tool checks every expression in the function based on a set of detection rules, which may require the front end to provide dependence information or compute slicing. After analyzing a function, a constraint model of the function is generated, which is used to check corresponding function-call expressions?

3.2   Design of Functional Modules

Figure 2 indicates that MAQAT supports some essential activities of mobile applications software quality assurance. A software engineer can utilize the source code analysis tool set to perform the automated static inspection. The automated code-style checking and defect detection is an important complementarily of manual inspection. And the generated visualization documents are valuable to fill in the gap between design models and code implementations. Then, he may produce combination test cases for different combinatorial testing criterions with the combination test case generation tools. After the testing executions, he can use the testing analysis tools to evaluate testing sufficiency, find out the bottleneck of the program performance, or replay the specific execution for debugging. Besides, the software complexity measurement tools are helpful to evaluate the software quality and make further testing plans.

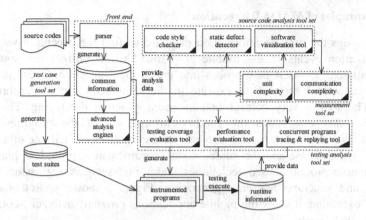

Fig. 1. Architecture of Mobile Applications Quality Assurance Tool

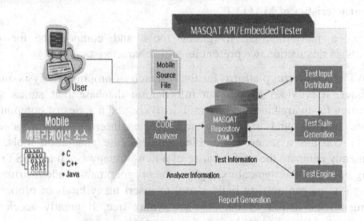

Fig. 2. Overall Behavior of MASQAT

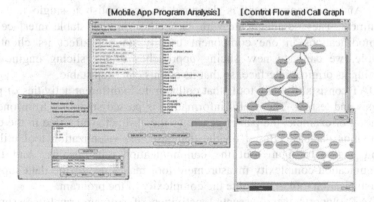

Fig. 3. Examples of MASQAT Execution

3.3   Examples of MAQAT Execution

MAQAT scans the runtime information database to find the execution sequence of synchronization events in the mobile program. Then it utilizes the source code instrumentations to insert new probes into the original program. These probes can force the annotated program to execute in the same sequence of synchronization events. The tool is very helpful in concurrent program debugging, The *runtime information database* stores the runtime information of the program dynamic behaviors. We also defined some database access routines to facilitate other tools to access it. The database and the source code instrumentation provide a platform for other dynamic program-based techniques and tools, such as regression test case selection and structural test case generation. Figure 3 shows the set of examples MAQAT execution, it show the mobile applications program analyzer , control flow and call(called) graph.

3.4   Characteristics of MAQAT

MAQAT is a platform that integrates tools and components for different requirements. In this section, we present its basic characteristics.

- MAQAT is a powerful platform for the research of program analysis and testing techniques. It provides a common information database that stores sufficient information for many kinds of program analysis, and a series of components that facilitate building and examining software engineering tools. For example, MAQAT contains a series of combination test case generation tools. We can conveniently compare the performance of a new strategy (such as PSST) with the existing ones. Another typical example is the programmable code instrumentation. Based on it, we can quickly build a tool to insert many kinds of probes without knowing all the details of the abstract syntax tree. It greatly accelerates the development of advanced analysis and testing tools.
- MAQAT has a flexible architecture that facilitates incremental development. The system is designed to be composed of a series of independent components and tools. And each component is designed to accomplish a single and specific assignment. They communicate with each other through stable interfaces. Thus, the modifications in one component usually do not affect its clients. For example, we can add new slicing approaches to the slicing engine without changing its original interface, so that its clients can keep stable.
- MAQAT consists of many tools that collaborate in different activities of program analysis and testing. The useful information is passed smoothly from one tool to another. For example, the parser generates the abstract syntax tree in the common information database. Based on the database, the visualization tool utilizes the slicing engine to figure out the communication relationships. And then the communication complexity measurement tool makes use of the data supplied by the visualization tool to compute the complexity of the program.
- MAQAT supports many essential activities of software quality assurance. It provides different components and tools to help software engineers to assure the

quality of the programs. This characteristic also helps researchers to implement some complex techniques. For example, the evolutionary testing tool may require the abilities to analyze the program structure, generate test cases, monitor execution paths, compute the testing coverage, and evaluate the runtime performance, which are difficult to be supported by a single tool. Fortunately, MASQAT has provided the basic components and core functions for the most foregoing requirements. It evidently reduces the cost of the development.

4   Conclusions and Future Works

We have developed a Mobile Applications Software Quality Assurance platform named MAQAT, which consists of a front end and four tool sets for mobile source code analysis, test case generation, testing analysis, and software measurement. The platform facilitates the implementation and examination of software engineering tools. Its flexible architecture is helpful for the incremental development.

We have future studies as followings;

- We are developing an evolutionary testing tool by using MAQAT as a platform. The tool is designed to generate test cases that reach full coverage for the structural criterion. We plan to build more probes and analysis engines for its implementation
- We are planning to implement a new parser for Java and AspectJ. We will refactor the front end to support the features of object-oriented and aspect-oriented programs. Because the abstract syntax tree and the program dependence graph are designed as language independent representations, most codes of the front end can be reused.

Acknowledgement. This work (Grants No.C0024433) was supported by Business for Cooperative R&D between Industry, Academy, and Research Institute funded Korea Small and Medium Business Administration in 2012.

References

1. Keogh, J.: J2ME: The Complete Reference. Osborne/McGraw-Hill (2003)
2. Juntao Yuan, M.: Enterprise J2ME: Developing Mobile Java Applications. Prentice Hall PTR (2003)
3. García Serrano, A.: Programación de juegos para móviles en J2ME (2011)
4. http://developers.sun.com/mobility/midp/articles/api/
5. http://www.netrino.com/images/articles/KVM_J2ME_figure2.gif
6. http://www.roseindia.net/j2me/midlet.gif
7. Tai, K.C., Lei, Y.: A Test Generation Strategy for Pairwise Testing. IEEE Trans. on Software Engineering 28(1) (January 2002)

8. Xu, B., Nie, C., Shi, Q., Lu, H.: An Algorithm for Automatically Generating Black-box Test Cases. Journal of Electronics 20(1) (January 2003)
9. Shi, L., Xu, B., Nie, C.: Combinational Design Approaches for Automatic Test Generation. Journal of Electronics 22(3), 205–208 (2005)
10. Xu, B., Zuo, F., Zhou, X., Shi, L.: Event-based Visualization Debugging on Concurrent Program. In: Proc. of the 16th IASTED International Conference on Parallel Distributed Computing and Systems, PDCS (November 2004)
11. Zhou, Y., Xu, B.: Measuring Structure Complexity of UML Class Diagrams. Journal of Electronics 20(3), 227–231 (2003)

SAT Solving Technique for Semantic Web Service Composition*

Hyunyoung Kil[1] and Wonhong Nam[2],**

[1] Korea Advanced Institute of Science & Technology, Daejeon 305-701, Korea
hkil@kaist.ac.kr
[2] Konkuk University, Seoul 143-701, Korea
wnam@konkuk.ac.kr

Abstract. The Web Service Composition (WSC) problem aims to find an optimal composition of web services to satisfy a given request using their syntactic and/or semantic features when no single service satisfies it. In particular, the semantics of services can help a composition engine find more correct, complete, consistent and optimal candidates as a solution. In this paper, we study the WSC problem considering semantic aspects, e.g., exploiting the semantic relationship between parameters of web services. Given a set of web service descriptions, an ontology and a requirement web service, we find the optimal composition which contains the smallest number of semantically well connected web services, by using semantic matchmaking and a boolean satisfiability solver. In a preliminary experiment, our proposal can find optimal compositions of web services efficiently.

Keywords: Web service composition, Semantic web, SAT.

1 Introduction

Web services are software systems designed to support machine to machine interoperations over internet. Recently, many researches have been carried out for the web service standard, and these efforts significantly have improved flexible and dynamic functionality of *service oriented architectures* in the current semantic web services. However, a number of research challenges still remain; e.g., automatic web service discovery and web service composition. Given a set of available web services and a user request, a *web service discovery problem* is to automatically find a web service satisfying the request. Often, the client request cannot, however, be fulfilled by a single pre-existing service. In this case, one desires *web service composition (WSC)* which combines some from a given set of web services to satisfy the requirement, based on their syntactic and/or semantic features.

Semantics is one of the key elements for the automated composition of web services since this machine-readable description of services can help a composition engine find a correct, complete, consistent and optimal plan as a solution. Semantic description is

---

* This research was supported by the MKE, Korea, under the ITRC support program supervised by the NIPA (NIPA–2012–H0301–12–3006.)
** Corresponding author.

T.-h. Kim et al. (Eds.): SIP/WSE/ICHCI 2012, CCIS 342, pp. 167–172, 2012.
© Springer-Verlag Berlin Heidelberg 2012

mainly represented with an ontology. An ontology is a formal knowledge base specified with a set of concepts within a domain, properties of each concepts, and the relationships among those concepts. Based on the ontology, programs can reason about the entities within that domain and find more candidate web services which are not only syntactically but also semantically appropriate for composition. As a result, we can obtain a composite service with high quality.

In this paper, we propose a novel technique to find an *optimal* composition for the semantic web service composition problem. Given a set of semantic descriptions of web services and a requirement web service, our algorithm identifies the *shortest sequence of web services* such that we can legally invoke the next web service in each step and achieve the desired requirement eventually. We first reduce the composition problem into a *reachability problem* on a *state-transition system* where the shortest path from the initial state to a goal state corresponds to the shortest sequence of web services. To solve the reachability problem, we employ a state-of-the-art SAT solver. We report on a preliminary implementation and experiment for our solution, which demonstrate that our technique finds optimal compositions for 5 modified examples for the WSC'09 competition [1].

2 Semantic Web Service Composition

In this section, we formalize the notion of web services and their composition we consider in this paper. A *web service* is a tuple $w = (I, O)$ where I and O are respectively a finite set of *input parameters* and a finite set of *output parameters* for w. Each input/output parameter $p \in I \cup O$ is a concept referred to in an ontology Γ through OWL-S [2] or WSMO [3]. We assume that when a web service w is invoked with all the input parameters $i \in I$, w returns all the output parameters $o \in O$.

To decide invocation relationship from $w_1(I_1, O_1)$ to $w_2(I_2, O_2)$ in the composition, it is necessary to semantically compare outputs O_1 of w_1 with inputs I_2 of w_2. For this, we need to compute a semantic similarity between two parameters; that is, we have to find a relationship between two knowledge representations encoded using Γ. A causal link [4] describes the semantic matchmaking between these two parameters with the matchmaking function $Sim_\Gamma(p_1, p_2)$ which identifies the matching level of p_1 and p_2 based on a given ontology Γ. In a number of web service composition models [5,6,7], Sim_Γ is reduced to the following matching levels.

- *exact* if two parameter p_1 and p_2 are equivalent concepts; i.e., $\Gamma \models p_1 \equiv p_2$.
- *plug-in* if p_1 is sub-concept of p_2; i.e., $\Gamma \models p_1 <: p_2$.
- *subsume* if p_1 is super-concept of p_2; i.e., $\Gamma \models p_1 :> p_2$.
- *disjoint* if p_1 and p_2 are not compatible.

The *exact* matching means that p_1 and p_2 can substitute for each other since they refer to equivalent concepts. The *plug-in* matching is also a possible match to substitute p_1 for p_2 everywhere since p_1 is more specific than p_2. In other words, p_1 is more informative than p_2. The *subsume* matching is the converse relation of the plug-in matching. The *Disjoint* matching informs the incompatibility of two web service parameters. Thus, it cannot give any contribution to connect the services.

We assume that the ontology Γ is given, e.g., specified in OWL. Given two web services $w_1(I_1, O_1)$ and $w_2(I_2, O_2)$, we denote $w_1 \sqsupseteq_I w_2$ if w_2 requires less informative inputs than w_1; i.e., for every $i_2 \in I_2$ there exists $i_1 \in I_1$ such that $i_1 <: i_2$. Given two web services $w_1(I_1, O_1)$ and $w_2(I_2, O_2)$, we denote $w_1 \sqsubseteq_O w_2$ if w_2 provides more informative outputs than w_1; i.e., for every $o_1 \in O_1$ there exists $o_2 \in O_2$ such that $o_2 <: o_1$. A *web service discovery problem* is, given a set W of available web services and a request web service w_r, to find a web service $w \in W$ such that $w_r \sqsupseteq_I w$ and $w_r \sqsubseteq_O w$.

However, it might happen that there is no single web service satisfying the requirement. In that case, we want to find a sequence $w_1 \cdots w_n$ of web services such that we can invoke the next web service in each step and achieve the desired requirement eventually. Formally, we extend the relations, $\sqsupseteq_I$ and $\sqsubseteq_O$, to a sequence of web services as follows.

- $w \sqsupseteq_I w_1 \cdots w_n$ (where $w = (I, O)$ and each $w_j = (I_j, O_j)$ and $I, O, I_j, O_j \subseteq \Gamma$) if $\forall 1 \leq j \leq n$: for every $i_2 \in I_j$ there exists $i_1 \in I \cup \bigcup_{k<j} O_k$ such that $i_1 <: i_2$.
- $w \sqsubseteq_O w_1 \cdots w_n$ (where $w = (I, O)$ and each $w_j = (I_j, O_j)$ and $I, O, I_j, O_j \subseteq \Gamma$) if for every $o_1 \in O$ there exists $o_2 \in \bigcup_{1 \leq j \leq n} O_j$ such that $o_2 <: o_1$.

Finally, given a set of available web services W, an ontology Γ and a service request w_r, a *semantic web service composition problem* $WC = (W, \Gamma, w_r)$ we focus on in this paper is to find a sequence $w_1 \cdots w_n$ (every $w_j \in W$) of web services such that $w_r \sqsupseteq_I w_1 \cdots w_n$ and $w_r \sqsubseteq_O w_1 \cdots w_n$. The optimal solution for this problem is to find a sequence with the minimum value for n.

3 Solving with SAT Solver

To solve a semantic web service composition problem with a boolean satisfiability solver, we first explain how this problem can be reduced into a reachability problem on a state-transition system. Then, we present our encoding to a CNF (Conjunctive Normal Form) formula which is true if and only if there exists a path of length k from an initial state to a goal state of the state-transition system. Finally, we propose our algorithm to find an optimal solution for the problem.

3.1 Reduction to Reachability Problem

Given a semantic web service composition problem $WC = (W, \Gamma, w_r)$, the problem can be reduced into a reachability problem on a state-transition system. The *state-transition system* is a tuple $S = (X, \Sigma, T)$ where

- X is a finite set of *boolean variables*; a *state* q of S is a valuation for all the variables in X.
- Σ is a set of *input symbols*.
- $T(X, \Sigma, X')$ is a *transition predicate* over $X \cup \Sigma \cup X'$. For a set X of variables, we denote the set of primed variables of X as $X' = \{x' \mid x \in X\}$, which represents a set of variables encoding the successor states. $T(q, a, q')$ is *true* iff q' can be the next state when the input $a \in \Sigma$ is received at the state q.

In addition, from a given requirement web service $w_r = (I_{w_r}, O_{w_r})$, we encode an *initial state predicate* $Init(X)$ and a *goal state predicate* $G(X)$.

Intuitively, we have an initial state where we possess all the data instances corresponding to the input of w_r as well as one corresponding to their supertypes. As goal states, if a state is more informative than the outputs of w_r, it is a goal state. Finally, given a type-aware web service composition problem $WC = (W, \Gamma, w_r)$, we can reduce WC into a reachability problem $R = (S, Init, G)$ where the shortest path from an initial state to a goal state corresponds to the shortest sequence of web services.

3.2 Encoding to CNF Formula

Now, we study how to construct a formula $[[R]]_k$ which is true if and only if there exists a path $q_0 \cdots q_k$ of length k for a given reachability problem $R = (S, Init, G)$. The formula $[[R]]_k$ is over sets $X_0, \cdots, X_k$ of variables and $W_1, \cdots, W_k$ where each X_j represents a state along the path and W_j encodes a web service invoked in each step. It essentially represents constraints on $q_0 \cdots q_k$ and $w_1 \cdots w_k$ such that $[[R]]_k$ is satisfiable if and only if q_0 is the initial state, each q_j evolves according to the transition predicate for w_j, and q_k reaches to a goal state. Formally, the formula $[[R]]_k$ is as follows:

$$[[R]]_k \equiv Init(X_0) \wedge \bigwedge_{0 \leq j < k} T(X_j, W_{j+1}, X'_{j+1}) \wedge G(X_k)$$

Since each X_j is a finite set of boolean variables, Σ and W_j are finite, and $Init$, T and G are predicates, we can easily translate $[[R]]_k$ into a CNF formula which is the standard input format for conventional SAT solvers.

3.3 Algorithm for the Optimal Solution

Since we can use a SAT solver with $[[R]]_k$ to check whether there exists a path of length k from the initial state to a goal state, we are able to find a shortest path simply by increasing the value k from 0 to $|W|$. In the worst case, we check the formula until only $|W|$ as k since multiple executions of any $w \in W$ do not provide more data instances than a single execution of w.

Algorithm 1 presents our semantic web service composition. Given a set W of web services, an ontology Γ and a requirement web service w_r, the algorithm first reduces them into a state-transition system, and initial and goal predicates as Section 3.1 (line 1), and it begins with 1 as the value of k. For each loop, it constructs a CNF formula for k as Section 3.2 (line 3), and checks it with an off-the-shelf SAT solver (line 4). If the formula is satisfiable, the SAT solver returns a truth assignment; otherwise, it returns *null*. Once the algorithm finds a path of the length k, it extracts a web service sequence from the path, and returns the sequence (line 5).

4 Preliminary Experiment

We have implemented an automatic tool for the semantic web service composition algorithm in Section 3.3. Given an ontology in an OWL file, and a set of available web

---

Algorithm 1. SemanticWebServiceComposition

Input : a set W of web services, an ontology Γ and a web service w_r.
Output: a sequence of web services.

1 $(S, Init, G) := ReduceToReachabilityProblem(W, \Gamma, w_r)$;
2 **for** $(k := 0; k \leq |W|; k := k + 1)$ **do**
3     $f := ConstructCNF(S, Init, G, k)$;
4   **if** $((path := \text{SAT}(f)) \neq null)$ **then**
5 | **return** $ExtractWSSequence(path)$;
6   **endif**
7 **endfor**

Table 1. Experiment result

Problem	Parameters	Web services	Solution length	Time (sec.)
p_1	100	30	3	0.1
p_2	500	50	6	1.1
p_3	1000	150	9	14.8
p_4	2000	300	7	46.9
p_5	5000	300	7	106.2

services and a query web service in WSDL files, our tool generates a web service sequence in WSBPEL to satisfy the request. To demonstrate that our tools efficiently identify an optimal solution, we modified the examples generated by the WSC 09 [1] testset generator to map parameters to concepts, and then we have experimented on 5 examples which includes upto 5,000 parameters and 300 web services. For an off-the-shelf SAT solver, we employ zChaff [8] which achieved promising success in the boolean satisfiability problem literature. All experiments have been performed on a PC using a 2.93GHz Core i7 processor and 4GB memory. Figure 1 presents the total execution time in seconds for our preliminary experiment of our algorithm.

5   Conclusion and Future Work

For the semantic web service composition problem, we have proposed a novel solution that finds the shortest sequence of web services to satisfy a given requirement considering semantic aspect. To identify the optimal solution, the technique is based on a semantic matchmaking of service parameters and a boolean satisfiability solving. Our preliminary experiments present promising results where the tool finds the shortest sequence efficiently.

There are several directions for future work. First, we want to optimize the current version of our implementation. Second, it is worth pointing out that, while our implementation uses SAT-based state-space exploration, the approach can easily be adapted to permit other model checking strategies such as BDD-based model checking [9] and counter-example guided abstraction refinement [10].

References

1. Kona, S., Bansal, A., Blake, B., Bleul, S., Weise, T.: WSC-2009: a quality of service-oriented web services challenge. In: The 11th IEEE Conference on Commerce and Enterprise Computing, pp. 487–490 (2009)
2. Martin, D.: OWL-S: Semantic Markup for Web Services (2004), http://www.w3.org/Submission/OWL-S
3. Fensel, D., Kifer, M., de Bruijn, J., Domingue, J.: Web Service Modeling Ontology (WSMO). W3C member submission (2005)
4. Russell, S., Norvig, P.: Artificial Intelligence: a modern approach. Prentice-Hall (1995)
5. Paolucci, M., Kawamura, T., Payne, T.R., Sycara, K.: Semantic Matching of Web Services Capabilities. In: Horrocks, I., Hendler, J. (eds.) ISWC 2002. LNCS, vol. 2342, pp. 348–363. Springer, Heidelberg (2002)
6. Zhang, R., Arpinar, I.B., Aleman-Meza, B.: Automatic composition of semantic web services. In: Proceedings of the 10th International Conference on Web Services, pp. 38–41 (2003)
7. Sirin, E., Parsia, B., Hendler, J.A.: Filtering and selecting semantic web services with interactive composition techniques. IEEE Intelligent Systems 19(4), 42–49 (2004)
8. Zhang, L., Malik, S.: The Quest for Efficient Boolean Satisfiability Solvers. In: Brinksma, E., Larsen, K.G. (eds.) CAV 2002. LNCS, vol. 2404, pp. 17–36. Springer, Heidelberg (2002)
9. Clarke, E., Grumberg, O., Peled, D.: Model checking. MIT Press (2000)
10. Clarke, E., Grumberg, O., Jha, S., Lu, Y., Veith, H.: Counterexample-guided abstraction refinement. In: Proceedings of the 12th Computer Aided Verification, pp. 154–169 (2000)

Byzantine Fault Tolerance as a Service

Hua Chai and Wenbing Zhao

Department of Electrical and Computer Engineering
Cleveland State University, Cleveland, OH 44115
wenbing@ieee.org

Abstract. In this paper, we argue for the need and benefits for providing Byzantine fault tolerance as a service to mission critical Web applications. In this new approach to Byzantine fault tolerance, an application server can partition the incoming requests into different domains for concurrent processing, decide which set of messages that should be totally ordered, or not at all, based its application semantics. This flexibility would reduce the end-to-end latency experienced by the clients and significantly increase the system throughput. Perhaps most importantly, we propose a middleware framework that provides a uniform interface to the applications so that they are not strongly tied to any particular Byzantine fault tolerance algorithm implementation.

Keywords: Byzantine fault tolerance, Web services, service oriented computing, application semantics, business activities.

1 Introduction

In the past decade or so, we have seen tremendous efforts to bring Byzantine fault tolerance (BFT) to distributed systems (such as [1–3, 11, 12]). The BFT algorithms based on the basic client-server model have advanced to the extent that very little room is left for further improvement [7]. On the other hand, practical applications often involve much more complicated system models, as such, a naive use of a BFT algorithm not only would incur unnecessarily high runtime overhead, but might render the resulting system to function incorrectly (*e.g.*, a deadlock might occur if the total order imposed on the messages did not respect the causal relationship among some of the messages).

To avoid this problem, the application semantics must be considered so that the correct message ordering and execution rules can be specified. Furthermore, the application might need to reach a Byzantine agreement on values other than the message ordering, *e.g.*, a transaction processing application will want to ensure that all non-faulty coordinator replicas agree on the same outcome (commit or abort) for each distributed transaction.

While it is possible for each application to customize a BFT algorithm implementation based on its need for optimal and correct operation, as we have done in [2, 11], we believe that it is much more desirable to separate out the components responsible for ensuring Byzantine agreement from the application logic, and create a Byzantine fault tolerance service for applications. Such a service

T.-h. Kim et al. (Eds.): SIP/WSE/ICHCI 2012, CCIS 342, pp. 173–179, 2012.

would provide interfaces for the application server replicas to reach Byzantine agreement on various values in addition to message total ordering, such as business decisions (mentioned above), random numbers, timestamps, and message identity (for messages that do not need total ordering). The application gets to decide when to use which interface to ensure Byzantine fault tolerance according to its need, much in the same way as when to use an appropriate cryptography primitive (such as encryption or digital signature) when building a secure system.

2   BFT as a Service Architecture

The objectives for the middleware framework enabling the use of BFT as a service include:

1. Provide a uniform interface to application servers to achieve Byzantine fault tolerance;
2. Provide a rich set of services to applications that go beyond simple total ordering;
3. Enables the registration of various BFT algorithm implementations and the selection of any particular BFT algorithm implementation by the applications.

Objective 1 decouples the application server from any particular BFT algorithm implementation and encapsulates the complexities of interaction with these BFT algorithms. Objective 2 enables applications that use sophisticated system models to enjoy Byzantine fault tolerance. This includes the ability of ensuring Byzantine fault tolerant total ordering of messages, as well as dynamic partitioning of the requests and ensuring total ordering of messages within each partition, and achieving Byzantine agreement on various values such as a business decision, random numbers, timestamps, or the identity of the message that does not need to be totally ordered. Objective 3 facilitate the registration of BFT agreement services and the selection of a particular BFT agreement service by an application service, via a registration service cluster.

The architecture of the middleware framework to enable BFT as a service is shown in Figure 1. The figure shows two different BFT agreement implementations running in two separate agreement clusters, and two application servers together with their clients. A BFT agreement cluster registers itself with the registration service so that the application server can discover that it is available for providing a Byzantine agreement service. Once an application server obtains sufficient information from the registration server, it is ready to request a service by communicating with a particular BFT agreement cluster directly on-demand based on its need.

In addition to the registration cluster, the framework consists of two Axis2 handlers, a lightweight handler to be plugged into the client side, and another handler to be plugged into the server side. The components in each handler are highlighted in Figure 2.

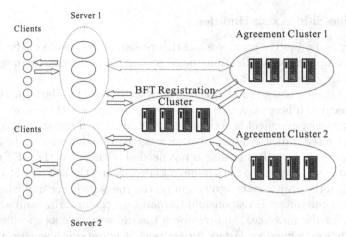

Fig. 1. Architecture for the BFT-as-a-service framework

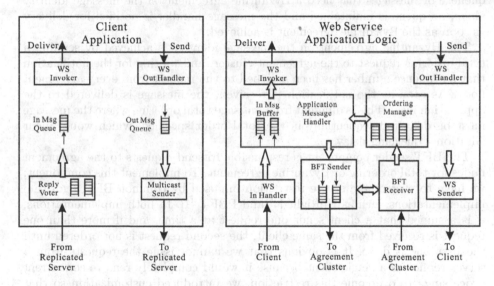

Fig. 2. Major components in the the client-side and server-side handlers

2.1 Registration Service

The registration service is replicated for Byzantine fault tolerance. It allows the BFT service providers to register their services and interested users to select a BFT service for Byzantine fault tolerance. To register a BFT service, the provider must provide information such as addressing and configuration parameters (e.g., replication degree, IP address, port number, and the public key for each agreement node. For each BFT service, the corresponding server-side Axis2 handler must be made available for the application to download. The server-side handler is customized for each BFT service provider. The client-side handler implementation is independent from any specific BFT algorithm implementation and does not need to be customized.

2.2 Service-Side Axis2 Handler

This handler embodies the main work of this research. It consists of the following four main components: application message handler, ordering manager, BFT sender, and BFT receiver.

The application message handler is responsible to partition the requests sent to the server, decide if it is necessary to totally order a message within its own domain, and if a Byzantine agreement is needed on the identity of a message, according to the application semantics. An incoming message can be delivered right away if a Byzantine agreement on the message is not needed. Otherwise, the BFT sender is instructed to send a request to the agreement cluster, and the delivery of a message is blocked until the appropriate agreement on the message is accomplished.

The ordering manager is responsible to maintain the ordering and agreement information for the messages, and reinforce the delivery rule as specified by the application message handler. For each partition, it maintains a separate message queue. For messages that need a Byzantine agreement on the message identity alone, no queue is maintained and the message handler is notified for delivery as soon as the Byzantine agreement is achieved.

The Byzantine agreement on the message identity is achieved by sending a total ordering request to the agreement cluster, and waiting for the notification that a sequence number has been assigned to the request from every agreement node. As soon as the notification is received, the message is delivered to the application logic. This is different from message total ordering where the message must be delivered sequentially in the total order specified, which would incur additional queueing delay.

The BFT sender component is responsible to send requests to the agreement nodes for total ordering or Byzantine agreement. To implement this component, we have to overcome a severe restriction imposed by common BFT algorithm implementations such as UpRight [4] and PBFT [1]. In both implementations, it is assumed that a client sends one request at a time, and if more than one request is received from the same client, the second request is not ordered until the first one is done. It is obvious that we cannot issue the requests from a server replica as a single client because it would completely remove concurrent processing. To overcome this restriction, we introduced customization so that the BFT sender can act as the proxies for the original senders of the requests (one for each client).

The BFT receiver component receives ordering notifications for the requests sent by the BFT sender. Upon receiving such a notification, the BFT sender is informed so that it stops the possible retransmission of the corresponding request. This logic is rather different from that of the normal client-side and server-side BFT libraries.

2.3 Client-Side Axis2 Handler

The client-side handler is generic and very lightweight. It contains a multicast sender component to facilitate the sending of a request to all sever replicas (in place of the point-to-point sender component in typical non-replicated Web service client), and a voter component to perform majority voting on the reply messages sent by the server replicas.

3 Performance Evaluation

Our middleware framework is specifically implemented for the Axis2 Web services platform. The server-side handler is customized for the UpRight library [4], which implements the Zyzzyva BFT algorithm [7]. The test application is a travel reservation application supported by an open source coordination framework (*i.e.*, Kandula2) conforming to the Web service business activity (WS-BA) standard [6]. Due to space limitation, the description of the test application is omitted. Interested readers are referred to [2] for details. During our experiments, only the WS-BA coordinator is replicated for Byzantine fault tolerance protection. The replication degree is fixed at three (that is, three replicas are used to protect against up to one Byzantine faulty replica). The replication degree of the agreement cluster is set to tolerate a single Byzantine fault as well.

The performance evaluation results are summarized in Figure 3. The measurements compare the end-to-end latency (measured at the client) and the system throughput (measured at the server replica) under the following three configurations:

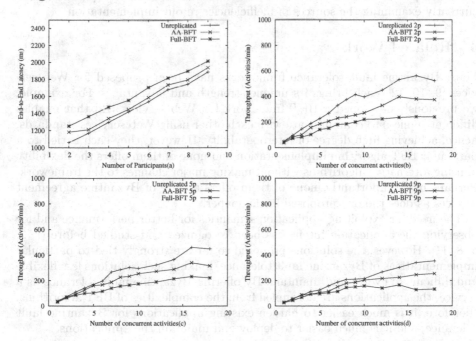

Fig. 3. End-to-end latency and throughput measurement results. (a) End-to-end latency in the presence of a single business activity. (b) Throughput under various number of concurrent clients for 2 participants in each business activity. (c) Throughput for 5 participants in each activity. (d) Throughput for 9 participants in each activity. The scales for the three throughput figures are kept the same for ease of comparison.

- Unreplicated application. For a fair comparison, all messages exchanged are protected with HMAC.
- Application-aware Byzantine fault tolerance (denoted as AA-BFT in the figure). By studying the semantics of the application and the WS-BA standard, we have proved that it is sufficient to use source ordering instead of total ordering for the incoming messages. However, a Byzantine agreement on the identity of the messages that are sent to the WS-BA coordinator is still necessary.
- Full Byzantine fault tolerance (denoted as Full-BFT). In this configuration, every incoming message to the WS-BA coordinator is totally ordered and delivered sequentially according to the total order.

The end-to-end latency measurement is done with a single activity taking place for various number of participants. It is somewhat surprising that the runtime overhead on the end-to-end latency (as shown in Figure 3(a)) is rather small for both AA-BFT and Full-BFT. This reflects the highly optimized operation of the Zyzzyva algorithm.

However, the throughput measurement results (in Figure 3(b)-(d)) show significant throughput reduction for Full-BFT. This is expected because of the sequential delivery of requests. The results for AA-BFT are worse than what we had expected because there are noticeable reduction in throughput. We are currently examining the sources of inefficiencies in our implementation.

4   Related Work

Many Byzantine fault tolerance frameworks have been proposed for Web services [9, 10, 12], each brings its unique strength and advantages. For example, we previously developed a BFT framework for Web services [12] that enables different replicas to communicate with each other using Web services standards, hence, achieving high degree of interoperability. However, they each is tied to a particular BFT algorithm implementation and none of them offers the flexibility of using alternative algorithms without making major changes to the framework. Perhaps most importantly, none of them offers a suite of Byzantine agreement services as does the one proposed in this paper.

The need for exploiting application semantics for better performance and for observing the application intent has been recognized and studied before [1, 2, 5, 8, 11]. However, the solutions proposed so far are strongly tied to particular implementations of Byzantine fault tolerance, making such solutions less flexible and difficult to evolve and maintain. By offering Byzantine fault tolerance as a service, the applications are decoupled from the complexities of BFT algorithms, therefore, it is much easier to harden existing applications for Byzantine fault tolerance, and it is much easier to deploy and maintain the applications.

5   Conclusion and Future Work

In this paper, we presented our arguments on the need for providing Byzantine fault tolerance as a service due to the many benefits of the approach. We further documented the design and implementation of a middleware framework that can be used to render an existing application Byzantine fault tolerant with minimum modifications.

For future work, we are planning to add support for a number of other BFT algorithm implementations such as PBFT [1], enhance our current implementation for more robustness and efficiency, and validate our framework with more applications.

Acknowledgements. This work was supported in part by NSF grant CNS 08-21319, and by a CSUSI grant from Cleveland State University.

References

1. Castro, M., Liskov, B.: Practical Byzantine fault tolerance and proactive recovery. ACM Transactions on Computer Systems 20(4), 398–461 (2002)
2. Chai, H., Zhang, H., Zhao, W., Melliar-Smith, P.M., Moser, L.E.: Toward trustworthy coordination for web service business activities. IEEE Transactions on Services Computing (to appear)
3. Clement, A., Wong, E., Alvisi, L., Dahlin, M.: Making Byzantine fault-tolerant systems tolerate Byzantine faults. In: Proceedings of the 6th Symposium on Networked Systems Design and Implementation, Boston, MA (2009)
4. Clement, A., Kapritsos, M., Lee, S., Wang, Y., Alvisi, L., Dahlin, M., Riche, T.: Upright cluster services. In: Proceedings of the ACM SIGOPS 22nd Symposium on Operating Systems Principles, SOSP 2009, pp. 277–290. ACM, New York (2009), http://doi.acm.org/10.1145/1629575.1629602
5. Distler, T., Kapitza, R.: Increasing performance in Byzantine fault-tolerant systems with on-demand replica consistency. In: Proceedings of the Sixth Eurosys Conference (2011)
6. Freund, T., Little, M.: Web services business activity version 1.1, OASIS standard (April 2007), http://docs.oasis-open.org/ws-tx/wstx-wsba-1.1-spec-os/wstx-wsba-1.1-spec-os.html
7. Kotla, R., Alvisi, L., Dahlin, M., Clement, A., Wong, E.: Zyzzyva: Speculative Byzantine fault tolerance. In: Proceedings of 21st ACM Symposium on Operating Systems Principles (2007)
8. Kotlan, R., Dahlin, M.: High throughput Byzantine fault tolerance. In: Proceedings of International Conference on Dependable Systems and Networks (2004)
9. Merideth, M., Iyengar, A., Mikalsen, T., Tai, S., Rouvellou, I., Narasimhan, P.: Thema: Byzantine-fault-tolerant middleware for web services applications. In: Proceedings of the IEEE Symposium on Reliable Distributed Systems, pp. 131–142 (2005)
10. Pallemulle, S., Thorvaldsson, Goldman, K.: Byzantine fault-tolerant web services for n-tier and service oriented architectures. In: Proceedings of the 28th International Conference on Distributed Computing Systems (2008)
11. Zhang, H., Chai, H., Zhao, W., Melliar-Smith, P.M., Moser, L.E.: Trustworthy coordination for web service atomic transactions. IEEE Transactions on Parallel and Distributed Systems 23, 1551–1565 (2012)
12. Zhao, W.: Design and implementation of a Byzantine fault tolerance framework for web services. Journal of Systems and Software 82, 1004–1015 (2009)

Interaction Patterns for Byzantine Fault Tolerance Computing

Hua Chai and Wenbing Zhao

Department of Electrical and Computer Engineering
Cleveland State University, Cleveland, OH 44115
wenbing@ieee.org

Abstract. In this paper, we present a catalog of application interaction patterns with the corresponding message ordering and execution rules for Byzantine fault tolerance computing. For each pattern, a set of rules are defined to determine whether or not an inbound message should be ordered and in what particular order, and which set of messages should be delivered sequentially, concurrently, or selectively concurrently under various scenarios. This catalog could serve as the design patterns for constructing practical Byzantine fault tolerance applications that may use much more sophisticated system models than the basic client-server state machine model. The set of patterns will make it easier and less error-prone when applying the Byzantine fault tolerance techniques for practical systems, in particular, Web based applications.

Keywords: Byzantine fault tolerance, Web services, cloud computing, interaction patterns, application semantics.

1 Introduction

Distributed systems are playing an increasingly important role in our society and our lives. For example, many major technology companies (such as Apple, Microsoft and Amazon) have offered various cloud-based services to both consumers and businesses. The dependability requirement on such services is undoubtedly becoming higher because any extended downtime or incidents of data corruption would result in significant loss of revenue and reduced reputation. In the past decade or so, we have seen tremendous efforts to bring Byzantine fault tolerance (BFT) to practical distributed systems (such as [3–5, 12, 15]).

However, we have yet to see widespread adoption of the Byzantine fault tolerance technology in practice. Even though it may be due to a multitude of reasons, such as the concerns of the resources cost and the performance uncertainty during non-optimal conditions, we believe that an important obstacle is that the system models used in the state-of-the-art BFT algorithms are often much too simple for many practical applications, such as business processes [1] and groupware applications [14], which often involve concurrent processing and asynchronous invocations, and impose various dependencies among inbound messages. For example, in existing BFT algorithms, a total order is imposed on all

T.-h. Kim et al. (Eds.): SIP/WSE/ICHCI 2012, CCIS 342, pp. 180–188, 2012.

inbound messages (or those within the same partition), and a linearizable execution of these messages is ensured (except for those independent of each other as an optimization). For some applications, however, such an execution order might lead to deadlocks when the actual dependency among the messages is not respected [13].

That said, it does not mean that the existing BFT algorithms cannot be used at all for such applications. On the contrary, as shown in our previous work [4, 12], they can serve as powerful building blocks for any sophisticated BFT application, much in the same way as how cryptography primitives (e.g., encryption/decryption and digital signatures) can be used to build a secure system. What is needed is to determine appropriate message ordering and execution rules for the application, such as when a Byzantine agreement is necessary and for what value, and when concurrent processing must be enabled and how to do that while ensuring replica consistency. Such rules cannot be designed without the knowledge of application semantics. The open research issue then is to determine what application semantics is needed and how to exploit such knowledge to enable the applications to operate as they have been designed with minimum runtime overhead. What is more challenging is how to enable the discovery of application semantics and the design of message ordering and execution rules automatically or semi-automatically with minimum per-application development cost. This obviously is a grand research goal. The first step towards the goal is the compilation of a comprehensive application interaction patterns catalog because these patterns would serve as the foundation for the formulation of the execution rules and automated application semantics discovery. This paper presents our preliminary work in building such a catalog of interaction patterns. All patterns presented are highly relevant for Web based applications.

2 Basic Request-Reply Interaction Patterns

Figure 1 shows three basic request-reply interaction patterns commonly used in Web based applications. Pattern I.a involves a client sending a request to the replicated server and waiting for the reply synchronously. An implicit assumption here is that requests sent by different clients are uncorrelated except that they might query/update the same state variables.

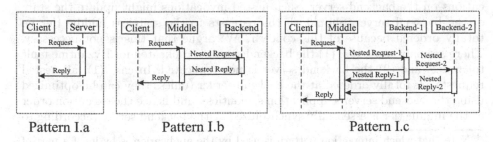

Pattern I.a   Pattern I.b   Pattern I.c

Fig. 1. Basic request-reply interaction patterns

- *Scenario 1: no knowledge of application semantics*[1]. All requests are assumed to involve update operations, and therefore, they are totally ordered and they must be executed at the server replicas sequentially in the same total order [3].
- *Scenario 2: read-only request.* A read-only request is delivered immediately for execution without the need for total ordering [3].
- *Scenario 3: partitionable requests*: Requests within the same partition must be totally ordered and executed linearly, and those belong to different partitions can be handled in parallel [2, 10]. In some cases, there exist cross-border requests that access/update multiple parts of the state [6, 8], which would make the total ordering of all requests necessary to ensure causal ordering. However, non-cross-border requests could still be executed in parallel as long as the partial ordering is respected [8].
- *Scenario 4: commutative requests.* Commutative requests can be executed in parallel. However, if cross-border requests exist, all requests would still need to be totally ordered to ensure causal ordering.
- *Scenario 5: stateless server.* In this case, a request can be delivered immediately without the need for total ordering because the execution for different requests is completely independent.

Pattern I.b describes synchronous request-reply interactions in a three-tier application, where the replicated server (termed as "Middle" in the figure) on which the client invokes would issue one or more nested requests to a backend server and waits synchronously for the corresponding replies. There is no assumption as to whether or not the backend server is replicated. If it is, then each middle-tier replica should collect $f + 1$ consistent nested replies before it accepts them, where f is the number of faulty replicas tolerated by the application.

If no application semantics is known, not only the requests to the middle-tier replicas must be totally ordered, so do the nested replies to ensure replica consistency [9] unless the backend server is replicated as well. Furthermore, all inbound messages should be executed sequentially according to the total order. For read-only operations, the requests and nested replies can be delivered immediately without total ordering. The rules for the scenarios with partitionable and commutative requests are rather similar to those for pattern I.a.

In pattern I.b with a stateless middle tier, the middle tier issues nested invocations on the backend server. Such nested invocations might update the state of the backend server. Should all the requests to the stateless middle tier be totally ordered because of this concern? We argue that this is not necessary. There are only two cases: (1) the backend server is replicated for Byzantine fault tolerance, and (2) the backend server is not replicated. In case (1), all nested requests are totally ordered at the backend server (unless they can be optimized using the backend server's application semantics), and hence the execution order at the middle tier is essentially synchronized at the backend server (according to

---

[1] Note that which interaction pattern is used by the application is by itself a part of the application semantics. Thus, the phrase "no knowledge of application semantics" actually means that no application semantics is known other than the interaction pattern.

the total order). In case (2), the execution order of requests (to the middle tier) with conflicting nested invocations is naturally synchronized at the unreplicated backend server, and no constraint is imposed by the system on the execution order of other requests.

Pattern I.c highlights the cases when asynchronous invocations (on the backend servers) are used at the middle tier. In this pattern, the middle-tier server issues two or more nested requests to different backend servers. It then collects all the corresponding replies before it generates a reply to the client. The same set of scenarios as those in Pattern I.b could occur and the handling is similar except that the relative ordering among the nested replies is not important. However, if the backend servers are not replicated, a Byzantine agreement is needed on the identity of the nested reply message itself to prevent a faulty backend server from sending conflicting nested replies to the middle-tier replicas without being detected.

3   Oneway Interaction Patterns

The oneway interaction patterns are illustrated in Figure 2. Pattern II.a is common to even-driven applications (for event stream processing, for example) where one process (*i.e.*, event producer) periodically sends events (*i.e.*, oneway notifications) to an event processing agent for processing [7]. The agent might transform the events received and pass the transformed events to another agent for further processing or to an event consumer. The agent might also carry out tasks such as pattern matching and generate an alert when certain predefined criteria is met.

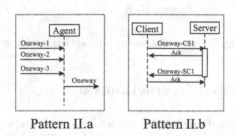

Pattern II.a   Pattern II.b

Fig. 2. Oneway interaction patterns

Without any knowledge on application semantics, all oneway messages should be totally ordered and delivered sequentially according to that order. Once the type of operation on the event is known, many optimizations can be made, for example, if a stateless transformation is involved, the optimization laid out for stateless servers (in patterns I.a and I.b) can be employed. For this type of applications, the events arrive periodically and the execution of each event is typically very fast, which suggests that more priority should be given on the optimization of the ordering stage rather than the execution stage.

Pattern II.b is commonly used in Web services applications in which the client sends a oneway request to a server and *asynchronously* waits for the corresponding reply. In response to receiving a oneway message, an acknowledgment is sent so that the sender of the oneway message is informed of the fact. This is often referred to as synchronous oneway messaging (asynchronous oneway messaging without the explicit acknowledgment is also possible in Web services). The oneway messages should be handled in a similar way to those in Pattern II.a. For both Pattern II.a and Pattern.b, the tricky issue is to determine when it is safe to deliver the next oneway message to the application. If the upcall for delivery is synchronous, *i.e.*, the call returns only after the message is fully executed, the next message can be delivered subsequently. However, if the upcall for delivery is asynchronous, a hook must be injected into the application so that the infrastructure knows when the current message is fully executed. For Pattern II.b, the sending of oneway message Oneway SC1 by the server application could be used as the signal that the server is done processing the previous oneway message.

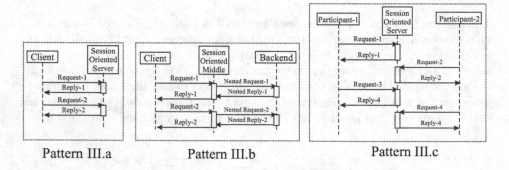

Pattern III.a   Pattern III.b   Pattern III.c

Fig. 3. Session-oriented interaction patterns

4   Session-Oriented Interaction Patterns

Many Web-based applications involve session-oriented interactions between each client and the server, as shown in patterns III.a and III.b in Figure 3, or between the server and a finite number of participants, as shown in pattern III.c in Figure 3.

Normally, the creation of a session is triggered by a request from a client or one of the participants (acting as the initiator). For multi-participant session-oriented interactions (in pattern III.c), participants must register with the server to join the session. All messages exchanged within a session carry a unique session identifier. Different sessions may share state, but only through the backend servers. Hence, the requests to the session-oriented server can be partitioned, *i.e.*, the requests that belong to different sessions can be handled in parallel. As argued in pattern I.b, the execution in different sessions will be synchronized at the backend server if some state is shared among these sessions.

In pattern III.a, each session involves a single client, hence, source ordering on the requests within the session is sufficient. In fact, it is unnecessary to ensure the Byzantine agreement on the identity of each request (*i.e.*, the same request is delivered to all non-faulty replicas) because the execution of conflicting requests sent by a faulty client would only impact the client itself and the corresponding session state, which is limited to this particular session. In pattern III.b, the session-oriented server interacts with the backend server in response to the client's request. Although source ordering on the requests is sufficient, all non-faulty replicas must reach a Byzantine agreement on which request is to be delivered.

In pattern III.c, multiple participants are involved in each session. Without any knowledge on application semantics, all requests sent to the server should be totally ordered and executed sequentially in the total order imposed. However, if it is known that some operations invoked by different participants are commutative, such as the registration and voting operations in a Web services atomic transaction [12], requests for these operations can be delivered immediately without imposing a total order among them except that Byzantine agreement on the identity of such messages is still needed.

The Byzantine agreement on the identity of a request requires less sophisticated mechanisms compared with the Byzantine agreement on message total ordering, because it can be done to each message individually without the concern of the relative ordering of different messages. Although the latency for the Byzantine agreement on the identity of a message would be similar to that on message total ordering during normal operation, the view change, if one is needed, could be faster because there is less information to be collected and carried over from one view to another. Furthermore, the Byzantine agreement on the identity of multiple messages can be batched together and piggybacked with other Byzantine agreement instances if it is allowed by the application semantics, which is indeed the case for Web services atomic transactions [12].

5   Multi-process Interaction Patterns

In all previous patterns, exploiting application semantics only offers better performance (*i.e.*, less runtime overhead for BFT). The patterns IV.a and IV.b shown in Figure 4 reveal that the application might not operate correctly (*e.g.*, a deadlock could occur) if the application semantics is not considered when multiple processes interact with each other in a peer-to-peer fashion.

Pattern IV.a illustrates a typical interaction involved in groupware applications [14] (*e.g.*, multiple users collaborate on the same document) where process-1 applies an update to a shared document and propagates the change to its collaborators process-2 and process-3, process-2 receives this update and applies further changes to the document, and disseminates the latest change to process-1 and process-3. Apparently the update notification-1 (from process-1) causally precedes the update notification-2 (from process-2) and the two notifications should be processed at process-3 in this causal order. However, without considering the application semantics, the ordering on these two notifications will

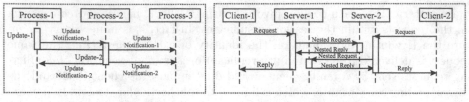

Pattern IV.a   Pattern IV.b

Fig. 4. Multi-process interaction patterns

be determined at the primary replica based on the time of arrival according to existing BFT algorithms. If the update notification-2 happens to arrive *before* notification-1, and the two messages are ordered that way, the changes made by process-1 would be lost, which would violate the intention of the application.

Pattern IV.b highlights an interaction pattern we observed in a distributed transaction application [13]. In response to the request from client-1, server-1 issues a nested invocation on server-2. At the same time, client-2 sends a request to server-2, which causes server-2 to issue a nested invocation on server-1. The application itself can cope with this situation because the nested invocation can be handled concurrently with the invocations from the clients. However, if all requests to each of the servers are to be totally ordered and executed sequentially in that total order, a deadlock would occur. To avoid the deadlock, application semantics must be considered so that the nested request is delivered before the previous request (from the client) is fully processed. However, it is non-trivial to determine when it is safe to deliver another request concurrently with the previous request, which requires further application semantics to determine the execution order rule.

6   Related Work

We are not aware of any other work that aims to compile a catalog of application interaction patterns in the context of Byzantine fault tolerance computing. A few research works [3, 4, 6, 8, 12], including our own [4, 12], have relied on specific interaction patterns in order to enable concurrent execution of some requests, and in some cases, reduce or avoid the use of totally ordering on some or all requests, for systems such as networked file/storage systems [3, 6, 8] and a number of Web services applications [4, 12]. However, none of the above work recognized the benefits of abstracting out the related interaction patterns and designing BFT solutions accordingly.

The most interesting work related to ours is [11]. The paper documented a list of communication patterns and workflow patterns for Web services composition. Asynchronous and synchronous communications are considered separately. Some communication patterns considered in [11] are identical to ours, such as those in the basic interaction patterns. However, some communication patterns such as publish-subscribe and broadcast, are not considered in our paper. We plan to enrich our set of patterns by incorporating these additional patterns introduced in [11].

7 Conclusion and Future Work

In this paper, we documented a set of application interaction patterns we have compiled so far, with limited analysis for each pattern. These include a number of basic interaction patterns, the oneway communication, and several session-oriented interaction patterns commonly used by most Web based applications, and also a number of multi-process interaction patterns used in more sophisticated systems such as the Web services transaction processing systems. We believe that these patterns would serve as an important foundation to carry out further work on the automation of application semantics discovery.

For future work, we are planning to compile more interaction patterns, and for each interaction pattern, to consider more detailed analysis on the possible scenarios. In particular, we will incorporate the communication patterns discussed in [11] and explore the possibility of combining both communication patterns and workflow patterns to capture more application semantics.

Acknowledgements. This work was supported in part by NSF grant CNS 08-21319, and by a CSUSI grant from Cleveland State University.

References

1. SOA best practices: The BPEL cookbook,
   http://www.oracle.com/technetwork/articles/soa/index-095969.html
2. Adya, A., Bolosky, W.J., Castro, M., Cermak, G., Chaiken, R., Douceur, J.R., Howell, J., Lorch, J.R., Theimer, M., Wattenhofer, R.P.: Farsite: Federated, available, and reliable storage for an incompletely trusted environment. In: Proceedings of the 5th Symposium on Operating Systems Design and Implementation, pp. 1–14 (2002)
3. Castro, M., Liskov, B.: Practical Byzantine fault tolerance and proactive recovery. ACM Transactions on Computer Systems 20(4), 398–461 (2002)
4. Chai, H., Zhang, H., Zhao, W., Melliar-Smith, P.M., Moser, L.E.: Toward trustworthy coordination for web service business activities. IEEE Transactions on Services Computing (to appear)
5. Clement, A., Wong, E., Alvisi, L., Dahlin, M.: Making Byzantine fault-tolerant systems tolerate Byzantine faults. In: Proceedings of the 6th Symposium on Networked Systems Design and Implementation, Boston, MA (2009)
6. Distler, T., Kapitza, R.: Increasing performance in Byzantine fault-tolerant systems with on-demand replica consistency. In: Proceedings of the Sixth Eurosys Conference (2011)
7. Etzion, O., Niblett, P.: Event Processing in Action. Manning Publications (2010)
8. Kotlan, R., Dahlin, M.: High throughput Byzantine fault tolerance. In: Proceedings of International Conference on Dependable Systems and Networks (2004)
9. Pallemulle, S., Thorvaldsson, G.K.: Byzantine fault-tolerant web services for n-tier and service oriented architectures. In: Proceedings of the 28th International Conference on Distributed Computing Systems (2008)
10. Rhea, S., Eaton, P., Geels, D., Weatherspoon, H., Zhao, B., Kubiatowicz, J.: Pond: The oceanstore prototype. In: Proceedings of the 2nd Conference on File and Storage Technologies, pp. 1–14 (2003)

11. Wohed, P., van der Aalst, W.M.P., Dumas, M., ter Hofstede, A.H.M.: Analysis of web services composition languages: The case of BPEL4WS. In: Song, I.-Y., Liddle, S.W., Ling, T.-W., Scheuermann, P. (eds.) ER 2003. LNCS, vol. 2813, pp. 200–215. Springer, Heidelberg (2003), http://eprints.qut.edu.au/1776/
12. Zhang, H., Chai, H., Zhao, W., Melliar-Smith, P.M., Moser, L.E.: Trustworthy coordination for web service atomic transactions. IEEE Transactions on Parallel and Distributed Systems 23, 1551–1565 (2012)
13. Zhao, W., Moser, L., Melliar-Smith, P.M.: Deterministic scheduling for multi-threaded replicas. In: Proceedings of the IEEE International Workshop on Object-oriented Real-time Dependable Systems, Sedona, AZ, pp. 74–81 (2005)
14. Zhao, W.: Concurrency control in real-time e-collaboration systems. In: Kock, N. (ed.) Encyclopedia of E-Collaboration, pp. 95–101. Idea Group Publishing (2008)
15. Zhao, W.: Design and implementation of a Byzantine fault tolerance framework for web services. Journal of Systems and Software 82, 1004–1015 (2009)

HTML5 Standards and Open API Mashups for the Web of Things

Si-Ho Cha[1] and Yoemun Yun[2,*]

[1] Dept. of Multimedia Science, Chungwoon University
Daehakgil-25, Hongseong, Chungnam, 350-701, South Korea
[2] Dept. of Applied Music, Chungwoon University
Daehakgil-25, Hongseong, Chungnam, 350-701, South Korea
{shcha,hippie740}@chungwoon.ac.kr

Abstract. This paper describes why the Web of Things is required and how HTML5 technologies and Open API mashups can be used for the Web of Things. The Web of Things is to use Web technologies to provide value-added services through communications between smart things or between them and their users. Today, consumer electronics (electronic things) is closely related to our lives, and are becoming increasingly smart. However, these things should be able to easy access to provide services that users want, rather than smart independently. Problem is can't to create interactive applications to easily combine the various heterogeneous things. HTML5 Web standards and Open APIs mashups can provide the develop methods that are simple, lightweight, loosely-coupled, scalable, and flexible for developing those applications.

Keywords: The Web of Things, HTML5, WebSocket, REST, Open API Mashups, M2M.

1 Introduction

ITU-T (International Telecommunication Union-Telecommunication Standardization Sector) predicted that it will be possible using a variety of services through sending or receiving information between persons as well as things on the future Internet by the report "the Internet of Things [1]" in 2005. Today, a large number of different means are used to enable communication between heterogeneous devices. In general, they are referred to as the Internet of Things or machine-to-machine (M2M). The Internet of Things refers to uniquely identifiable objects (things) and their virtual representations in an Internet-like structure [2]. The Internet of Things has usually focused on establishing connectivity in various challenging and constrained networking environments. M2M is the technology that establishes intelligent communication between things.

Many efforts are currently going towards networking smart things from the physical world (e.g. RFID, wireless sensor and actuator networks, embedded devices)

---

* Corresponding author.

T.-h. Kim et al. (Eds.): SIP/WSE/ICHCI 2012, CCIS 342, pp. 189–194, 2012.

on a larger scale [3]. In particular, the Internet of Things has essentially explored the development of applications built upon various networked physical objects [3]. Because there is no standard protocol for accessing dedicated sets of functionality of each object, the development of applications controlling for each protocol is really impossible. Those objects can't be controlled without using dedicated applications and proprietary protocols. For this reason, M2M is still suffering from the limitations. As a consequence, smart things (objects) are hard to integrate into the Internet of Things. Web technologies (e.g. browsers, caching systems, protocols) and languages (e.g. HTML, JavaScript, mashups) provide accessible from anywhere, at any time, easy to install and upgrade, simple to use, comprehensive, lightweight, non-restrictive, and flexible way to integrate smart things efficiently.

The Web of Things is to use Web technologies to provide value-added services through communications between smart things or between them and their users on the upper layer of the Internet of Things. In the Web of Things, smart things are inhabitants of the Web. Therefore, the Web of Things is a special case of the Internet of Things by integrating smart things not only to the Internet, but also to the Web. REST is actually core to the Web and uses URIs for encapsulating and identifying services on the Web. In its Web implementation it also uses HTTP as a true application protocol. It finally decouples services from their presentation and provides mechanisms for clients to select the best possible formats. This makes REST an ideal candidate to build an "universal" API for smart things [3]. This paper describes why we need the Web of Things and the mashups HTML5 technologies and Open APIs that can be used in the Web of Things for smart things. This paper also shows that HTML5 Web standards and Open APIs mashups can provide the develop methods that are simple, lightweight, loosely-coupled, scalable, and flexible for developing those applications.

The rest of the paper is organized as follows. Section 2 discusses related works to this paper, and Section 3 introduces HTML5 Web standards and Open APIs mashups for the Web of Things. Finally, in Section 4, conclusions are made including the future research.

2   Related Works

The advantages of the Web are quick and easy updates, reach anybody and anywhere, available anytime and cross-platform, always up-to-date, zero install, and reduce business costs.

Y.2002 [4] that is the ITU-T Recommendation of the Internet of Things has been specified open Web-based service environment as one of the core competencies to support a ubiquitous networking. The Web of Things is a special case of the Internet of Things and it is to use Web technologies to incorporate smart things to the Web. This linking of physical things to the Web is not a new idea. An early approach was to provide a virtual counterpart of the physical things on the Web. And another approach was to embed Web servers on the physical things [5]. JXTA is a set of open protocols for allowing devices to collaborate in a peer-to-peer fashion, and was eventually the first attempt to bridge the physical thing world over the Internet [3]. Web services (SOAP, WSDL, etc.) were proposed to deploy them on embedded devices and sensor networks [6]. Current approaches are to apply the REST (Representational State Transfer) style to the physical world. The essence of REST is to focus on creating loosely coupled services on the Web so that they can be easily reused [7]. The motivation for REST was to capture the characteristics of the Web which made the Web successful. Subsequently these characteristics are being used to guide the evolution of the Web. REST is actually core to the Web and uses URIs for encapsulating and identifying services on the Web [3]. Central to the RESTful architecture is the concept of resources identified by universal resource identifiers (URIs). These resources can be manipulated using a standard interface, such as HTTP, and information is exchanged using representations of these resources [8].

WebSocket [9] enables the HTML5-based monitoring system to monitor WSNs in electronic engineering directly over the Web. The WebSocket is a web technology providing for bi-directional, full-duplex communications channels, over a single Transmission Control Protocol (TCP) socket giving clients and servers a simple way to communicate over a persistent stream without the need for third-party plugins or hacks. Additionally, it serves a purpose for Web applications that require real-time bi-directional communication.

3   New Technologies for the Web of Things

The advantages of the Web are quick and easy updates, reach anybody and anywhere, available anytime and cross-platform, always up-to-date, zero install, and reduce business costs. The Web of Things [10] is about re-using the Web standards to connect the quickly expanding eco-system of embedded devices built into everyday smart objects. To accomplish the Web of Things, we can use REST, HTML5 standard technologies and Open API meshups.

3.1   REST

Recent developments in the Web of Things show that existing methods such as XML-RPC and SOAP-based web services don't cover all available web services. One alternative is REST (Representational State Transfer). REST is to describe an architecture style of networked systems [11]. The Web is comprised of resources. A resource is any item of interest. REST is intended to evoke an image of how a well-designed Web application behaves: a network of web pages (a virtual state-machine), where the user progresses through an application by selecting links (state transitions), resulting in the next page (representing the next state of the application) being transferred to the user and rendered for their use [11]. REST-enabled devices would not require any additional API or descriptions of resources/functions. It does not deal with implementation details (e.g., using JavaServlet or CGI to implement a Web service). Here are the characteristics of REST [12]:

- Client-Server: a pull-based interaction style: consuming components pull representations.
- Stateless: each request from client to server must contain all the information necessary to understand the request, and cannot take advantage of any stored context on the server.
- Cache: to improve network efficiency responses must be capable of being labeled as cacheable or non-cacheable.
- Uniform interface: all resources are accessed with a generic interface (e.g., HTTP GET, POST, PUT, and DELETE).
- Named resources - the system is comprised of resources which are named using a URL.
- Interconnected resource representations - the representations of the resources are interconnected using URLs, thereby enabling a client to progress from one state to another.
- Layered components - intermediaries, such as proxy servers, cache servers, gateways, etc, can be inserted between clients and resources to support performance, security, etc.

RESTful web services are services built using the RESTful architectural style. Building web services using the RESTful approach is emerging as a popular alternative to using SOAP-based technologies for deploying services on the internet, due to its lightweight nature and the ability to transmit data directly over HTTP.

3.2   HTML5 Standards

Most of the existing Web-based approaches use HTTP to transport data between devices. HTTP is half duplex, and functions as a request-response protocol in the client-server computing model. In HTTP, a browser acts as a client, while an application running on a computer hosting a Web site functions as a server [13]. Ajax is a group of interrelated web development techniques used on the client-side to create asynchronous web applications. With Ajax, web applications can send data to, and retrieve data from, a server asynchronously without interfering with the display and behavior of the existing page. Data is usually retrieved using the XMLHttpRequest object.

WebSocket [9] technology provides similar functionality to regular connections to the web with some additional protocol overhead while multiplexing several WebSocket services over a single TCP port. Before the implementation of WebSocket, such bi-directional communication was only possible using Comet channels; however, a Comet is not trivial to implement reliably, and due to the TCP handshake and HTTP header overhead, it may be inefficient for small messages [14]. However, WebSocket is a web technology providing for bi-directional, full-duplex communications channels, over a single TCP socket giving clients and servers a simple way to communicate over a persistent stream without the need for third-party plugins or hacks. Additionally, it serves a purpose for Web applications that require real-time bi-directional communication. WebSocket requires its own backend application to communicate with (server side). Therefore, Node.js is used to develop WebSocket server. Node.js [15] is a platform built on Chrome's JavaScript runtime for easily building fast, scalable network applications. Node.js uses an event-driven, non-blocking I/O model that makes it lightweight and efficient, perfect for data-intensive real-time applications that run across distributed devices. Node.js itself doesn't have support for WebSocket but there are already some plugins that implement WebSocket protocols.

We can use Canvas API, Geolocation API, Chart API, and various other new techniques of the HTML5 standards to represent data from physical world, easily and efficiently. In the Web of Things, embedded devices can be interacted with WebSocket API and their status and functions can be monitored on Canvas through Geolocation and Chart APIs. Canvas API provides scripts with a resolution-dependent bitmap canvas, which can be used for rendering graphs, or other visual images on the fly. The Canvas enables the Web browser to natively manipulate, compose, and layer image, video, and chart data. The Geolocation API defines a high-level interface to location information associated only with the device hosting the implementation, such as latitude and longitude. We can perform the deployment of smart things and the configuration management of them through mash-up of the Geolocation API and Google Maps API. RGraph [16] is a HTML5 JavaScript Charts library to represent the data gathered from smart things. RGraph is supports over 20 different types of JavaScript based charts. Using the HTML5 Canvas tag, RGraph creates these charts in the Web browser, meaning quicker pages and less Web server load.

3.3   Mashup Service

In the Web of Things, embedded devices or consumer electronics are connected by fully integrating them to the Web. Fig. 1 shows the basic model that the Web of Things is applied to various smart things [17]. In terms of applications, each thing is only shown a Web resource or service. Therefore, the things are accessed and exploited through Web technologies. As shown in Fig. 1, the Web of Things should provide with desired services through the mashup services to prepare proper services for various smart things and/or users.

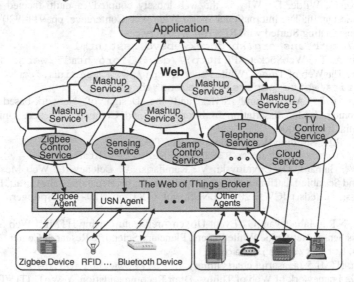

Fig. 1. Applying model of the Web of Things [17]

4   Conclusion

In this paper, we described new technologies for the Web of Things such as REST, HTML5 standards, and Open API mashups. RESTful architectures are becoming one of the most ubiquitous and lightweight integration architecture. And by utilizing the WebSocket, Canvas, Geolocation, Chart, and various other new techniques provided by HTML5, the Web of Things can be implemented in with the loose-coupling, simplicity, and scalability. The advantages offered by introducing support for HTML5 standards directly at the device-level are beneficial for developing a new generation of networked devices that are much simpler to program and reuse. Furthermore, as most mobile things such as Smartphone have already Web connectivity and Web browsers, and most programming languages support HTTP, HTML5 standards and Open APIs can provide the Web of Things.

References

1. ITU-T: the Internet of Things – Executive Summary. Internet Report (2005)
2. Wikipedia: Internet of Things,
   http://en.wikipedia.org/wiki/Internet_of_Things
3. Guinard, D., Trifa, V., Wilde, E.: Architecting a Mashable Open World Wide Web of Things. Technical Report No. 663, Department of Computer Science, ETH Zurich (2010)
4. ITU-T: Overview of Ubiquitous Networking and of Its Support in NGN. Y.2002 (2009)
5. Duquennoy, S., Grimaud, G., Vandewalle, J.-J.: The Web of Things: Interconnecting Devices with High Usability and Performance. In: The International Conference on Embedded Software and System (ICESS 2009), pp. 323–330 (2009)
6. Priyantha, N.B., Kansal, A., Goraczko, M., Zhao, F.: Tiny Web Services: Design and Implementation of Interoperable and Evolvable Sensor Networks. In: The ACM Conference on Embedded Network Sensor System, pp. 253–266 (2008)
7. Pautasso, C., Wilde, E.: Why is the web loosely coupled? a multi-faceted metric for service design. In: The International World Wide Web Conference, pp. 911–920 (2009)
8. NetBeans: Getting Started with RESTful Web Services,
   http://netbeans.org/kb/docs/websvc/rest.html
9. Hickson, A.: The WebSocket API, http://dev.w3.org/html5/websockets/
10. Tridium: The Web of Things. White Paper, http://www.tridium.com/galleries/white_papers/WP-SedonaWeb.pdf
11. Fielding, R.T.: Architectural Styles and the Design of Network-based Software Architectures. Ph.D. dissertation in Information and Computer Science, University of California, Irvine (2000)
12. Costello, R.L.: Building Web Services the REST Way,
    http://www.xfront.com/REST-Web-Services.html
13. Trifa, V., Guinard, D., Davidovski, V., Kamilaris, A., Delchev, I.: Web Messaging for Open and Scalable Distributed Sensing Applications. In: Benatallah, B., Casati, F., Kappel, G., Rossi, G. (eds.) ICWE 2010. LNCS, vol. 6189, pp. 129–143. Springer, Heidelberg (2010)
14. Swamy, N.R., Mahadevan, G.: Event Driven Architecture using HTML5 Web Sockets for Wireless Sensor Networks. White Papers, Planetary Scientific Research Center (2011)
15. Node.js, http://nodejs.org/
16. RGraph: HTML5 Javascript charts library, http://www.rgraph.net/
17. In, M.G.: Framework of Web of Things. Draft Recommendation, Y.WoT, ITU-T (2011)

Effectiveness of Web-Based Instruction for Creativity Education in University Student

Kyung-hwa Lee[1] and Kyoung-hoon Lew[2,*]

[1] Dept. of Lifelong Education, SoongSil University
511 Sangdo-dong, Dongjak-Gu, Seoul, 156-743,
Republic of Korea
[2] Graduate School of Education, SoongSil Univ.
511 Sangdo-dong, Dongjak-Gu, Seoul, 156-743,
Republic of Korea
Lewkh@ssu.ac.kr

Abstract. The purpose of this research was to analyze the creative thinking ability of university students in web-based instruction. Up to now the subject 'Creativity and Problem-solving' has been lectured face-to-face in a class as a general education curriculum, but it was developed newly as a web based online lecture. And after conducting it for a semester, the effectiveness of this lecture on the improvement of the creative thinking ability of university students was validated. The participants were 176 university students who were selected among the classes for creativity conducted at Seoul area in Korea. The creativity test was developed to measure the participants' creative thinking ability, and the collected data were analyzed by t-test. The results showed that the creative thinking ability with 6 sub-factors were not significantly different between two groups. In addition, the methods of the creativity classes significantly influenced on creative thinking ability. The result of this research implies the direction for creativity education in future.

Keywords: Creative thinking ability, university student, web-based instruction, face-to-face lecture, t-test.

1 Introduction

The ability to generate novel and useful ideas and solutions to everyday problems is an important competence of creativity (Amabile, 1996; Sternberg & O'Hara, 1999; Sternberg, 2004). Social and cultural environment where creativity can be expressed out is very important to produce creative outputs. Therefore, creativity can be defined as an ability of an individual, integrated with his or her character, to create products new, unique and appropriate to contemporary situation.

Guilford(1967) considered creativity as an intellectual ability and a thinking process that needs divergent thinking. He suggested sensitivity to problem, fluent of thinking, originality, elaboration and redefinition as its components.

---

* Corresponding author.

T.-h. Kim et al. (Eds.): SIP/WSE/ICHCI 2012, CCIS 342, pp. 195–202, 2012.
© Springer-Verlag Berlin Heidelberg 2012

Torrance defined that 'creative thinking ability is the aggregation of generalized spiritual ability deemed to be working when making a creative achievement. He suggested fluent of thinking, flexibility, originality and elaboration as the subsets of creative thinking.

Runco(2004) asserts that creativity develops and creative behavior can be developed through education. He emphasizes that there is difference in creativity between childhood and adulthood, but creativity education is very important and it should be conducted in different ways (Sternberg & Lubart, 1999). It is also noticeable that enterprises are demanding more creative talents as the era of creativity-based competition comes. Thus, university education is also requested to be changed according to such change in enterprise culture and competition system. Especially the creative education for university students has a tendency to emphasize its role as one of basic elements of employment and to consider creativity as an individual ability essential to perform tasks in enterprises. This tendency can be verified through the fact that recently many enterprises are requesting creativity and problem-solving ability in their recruiting process for new employees.

Rose and Lin(1984); Scott, Leritz and Mumford(2004) made a meta-analysis on the experiments related to creativity improvement and found creativity could be improved. Many of scholars in Korea also made positive reports to support this in their researches (Lew & Park, 2009). Regarding the education for university students, there are researches conducted by Baek(2006), Lee and Lew(2010) and Lee, Lew and Kim(2012) but the effectiveness of the education was all measured only for face-to-face lectures in classes. Considering the fact that such class for creativity education can accommodate up to 30 to 60 students only (Baek, 2006; Lee & Lew, 2011). it is deemed to be necessary to review and make an innovative change in the methods for creativity education so as to make the education effective to more students.

Modern society has been changed rapidly by the development of scientific technology. Especially the advancement of information & communication technology has made a significant and overall impact on our society. Web-based learning enables not only the simultaneous interaction of the conventional lecturing system or face-to-face lectures in class but also non-simultaneous interaction beyond time and space and, above all, it has an advantage of accommodating many students simultaneously without any limit of education space. Web-based instruction (WBI) is a hypermedia-based teaching method that utilizes the characteristics of the Web and the materials provided through the Web(Kahn, 1997). In this research, it means the teaching activity performed under the Web environment with a Web-based teaching program developed by the authors of this research. The characteristics of contemporary university students can be called as a net-work(N) generation, and according to Tapscott(1999), N generation has an attitude to accept diversity, curiosity for various aspects, solid self-assertiveness and strong dependence. Especially they are excellent in computer-assisted learning ability, good at manipulating a mouse and well developed in their identity so that they prefer to learn by themselves rather than through teacher's explanation and show a tendency to think logically.

In this research, a WBI program was developed and applied for the creativity education of university students in order to investigate whether there could be any difference in the development of creative thinking ability between WBI lecture and face-to-face lecture. At this point in time that most of creativity educations are conducted with face-to-face lectures and seldom with Web-based teaching programs, the result of this research shall be able to give an implication to the application of onsite teaching formats that can improve the creativity of university students.

For this research, after establishing a WBI class 'Creativity and Problem-solving', following research subject was selected to investigate how different this WBI is from existing face-to-face lecture.

Research subject is as follow. Is the WBI class 'Creativity and Problem-solving' effective in improving the creativity of university students?

2   Method

2.1   Participants

The participants of this research were 176 university students from first to fourth graders, who were selected among the students of "Creativity & Problem-solving" class. WBI students were 124(67 males and 55 females) and face-to-face lecture students were 52(30 males and 22 females).

2.2   Instruments

Group Integrative Creative Test. Korean-Type Creative thinking ability test developed by Lee & Lew(2012). It tests creative thinking ability with 5 questions for six-factors (fluency, flexibility, originality, imagination, sensitivity, elaboration). Each sub-factor's score is up to 10 and the total score of the scale ranges from 0 to 60. Higher score means more creative thinking ability level.

This experiment, which has been developed to be used for from elementary school students to adults, can measure both creative thinking ability and creative personality. But only creative thinking ability was selected and measured in this research, and the grading for the experiment was conducted directly by these researchers. The Cronbach's Alpha of this experiment was .896.

In this research, fluency of thinking was .57, flexibility .68, originality .48, imagination .81, sensitivity to problem .58, elaboration .66 and total Cronbach's Alpha was .823.

2.3   Procedure

The experiment was conducted for 16 weeks during the first semester of 2011 and the design of experiments and lecture content are shown in <Table 1> and <Table 2>..

Table 1. Design of experiments

group	pre-test	experiment	post-test
G_1	O_1	X_1	O_2
G_2	O_1	X_2	O_2

G1: experimental group/ G2 : control group
O1, O2: creativity test
X_1: WBI / X_2: Face-to-face lecture

'Creativity and Problem-solving' WBI class development

The lecture goal, process and content of the class 'Creativity and Problem-solving' in the WBI class that this research made experiment on and the face-to-face lecture are as follows;

Table 2. Developed WBI course

week	Key sentence	contents
1	What is creativity?	Understand the concept of creativity and elements of creativity.
2	Who is creative person?	Analyze and understand oneself through the activity to check own creativity and multi-intelligence.
3	How can we develop creativity?	Know various teaching-learning models to develop creativity and actually utilize them.
4	What is creative thinking skill?	Understand creative thinking skill and practice applying it to real life.
5	Creative thinking method 1	• practice (1) – Brain Storming, Brain Writing
6	Creative thinking method 2	• practice (2) – SCAMPER, Synectics
7	Creative thinking method 3	• practice (3) - Lotus, SixThinking Hats
8	Developmental trends of Creativity.	Growth of creativity for adult and child
9	Art & Creativity	Find creative ideas through art works and movies.
10	Creative Problem Solving(CPS) 1	Stage 1: Fact Finding, Problem Finding
11	CPS-2	Stage 2: Idea Finding, Solution Finding
12	CPS-3	Stage 3: Acceptance Finding, Presentation
13	Finding creativity in product	Find creativity in music, art, movie, literature.
14	Finding creativity in life	Find creative ideas, creative products, creative activities in daily life.

2.4   Data Analysis

Data was collected during the period from September 1, 2011 to December 14, 2011. The researcher explained the purpose of this survey to the participants. Data analysis was carried out by using SPSS WIN 17.0 program.

First, after descriptive statistics (Mean, standardize deviation), t-test was carried out for the gap of creative thinking ability pre-test between two groups. Second, t-test was carried out for the gap of creative thinking ability post-test between two groups. Third, t-test was carried out for the gap of creative thinking ability pre-test and post-test between two groups.

3   Results

3.1   Homogeneity Test of Creative Thinking Ability Pre-test

The result of difference of the total creative thinking ability level between two groups is as follows. The result of t-test for the technical statistics (M, SD) of creative thinking ability pre-test on the experimental group and control group showed no significant difference between these two groups.

Table 3. Difference of creative thinking ability scores between two groups

sub-factors	WBI group (N= 124)	FtoF group (N= 52)	t
fluency	5.15(1.38)	5.06(1.48)	.452
elaboration	3.35(1.49)	3.23(1.59)	.678
flexibility	4.42(1.39)	4.65(1.33)	.798
originality	4.03(1.38)	4.35(1.18)	1.01
sensitivity	3.85(1.27)	3.90(1.47)	.652
imagination	3.66(1.61)	3.64(1.51)	.348
total	24.46(5.29)	24.83(5.99)	.692

3.2   Homogeneity Test of Creative Thinking Ability Post-test

In ordered to evaluate the efficacy of lectures between the experimental group (WBI lecture) that took the class of creativity for a semester (16 weeks) and the control group (Face-to-face lecture), the average difference of post-test was investigated. The result is shown in <table 4> and <Table 5>.

3.3   Comparison of Creativity Improvement by Group

The result of t-test showed that the post creative ability score had a significant difference (p<.05) between the experimental group and the control group in several sub-factors. Further analysis on the result of this research showed that the prior and post creative thinking ability had a significant difference between two groups in fluent of thinking, originality and sensitivity to problem. It was also found that the ability to express various ideas could be improved through the classes for creativity.

Table 4. Technical statistics of creativity post-test by group

sub-factors	experiment group (N= 124)	control group (N= 52)	t
fluency	7.72(1.48)	7.77(1.42)	.870
elaboration	3.38(1.37)	3.30(1.41)	.664
flexibility	4.45(1.25)	4.64(1.38)	1.432
originality	6.03(1.52)	6.75(1.38)	1.212
sensitivity	5.75(1.37)	5.70(1.37)	.240
imagination	4.01(1.30)	3.97(1.47)	.146
total	31.3(5.38)	32.13(6.23)	.692

Table 5. Difference of creative thinking ability

	Group	Pre-test	Post-test	t
fluency	Experimental(N= 124)	5.15(1.38)	7.72(1.48)	2.40**
	Control(N= 52)	5.06(1.48)	7.77(1.42)	2.43**
originality	Experimental(N= 124)	4.03(1.38)	6.03(1.52)	3.50***
	Control(N= 52)	4.35(1.18)	6.75(1.38)	4.17***
sensitivity	Experimental(N= 124)	3.85(1.27)	5.75(1.37)	3.72**
	Control(N= 52)	3.90(1.47)	5.70(1.37)	3.03**

** $p < .01$, *** $p < .001$

The result of t-test on prior originality and post originality showed a significant difference in prior and post score of the groups. It was also found that the ability to create unique and ingenious ideas could be significantly improved through a training to exercise absorbing thoughts of other students and creating own ideas.

Such result is identical with the result of the research conducted by Firestein & Lunken(1993), Baek et al.(2006) and Lee & Lew(2011) who reported that creativity had been improved after the lecture for creativity.

4   Conclusions

In this research an experiment was conducted to verify whether the creativity of university students could be improved through WBI lecture for creativity and the conclusion based on the result is as follows;

First, WBI class 'Creativity and Problem-solving' was effective in improving the creativity of university students and particularly fluent of thinking and originality were significantly improved. This result is identical to the result that fluent of thinking, originality and elaboration were significantly improved in the experiment of

Baek et al.(2006) carried out through the classes for creativity in association with the classes for major subjects of engineering department students. In the class-room instruction of Lee & Lew(2011), fluent of thinking and originality were improved and originality is a creativity element that belongs to the high level in creativity sector. It is deemed that if students are given with various substantial missions to collect various ideas and make presentations for them together with classes for theory every week, the classes are carried out in a way to share such output together and such experiences stimulate them to expand their way of expressing unique and new ideas. Bull, Montgomery & Balloche (1995) also emphasized that treating the outputs related to insight or innovation would be important when carrying out lectures for creativity.

The activities to suggest several subjects and make students discuss about them might have helped the improvement in fluent of thinking. In the classes, various creativity techniques were explained to students and they were asked to perform the activities actually, from which the students felt the effectiveness in developing their ideas.

This research showed that the WBI class 'Creativity and Problem-solving' for university students were very effective to the improvement of creativity. In general, face-to-face lecture for creativity education in a class-room is effective but it turned out that also WBI class for creativity education would improve creativity.

For university students, it would not be easy to take the class for creativity because they have to study their own major subjects. However, creative problem-solving ability in their major sector or in their life would be very essential ability and even enterprises are now beginning to consider creative thinking ability as one of the essential abilities for new employee. Therefore, university institutions have to review the establishment and operation of WBI class for creativity education and execute it for many students as soon as possible.

This research might have its limit in the fact that a class for creativity was developed simply in WBI and the selection of students for the experiment was not random. In addition, there need researches to investigate the effectiveness of creativity lecture not only for creative thinking ability but also including creative personality factor.

References

1. Amabile, T.M.: Creativity in context: Update to the social psychology of creativity. Boulder, Co., Westview (1996)
2. Baek, Y.S., et al.: Achievements in the Creativity Education through Freshmen Engineering Design. Journal of Educational Technology 9(2), 5–20 (2006)
3. Bull, K.S., Montgomery, D., Baloche, L.: Teaching creativity at the college level: A synthesis of curricular components perceived as important by instructors. Creativity Research Journal 8(1), 83–89 (1995)
4. Tapscott, D.: Growing Up Digital: The Rise of the Net Generation. McGraw-Hill Companies, Inc. (1999)

5. Firestein, R.L., Lunken, H.P.: Assessment of the long term effects of the master of science degree in creative studies. Journal of Creative Behavior 27(3), 188–199 (1993)
6. Guilford, J.P.: The nature of human intelligence. McGrow-Hill, NewYork (1967)
7. Kahn, B.H.: Web-based insruction (WBI): Whatis it and why is it? In: Khan, B.H. (ed.) Web-based Instruction, pp. 5–8. Educational Technology Publications, NJ (1997)
8. Lee, K.H., Lew, K.H., Kim, E.K.: Creative thinking ability of university students. Korean Society for Creativity Education 12(1), 29–47 (2012)
9. Lee, K.H., Lew, K.H.: The Effect of Creative Instruction on the Creativity of University Students. The Journal of Korean Society for the Gifted and Talented 9(3), 5–20 (2010)
10. Lee, K.H., Lew, K.H.: Development and Standardization of Group Integrative Creative Test for Korean Elementary schools and Middle/high schools Students. The Korean Journal of Educational Psychology 26(1), 1–15 (2012)
11. Lew, K.H., Park, S.H.: The Effect of Verbal Feedback on Improving the Creative Thinking Ability and Creative Personality. The Journal of Korean Society for the Gifted and Talented 8(3), 133–150 (2009)
12. Rose, L.H., Lin, H.T.: The meta-analysis of long term creativity training programs. Journal of Creative Behavior 18, 11–22 (1984)
13. Runco, M.A.: Creativity. Annual Review of Psychology 55, 657–687 (2004)
14. Scott, G., Leritz, L.E., Mumford, M.D.: The effectiveness of creativity training: A quantitative review. Creativity Research Journal 16(4), 361–388 (2004)
15. Sternberg, R.J., Lubart, T.I.: The concept of creativity: Prospect and paradigms. In: Sternberg, R.J. (ed.) Handbook of Creativity. Cambridge University Press, New York (1999)
16. Sternberg, R.J., O'Hara, L.: Creativity and intelligence. In: Sternberg, R.J. (ed.) Handbook of Creativity, pp. 251–272. Cambridge University Press (1999)
17. Sternberg, R.J.: Wisdom, Intelligence and Creativity. Cambridge University Press (2003)

Sensor Web for Supporting Mobility in Sensor Networks

Chang-Hong Park[1], Jungwon Cho[2], and Do-Hyeun Kim[1,*]

[1] Dept. of Computer Engineering, Jeju National University, Jeju, Republic of Korea
kimdh@jejunu.ac.kr
[2] Dept. of Computer Education, Jeju National University, Jeju, Republic of Korea
jwcho@jejunu.ac.kr

Abstract. The sensor web supports finding, accessing and controlling repositories by utilizing data collecting devices such as conventional sensors, cameras and measuring equipment and those data collected from them. Sensor web is designed to store, manage and provide sensing data on the basis of sensor network for users on the internet. Accordingly, this paper presents mobile sensor web to support mobility of sensor node in sensor networks. We provide the context information of mobile sensor node included RFID tag, sensor, GPS, camera on web service. In future, this study will become the basic reference system for supporting mobile ubiquitous service.

Keywords: Mobility, Sensor Web, Sensor Networks.

1 Introduction

Recently, advanced information technology have led to the conceptualized notion of a "web" of sensors, interconnected and interacting with one another to provide observations and measurements of geophysical phenomena, and routing data. This concept is sensor web. The sensor web is an emerging trend which makes various types of web-resident sensors, instruments, image devices, and repositories of sensor data, discoverable, accessible, and controllable via the World Wide Web. A lot of effort has been invested in order to overcome the obstacles associated with connecting and sharing these heterogeneous sensor resources[1][2].

The sensor web standard defined by the Open Geospatial Consortium (OGC), that we call the Sensor Web Enablement (SWE)[3]. The SWE has a number of standards that define formats for sensor data and metadata as well as sensor service interfaces. SWE consists of a set of standard services to build a unique and revolutionary framework for discovering and interacting with web-connected sensors and for assembling and utilizing sensor networks on the Web. SensorMap is a portal web site for real-time real-world sensor data. The SensorMap at Microsoft Research aims to address these challenges by providing a research web portal and a set of tools for data owners to easily publish their data and users to make useful queries over the live data sources[4].

---

* Corresponding author.

T.-h. Kim et al. (Eds.): SIP/WSE/ICHCI 2012, CCIS 342, pp. 203–208, 2012.
© Springer-Verlag Berlin Heidelberg 2012

Existed sensor web does not support mobility of sensor node for roaming sensor networks. This paper proposes the mobile sensor web architecture of effective collecting context data and distributing to the business application services based on large-scale sensor networks.

The rest of this paper is structured as follows. In Section 2, we detail the related work of the sensor web. In Section 3, we describe our proposed mobile sensor web and show how our design addresses. Finally we conclude in Section 4.

2   Related Works

The Open Geospatial Consortium (OGC) develops the geospatial standards that will make the sensor web vision a reality. OGC have been centered to research sensor web so far. The sensor web concept is at least one generation beyond the popular sensor network, which is a relatively straight forward interconnection of sensors that route measurements to a central data collection point. OGC suggests open sensor web structure in which sensor web research based on sensor network. There are five specifications suggested, and two of the specifications are sensor ML (sensor model language) and O&M (observation and measurement) in terms of XML data specification. The other three specifications suggest SCS (Sensor Collections Service), SPS (Sensor Planning Service) and WNS (Web Notification Service) in terms of behavior specification. Open sensor web structure which suggested by OGC is shown figure 1 as below[3].

Also, GeoICT Research Lab in OGC implement project relevant to open sensor web structure. The ongoing project collects data such as the amount of rainfall, humidity, temperature, velocity, direction of the wind and air pressure through wireless sensor network and shows it on the web.

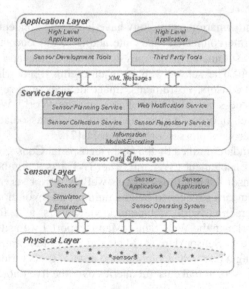

Fig. 1. OGC's open sensor web structure [3]

Also, GeoICT Research Lab in OGC implement project relevant to open sensor web structure. The research to visualize data collected by sensor network on the internet is in the progress by Sensor Map of Microsoft[4]. To geography simulator, GIS 3D technique is used to provide better GUI interface to implement real geographical features. Information collected by sensor network is provided through web page as following figure 2.

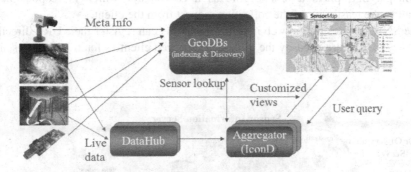

Fig. 2. Relation map of SensorMap components [4]

SensorMap system is consists of four components – GeoDB, DataHub, IconD and SenseWeb Client. GeoDB contains sensor device information such as sensor type, data rate, sensor owner, and visualization option, not data which collected by sensor. Data hub supports interface that provide collected data by sensor network as web service or interface that store data in data base. IconD is aimed for generating icon and query in server. Consequently, it generates icon which is shown in sensor web interface. SenseWeb is web client developed by Window Live Local mashup technology to process inquiries from users. Information provided by Sensor Map is the data collected by wireless sensor network, traffic report, local data and environmental information [4].

3   A Proposed Mobile Sensor Web

The mobile sensor web platform consists of the following four components (Figure 3): a Sensor Name Server (SNS) indexes the data so that it can be queried efficiently. SNS includes the location manager which support a mobility of sensor node based on sensor web in sensor networks. The Sensor Information Server (SIS) provides information of sensor node and real-time sensor data. The Sensor Provider Server (SPS) supports the sensor GUI that lets users query data sources and view results on the map. A Sensor Observation Server (SOS) is used to fetch observations from a sensor or a constellation of sensors.

The SOS is the fundamental and unique component that needs to communicate directly with sensor networks, which is responsible for collecting real time sensing data and then translating the raw information. In other words, SOS is the middleware for entering into the sensor networks from outside clients.

The SIS is a database housing sensor metadata and real-time sensing data. The metadata includes information such as sensor node name, sensor location, sensor name, sensor type, data type, unit, etc.

The SPS is intended to provide an interface to handle asset management that uses and manages available information sources (sensors, sensor platforms) in order to collect sensing data. SPS supports a representing sensor data that can be mashed up with maps. SPS plays a crucial role as a coordinator which is responsible for evaluating the feasibility of the collection request from the client.

The SNS provides public web interfaces, and this can register their URL directly to SIS. These URLs are used by the mobile sensor web client to fetch real-time sensing data.

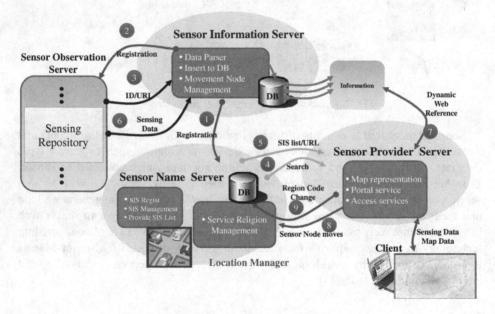

Fig. 3. Proposed mobile sensor web configuration

We propose sequence diagram of real-time mobile sensor web for supporting mobility of sensor nodes on map. Figure 4 illustrates how the client can be used in order to achieve real-time mobile sensing data using search functionality. Figure 4 depicts a sequence diagram that shows a client access the SPS to display a sensing data of mobile sensor nodes, the SPS can request SNS for discovering the SIS. The SNS checks the activity of the SIS and then returns directory list. The client searches PoI(Point of Interest) and sensor node and select the URL and IP port number of registered SIS. If a client requests sensing data of mobile sensor node, the SPS access the SNS to discovery mobile sensor node.

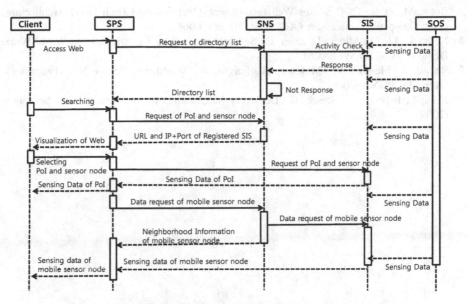

Fig. 4. Proposed sequence diagram for real-time mobile sensor web

4   Conclusions

The sensor web is an emerging trend which makes various types of web-resident sensors, instruments, image devices, and repositories of sensor data, discoverable, accessible, and controllable via the World Wide Web. A lot of effort has been invested in order to overcome the obstacles associated with connecting and sharing these heterogeneous sensor resources. However, there is still one challenge left that has to be addressed within this context: the mobility of sensors and SWE services. In this paper, we propose the real-time mobile sensor web for displaying to user various context information on Internet Web based on map. It will be an important basis for further developments and approaches in the context of mobile sensor web.

Acknowledgments. This work was supported by the Industrial Strategic Technology Development Program funded by the Ministry of Knowledge Economy (MKE, Korea). [10038653, Development of Semantic based Open USN Service Platform]. This work was supported by the National Research Foundation of Korea(NRF) grant funded by the Korea government(MEST) (No. 2011-0015009).

References

1. Moe, K., Smith, S., Prescott, G.: Sensor Web Technologies for NASA Earth Science. In: Aerospace Conference. IEEE (2008)
2. Chu, X., Buyya, R.: Service Oriented Sensor Web. Sensor Networks and Configuration. Springer (2007)

3. Botts, M., et al.: OGC Sensor Web Enablement: Overview and High Level Architecture, Open Geospatial Consortium. OGC White Paper (2006)
4. Nath, S., Liu, J., Miller, J., Zhao, F.: SensorMap: A Web Site for Sensors World-Wide. Demo at ACM SenSys (2006)
5. Rhead, I., Merabti, M., Mokhtar, H., Fergus, P.: Worldwide Sensor Web Framework Overview. PGNet (2008)
6. Jirka, I., Bröring, A., Stasch, C.: Discovery Mechanisms for the Sensor Web. Sensors 9 (2009)

Users' Personality Traits as Predictors of UCC Usage on the Internet

Yun Ji Moon[1], Sora Kang[2], Chris Rowley[3], Juhee Han[4], and Min Sun Kim[5,*]

[1] Department of Management Information Systems, Catholic University of Pusan,
South Korea
[2] Division of Digital Business, Hoseo University, South Korea
[3] Centre Research on Asian Management, City University, London, UK
HEAD Foundation, Singapore
[4] College of Social Sciences, Chung-Ang Universiy, South Korea
[5] Department of Distribution Management, Hyupsung University, South Korea
sunnyminkim@hanmail.net

Abstract. There has been the growth on the internet of businesses and websites more reliant on content actually created by the users themselves, so-called UCC. We are interested in why individuals engage in this 'free' content creation behavior with no specific financial rewards. Consequently, our study focuses on the inter-relationships between factors that promote UCC usage. We propose an individual's personality is a stimulus to UCC, but that perception of ease of use and usefulness and emotional pleasure mediate this. Based on a survey of over 500 UCC site users our results suggest a significant correlation between individual personality traits, emotional pleasure and ease of use and usefulness toward UCC usage. Those with high UCC involvement display more significant pleasure in their UCC usage. Our study has implications for theory and practice, not least in terms of future models of business and development in the service sector.

Keywords: UCC (user-created content), Perceived usefulness, Perceived ease of use, Stimulus-Organism-Response (S-O-R) paradigm.

1 Introduction

The term 'Web 2.0' is taken to represent a change towards a new digital era, one that facilitates more interactive information sharing, inter-operability, user-centered design and collaboration on the internet. A typical feature of Web 2.0 is the creation of non-standardized, user-centric content based on website user participation and sharing of the information created [1]. Typical examples of this include blogs, wikis, social bookmarking, multimedia sharing and podcasting [2]. One of the most common forms of such behavior is user-created content (UCC), which exists on web platforms to enable user-created text, photos or video content to be shared with other users [3].

---

* Corresponding author.

T.-h. Kim et al. (Eds.): SIP/WSE/ICHCI 2012, CCIS 342, pp. 209–216, 2012.
© Springer-Verlag Berlin Heidelberg 2012

Thus, UCC is defined as content made publicly available over the internet, which reflects a certain amount of creative effort and which is created outside of professional routines and practices [4].

To increase the economic efficiency of Web 2.0-based UCC, the number of UCC users needs to reach a certain threshold. This phenomenon is related to a network effect. This refers to the theory that the value a consumer obtains from a product or service increases as more people use it [5]. As more people use a product or service, the number of suppliers providing it will increase, and this growth, in turn, will enhance the value of the product or service. Such a network effect can also be applied to the Web 2.0 UCC domain. Participation, sharing and openness, which are the principles that inform Web 2.0, can be understood as the engine that drives the value of a network. As the number of participants in a given network escalates, the more users will share data and the network's openness will improve due to the higher frequency of free usage and search. More users contributing content, more contributors possessing more knowledge and information and more contributors intending to share content, will all lead to a greater network effect. In order to obtain the economic efficiency of such sites (e.g., Youtube and Facebook), the sites' number of UCC users should have reached an appropriate threshold. Therefore, it is important for businesses to understand what elements are important to attract UCC users and to lead them to use UCC sites. So, understanding the affecting factors on UCC usage, this study sets out to examine the impact of individual characteristics – personality traits.

For many years the issue of individual characteristics received little attention in the IS literature. One domain of individual differences that has received limited attention in the IS literature is personality [6]. However, recent advances in personality psychology suggests a fruitful way to integrate individual traits into IS models [7][8]. Our paper examines the relationship between personality and the Technology Acceptance Model (TAM) because the basic concept underlying this model places significant focus on individual reactions to technology, in which personality can be expected to play a part. In addition, we also include the relationship between personality and emotions. The existence of a relationship between personality and emotions is well documented, especially between extraversion and neuroticism [9]. Thus, people's attitudes, cognitions, emotions, and behaviours are in part determined by individual personality. That is, psychological predispositions have important effects upon a number of individual level variables. Therefore, our study attempts to replicate and extend the previous findings showing that personality influences users' perceptions, emotions, and behaviours in the UCC area.

Additionally, our study takes into consideration UCC involvement as a control variable in the relationships between emotions, perceptions and UCC usage. Unlike an IS within organizations, compulsive factors are excluded in UCC. So, the level of activity varies depending on the individuals' involvement in UCC activities, namely the level of immersion. Therefore, the effects of the emotions or perceptions on usage cannot help but change according to UCC involvement. Bitner [10] suggested that a single personal factor takes effect to moderate the impact of an individual's emotional and perceptional factors on their behavior. Consequently, our study includes a user's involvement as a moderating variable.

Our study is important for several reasons. As such new internet and web trends better absorb users who were forms relatively alienated in the production of web content, it may encourage and enable more of the broader public to participate. The impact on society would then increase considerably. Our study also crosses subjects and areas, not only organizational behavior and psychology, but also IS and management more generally. It also uses some well known ideas but also applies them in a relatively under-utilized research context.

2   Research Model and Hypotheses

The conceptual research model used in our study is set out in Figure 1. It is concerned with individual personality factors which influence a user's perception and behavior in UCC usage, such as emotional pleasure, Perceived Ease of Use (PEU) and Perceived Usefulness (PU). In addition, our study examines the relationship between PEU and PU based on the Technology Acceptance Model (TAM). Finally, our model shows a relationship where individual assessment of emotional pleasure, PEU and PU influences UCC usage differently, depending on users' involvement in UCC formation.

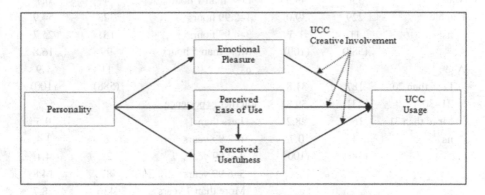

Fig. 1. Research Model

Hypothesis 1: UCC website users' extraversion will have a positive impact on emotional pleasure.

Hypothesis 2: UCC website users' neuroticism will have a negative impact on emotional pleasure.

Hypothesis 3: UCC website users' extraversion will have a positive impact on their PEU.

Hypothesis 4: UCC website users' neuroticism will have a negative impact on their PEU.

Hypothesis 5: UCC website user's extraversion will have a positive impact on PU.

Hypothesis 6: UCC website user's neuroticism will have a positive impact on PU.

Hypothesis 7: UCC website users' PEU of a website will have a positive impact on their PU of the site.

Hypothesis 8: The greater the emotional pleasure a UCC website offers, the higher is the users' UCC usage.

Hypothesis 9: As the users' PEU of UCC website improves, the user's UCC usage will increase.

Hypothesis 10: As the users' PU of UCC website improves, the user's UCC usage will increase.

Hypothesis 11: The impact of emotional pleasure on UCC usage affects more significantly the high involved group than the low involved group in creating UCC.

Hypothesis 12: The impact of PEU on UCC usage affects more significantly the high involved group than the low involved group in creating UCC.

Hypothesis 13: The impact of PU on UCC usage affects more significantly the high involved group than the low involved group in creating UCC.

3   Research Methodology and Result

Table 1. Demographic characteristics of samples

Category	Freque	Percentage	Category	Frequenc	Percentag
Gender			Average Internet usage		
Male	350	59.5	Less than 1 hour	4	0.7
Female	229	39.0	1–2.99 hours	323	54.9
ns	11	1.5	3–4.99 hours	151	25.7
	(588)	(100)	More than 5 hours	99	16.8
Age			ns	11	1.9
Less than 20	187	31.8		(588)	(100)
21–30	231	39.3	Internet experience		
More than 31	166	28.2	Less than 1	3	0.5
ns	4	0.7	1–2.99 years	8	1.4
	(588)	(100)	3–4.99 years	24	4.1
			5–6.99 years	87	14.8
			More than 7 years	436	78.7
			ns	3	0.5
				(588)	(100)

Table 2. Factor analysis results and Cronbach's alpha[a]

Items	Standardized coefficient (*t*-value)	AVE	CCR	Item-to-Total Correlation	Cronbach's α
[1] Extroversion		.51	.86		.83
Extroversion 1	.64(fixed= 1.0)			.56	

Table 2. (*continued*)

Extroversion 2	.80(14.60)			.71	
Extroversion 3	.77(13.97)			.65	
Extroversion 4	.74(13.50)			.64	
Extroversion 5 (excluded from reliability test)	–	–	–	–	–
Extroversion 6	.63(10.94)			.50	
Extroversion 7	.67(12.76)			.59	
Extroversion 8 (excluded from reliability test)	–	–	–	–	–
[2] Neuroticism					.81
Neuroticism 1	.70(fixed= 1.0)	.50	.85	.55	
Neuroticism 2	.68(11.67)			.50	
Neuroticism 3	.76(13.31)			.62	
Neuroticism 4	.76(13.31)			.63	
Neuroticism 5 (excluded from factor analysis)	–	–	–	–	–
Neuroticism 6	.66(11.40)			.54	
Neuroticism 7	.66(11.44)			.41	
Neuroticism 8 (excluded from factor analysis)	–	–	–	–	–
[3] Pleasure		.71	.88		.87
Pleasure 1	.79(fixed= 1.0)			.71	
Pleasure 2	.92(22.98)			.82	
Pleasure 3	.81(20.91)			.74	
Pleasure 4 (excluded from reliability test)	–		–	–	
[4] PEU		.78	.91		.91
PEU1(excluded from reliability test)	–	–	–	–	
PEU2	.85(fixed= 1.0)			.80	
PEU3	.95(28.40)			.87	
PEU4	.83(24.97)			.79	
[5] PU		.76	.93		.93
PU 1	.81(fixed= 1.0)			.80	
PU 2	.85(24.28)			.84	
PU 3	.92(27.63)			.86	
PU 4	.91(27.24)			.85	
[6] UCC usage		.64	.84		.81
Usage 1	.76(fixed= 1.0)			.64	

Table 2. (*continued*)

Usage 2	.83(18.73)	.74
Usage 3	.80(18.30)	.69

Note: CCR = composite construct reliability; AVE = average variance extracted
[a] Hypothesized model with standardized parameter estimates for the full sample ($N = 588$)
$\chi^2 = 801.23$, $df = 309$ (p < .001); CFI = .94; RMSEA = .05; NFI = .90; TLI = .92.

Table 3. Discriminant validity analysis results

	1	2	3	4	5	6	M	SD
1. Extroversion	.51						4.54	1.05
2. Neuroticism	.28**	.50					4.33	1.06
3. Pleasure	.22**	.19**	.71				4.66	0.98
4. PEU	.02^{ns}	.04^{ns}	.01^{ns}	.77			4.26	1.57
5. PU	.27**	.23**	.48**	.07^{ns}	.76		4.31	1.48
6. UCC usage	.17**	.16**	.49**	.55**	.07^{ns}	.64	2.41	1.11

[a] Diagonals: AVE from the observed variables by the latent variables
[b] Off-diagonals: construct-level correlation = (shared variance) $^{1/2}$ *p < 0.05; **p < 0.01

Table 4. Hypotheses test results

Hypotheses	Research Model		
	Standardized path coefficient	t-value	results
H1 Extroversion → Pleasure (+)	.22***	4.30	supported
H2 Neuroticism → Pleasure (-)	-.16**	3.12	supported
H3 Extroversion → PEU	.07^{ns}	1.48	rejected
H4 Neuroticism → PEU (-)	.07^{ns}	1.27	rejected
H5 Extroversion → PU (+)	.26***	5.25	supported
H6 Neuroticism → PU (+)	.18***	3.58	supported
H7 PEU → PU (+)	.34***	8.04	supported
H8 Pleasure → UCC usage (+)	.32***	7.32	supported
H9 PEU → UCC usage (+)	.03^{ns}	0.72	rejected
H10 PU → UCC usage (+)	.47***	10.18	supported

***$P < .001$, **$P < .01$, χ^2 (264) = 808.85, $p < .001$; CFI = .93; TLI = .91; RMSEA = 06.

Table 5. Multiple group analysis results

Hypotheses	Standardized path coefficient (t-value)		$\Delta\chi^2$	Goodness of Fit Indices
	High involvement group	Low involvement group		

Table 5. (*continued*)

H11 Pleasure → UCC usage	.41 (5.60)***	.20 (2.80)**	3.98 (p < .05)	CFI = .90
H12 PEU → UCC usage	.06 (0.93)^{ns}	.02 (0.35)^{ns}	.84 (ns)	TLI = .90
H13 PU → UCC usage	.36 (5.23)***	.42 (5.15)***	2.13 (ns)	RMSEA = .04

***$P < .001$, **$P < .01$, *$P < .05$, $\chi2$ (529) = 1140.55, $p < .001$

4   Discussion

Our paper makes several important contributions. It sheds some light on the question: what is it that makes people actively participate in UCC usage which offers no specific extrinsic financial or social rewards? This issue is important because it is difficult for websites to be successful without securing a certain level of users. From this perspective, even if UCC is expanding its user base and absorbing more people as the main agents of creation, it would still be challenging for businesses to develop without an understanding of the specific reason as to why users participate and the accompanying problems in this. Therefore, it is important to explore the dominant drivers encouraging users' participation in UCC. In our study the search for the reason as to why individuals use UCC websites is not limited to compensation aspect like in previous studies. Instead, we explored users' responsive actions according to the interaction in the personal, more fundamental personality, emotion and perception aspects.

References

1. Lazar, I.: Creating Enterprise 2.0 from Web 2.0. Business Communications Review 37(8), 14–16 (2007)
2. Anderson, P.: What is Web 2.0? Ideas, technologies and implications for education. Joint Information Systems Committee Technology and Standards Watch Report 1-64 (2007)
3. Kolbitsch, J., Maurer, H.: The transformation of the web: How emerging communities shape the information we consume. Journal for Universal Computer Science 12, 187–213 (2006)
4. Vickery, G., Wunsch-Vincent, S.: Participative web and user-created content: Web 2.0 wikis and social networking. Organization for Economic Co-operation and Development, Paris (2006)
5. Katz, M., Shapiro, C.: Network externalities, competition and compatibility. American Economic Review 75(3), 424–440 (1985)
6. Devaraj, S., Easely, R.F., Crant, M.: How does personality matter? Relating the Five-Factor Model to technology acceptance and use. Information Systems Research 19(1), 93–105 (2008)
7. Bono, J.E., Judge, T.A.: Personality and transformational and transactional leadership: A meta-analysis. Journal of Applied Psychology 89(5), 901–910 (2004)

8. Judge, T.A., Bono, J.E., Ilies, R., Gerhardt, M.W.: Personality and leadership: A review and test of theoretical propositions. Journal of Applied Psychology 89, 542–552 (2002)
9. Mardaga, S., Hansenne, M.: Do personality traits modulate the effect of emotional visual stimuli on auditory information processing? Journal of Individual Differences 30(1), 28–34 (2009)
10. Bitner, M.J.: Servicescape: The impact of physical surroundings on customers and employees. Journal of Marketing 56(2), 57–67 (1992)
11. Eysenck, S.B.G., Eysenck, H.J., Barrett, P.T.: A revised version of the psychoticism scale. Personality and Individual Differences 6, 21–29 (1985)
12. Mehrabian, A., Russell, J.A.: An approach to environmental psychology. MIT Press, Cambridge (1974)
13. Ryu, K., Jang, S.: The effect of environmental perceptions on behavioral intentions through emotions: The case of upscale restaurants. Journal of Hospitality & Tourism Research 31(1), 56–72 (2007)
14. Venkatesh, V., Davis, F.D.: A theoretical extension of the technology acceptance model: Four longitudinal field studies. Management Science 46, 186–204 (2000)
15. Chun, H.M., Yoon, J.S.: A study on web 2.0 and UCC: The evolving trends and strategic implication. KSCI Review 15(1), 91–98 (2007)
16. Childers, T.L., Carr, C.L., Peck, J., Carson, S.: Hedonic and utilitarian motivations for online retail shopping. Journal of Retailing 77(4), 511–535 (2001)
17. Menon, S., Kahn, B.: Cross-category effects of induced arousal and. pleasure on the Internet shopping experience. Journal of Retailing 78(1), 31–40 (2002)

Path Analysis for Attachment, Internet Addiction, and Interpersonal Competence of College Students

Jeonghoon Kang[1,*], Hyungsung Park [2,*], Taesoo Park[1], and Junghwan Park[1,**]

[1] Jeju National University, South Korea
peaceallyo@naver.com, {yosan,edu114}@jejunu.ac.kr
[2] Korea National University of Education, South Korea
hyungsung@gmail.com

Abstract. The purpose of this research was to investigate the attachment of university students and interpersonal relationship ability, and correlations with internet addiction. The results of this study were as follows: First, attachment avoidance has a significant influence on interpersonal competence as well as on internet addiction. On other hand, attachment anxiety has not influence on interpersonal competence but has a significant influence on internet addiction. Second, a self report questionnaire was used to measure the variables of attachment anxiety, attachment avoidance, interpersonal competence and internet addiction. The self report questionnaire cannot neglect the subjectivity of the participants, and cannot control the influence of tendency to be seen socially righteous in the examination attitude of the participants.

Keywords: Attachment, internet addiction, interpersonal competence.

1   Introduction

Information and communication technologies such as the Internet affect society as a whole, and the user target is increasing across gender and age. Internet addiction status survey presented by National Information Society Agency [1] shows a growing rate of internet addiction for the case of university students (20-24 years) with the figures of 8.3% in year 2008, 8.5% in 2009, 10% in 2010. The increase in rate of internet addiction shows high risk of addiction considering the environment of university students with easy access and utilization of Internet.

Attachment theory is argued by Bowlby [2] which emphasized the importance of interpersonal relationships a man makes for the first time right after birth. Bowlby [2][3] has carried out various numbers of studies to understand the relationship between attachment and various social consequences since he has proposed the attachment concept and internal execution model concept to define the characteristics of the relationship between early life infants and parents.

---

* First authors: Two authors made equivalent contributions.
** Corresponding author.

T.-h. Kim et al. (Eds.): SIP/WSE/ICHCI 2012, CCIS 342, pp. 217–224, 2012.
© Springer-Verlag Berlin Heidelberg 2012

Attachment can have a significant impact on interpersonal relationships. According to Wiggins [4] and Kiesler [5], interpersonal relationships not only form and develop a unique form of ego as a source of personal development and to develop but also satisfies the desire for affiliation and affection. Young et al. [6] argues that the expectation of being able to have a conversation with others or play games through the internet appeals to people not in good interpersonal relationship with others in real life and increases the use of internet. Lee [7] has reported that both family relationship and friendship among interpersonal relationship variables have significant influence to internet addiction.

Attachment styles formed in early life as the form of an internal working model, acts as the foundation of interpersonal relationships with others and acts with consistency in relationship with others. They also influence expectations and behaviors towards oneself and others and interpersonal relationships. Depending on the type of attachment theory, attachment theory is being usefully recognized to understand the way people make relationships and what type of people form and maintain intimate relationships or have difficulty in making relationships [8].

Looking at the researches on youth internet addiction and attachment, Mok [9] has pointed out that not the attachment of the parents but that of the peer friends has a significant influence to internet addiction. Internet addiction had high marks for the type of attachment. According to the research result of Shin [10], attachment avoidance and attachment anxiety has negative correlations with interpersonal relationship skills. Jeong [11] said that unstable attachment had significantly higher level of psychological symptoms and the level of interpersonal relationship problems than stable attachment.

Previous researches focused on studying the influence attachment gives to interpersonal relationship and internet addiction. On the other hand, there is no research on a structural model between variables through path analysis on attachment, interpersonal competence and internet addiction. Therefore, the purpose of this research lies on investigating the attachment of university students and interpersonal relationship ability, and correlations with internet addiction.

2   Theoretical Discussion on Variables

Looking at the relationship between the variables through an advanced research is as follows. Lee [12] argued that attachment anxiety does not directly affect interpersonal competence but influences the interpersonal competence with through the medium of negative emotion and cognitive biases. According to the content of theses on interpersonal relationships and relationship between internet addiction, conversation with others has been reduced due to internet resulting in deterioration of interpersonal relationship [13], and youth internet addiction composes social discomfort affecting their interpersonal relationship and may lead to mal-adaptation in interpersonal relationships [14]. It shows that contact with family, friends and surrounding people gets reduced in real world as getting immersed in the internet and thus miss the opportunities to acquire social skills to solve interpersonal relationship problems.

Once addicted to the internet, we seek for compensation in the virtual space for the unsmooth interpersonal relationship unsatisfied in reality. Yang [15] said that it showed that the severe the internet addiction, the lower the activity and satisfactory level of the interpersonal relationship. Also, Kim et al. [16] said that students addicted to the internet showed more positive interpersonal relationship online than when directly met. Additionally, Kraut et al. [17] assert that online interpersonal relationship via the internet is limited relative to relationships through physical approaches, and even ordinary people are led to reduction in social support network or qualitative change of interpersonal relationship if such relationships are repeated. Such results, in the research of Young [18] can be seen as being associated to people showing addictive characteristics escape from real life and appeal inappropriateness and difficulties.

3   Research Method

3.1   Participants and Analysis Method

Participants were sophomore students of J University located in South Korea. The research purpose, consuming time, methods and cautions were sufficiently explained to the participants. A total of 950 copies of questionnaires were distributed to 10% of the total students of 9584, and 783 copies of them were used as valid questionnaires utilized for research analysis, excluding the 167 copies responded insincerely to the test items. SPSS for Window and AMOS were used to analysis the data. The correlations among the variables of attachment, interpersonal competence and internet addiction were analyzed. Maximum likelihood was used to analyze the structure equation.

3.2   Research Model

The hypothetical model set in this research based on the advanced research is as following Figure 1.

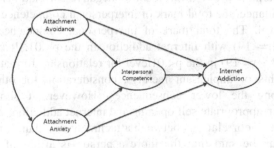

Fig. 1. Path model among variables

3.3   Research Tools

Experiences in Close Relationship–Revised Scale. ECR-R developed my Fraley, Waller and Brennan [19] was used as the tool for measuring attachment. In this research, .85 was attachment avoidance and .89 was attachment anxiety for the *Cronbach's α.*

Interpersonal Competence Scale. It was developed by Buhrmester, Furman, Wittenberg and Reis [20] was used to measure the interpersonal relationship ability. The *Cronbach's α* in this research were; .86 for forming and opening a relationship, .79 for insistence for right or unpleasant feeling, .81 for consideration towards others, .68 for conflict management, .57 for appropriate self management.

Adult Internet Addiction for Self Report Scale. A-scale was developed by Korea Agency for Digital Opportunity and Promotion [1] was used as the internet addiction measurement tool for the university student. A-scale was made to measure the proneness to internet addiction of adults and to propose the classification criteria. .86 for orientation to virtual world, .84 for positive expectation, .85 for internal character, immersion and .86 self cognition about internet for the *Cronbach's α* in this research.

4   Results and Analysis

4.1   Interrelationship between the Variables

A correlation analysis was performed to determine the relationship among all the variables. Table 1 shows the correlation coefficient among variables.

The relationship between the independent variables attachment anxiety and attachment avoidance shows positive correlations (r=.586) in p<.01 level. Attachment avoidance among independent variables and internet addiction which is a dependent variable shows positive correlations in p<.01 (r=.324). It shows negative correlations (r=-.32 ~ r=-.19) in attachment anxiety, the total mark of interpersonal competence and in the lower variable p<.01 level. It shows negative correlations (r=-.44 ~ r=-.25) in attachment avoidance, the total mark of interpersonal competence and in the lower variable p<.01 level. The total mark of interpersonal competence has a negative correlation level (r=-.19) with internet addiction in the p<.01. It shows a negative correlation (r=-.12 ~ r=-19) in the p<.01level for relationship formation and opening, insistence for rights or unpleasant feelings, consideration for others and conflict management among the lower consequences. However, it shows there is no correlation between appropriate self opening and internet addiction.

From the result of correlations between attachment avoidance and interpersonal competence, it can be said that the more a person is afraid of getting close to others showing tendency to avoid attachment, the lower the interpersonal competence.

Table 1. Correlation coefficient between variables (*N=783*)

	1	2	3-1	3-2	3-3	3-4	3-5	3	4-1	4-2	4-3	4-4	4
1. Attachment avoidance	—	.586**	-.479**	-.248**	-.333**	-.263**	-.386**	-.439**	.300**	.278**	.254**	.308**	.324**
2. Attachment anxiety		—	-.314**	-.256**	-.223**	-.193**	-.233**	-.317**	.376**	.316**	.365**	.331**	.401**
3-1. Relationship			—	.557**	.604**	.457**	.514**	.841**	-.150**	-.157**	-.143**	-.163**	-.174**
3-2. Rights				—	.574**	.396**	.535**	.791**	-.081*	-.112**	-.125**	-.112**	-.123**
3-3. Others					—	.645**	.402**	.843**	-.208**	-.161**	-.071	-.148**	-.165**
3-4. Conflict						—	.375**	.732**	-.245**	-.160**	-.109**	-.155**	-.191**
3-5. Open up							—	.657**	-.022	-.054	-.081*	-.052	-.061
3. Interpersonal competence								—	.192**	.175**	.141**	.172**	.193**
4-1. Virtual									—	.720**	.674**	.686**	.887**
4-2. Expectation										—	.667**	.659**	.858**
4-3. Internal characteristic											—	.686**	.886**
4-4. Cognition												—	.856**
4. Internet addiction													—

*Correlation is significant at the 0.05 level.
**Correlation is significant at the 0.01 level.
***Correlation is significant at the 0.001 level.

4.2   Structural Equation Model Analysis in the Relationship between Attachment of University Students and Internet Addiction

Prior to the hypothesis model set in this research to be verified, the goodness of fit of the model as to the relationship between the variables was verified by composing a measuring model. The goodness of it of the measurement model of the variables related to internet addiction were χ^2 (56) = 301.594, p>.001, χ^2/df = 5.386, GFI =.945, TLI=.938, CFI=.956, RMSEA=.075 (.067, .083) which the goodness of fit indexes satisfied the basis >.90. The RMSEA value also satisfied the basis <.08 and the confidence interval (.067, .083) were also appropriate. Based on the advanced research, it could be known that the overall coincidence of the hypothesis model of the research which the paths for relationship between the variables related to attachment, interpersonal competence and internet addiction were connected, the indices also corresponded to the criteria. Therefore, the hypothesis model was selected as the final model. The effects of direct and indirect paths between each variable are proposed in Table 2.

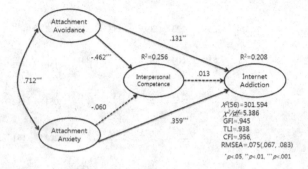

Fig. 2. The path analysis model

As proposed in Figure 2 and Table 2, attachment avoidance is explained directly significant to internet addiction (β=.131, p<.01), and is also explained directly significant in interpersonal competence (β=-.462, p<.001). However, internet addiction is not significantly explained in interpersonal relationship, Therefore mediated effect is not valid. Although attachment anxiety is explained directly significant to internet addiction (β=.359, p<.001), not explained significantly in interpersonal relationship ability.

Table 2. Path coefficient on research model and direct-indirect effect analysis

Reference variable	Predicted variables	Estimate	S.E	C.R	Total effect	Direct effect	Indirect effect	R^2
Interpersonal competence	Attachment avoidance	-1.211	.173	-6.984	-.462	-.462***		.256
	Attachment anxiety	-.103	.107	-.963	-.060	-.060		
Internet addiction	Attachment avoidance	.505	.251	2.016	.125	.131**	-.006	
	Attachment anxiety	.897	.151	5.936	.358	.359***	-.001	.208
	Interpersonal competence	.020	.066	.296	.013	.013		

**Correlation is significant at the 0.01 level.   ***Correlation is significant at the 0.001 level.*

5   Discussion and Conclusion

Summarizing the research result, attachment avoidance has a significant influence on interpersonal competence (β=-.462, p<.001) as well as on internet addiction (β=.131, p<.01). On other hand, attachment anxiety has not influence on interpersonal competence but has a significant influence on internet addiction (β=.359, p<.001).

This corresponds to the research result of Jeon [21] who has argued that it is more likely to be addicted to internet for those in attachment anxiety, and lies in the same context with the research result argued by Kim et al. [22] of which negative nursing attitude explains internet addiction more significantly. These are results which portray higher the attachment lower the risk of internet addiction, and they show attachment has influence on internet addiction. Proposals for sequel researches are as follows; the research should allow more intensive qualitative research methods be integrated regarding internet addiction of university students for an empirical research, by expanding the research target sampling on the internet addiction group (high risk group). Secondly, a self report questionnaire was used to measure the variables of attachment anxiety, attachment avoidance, interpersonal competence and internet addiction. The self report questionnaire cannot neglect the subjectivity of the research target, and cannot control the influence of tendency to be seen socially righteous in the examination attitude of the research target. Therefore, the parts which perception was limited looking at the content of the questionnaire should be supplemented through intensive interviews of the internet addiction group by supplementing the limit of self report format.

References

1. National Information Society Agency: 2010 Internet using survey (2010)
2. Bowlby, J.: The nature of the child's tie to his mother. International Journal of Psycho-Analysis XXXIX, 1–23 (1958)
3. Bowlby, J.: Attachment and loss, vol. 1: Attachment. Basic Books, New York (1969)
4. Wiggins, J.S.: A psychological taxonomy of trait-descriptive terms: The interpersonal domain. Journal of Personality and Social Psychology 37, 395–412 (1979)
5. Kiesler, J.: Contemporary interpersonal theory and research: Personality, psychopathology, and psychotherapy. John Wiley & Son, New York (1996)
6. Young, K., Pistner, M., Buchanan, J., O'Mara, J.: Cyber-Disorders: The Mental Health Concern for the New Millenium. Cyber Psychology and Behanior 3(5), 475–479 (2000)
7. Eun Youn, L.: Relationship between Impulsiveness and Internet Addiction in Elementary School Students: Mediating Effects of Interpersonal Relation. Graduate School of Duksung Woman University (2010)
8. Lopez, F.G., Brennan, K.A.: Dynamic process underlying adult attachment organization: Toward an attachment theoretical perspective and the healthy and effective self. Journal of Counseling 47(3), 283–300 (2000)
9. Jun Seon, M.: The Relationship of internet addiction to attachment, school adjustment and self-control among adolescents. Graduate School of Kyeong Nam University (2004)
10. Ji Uk, S.: The Path Analysis of the Relationship of Attachment, Emotion, and Interpersonal Competence. Master's thesis. Graduate School of EWha Woman University (2006)
11. Da Un, J.: The relation of attachment and Internet intoxication of youth. Master's thesis. Graduate School of Han Nam University (2010)
12. Jung Hee, L.: Structural analysis of interpersonal relationships by the adult attachment styles. Doctoral dissertation. Graduate School of Bu san University (2005)
13. Se Young, K.: Study on the difference in Internet activities, self-control, self-regulated learning and academic achievement. Graduate School of EWha Woman University (2005)

14. Bo Ram, K.: Analysis on the effect that internet addiction has on the formation of personal relations: Centering on high schools in Anyang areas. Graduate School of EWha Woman University (2003)
15. Don Kyu, Y.: The Differences of Adolescents' Activity and Satisfaction of Interpersonal Relationship according to the Internet Addiction Tendency. Korean Journal of Youth Studies 10(3), 481–500 (2003)
16. Kwang Ung, K., Mi Suk, R., Ji Hang, L.: Effects of Internet Addiction on On-line and Off-line Interpersonal Relationships. Journal of Children Care 25(2), 109–120 (2004)
17. Kraut, R.E., Patterson, M., Lundmark, V., Kiesler, S., Mukhopadhyay, T., Scherlis, W.: Internet paradox: A social technology that reduces social involvement and psychological well-being? American Psychologist 53(9), 1017–1032 (1998)
18. Young, K.S.: Cyber-disorder: The mental health concern for the new millennium. Paper presented at the 107th APA Convention. Cyber Psychology & Behavior, August 20 (1999)
19. Fraley, R.C., Waller, N.G., Brennan, K.A.: An item response theory analysis of self-report measures of adult attachment. Journal of Personality and Social Psychology 78, 350–365 (2000)
20. Buhrmester, D., Furman, W., Wittenberg, M.T., Reis, H.T.: Five Domains of Interpersonal Competence in Peer Relations. Journal of Personality and Social Psychology 55(6), 991–1008 (1988)
21. Hyo Jung, J.: The attachment style and psychological Characteristics of Internet Addiction among College Students. Korean Journal of Youth Studies 13(3), 137–159 (2006)
22. Young Hae, K., Hyun Mi, S., Young Ok, Y., Young Lan, J., Ne Young, L.: Relation between Internet Game Addiction in Elementary School Students and Student's Perception of Parent-Child Attachment. Journal of Korean Academy of Child Health Nursing 13(4), 383–389 (2007)

Study of the Components of Brand Valuation and Effectiveness

Jung-Hee Yi

Department of Design, Seoil College, Korea
junghee4974@lycos.co.kr

Abstract. Brand is a concept like an equity which is continuously cultivated and accumulated for a long time. As the result of K-BPI supervised by KMAC, Morning Glory is at the top of high-royalty brand in the general category of consumer goods by taking the first for 11 years in succession, in the part of general stationary among the consumer goods' general parts. After extracting components of brand valuation, main characteristics of Morning Glory are arranged and current environment of brand is examined, so this study will be a guidance to establish the direction of brand policy.

Keywords: Brand Valuation, Component and Effectiveness, Morning Glory.

1 Introduction

The standard of brand's middle and long term strategy was 10 years 5 years ago, but it was reduced to 3 years recently. It's not surprised if reflecting the actual situation of Korean industry which judges the success of product and decides maintenance or abolition within 1 year. However, brand is a concept like an equity which is continuously cultivated and accumulated for a long time. It can neither beat competitive brand nor take the first place with the investment of one moment. And, it's premised by long-term discernment and continuous investment.

The model of valuation doesn't have absolutely accurate answer. In other words, there can be several approaches for the evaluation of brand value and there is no complete approach of valuation which can satisfy all of various desires or purposes.

The study on brand valuation is varied by researchers. In other words, evaluation items and variables are changed by the concept of brand value defined by research and evaluation method is various by each purpose.

In 2011, 5-year survival of new restaurants or accommodations was about 29%, but that of Morning Glory franchises was more than 72% as a leading company of general stationary for about 30 years in [Figure 1].

This study intends to establish successful direction of brand policy by discussion components and utility of brand valuation through the successful foundation strategy of Morning Glory.

T.-h. Kim et al. (Eds.): SIP/WSE/ICHCI 2012, CCIS 342, pp. 225–231, 2012.
© Springer-Verlag Berlin Heidelberg 2012

Fig. 1. Shop of Morning Glory (L.A., Australia (Brisbane), New York)

1.1   Components of Brand Valuation

Brand valuation by scholars is achieved mainly from the viewpoint of customers. The axis of brand valuation started from the viewpoint of consumers and provides useful information for brand management, so it has a great utility.

If analyzing the discussion of scholars, there is no opinion in accord among the researchers, for the components of brand valuation.

Based on the documentary researches which have been conducted until now, this study intends to draw factors of brand awareness, perceived quality, associated image, perceived value, confidence, customer satisfaction, leadership, differentiation, distribution coverage, brand preference and other equities which are considered to be suitable for the valuation of Morning Glory, a general stationery brand, among the components of brand valuation suitable for general products and utilize them to brand valuation of Morning Glory.

2   Paper Preparation

2.1   The Object of Studying

Under the changes of worldwide management environment and our firms, K-BPI supervised by KMAC has provided an index to prepare the foundation of brand management environment for the first time in Korea and contributed to the global competitiveness of domestic brands since 1999. After starting with the investigation of total 79 industrial groups in 1999, it was progressed for 196 industrial groups in the 13th investigation of 2011.

The object of studying, Morning Glory, shows less than 50 points between the second brand among the general stationery industrial groups and total points of K-BPI, in most of consumer good groups.

In the part of general stationery among the parts of general consumer goods, Morning Glory has been at the top of highest loyalty in general category of consumer goods for 11 years in succession.

Table 1. The result of Korean industry's K-BPI
※ less than 50 points of the gap with total points of K-BPI

Big division	Industrial group	The first brand	The second brand
	Beer	Hite	Cass
	Shampoo	Elastin	Miseenscéne
	Ice-cream	Bravo corn	World corn
	Female basic cosmetics	Seolhwasoo	Hera
Consumer goods	Female color cosmetics	Hera	Seolhwasoo
	Hair dye	Miseenscéne	L'Oréal
	Meat processed ham	Spam	Mokwoochon ham
	General stationery	Morning Glory	Monami
	Cigaret	ESSE	Dun Hill
Durable goods	Digital camera	Samsung digital camera	Canon digital camera

In conclusion, brands who have established brand equity with long-term continuous investment are in the position of No.1 brand.

2.2   Operant Variable of Studying

The first is to study qualitatively with the factors of Morning Glory's brand valuation, brand awareness, perceived quality, associated image, perceived value, confidence, customer satisfaction, leadership, differentiation, distribution coverage, brand preference and other equities.

The second, measures are studied for unique differentiation of Morning Glory's brand valuation.

3   Results of Studying

3.1   Study for Material and Color

The first is brand awareness and preference.

Morning Glory unified company name and brand name for their brand power and pursued single brand strategy without any separated brand while producing about 3000 kinds of products. By applying same brand image to developed products, sales vehicles and all of internal/external shop signs, they emphasized CIP(Corporate Identity Program) unifying the image of Morning Glory and maximized exposure so that consumers can be familiar to Morning Glory. [Figure 2]

Fig. 2. Morning Glory CIP

The second, Morning Glory places Korean image on the brand value, with associated image and perceived value. The purpose of Morning Glory is to be the company of worldwide design stationery. Morning Glory means not only glory of morning but also morning-glory flower. Morning Glory whose basic symbol is morning-glory flower has the purpose, reliable society where consumers can select products with belief. Morning Glory values 'the image of Korea' which is the country of silent morning. They gave positive image to cosmopolitans with superiority and beauty of Korean spirit and furthermore, upgraded Korean image in the world so as to improve good feeling of Korean products and play a core roles for the development of Korean design. It's also the reason for that products are produced by only Korean own character and lyrical art property without import of character.

The third, customer satisfaction. Morning Glory has enterprise policy reflecting customer's opinion actively.

In this period, consumers purchase products made by company unilaterally. While the number of smart consumers is increased, the number of firms who obtain product idea from them is increased and new word, 'Cresumer' meaning 'Creative Consumer', was born and used.

Morning Glory developed 'notebook which is convenient to be written', hit product, in [Figure 3] through the 'supporters activity of Morning Glory' who are consumer monitering members.

By reflecting the opinion of supporters, that the spring on the side of spring note prevents writing, they developed the product which is convenient to write without the spring in the middle of note and increased the sales. [Figure 4]

Fig. 3. Supporters of Morning Glory

Fig. 4. Write a comfortable note

The fourth is for the differentiation, there is product development caused by Morning Glory's Employee Empowerment. With the design management strategy focusing on design-first management policy and customer satisfaction, design laboratory was established and organized as the division under intermediate control of CEO in 1996. It's operated by the system one designer is in charge of all things such as product design, market survey, planning, design, production, warehousing and purchase for the product he designed. For the strength of Employee Empowerment, a designer promotes his works for himself, so he displays creativity and assumes responsibility for products. Therefore, his occupational satisfaction is improved. In addition, it grasps consumers' desire the mostly and applies it to the product, prevents the distortion of designing intention during the production and releases consumer-oriented products emphasizing customer satisfaction the mostly. For the effects of Employee Empowerment, it can treat directly to consumers' requirements. Therefore, they realized that white color of notebook lays a burden on eyes so much and worried about the idea minimizing eyes' fatigue, so they developed 'Morning non-glazed paper' which is note paper and 'eye soft zone' reducing eyes' fatigue. [Figure 5]

Fig. 5. Morning Glory's notebook of eye soft zone

The fifth is distribution coverage. It's branch sales of Morning Glory. Since they opened stationery center arranging and selling products generally in 1981, the structure of agency structure that other domestic competitors don't have was built. In contrary to the fact existing domestic stationery companies don't have independent structure of distribution, they have 55 branches in the whole country and about 160 Morning Glory chain stores and scores of thousands of general retail stores are operated. Chain stores of Morning Glory were built so as to possess distribution stores selling Morning Glory products at the stage of retail stores.

The sixth is perceived quality and confidence. Morning Glory progresses investigation and improvement of strict standard and quality by placing QC division under the immediate control of CEO with the company motto, 'more value trifling things'. With the activities of product development, they could secure the quality superior than other competitors in same field and their products could be differentiated.

The seventh is leadership. From the early stage of overseas advance, they have rejected OEM and insisted the export of their own brand products until now. They firstly introduced the concept of design to domestic weak market of stationery and are showing strong leadership in the field with continuous development of new products and design power leading the market. They establish shops continuously in overseas areas with leading commercial supremacies and big-sized shops in Beijing Sidan and Yeji who are growing in earnest. And, they have a plan to establish extra-large shop in superior commercial supremacies such as Shanghai, Hangzhou, etc.

4   Conclusions

Joseph Alois Schumpeter which is a representative of enterprise management strategy defined enterprise's instinct as a growth and emphasized creative destruction for going concern.

If considering hundreds of thousands of brands in the investigation of consumer awareness, it's result assuming lots of efforts and extraordinary cost of studying, such as brand restructuring, renewal of products and service, combined communication, etc. They actualized the first brand status based on the consumers' love and confidence by enduring fatigue of awareness and creating revitalization of loyalty. They are forming market hegemony by keeping No.1 leadership grasped once with continuous transformation.

Until now, we examined components and utility of brand valuation. However, worldwide standard for brand valuation is not established yet because brand power is caused by consumers' awareness and mindset rather than tangible materials possessed by enterprise. Thus, through the brand valuation method which can measure consumer's awareness for the brand which is difficultly measured, they induce consumers to purchase products effectively and provide judgement grounds of investment, strategy, etc. to enterprise. Studies intending to evaluate object brand value which has an utility for brand valuation should be continued.

References

[1] Jung, H.J.: Brand valuation and brand management. Management Research, vol. 26 (2006)
[2] Schumpeter, J.A.: Entrepreneurship, Style, and Vision. Jürgen G. Backhaus (2003)
[3] Yi, J.H.: The Component and Effectiveness of Brand Valuation - Focused on Morning Glory. In: Proceedings of the KAIS Fall Conference. The Korea Academia-Industrial Cooperation Society, pp. 162–165 (2012)

Advanced AVB Method for IPTV Service Provision

Yong-do Choi[1], Min-Jun Kim[2], Jae-hyun Jun[2], Zhi-bin Yu[2],
Sung-ho Kim[3], and San-ryul Ryu[4]

[1] Mobile Communication Engineering, Kyungpook National University,
Daegu, Korea
ydchoi@mmlab.knu.ac.kr
[2] Electrical Engineering and Computer Science, Kyungpook National University,
Daegu, Korea
{zbyu,jhjun}@mmlab.knu.ac.kr
[3] School of Computer Science and Engineering, Kyungpook National University,
Daegu, Korea
shkim@knu.ac.kr
[4] Computer Science, Chungwoon University, Chungcheongnam-do, Korea
rsr@chungwoon.ac.kr

Abstract. Network applications are increased in both quality and quantity by
advanced network technology and hardware. Especially, multimedia streaming
such as IPTV has increased grown exponentially by customer demand. In order
to provide IPTV services competently, it is necessary to secure network resources stably. In this paper, we propose a method guaranteeing competent
QoS, based on traditional AVB, for reserving network resources for IPTV services. We propose a time synchronization with single time-sync frame and
mean propagation delay symmetry, and an enhanced AVB with considering
reservation failure situations, and guarantee QoS for IPTV services. For performance analysis, we make a enhanced AVB simulation model, and measure
accuracy of time synchronization, end-to-end delay, and utilization with
OPNET.

Keywords: AVB, Guaranteeing QoS, Time Synchronization.

1 Introduction

The growth of high speed Internet causes an increment of network traffics and applications which used voice, data, multimedia services, and depending on development
of terminal device which can support multimedia services (Mp3 player, Portable Multimedia Player (PMP), smart phone, and navigation etc.) many network application
services are appeared. Video Streaming service such as Internet Protocol TeleVision
(IPTV) and Video on Demand (VoD) is rapidly increasing in the world. A sufficient
resource of network is needed for supporting video streaming service. However, current network resource is an insufficient due to a heavy Peer-to-Peer (P2P) traffic and
other traffic is getting into network, and sometimes normal network service is an impossible due to malicious traffics such as Distributed Denial of Service (DDoS).

T.-h. Kim et al. (Eds.): SIP/WSE/ICHCI 2012, CCIS 342, pp. 232–239, 2012.

To support stable video streaming service against harmful traffics, network bandwidth reservation is needed. Current video streaming service is guaranteed Quality of Service (QoS) from Internet Service Provider (ISP) to subscriber network, but not guaranteed QoS from subscriber network to each user because of network transmission policy is a best-effort [1].

The Institute of Electrical and Electronics Engineers 802.1 Audio/Video Bridging Task Group (IEEE 802.1 AVB TG) is carrying out research among digital media devices based on the Ethernet. First, high quality synchronization services are provided among several digital media devices in the LAN. Second, there is a mechanism to make reservation resources for each service and sets of default rules for managing the resources. This reservation manage mechanism is called Multiple Stream Registration Protocol (MSRP). A third kind of research is traffic forwarding method through reserved bandwidth [2]. Our study is using time-synchronization and resource reservation for support IPTV service. We used single-TimeSync Frame instead of AVB time-sync frame. Therefore, original MSRP mechanism can't handle many situations when the bandwidth reservation and withdraw reservation bandwidth of the service, so we suggested Active MSRP.

The remainder of the paper is organized as follows. Section II, we introduce the relative time synchronization and bandwidth reservation methods. Section III, we propose processes for time-synchronization with single-TimeSync frame and Active MSRP, followed by simulation and numerical results in Section IV. Section V presents the concluding remarks.

2   Relative Work

2.1   Time Synchronization

The most prominent time-synchronization method is the network time protocol (NTP) proposed by Mills and the Internet Engineering Task Force (IETF) group. A subset of NTP, called the Simple Network Time Protocol (SNTP), is protocol compatible with NTP. The NTP provides to transmitting Coordinated Universal Time (UTC) to hierarchical intermediate time servers. The intermediate time server synchronizes time in located their sub-network, adjust local time for individual device [3]. However NTP does not compensate jitter, so it cannot support the exact time synchronization.

IEEE 1588 PTP and IEEE 802.1AS was approached to handle the problem of NTP. IEEE 1588 PTP defines a protocol enabling precise synchronization of clocks in measurement and control systems implemented with technologies such as network communication, local computing and distributed objects. The protocol is applicable to systems communicating via packet networks, and it supports system-wide synchronization accuracy in the sub-microsecond range with minimal network and local clock computing resources [4].

IEEE 802.1AS specifies the protocol and procedures used to ensure that the synchronization requirements are met for time sensitive applications. It specifies the use of IEEE 1588 specifications where applicable in the context of IEEE Stds 802.1D and 802.1Q. IEEE 802.1AS's the synchronization process uses propagation times measured by the master and slaves on all the wired links by exchanging Pdelay_Req, Pdelay_Resp, and Pdelay_Resp Follow Up messages. The synchronization process also uses the residence times measured at the P2P slaves. Figure 1 illustrates the propagation time measurement by one node at the end of a link, referred to as the Requestor. For purposes of measurement, the other node is the Responder. A similar measurement occurs in the opposite direction, with the Requestor and Responder interchanged and the directions of the messages in Figure 1 reversed.

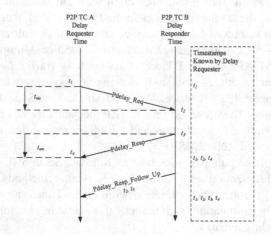

Fig. 1. Propagation time measurement using Pdelay mechanism

2.2   Bandwidth Reservation

The established bandwidth reservation method is Resource Reservation Protocol (RSVP). The RSVP that Integrated Service (IntServ) is operated on the transport layer. The RSVP can designate a Quality of Service (QoS) for each user. Every device, however, must support RSVP in all paths between senders and receivers. These devices must remember bandwidth reservation status for each flow between terminals [5].

Therefore, it is difficult to realize in the internet environment that is not fixed a path of packets. For these reasons, there are few examples in which using RSVP is completed by standardization. To make up for the problems of RSVP, Differentiated Service (DiffServ) technology provides QoS by the priority of traffic are appears. The IEEE 802.1p, DiffServ method, is operated on datalink layer, it provides QoS by priority of frame on the Ethernet. However, the method based on priority of Frame doesn't provide fairness for non-time sensitive traffics, and the hop transmission is increase more, the time sensitive traffics are delayed more by other kinds of traffic. Because QoS guarantee of DiffServ is not completely consistent well, MSRP is studying by the bandwidth reservation method in AVB TG. The MSRP builds the sub-spanning tree and reserves the traffic bandwidth in the Ethernet [6]. Because it is operated in a data link layer, the paths are fixed. Furthermore, it has an advantage in that guaranteed traffic does not interfere with other kinds of traffic, because it is IntServ that reserves each kind of requested traffic.

3   AVB Time Synchronization and Bandwidth Reservation

3.1   Time Synchronization with Single Time-Sync Frame

In the previous section, the method of timing and synchronization was described. The above technologies provide precise time accuracy and compensation. IEEE 1588 PTP and IEEE 802.1AVB, however, have problems where there are too many messages in LAN. Therefore, we propose a method of propagation delay measurement for time sensitive applications using a single time-sync frame in bridged LANs.

This method is able to reduce network overload by too many messages and process complexity of the network devices. Also this has an advantage in that it does not affect the time accuracy, but just provides the required simple process in each network device. Within this paper, all functions are encapsulated in a single time-sync frame, minimal Ethernet frame size. Each device emits these frames at their link-dependent interval. Within IEEE 802.1AS, too many function/direction specific frames are transmitted. IEEE 1588 PTP and IEEE 802.1AS involve seven separate frame transmissions (as opposed to two). For this illustration, we can assume that both master and slave devices desire to calibrate link delays, to minimize topology-change transients. In a full-duplex Ethernet model, the single time-sync frame facilitates synchronization of neighboring clockslave stations. This frame, which is normally sent at 10ms or 100ms intervals, includes time stamp information and the identity of the network's clock master.

For time synchronization with propagation measurement, grandTime, requestTxTime, responseRxTime, and responseTxTime fields are used. The grandTime field specifies grandmaster synchronized time. The requestTxTime field specifies the local free-running time within the source station, when the previous a single time-sync frame has been transmitted on the opposing link. The responseRxTime specifies the local free-running time within the target station, when the previous a single time-sync frame was received on the opposing link. The responseTxTime specifies the local free-running time within the neighbor station, when the previous a single time-sync frame has been transmitted on the incoming link.

Synchronization accuracy is affected by the transmission delays associated with transmission delays, and the receive port is responsible for compensating (*grandTime*, *baseTime*) affiliations by frame-transmission delay. The clock-slave entity uses the computed cable-delay measurement and is therefore responsible for initiating such measurement. Cable-delay measurements begin with the transmission of frame F1 between the clock-slave and clockmaster nodes and conclude with the clock-master response, a transmission of frame F2 between the clock-master to clock-slave nodes.

Based on the preceding listed values, Equation (1) defines the computations for computing mean propagation delay, D_{mp}. Although not explicitly stated, the best accuracy can be achieved by performing this computation every cycle.

$$D_{mp} = ((t4 - t1) - (t3 - t2))/2 \tag{1}$$

A D_{mp} value was saved in each port at 100ms after it had calculated each port in the device, because the propagation delay update period is 100ms.

When the single time-sync frames arrive at their final destination slave clocks, the sum of the correction fields in this frame is a measure of the total residence time in all the intervening devices, plus the propagation times on all the links except the final ingress link at the destination.

3.2   Bandwidth Reservation

The Bandwidth reservation failure situation can be one of three separate cases. First, available bandwidth is insufficient in the path from the Talker to the Listener. Second, the Listener already receives a similar stream service from other Talkers. Last, the state of bridge port is changed.

If Listener receives similar stream by from other Talkers or the port of bridge has insufficient bandwidth when a Talker sends the Talker Advertise message, the control process was necessary. In this case, the Listener generates an Asking Failed message with same streamID in the Talker Advertise message then sends it to the Talker.

The bandwidth reservation failure situation can occur in the bridge along the path from the Talker to the Listener. In this case, we separate two sub-cases. The bandwidth reservation failure occurred while forwarding the Talker Advertise message. The other sub-case is that available bandwidth is sufficient while forwarding the Talker Advertise message but the available bandwidth is insufficient when the Listener Ready message is forwarding to the Talker. The first sub-case has already been described in the previous section. The Talker Advertise message is changed to Talker Failed message. It is composed by adding a FailureInformation field to the Talker Advertise message. Talker Failed message is forwarding to the Listener-side.

The second sub-case is bandwidth reservation failure while actual bandwidth reservation is taking place. In this case, the bridge on which the bandwidth reservation failed sends a Listener Asking Failed message to Talker as if Listener already received service from other Talkers and sends a Talker Failed message to Listener as if the Talker had stopped the service. The reason for doing this, is it simplifies reservation processing. In Figure 2 shows the process of bandwidth reservation failed while Listener Ready message is forwarding.

In the case of a Listener which receives service from the same Talker that exists in another port in the Bridge, although the Listener requests reservation withdrawal, reserved bandwidth withdraw at port which received message by the Listener. Therefore the port sends the message to Talker-side port. The Talker-side port decrease one from the number of Listener-side port which receives service from the same Talker. The reservation state of Talker-side port is also changed from Listener Ready to Listener Ready Failed. If the reservation state is Listener Ready Failed, state is not changed. After decrease one, the number of Listener-side port is 0. In this case the reservation state of Talker-side port is changed to Listener Asking Failed and port sends the message to the Talker. We describe this process in Figure 3.

Next the port which transports the stream from the Talker to Listener can block by changing the state of the Spanning Tree Instance. The processing is same with bandwidth reservation failed while Listener Ready message is forwarding in this case.

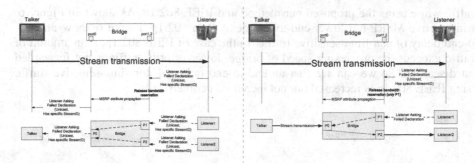

Fig. 2. Bandwidth reservation withdrawal process by all Listener request

Fig. 3. Bandwidth reservation withdrawal process by a part of Listener request

4   Simulation Result

To experiment the proposed methods (We denote our mechanism to single time-sync frame, and Active MSRP), we use the network simulator OPNET. We compared multicast streaming using traditional IGMP and our suggestion. We set up network environment using 6 L3 switchs which is intermediate devices, 10 terminal nodes, and the load time-sensitive traffic, non-time-sensitive traffic at each link and used time-sensitive traffic with voice and video traffic.

We tested the end-to-end delay vs. hop count for time synchronized. The proposed method, however, has lower end-to-end delay because of using just one frame. The proposed method also has advantages in processing complexity, due to a simple processing mechanism in every device (endpoints and intermediate bridges). We showed this in Figure 4.

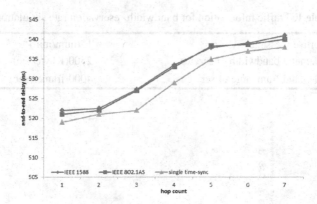

Fig. 4. End-to-end delay with three methods

To compare Active MSRP performance with other protocol, we measured the end-to-end delay for time-sensitive traffic and non-time-sensitive traffic. In addition we experiment the use rate of reserved bandwidth for each traffic while bandwidth reservation failed situation. Figure 5 show an end-to-end delay of time-sensitive traffic while using the proposed our method and IEEE 802.1p. As shown in Figure 6, using Active MSRP has lower end-to-end delay then 802.1p. Figure 6 show an end-to-end delay of non-time-sensitive traffic. In the case of IEEE 802.1p, if an amount of traffic exceeds the processing speed of bridge, lower priority traffic is not forwarded but discarded. So we can see that an end-to-end delay of non-time-sensitive traffic using IEEE 802.1p is increased but not increased geometrically.

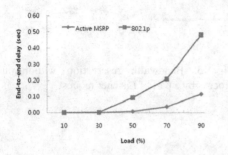

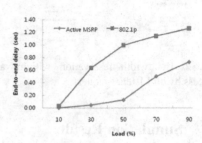

Fig. 5. End-to-end delay of time-sensitive traffic

Fig. 6. End-to-end delay of non-time-sensitive traffic

The original MSRP can process only a few bandwidth reservation failed situations. In this case, no used reservation bandwidth can exist. This causes low efficiency of the network utilization. However, Active MSRP can process all bandwidth reservation failed situations, preventing the waste of not using bandwidth. We experiment the rate of reservation bandwidth and using reservation bandwidth for Active MSRP and origin MSRP. For this experiment, we use only one video type time-sensitive traffic and it is sent after bandwidth reservation. We measured network utilization for Active MSRP and origin MSRP. We describe the traffic parameter and the result each Table 1, Figure 7.

Table 1. Traffic information for bandwidth reservation rate simulation

Talker Advertise message	15(num/min)
Maximum demand bandwidth of service	2500(Kbyte/sec)
Maximum demand frame rate of service	4000(frames/sec)

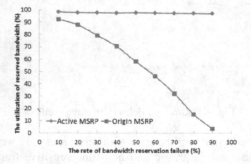

Fig. 7. The throughput of reserved bandwidth with Active MSRP and origin MSRP

In original MSRP, reserved bandwidth withdrawal is only when a Talker sends Talker Failed message. However, Active MSRP can process reserved bandwidth withdrawal in all situations, the network utilization is fixed. The network utilization is not 100%. Because reserved bandwidth is maximum value per unit time, but the each video traffic packet size is not uniform.

5   Conclusion

Nowadays digital media devices that generate and play time sensitive traffic are increasing exponentially. Because services that use these devices are sensitive to delay, the technology that can guarantee a low delay in the LAN is required. IEEE 802.1 AVB TG discusses three topics that are time synchronization, resource reservation, and traffic forwarding.

We proposed a method of time synchronization using a single time-sync frame and active MSRP in bridged LANs. In the experiment results, All nodes are synchronized in 7 hops and the number of control frames is decreased by 47% using the single time-sync frame as compared to the IEEE 802.1AS, and Active MSRP is higher throughput than original MSRP under bandwidth failure situation.

Acknowledgement. This research was supported by Basic Science Research Program through the National Research Foundation of Korea (NRF) funded by the Ministry of Education, Science and Technology (2012-0001829), and Kyungpook National University Research Fund, 2012.

References

1. Kerpez, K., Waring, D., Lapiotis, G., Bryan Lyles, J., Vaidyanathan, R.: IPTV Service Assurance. IEEE Communications Magazine 44(9), 166–172 (2006)
2. IEEE 802.1 Audio/Video Bridging Task Group Home Page (September 2008), http://www.ieee802.org/1/pages/avbridges.html
3. Mills, D.L.: Internet Time Synchronization: The Network Time Protocol. IEEE Transactions on Communications 39(10), 1482–1493 (1991)
4. IEEE 1588 Committee: IEEE P1588TM/D1-F Draft Standard for a Precision Clock Synchronization Protocol for Networked Measurement and Control Systems. IEEE WG IM/ST Committee (2007)
5. Zhang, L., Deering, S., Estrin, D., Shenker, S., Zappala, D.: RSVP: A New Resource ReSerVation Protocol. IEEE Network 7, 8–18 (1993)
6. IEEE Draft Standard for Local and Metropolitan Area Networks virtual bridged local area networks – Amendment 9: Stream Reservation Protocol (SRP), IEEE 802.1Qat (2009)

The Effects of Market Orientation, Entrepreneurial Orientation and Social Networks on the Social Performance of Non-profit Organizations

Jin-Hyuk Hong and Dong-Hwan Cho[*]

Department of Venture and Business, Gyeongnam National University of Science and
Technology, 150, Chilamdong, Jinjushi, Gyeongsangnamdo, Republic of Korea

Abstract. The main objective of this study is to analyze the effects of market
orientation, the entrepreneurial orientation and the social network on the social
performance of non-profit organizations and sector in Korea. In order to test
research hypotheses, field survey was designed, and by distributing
questionnaire survey data collection was performed. After collecting data,
hierarchical multiple regression analysis was performed. As a result, the market
orientation and the social network were shown to significant effect on the social
performance, the innovativeness of the entrepreneurial orientation was also
meaningful. In contrast, the risk-taking of the entrepreneurial orientation was
not shown to have a significant effect on the social performance.

Keywords: Non-Profit Organizations, Social Network, Entrepreneurial
Orientation, Market Orientation, Social Performance.

1 Introduction

Recently non-profit organizations(abbreviated as NPOs) was getting more interest in
Korea, and it has been getting more important the field of new academy. Especially,
the NPOs received attention with the quasi-public intensification. For example, they
are on rapid growth scale, expending subsidies, and representing civil rights(Lee,
2000)[1]. In this way, many previous studies have been making progress on the
increasing power of NPOs. The existing NPOs research mostly belongs to the leading
part of this research in the field of humanities and social science(Han and Moon,
2003)[2], and now the field of business administration started to investigate both the
inside of organization and the social phenomenon. Namely, the academic part mainly
discussed the effective management and administrative plan, and the management
approach was urgently needed about the new organization experiment and
effectiveness measures.

The main objective of this study is to analyze the effects of market orientation, the
entrepreneurial orientation and the social network on the social performance of non-
profit organizations and sector in Korea.

---

[*] Correspoding author.

T.-h. Kim et al. (Eds.): SIP/WSE/ICHCI 2012, CCIS 342, pp. 240–248, 2012.
© Springer-Verlag Berlin Heidelberg 2012

2   Theoretical Background and Research Hypotheses

2.1   Social Performance of Non-profit Organization

The non-profit organization is neither a legal nor technical definition but generally refers to organizations that use surplus revenues to achieve its goals rather than to distribute as profit or dividends(from Wikipedia, the free encyclopedia)[3].

The social performance is usually called as the corporate social performance in the literature. We used the more inclusive term of business social performance in this article. Lee(2007)[4] means the reinvestment of benefits that the internal side was offered to share the wealth and to prepare the welfare for the stakeholder and the employee, and the external side was provided to offer the social service activity in the make-work programs and the vocational training. This research suggests that social performance means the social standard(eg. the problem-solving, and the contributiveness) for the NPOs and it represents the social service(eg. the sharing wealth, and the distributing welfare) for the NPOs.

2.2   Market Orientation

The market orientation is the organizationwide generation of market intelligence pertaining to current and future customer needs, dissemination of the intelligence across department, and organizationwide responsiveness(Jaworski and Kohli, 1993)[5]. The market orientation is the business culture which is committed to the continuous creation of superior value for customers(Slater and Naver, 1994)[6].

Firstly, the customer orientation is the sufficient understanding of one's target buyers to be able to create superior value for them continuously. Secondly, the competitor orientation means that a seller understands the short-term strengths and weaknesses and long-term capabilities and strategies of both the key current and the potential competitors. Thirdly, the interfunctional coordination means the coordinated utilization of company resources in creating superior value for the target customers.

2.3   Entrepreneurial Orientation

Lumpkin and Dess(1996)[7] announced the dimensions of entrepreneurial orientations which were divided as the innovativeness, and openness towards risk-taking. Firstly, to capture new opportunities, risk-taking firms should seek opportunities without restraint in the resource and the environment. Thus, NPOs with an entrepreneurial orientation are often typified by risk-taking, such as incurring heavy debt or making large source commitments, in the interest of obtaining high returns by seizing opportunities in the market. Secondly, the innovativeness is concerned with supporting and encourages the new ideas, the experimentation and the creativity likely to results in the new products, the services or the process. In other words, the NPOs were asked to rate the extent to which they emphasize the technological development and seek to build a reputation for trying new methods and technologies. And, this important aspect of innovativeness is based on the survival company and the success in adopting new business.

2.4   Social Network

The social network included variables such as the acceptance of the idea of the venture in the public discourse, and existence or absence of support and infrastructure services. This dimension between the variables according to four sectors is for analytical purposes only and it is clearly not absolute(Moshe and Lerner, 2006)[8].

Firstly, the entrepreneur starts out depending on the resource of the network to which he belongs. Secondly, the entrepreneur proactively has creates the network and has to invest time and efforts in constructing it. The research implication can explore the possibility of receiving assistance in regarding to management and infrastructure from other organizations in the public sector from other non-profit organizations. And, it finding support assumption that within the framework of social networks may be applied measure for the business performance.

2.5   Hypotheses Development

Based on the literature review, the hypotheses were developed in the three theoretical backgrounds. Firstly, the market orientation can confirm the main variable for social performance(Narver and Slater, 1990[9]; Jasworski and Kohli, 1993[5]; Slater and Naver, 1994[6]; Matsuno et al., 2002[10]). Kohil and Jaworski(1990)[11] and Naver and Slater(1990)[9] announced that market orientation has positive effect on the organizational performance. Narver and Slater(1990)[9] suggest and reached that market orientation has positive effect on the profit improvement and creation in the company. Jaworski and Kohil(1993)[5] implied that market-based organizations has positive represent on the business performance. Also, Matsuno et al.(2002)[10] has positive effect on the business performance. Kara et al.(2004)[12] has directly effect on the between market orientation and organizational performance. Lee and Chae(2007)[13] also has positive conclude on the social performance for the social-base firms. According to the literature review, market orientation is the factors affecting social performance. Therefore, the following is the hypothesis showing the effect of market orientation on social performance.

H$_1$: Market orientation has positive effect on social performance of NPOs.

Secondly, as several previous studies on the relationship between the entrepreneurial orientation and the social performance, this research has the same direction between the two constructs(Lee, 2009[14]; Hwang, 2007[15]). Lee(2009)[14] suggests that market orientation can improve the social performance in Social company. Hwang(2007)[15] insisted that the woman social entrepreneurship has positive effect on the social performance. According to the literature review, the entrepreneurial orientation is the factors affecting the social performance. Therefore, the following is the hypothesis showing the effect of entrepreneurial orientation on the social performance.

H$_2$: Market orientation has positive effect on social performance of NPOs
  H$_{2-1}$: Risk-Taking has positive effect on social performance of NPOs.
  H$_{2-2}$: Innovativeness has positive effect on social performance of NPOs.

Thirdly, the social network are deemed to sustain the favorable relationship(eg. the industrial domain, the growth and development step, the industrial structure, the demand change, the competing intensity, and the government regulation) for the main step, the variable factors, and the main administration. Moshe and Lerner(2006) indicated that it is so valuable factors for the human resource, the school relation, the kinship, and the social position[8]. Social network has greatly process on the social company. It should be keep to sustain both the special step or administration and the hostile relation(Kwang Woo Lee, 2009)[14]. According to the literature review, the social network is the factors affecting the social performance. Therefore, the following is the hypothesis showing the effect of the social network on the social performance.

H$_3$: Social Network has positive effect on social performance of NPOs.

3   Research Methodology

3.1   Data Collection and Analysis Methods

Data for this study were collected from November 20, 2009 to December 03. A total of 142 questionnaires out of 200 were returned and have been valid for the analysis. They were certified as social enterprises by the Department of Labor(Republic of Korea). Cronbach's α coefficient was used to verify the reliability of measurement tools. Cronbach's α coefficient has a value of 0 to 1. If Cronbach's α coefficient is more than 0.6, the reliability is reported to be high. If it is lesser than 0.6, it is considered to lack internal consistency. In the reliability analysis, Cronbach's α of all variables were 0.8. Thus, overall reliability is higher and all configuration concepts used be seen as reliable. [Table 1] and [Table 2] shows the reliability and the validity analysis. Correlation analysis is an analytical technique to measure how closes two variables. The analysis is used to verify the muti-colinearity between the independent variables put together with the analysis of multivariate analysis. There is analyzed with the structural model since there are no muti-colinearity problems as shown in [Table 3].

This research was performed the hierarchical regression analysis. In hierarchical multiple regression analysis, the researcher determines the order that variables are entered into the regression equation. The researcher may want to control for some variable or group of variables. The researcher would perform a multiple regression with these variables as the independent variables. From this first regression, the researcher has the variance accounted for this corresponding group of independent variables. The researcher will run another multiple regression analysis including the original independent variables and a new set of independent variables(Flowers, 2012)[16].

Table 1. Reliability Test Results

Variables		Before Items	After Items	Cronbach's α
Market Orientation		5	5	.886
Entrepreneuria l Orientation	Risk-Taking	3	3	.815
	Innovativeness	3	3	.889
Social Network		7	5	.874
Social Performance		3	3	.875

Table 2. Validity Test Results

Variables		①	②	③	④	⑤
Market Orientation2		**.839**	.034	-.066	.159	.183
Market Orientation1		**.803**	.153	.234	.078	.152
Market Orientation3		**.771**	.021	-.153	.242	.167
Market Orientation4		**.755**	.213	.386	.031	.083
Market Orientation5		**.752**	.263	.272	.084	.127
Social Network3		.032	**.834**	.137	.089	.127
Social Network2		.042	**.805**	.173	-.011	.195
Social Network4		.139	**.787**	.176	.187	.146
Social Network5		.172	**.765**	.148	.030	.025
Social Network1		.214	**.662**	.042	.248	.197
Entrepreneurial Orientation	Innovativeness2	.142	.229	**.811**	.212	.212
	Innovativeness3	.130	.179	**.788**	.272	.235
	Innovativeness1	.104	.216	**.746**	.278	.187
	Risk-Taking1	.125	.122	.162	**.836**	.046
	Risk-Taking2	.085	.111	.283	**.821**	.152
	Risk-Taking3	.222	.116	.173	**.716**	.068
Social Performance2		.224	.249	.162	.176	**.823**
Social Performance3		.125	.249	.251	.059	**.804**
Social Performance1		.330	.216	.211	.080	**.758**
Eigen Value		3.471	3.467	2.516	2.326	2.325
Index of dispersion(%)		18.270	18.245	13.242	12.224	12.237
Cumulative Variance(%)		18.270	36.515	49.757	62.001	74.238

Table 3. Correlation Matrix

Variables	Mean	SD	①	②	③	④	⑤
Social Network	3.3239	.74671	1				
Risk-Taking	3.8310	.80311	.321**	1			
Innovativeness	3.7183	.92364	.474**	.512**	1		
Market Orientation	3.8437	.82758	.378**	.372**	.391**	1	
Social Performance	3.4742	.99036	.513**	.359**	.520**	.484**	1

** The correlation coefficient is significant on the level of 0.01(two-sided).

3.2   Hypotheses Testing

In this study, the proposed model for analysis is presented in [Figure 1]. Firstly, the results of hypothesis indicates the acceptance of H_1, which is that the market orientation appears to have positive influence on the social performance(t=3.56, p=.000). Secondly, H_2 was accepted the entrepreneurial orientation appears to have partial positive influence on the social performance. In other words, the risk taking appears to have not positive influence on the social performance(t=0.440, p=0.661), and the innovativeness appears to have positive influence on the social performance(t=3.24, p=.001). And lastly, H_3 was accepted as the social network appears to have positive effect on the social performance(t=3.61, p=.000). [Table 4] and [Table 5] is a summary on the results of hypothesis testing.

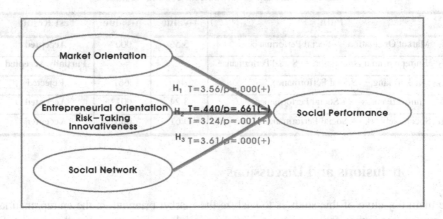

Fig. 1. Hypothesis Test Results

Table 4. Results of Hierarchical Multiple Regression Analysis

Independent Variables	Model ①				Model ②				Model ③			
	SE	β	t	sig.	SE	β	t	sig.	SE	β	t	sig.
(Constraint)	.328	-	3.69	.000								
SN*	.096	.513	7.07	**.000**								
(Constraint)					.374	-	.564	.574				
SN*					.097	.384	5.25	**.000**				
MO*					.087	.341	4.66	**.000**				
(Constraint)									.400	-	-.047	.639
SN*									.101	.275	3.61	**.000**
MO*									.089	.265	3.56	**.000**
EO* RT*									.096	.034	.440	.661
IN*									.089	.269	3.24	**.000**
R^2	.513				.603				.649			
Adj. R^2	.263				.363				.442			
$\triangle R^2$	.258				.354				.405			
Model F	50.079				39.635				24.989			

* MO:Market Orientation/ EO:Entrepreneurial Orientation /RT: Risk Taking/IN: Innovativeness/ SN: Social Network
▬ $P < 0.005$, $P < 0.001$

Table 5. Summary of Hypothesis Testing Results

Path	t-value	p-value	Test Results
H_1 : Market Orientation → Social Performance	3.56	.000*	Accepted
H_2 : Entrepreneurial Orientation → Social Performance	-	-	Partially Accepted
H_{2-1} : Risk Taking → Social Performance	.440	.661	Rejected
H_{2-2} : Innovativeness → Social Performance	3.24	.001*	Accepted
H_3 : Social Network → Social Performance	3.61	.000*	Accepted

4   Conclusions and Discussions

The main objective of this study is to analyze the market orientation, the entrepreneurial orientation, and the social network on the social performance by the non-profit organization. The followings are the main results of this study. Firstly, the market orientation showed the positive effect on the social performance. Secondly, the entrepreneurial orientation showed to have partial positive influence on the social performance. Thirdly, the social network showed to have positive influence on the social performance. In the result of empirical analysis, the market orientation and the social network showed the positive effect on the social performance[17]. But, the entrepreneurial orientation appears to have partial positive influence on the social performance[17]. In other words, the innovativeness is not only considering the social performance. And, the risk-taking was not able to analyze on the social performance.

The main objective of this study is to analyze the market orientation, the entrepreneurial orientation, and the social network on the social performance by the non-profit organization, and the research is to draw the implication. Firstly, the market orientation and the social network showed the positive effect on the social performance[5][9][10][17], and the entrepreneurial orientation as the innovativeness appears to have partial positive influence on the social performance[17]. Secondly, the non-profit organization and sector is significant to be considering the social performance[8][17]. Finally, this research was shown that the entrepreneurship was shown to have seeking more risk-taking than innovativeness in the NPOs environment[17].

This study has some limitations that may encourage further work. The first limitation is the sample size of 142, which limited my ability to draw conclusion about each the NPOs and sector. The future research should investigate whether the relationships found here hold in large samples and in each region of the NPOs and sector. The second limitations are invoked the measure items, which limited other the literature review. The future research should make the measure items for the NPOs and sectors. Finally, the model of this study considers the external stakeholders as a whole, despite the current situation in which the NPOs and sectors operate in a setting that imposes the several of research factors—the social responsibility, the reliability, the affinity, and the network property and so on.

References

1. Lee, H.T.: An analysis on the NGOs Support Project in the Local Government: forcing on the Buasn City. Korean Local Government Studies 4(1), 131–151 (2000)
2. Han, J.G., Moon, H.G.: Business Perspectives to Not-For-Profit Organizations: Research Trends and Future Directions. Korean Non-Profit Organization Research 2(2), 47–98 (2003)
3. http://en.wikipedia.org/wiki/Nonprofit_organization
4. Lee, D.J.: Policy Trends and Projects on the Corporate Social Responsibility. Korea Gas Corporation (Internal Document) (2007)
5. Joworski, B.J., Kohil, A.K.: Market Orientation: Antecedents and Consequences. Journal of Market 57(3), 52–70 (1993)
6. Slater, S.F., Narver, J.C.: Product-Market Strategy and Performance: An Analysis of the Miles and Snow Strategy Types. European Journal of Marketing 27(10), 33–51 (1994)
7. Lumpkin, G.T., Dess, G.G.: Clarifying the Entrepreneurial Orientation Construct and Linking it to Performance. The Academy of Management Review 21(1), 135–172 (1996)
8. Sharir, M., Lemer, M.: Gauging the Success of Social Ventures Initiated by Individual Social Entrepreneurs. Journal of World Business 41(1), 6–20 (2006)
9. Narver, J.C., Slater, S.F.: The Effect of a Market Orientation on Business Profitability. Journal of Marketing 54(4), 20–35 (1990)
10. Ken, M., Mentzer, J.T.: The Effects of Entrepreneurial Proclivity and Market Orientation on Business Performance. Journal of Marketing 66(4), 1–16 (2002)

11. Kohil, A.K., Jaworski, B.J.: Market Orientation: The Construct, Research Propositions and Managerial Implication. Journal of Marketing 54(2), 1–18 (1990)
12. Kare, A., Spillan, J.E., DeShields, O.W.: An Empirical Investigation of the Link Between Market Orientation and Business Performance in Non-Profit Service Providers. Journal of Marketing Theory and Practice 12(2), 59–72 (2004)
13. Lee, H.T., Chea, M.S.: The Relationship Between Entrepreneurship, IT Competency, Market Orientation, and Performance: Empirical Study Focused on Foreign Investment Firms. Journal of International Trade and Industry Studies 12(3), 205–229 (2007)
14. Lee, K.W.: An Empirical Study on the Success Factors of Sustainable Social Enterprise. PH. D Dissertation. Soongsil Univestiy (2009)
15. Hwang, M.A.: The Effects of Characteristics of Woman Entrepreneurs on Managerial and Social Performance. PH. D Dissertation. Soongsil Univestiy (2007)
16. Flowers, C.: Advanced Statistics (sub-note). The College of Education at the University of North Carolina at Charlott (2012)
17. Sung Hee, J., Yoon Joo, M.: The Effect Entrepreneurship and Market Orientation on Social Performance of Social Enterprise: Focused on the Gender Differences. Journal of Industrial Economics and Business 24(5), 2777–2802 (2011)

Relation between Children's Rough Physical Play and Using Social Language

Jisun Ma[1], Youngsik Kang[2], and Mijung Lee[3]

[1] Koje College, South Korea
jisunsky@hanmail.net
[2] Chungnam National University, South Korea
tlrdudrkd@yahoo.co.kr
[3] Kongju National University, South Korea
Cuty1215@hanmail.net

Abstract. This study is for understanding relation between rough physical play and social language use, providing basic data for developing program improving social language in the play. To achieve the goal, these study subjects are selected. First, what is relation between Rough physical play and social language use? Second, what is effect of Rough physical play of children to social language use?

Keywords: Rough Physical Play, Using Social Language.

1 Introduction

Children are growing as they interact with environment on their own ways through social experience and various plays. Many rough physical plays, which are enjoyed by children and bring positive effect, mean physical contact and chasing play like catching and tumbling with more than two children for just having fun without competition (Jeon So yeung, 2011). Meanwhile, despite many children enjoy rough physical play, adults have far short awareness for the play (Kim Yeong ah. 2007).

Compare to other play, Rough physical play is hard to be categorized with its feature (Pellegrini, 1987), considered as an unregulated behavior (Humphreys & Smith, 1984). With this, the play represents violent behavior with aggression, going against the value accepted by many teachers (Lee Jung suk, 2002; Johnson, Christie, & Yawky, 1999). Especially, the outlook of Rough physical play is similar to aggressive behavior including kicking, hitting, and chasing, considered to give negative effect to children (Pellegrini, 1989, Ko Yeo hun, Um Jung ae, 2010).

But, children have opportunities to grow physically and release energy through rough physical play, and even learn how to interact with others by controlling emotion, leaning skill for building social relation (Humphrey & Smith, 1987).

Rough physical play is focusing on behaviors appeared on the outlook, but there is social linguistic interaction on the play with peers. Social language means intentional utterance, so it can prevent the play becoming as a aggressive behavior, and effective inducing Rough physical play help establish more friendly social relation (Smith & Boulton, 1990).

T.-h. Kim et al. (Eds.): SIP/WSE/ICHCI 2012, CCIS 342, pp. 249–253, 2012.

With study results showing children participating in Rough physical play show better adaptation and higher popularity (Kim Yeong ah, 2007), and children with high popularity use more social language (Park Ga suk, 2001), it is understood there is interaction between rough physical play and social language use.

This study is for understanding relation between rough physical play and social language use, providing basic data for developing program improving social language in the play. To achieve the goal, these study subjects are selected.

First, what is relation between rough physical play and social language use?

Second, what is effect of Rough physical play of children to social language use?

2   Research Method and Procedure

2.1   Study Object

With 90 children in Kindergarten of N-si in Chungcheongnam-do and H kindergarten as the objects, the average age is 78 months with 49 boys and 41 girls.

2.2   Study Tool and Procedure

2.2.1   Study Tool
Rough physical play examine tool
Based on observation scope of Humphrey & Smith(1987), modified and supplemented tools for Korean context and tools used in Kim Hyun suk`s (2011) study are applied in this study.

Social language examine tool
For measuring social language of children, the tools used for this study is what Huh Jung soon (2007) used. The tools were used social analysis standard suggested by Pelligrini (1982) and translated by Park Ga suk (2001) with help from early childhood education expert for social analysis standard suggested by Pelligrini (1982). (Table 1)

Table 1. Scope of examine tool for social language

Demand					Conclusion						Response				Adjustment				Competition				Direction
Demand and information on	Demand maction on	Demand approval	Suggestion	Check	Signal	Internal expression	Evaluation	Estimation	Rule explanation	Reason on and cause explanation	Information demand and respond	Approval	Denial	Attention	Order r design nation	Confirmquestion	Manner expression	Argument	Complaint	Warning	Individual demand	Order

2.2.2   Study Procedure

Data for rough physical play and using social language of children was collected from July 2nd to 20th, and assistant teachers filmed morning free selective activity and afternoon outside play time that children make large or small groups. Video shooting was performed 20 minutes in morning, lunch time, and afternoon respectably in and outside. Researchers analyzed the recorded video. For collected data analysis, children`s Rough physical play was examined for 60 times and with 20 seconds of observance unit. Researcher observed each child independently based on recorded data. The observance was 1200 seconds per child (20 seconds*60 times) for 3 sessions.

For social language analysis, conversation was analyzed with 10 minutes as a unit, and the social language chart was filled for five minutes. The analysis was performed for 20 minutes per child (10 minutes*2 times) for 3 sessions.

3   Results and Analysis

3.1   Relation Rough Physical Play and Using Social Language of Children

In general, there`s positive correlation between Rough physical play and using social language of children (r=.385, p<.001). (Table 2) Especially, there`s positive correlation in the whole play with social language of conclusion (r=.215, p<.05), competition (r=.335, p<.001), and direction (r=.397, p<.001), and taunt (r=.292, p<.01), pushing and pulling (r=.220, p<.05), hitting and stab (r=.317, p<.01), falling (r=.400, p<.001), and catching (r=.251, p<.05) have positive correlation with whole social language.

3.2   Influence of Rough Physical Play over Using Social Language

Falling has 15%, 11% for hitting/stab, 3.5% for taunt, and lunging has 5.4% of negative influence, total 34.9% when it comes to Rough physical play having influence over using social language (Table 4).

In the low rank, falling has 11%, 6.1% for hitting/stab, and 5% for lunging, total 22% of positive influence when it comes to required language use. For conclusive language use, taunt has 12.5% of positive influence, 6.3% for falling, 5.1% for hitting/stab, and arm swinging has negative influence, total 29.6%. For adjusted language use, falling has 8.5% of positive influence, and 5.5% for hitting/stab, total 14%. For competitive language use, hitting/stab has 13# of positive influence, 4.4% for catching, 4% for taunt, and stalkingly scaring has 4.3% of negative influence, total 25.7%. For directive language use, falling has 16% of positive influence, 4.8% for pushing and pulling, and 3.5% for hitting/stab, total 24.3%.

4   Discussion and Conclusion

This study is for understanding the influence of Rough physical play of children over social language use. The central discussion for the results in study subject is as follows.

First, as a result of researching relation of the play and using social language of children, it is found that the more of the play, the more use of social language, especially conclusive, competitive, and directive social language. This result has the same context with previous studies saying the play has relation with social development (Koo Myung Sil 2007; Kim Young Ah, 2007; Lee Ji Young 2007; Wang Hye Won, 2012; Humphrey & Smith, 1987; Pellegrini, 1988, 1989; Periolat, 1998). This is a meaningful result showing social language can play an intermediate role for the play to be turned into pro-social play, not aggressive play.

The low rank of Rough physical play and social language type is as follows.

The entire play has positive correlation with low rank of social language including suggestion, evaluation, attention, order designation, warning, and order. The result allows inference that control function of social language inducing behavior of other children, restraining, directing, and guiding are effectively used (Huh Jung sun, 2007).

Second, as a result of studying the influence of Rough physical play over social language use, falling has the highest positive influence among the play, and hitting/stab and taunt have also have positive influence. Lunging has negative influence. It is a different result with Wang Hye Won (2012)`s study result that only escape and chasing have positive influence over pro-social leadership.

When it comes to influence of social language over low rank, it is found Rough physical play affects language use of demand, conclusion, adjustment, competition, and direction. Especially, falling and hitting/stab of the play evenly affect low ranks positively. This means falling, and hitting/stab of the play make children understand intention of others and use social language of demand, adjustment, and direction in the play making rough motion or inducing fight.

First, it is a result of quantitatively analyzing only Rough physical play and social language of children. Further study is required phenomenological approach that how social language makes the play pro-social play, not aggressive one.

Second, as the result shows, the play having positive influence over using social language is less aggressive behavior. As aggressive behaviors including arm swinging and stalkingly scaring have negative influence, for Rough physical play activity, development of rough physical play program is needed using rough play and social language appropriately.

References

1. Hun, K.Y., Ae, O.J.: An Investigation into the Aspects and Factors At Work in Children's rough and tumble play. Korea Journal of Child Studies 31(4) (2010)
2. Ah, K.Y., Young, S.H.: Aspects of Childern's Rough and Tumble Play during the Outdoor Play and Effects of Center and Social Competence. Korean Life Science Magazine 16(5) (2007)
3. Suk, K.H.: Relationship of Rough and Tumble Play to Social in Preschoolers. Major in Early childhood Education, Graduate school of Education, Gyeongin Natinal University of Education (2011)

4. Park, G.-S.: A Study on popular young children's social competence language. Major in Early childhood Education, Department of Education Graduate school of Education, Chung-Ang University (2001)
5. Won, W.H.: The Relationship between Rough and Tumble Play and Social Power of Children. Department of Physical Education Graduate school Pusan University (2012)
6. Sook, L.J.: Rough and Tumble Play in preschool children. Educational-industrial Laboratory Collected Papers, 22 (2002)
7. Young, L.J.: The Relationship between Boy's and Girl's Rough and Tumble Play and Peer Competence. Major in Early childhood Education of Duksung Women's University (2007)
8. Young, J.S.: A Comparison between Father Mother Perceptions of Young Children's Rough and Tumble. Major in Early childhood Education Graduate School of Edcation Pusan National University (2011)
9. Soon, H.J.: Children's Peer Competence and Social Language According to Peer Status. Major in Early childhood Education. Graduate School of Education of Sungshin Women's University (2007)
10. Coie, J.D., Kupersmith, J.B.: A Behavioral analysis of emerging social status in boys and girls groups. Child Development 54, 1400 (1983)
11. DiPietro, J.A.: Rough and Tumble Play. A function of gender. Developmental Psychology 17(1), 50–58 (1981)

Harmonic Frequency Test of Track Circuit's Return Current According to Electrical Rolling-Stock Operation

Baek Jonghyen, Jo Hyenjeong, Kim Geunyep, Lee Kangmi,
Kim Yongkyu, and Jang Donguk

Korea Railroad Research Institute, Woram-dong. #360-1,
Uiwang-si, Gyeonggi-do, South Korea
jhbaek@krri.re.kr

Abstract. Electric power used in electrical vehicles flows into the substation through the feedback circuit, track circuit. Due to this power conversion equipment in electrical railroads, return current contains harmonics, and it should not affect other communication lines. In this paper, based on the return currents, we measured harmonics and analyzed an influence in railway equipment due to the harmonics. For analysis, we utilize the measured values of return currents measured in track circuits, and predictive values of those compared to the earth methods between the existing electrified sections. Applying the regulations used for Gyeongbu HSL(High Speed Line), the results of measured harmonics have found to be acceptable.

Keywords: Track Circuit, Return Current, Harmonics, Electrical Railroad.

1 Introduction

Based on the past 2007, our country paid huge costs amounting to 24 trillion Won to traffic congestion costs, which is the huge amount reaching 3% of the entire gross domestic product(GDP). Recently, as we faced with the global warming problem and environmental problem, etc. all over the world, the railway is recounted as the sustainable means of transportation. However, in case of railway, it can be linked directly to the huge damage to the human lives and properties when any accident occurs, while simultaneously it is the most efficient means of transportation as the means of transportation suitable for the mass transport. Thus, the safety precaution against accident is the most important thing before everything. The current generated by the electrical rolling stock is associated with the signal, electricity, catenary and track system, and it is one of the most important elements which has to be handled to protect the electric system in relation to the railway in accordance with the safety of trackside staff and electrification. Especially, in case where the train control system which is responsible for the safety of train operation is malfunctioned by the influence of the harmonics of return current, it can cause serious problems such as the serious accident and discontinuation of train operation, etc. Moreover, since recent train control system is on a trend to be converted to the train control system realizing a

T.-h. Kim et al. (Eds.): SIP/WSE/ICHCI 2012, CCIS 342, pp. 254–260, 2012.

virtual block and moving block system caused by the wireless communication which applies ICT(Information and Communication Technology), it is necessary to analyze the inductive disturbance of system and system failure, etc. caused by the unbalance of return current and overcurrent state more seriously[1-7]. The load current used in the electrical rolling stock is flowed in the substation through impedance bonds by being divided into about 1/2 respectively since the impedance of both rails of track which is the return circuit is almost identical. The load current contains harmonics because of the power converter used in the electrical rolling stock, and this harmonic current shall not have an effect on the external communication line. Power converting system of the electrical rolling stock is consisted of the main power converter which performs the propulsion of vehicle and electrical braking by controlling the traction motor and the auxiliary power supply unit which supplies the power source of electric devices within the vehicle and the power sources necessary for the lighting fixtures and heating & cooling facilities for passenger car services. Power converting system has been equipped with excellent control capabilities in the aspects of high degree of performance and riding comfort, efficiency, safety and energy consumption owing to the technical development of power electronics technology, high-speed & large-capacity semiconductor devices and the microprocessor. However, due to the harmonics generated according to the use of high speed switching devices, it will have an effect on the substation, signaling system, data transmission and surveillance system as well as electrical vehicle[6-10]. Especially, the noise current generated at the frequency in the vicinity of multiples of power converter is call as the harmonics. This paper analyzed the relationship of harmonics of the return current in accordance with vehicle operation speeds in the electric railway section on the basis of the harmonics of return current which were measured and analyzed in accordance with the operation of rolling stock in the electric railway section newly established to check the harmonics of return current where the test must be performed according to the revised Railway Safety Act.

2 How to Measure the Harmonics of Track Circuit

To check whether there is any interference of harmonics in the track circuit in accordance with the operation of electrical rolling stock, we measured harmonics of return current by installing the Rogowski coil at the place where it is connected with the grounding to vehicle as shown in Figures 1 (a) and (b). We performed a FFT analysis by connecting current signals measured at the Rogowski coil with the notebook computer where the Labview 8.6 program for measurement was installed and by converting it to A/D.

Test criteria used at the time of stage 1 for the Gyeongbu High Speed Line were applied as its test criteria. This means that, when checking the interference of harmonics in the track circuit in accordance with the operation of electrical rolling stock, the harmonics measured at the central frequency(F0) and lateral frequency(F0±25Hz) by each basic frequency of track circuit(2040Hz, 2400Hz, 2760Hz, 3120Hz) shall not exceed harmonic limits by track circuit frequency listed in the Table 1 continuously for more than 1 second simultaneously[11]. The meaning of this criteria shows that, in case where the harmonics measured at the central frequency(F0) and lateral frequency(F0±25Hz) exceed harmonic limits by track circuit frequency continuously for more than 1 second simultaneously, there is a worry about disorders occurred in the transmission of information on train detection and speed limit.

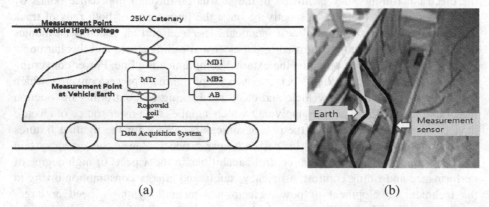

(a)   (b)

Fig. 1. Harmonic current measured point; (a) Harmonic current measured point, (b) Current sensor installed transformer earth cable

Table 1. Harmonic limits of track circuit frequency

Track circuit frequency	2040Hz	2400Hz	2760Hz	3120Hz
Harmonic limits of central frequency(F0)	228mA	192mA	156mA	121mA
Harmonic limits of lateral frequency(F0±25Hz)	80mA	60mA	52mA	45mA

3   Result of Measurement and Analysis on the Harmonics of Return Current

To check whether there is any interference of the track circuit in the harmonics in accordance with the operation of electrical rolling stock, we measured it by installing a current sensor at the high-voltage grounding side of the inside of KTX vehicle, and the effective values of harmonics measured at the central frequency(F0) and lateral frequency(F0±25Hz) by each basic frequency of track circuit(2040Hz, 2400Hz, 2760Hz, 3120Hz) did not exceed harmonic limits by track circuit frequency listed in Table 1 continuously for more than 1 second simultaneously. This paper presents total of 4 results of measurement and analysis methods for the one way trip of 170±5km/h and 1 round trip of 270±5km/h through which we obtained this conclusion.

3.1   Result of Measurement on the Train Driving at 170Km/h of Train Speed in the Up-Direction

The result of measurement on the harmonics of track circuit for the train driving at the speed of 170Km/h in the up direction was presented in Table 2. We may see that they do not exceed harmonic limits by basic track circuit frequency for more than 1 second. To analyze the effect according to the harmonics of return current by each basic frequency, we presented fluctuated values of return current according to the time in the graph by using the Sound & Vibration tool-kit of Labview 8.6 like Figure 2 and analyzing them. In case of Figure 2, it shows the result of analysis on the band of 2400Hz among 4 kinds of frequency used. In (a) of Figure 2, we analyzed portions where the harmonics measured at the central frequency(F0) and lateral frequency(F0±25Hz) exceed their limits by dividing them into two areas such as A and B in details like (b) and (c). Although there is a portion where the harmonic limit was exceeded for more than 1 second partially like the result of Table 2, there was no portion where harmonics measured at the central frequency(F0) and lateral frequency(F0±25Hz) exceeded their limits for more than 1 second simultaneously. Provided, in Figure 2, in case of lateral frequencies, they werc analyzed at F0±20Hz and F0±30Hz since it is impossible to analyze F0±25Hz in the unit of 0.1 second accurately.

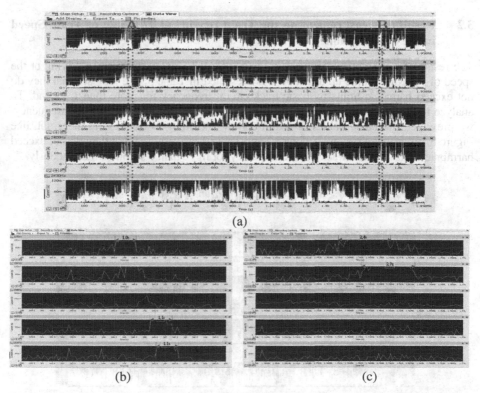

(a)

(b)   (c)

Fig. 2. Measuring result of up-direction on train velocity 170km/h; (a) Measuring data of harmonic current, (b) Analysis data of A section, (c) Analysis data of B section

Table 2. Up-direction 170km/h

Evaluation item	Judgment criteria		Test result	Remarks	Evaluation item	Judgment criteria		Test result	Remarks
1. 2040Hz	≦ 28mA	Do not exceed them for more than 1 second simultaneousl y at F0 and F0±25Hz	1. 2040Hz : Max. value 288mA 2 .2040Hz±25Hz : Max. value 332mA (Did not exceed them for more than 1 second simultaneously at F0 and F0±25Hz)	Suitable	5. 2760Hz	≦ 56mA	Do not exceed them for more than 1 second simultaneous ly at F0 and F0±25Hz	5. 2760Hz : Max. value259mA 6. 2760Hz±25Hz : Max. value 261mA (Did not exceed them for more than 1 second simultaneously at F0 and F0±25Hz)	Suitable
2. 2040Hz ± 25Hz	≦ 80mA				6. 2760Hz ± 25Hz	≦ 52mA			
3. 2400Hz	≦ 192 mA	Do not exceed them for more than 1 second simultaneousl y at F0 and F0±25Hz	3. 2400Hz : Max. value 284mA 4.2400Hz±25Hz : Max. value 287mA (Did not exceed them for more than 1 second simultaneously at F0 and F0±25Hz)	Suitable	7. 3120Hz	≦ 121 mA	Do not exceed them for more than 1 second simultaneous ly at F0 and F0±25Hz	7. 3120Hz : Max. value 219mA 8. 3120Hz±25Hz : Max. value 230mA (Did not exceed them for more than 1 second simultaneously at F0 and F0±25Hz)	Suitable
4. 2400Hz ± 25Hz	≦ 60mA				8. 3120Hz ± 25Hz	≦ 45mA			

3.2   Result of Measurement on the Train Driving at 270Km/h of Train Speed in the Up-Direction

The result of measurement on the harmonics of track circuit for the train driving at the speed of 270Km/h in the up direction was presented in Table 3. We may see that they do not exceed harmonic limits by basic track circuit frequency for more than 1 second. To analyze the effect according to the harmonics of return current by each basic frequency, we presented fluctuated values of return current according to the time in the graph like Figure 3. As with the results of Figure 2 and Table 2, we may see that they do not exceed harmonic limits by basic track circuit frequency for more than 1 second simultaneously.

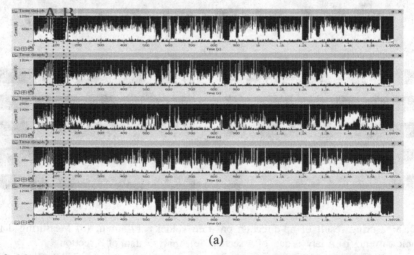

(a)

Fig. 3. Measuring result of up-direction on train velocity 270km/h; (a) Measuring data of harmonic current, (b) Analysis data of A section, (c) Analysis data of B section

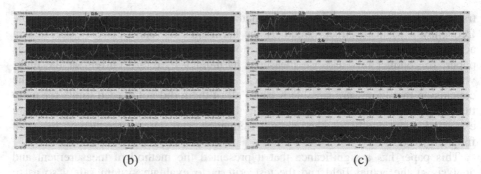

(b)   (c)

Fig. 3. (*continued*)

Table 3. Up-direction 270km/h

Evaluation item	Judgment criteria		Test result	Remarks	Evaluation item	Judgment criteria		Test result	Remarks
1. 2040Hz	≦ 228 mA	Do not exceed them for more than 1 second simultaneously at F0 and F0±25Hz	1. 2040Hz : Max. value 286mA 2. 2040Hz±25Hz : Max. value 517mA (Did not exceed them for more than 1 second simultaneously at F0 and F0±25Hz)	Suitable	5. 2760Hz	≦ 156 mA	Do not exceed them for more than 1 second simultaneously at F0 and F0±25Hz	5. 2760Hz : Max. value 309mA 6. 2760Hz±25Hz : Max. value 365mA (Did not exceed them for more than 1 second simultaneously at F0 and F0±25Hz)	Suitable
2. 2040Hz ± 25Hz	≦ 80mA				6. 2760Hz ± 25Hz	≦ 52mA			
3. 2400Hz	≦ 192 mA	Do not exceed them for more than 1 second simultaneously at F0 and F0±25Hz	3. 2400Hz : Max. value 282mA 4. 2400Hz±25Hz : Max. value 514mA (Did not exceed them for more than 1 second simultaneously at F0 and F0±25Hz)	Suitable	7. 3120Hz	≦ 121 mA	Do not exceed them for more than 1 second simultaneously at F0 and F0±25Hz	7. 3120Hz : Max. value 203mA 8. 3120Hz±25Hz : Max. value 371mA (Did not exceed them for more than 1 second simultaneously at F0 and F0±25Hz)	Suitable
4. 2400Hz ± 25Hz	≦ 60mA				8. 3120Hz ± 25Hz	≦ 45mA			

4   Conclusion

This paper presented results which were evaluated by measuring the harmonic current generated in the actual electrical rolling stock to check whether there is any interference of the harmonics in the frequency to be used at the track circuit due to the return current generated at the time of the operation of electrical rolling stock. This test is to check whether it can have an effect on the operation of track circuit which Is detecting the train occupation and transmitting the speed code to the antenna of vehicle. For this purpose, the criteria applied when testing the stage 1(Seoul-Dongdaegu) for Gyeongbu High Speed Line were applied, and we could see that the harmonics generated in the vehicle were suitable for the criteria.

In accordance with the Railway Safety Act which was revised recently, in case of the newly established line or improved line which can have an effect on the performance, the suitability of facilities must be checked by performing the general facility validation test. Especially, it is required to perform a test on harmonics of track circuit's return current to check whether it is possible to have an effect on the frequency used in the track circuit by the harmonics of return current generated in accordance with the operation of rolling stock in the electric railway section. In this paper, to conduct this test, we measured harmonics of return current at the high-voltage grounding side of rolling stock, and as a result, we could obtain the conclusion that they were suitable because all of them did not exceed limits for more than 1 second simultaneously, although there were cases where the limits were exceeded individually at the central frequency and lateral frequency by each frequency used.

This paper has a significance that it presented the method of measurement and analysis at the actual field and the test criteria to evaluate system safety so as to prevent the inductive disturbance of system and system failure caused by the return current, and we expect that it will contribute to the relative fields greatly in the future.

References

1. Baek, J.-H., Kim, Y.-G., Oh, S.-C., Cho, H.-J., Lee, G.-M.: Analysis on the return current according to the operation of rolling stock in the electric railway section. Journal of the Korea Academia-Industrial cooperation Society 12(9), 4112–4118 (2011)
2. Kim, Y.-G., Yoo, C.-G.: Effect of return current according to the application of joint grounding network in the 2×25kV power supply method. Journal of the Korean Institute of Electrical Engineers 51B(9), 509–514 (2002)
3. Lee, G.-N., Kim, Y.-G., Baek, J.-H., Yoo, C.-G.: Comparison of return currents according to the grounding type of electric railway system. Journal of the Academic Conference on Information and Control, 53–55 (2005)
4. Kim, Y.-G., Yang, D.-C., Yoo, C.-G.: Forecast on return current and impedance in the electrified section of Gyeongbu Line. Journal of the Summer Conference 2001 of the Institute of Electronics Engineers of Korea, 123–126 (2001)
5. Kim, Y.-G., Baek, J.-H., Yoo, C.-G.: A study on properties of track circuit according to the electrification of existing line. Journal of the Summer Conference 2004 of the Korean Institute of Electrical Engineers (2004)
6. Kim, Y.K., et al.: Estimation and Measurement of the traction return current on the electrified Gyeongbu Line. In: 2001 Proceedings of the International Conference on Control, Automation and Systems, pp. 1458–1461 (2001)
7. Lee, G.-N., Kim, Y.-G., Kim, J.-G., Kim, H.-R.: Joint grounding and single grounding interfaces at the track circuit. Journal of the Autumn Conference 2005 of the Korean Society of Railway (2005)
8. Kim, Y.-G., Baek, J.-H., Park, J.-Y.: Analysis on properties of tuning unit for the efficiency of maintenance of the track circuit. Journal of the Korea Academia-Industrial Cooperation Society 10(12), 3594–3599 (2009)
9. The Office of Railroads, Report on the action design for signalling equipment according to the electrification between Dongdaegu~Busan of Gyeongbu Line (1999)
10. The Office of Railroads, Report on the action design for power equipment according to the electrification between Dongdaegu~Busan of Gyeongbu Line (1999)
11. Eukorail, Core System Integration Test Procedure Phase A and B for the First Step of Gyeongbu High Speed Line: EMI (WBS No.: K690-0-C2300-EE-00+T-075) (2003)

Development of Sliding Step and Test Results

Euijin Joung

Korea Railroad Research Institute
ejjoung@krri.re.kr

Abstract. In the platform of the urban transit system, a certain gap is inevitably made between the subway vehicle and the platform, and the gap gets wider in the curved area of the platform. This gap contributes to decrease passengers' safety. Nowadays plug-in type doors are installed in the newly designed urban transit system. It is worldwide trend to reduce the noise coming from the outer side of vehicle. This plug-in door basically needs wider gap between door and platform and it maybe raise a serious accident. Sliding step is suggested to minimize gap and to overcome this safety problem at platform. In this paper, we presents development process for sliding step, trends of sliding step, development plan, technical description and test results.

Keywords: Advanced Electric Multiple Unit (EMU), Sliding step, The disabled.

1   Introduction

Existing transportation facilities give suffers for the disabled, elderly, pregnant women, infants and accompanying characters, and children because this system is usually fitted to the normal public. It is difficult for passenger to get on and off fast and easily because gap is formed between vehicles and platforms depending on the fluctuations of the vehicle. This gap increases the risk of accidents for a wheelchair wheel or the passenger's feet to fall and it is an obstacle for the disabled to move. Relieving the gap between the vehicle and platform, and increasing the safety of all passengers including the disabled, we have developed a sliding step to apply to the advanced Electric Multiple Unit (EMU). In this paper, differing to the existing platform attached gap filler, configuration and capabilities of the vehicle attached sliding step are described. Also developing concept and test results are described.

2   Needs and Technology Status of Sliding Step

2.1   Needs of Sliding Step

Eleven accidents have been recorded related to the gap between train and platform in Korea from 2003 to 2009. Two fatalities and nine severe injuries were occurred from those accidents. The figure below represented the press reports for those accidents.

T.-h. Kim et al. (Eds.): SIP/WSE/ICHCI 2012, CCIS 342, pp. 261–266, 2012.
© Springer-Verlag Berlin Heidelberg 2012

Fig. 1. Press reports for subway door a accidents

A newspaper said 459 stations have 50mm exceed gap between train and platform in the total 479 station. The 126 stations exceed 100mm gap and 32 stations exceed 150mm gap. This gap is made to prevent collision train to platform.

2.2   Technology Status

2.2.1   Vehicle Attached Type Step

Vehicle attached sliding step is already developed and commercialized in the countries in Europe. Numbers of related patents are registered and the technologies are continuously developed. Vehicle attached sliding step are generously applied when vehicle is first made. [1]-[4]

The step is categorized according to the installation sites and shapes. The steps installed on vehicle have three types such as sliding step, express ramp, and folding step.

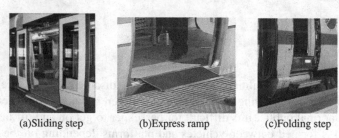

(a)Sliding step   (b)Express ramp   (c)Folding step

Fig. 2. Steps abroad

2.2.2   Platform Attached Type Step

Platform attached step is usually called as gap filler. Rubber type gap filler is attached in platform and installed in most of the station. But the platform attached rubber type sliding step has always certain fixed distance, so the type cannot flexibly respond to various vehicle models. Electric driving sliding step is considered to install to some platforms. The figure 3 shows the steps attached to platform in Korea.

3   Development Concept of Sliding Step

3.1   Gap between Vehicle and Platform

The platform of urban railway transit has to make a gap about 100mm between vehicle limit and platform limit considering the shake or disturbance of vehicle. The gap may

(a)Rubber type platform gap filter　　　　　　　(b)gap filter

Fig. 3. Steps installed in platform in Korea

not be a big problem for the general public, but when the weak and disabled ride on and off the vehicle, it can be dangerous such as wheel-off or misstep. Moreover, if the station is curved, a risk of accidents will be high due to unavoidable additional gap.

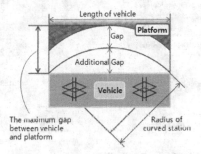

Fig. 4. Maximum gap between vehicle and platform in curved platform area

In addition, plug-in door were applied to the door to improve sound-proof, wind-proof, water-proof effect through completely sealed interior structure in the advanced EMU. The vehicle gap adopting plug-in door should include some gap that needs to operate the door because the door are projected to the outside and slid to the each side positions to open the door. Due to this reason, the gap between vehicle and platform in the advanced EMU is wider than that of the existing subway vehicle. It may cause passengers to higher risks of accidents. So the gap inevitably formed between the vehicle and the platform need to be removed by using the disabled-friendly technologies such as sliding step.

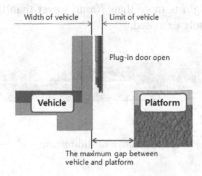

Fig. 5. Maximum gap between vehicle and platform adopting the plug-in door system

3.2   Driving Process of Sliding Step

Figure 6 represents sequence diagram of sliding step related to door system. Because the purpose of sliding step is to prevent passenger's misstep, the step is operated before the door is opened and the step is operated after the door is closed.

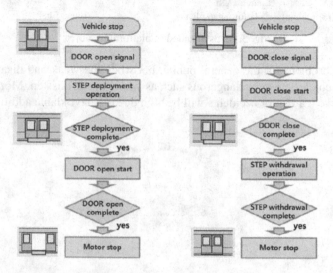

Fig. 6. Sequence diagram of sliding step

While operating sliding step, if the thresh hold bar of sliding step is contacted to the platform, the operation of sliding step is stopped. Because the platform height is not same to each platform, the hinge is installed for the clear operation of sliding step. Especially the hinge is installed to cope with the situation that the platform height is significantly lower than the floor of the vehicle. Because the height of hinge is 70mm, the sliding step can cover the same height difference between vehicle and platform. If the platform height is less than 70mm lower than the floor of the vehicle, the hinge is contacted to the platform sidewall and the extrusion operation of sliding step is limited. If the platform height is more than 70mm lower than the floor of the vehicle, the sliding step is completely extruded.

Fig. 7. Hinge of sliding step

4   Development of Sliding Step

4.1   Design Concept of Sliding Step

Sliding step is designed to facilitate to adjust to the various height of platform. The step assembly is modularized to easily get maintenance and mounting. In addition, it is designed not to require crew's additional operation by interlocking to the door system.

Fig. 8. Design of sliding step

4.2   Configuration of Sliding Step

Sliding step is configured and modularized of housing box, step assembly as an operation unit, locking devices, and checking cover. One of limit switches installed on step assembly as an operation unit is operated to know whether the sliding step is securely closed or opened. All behavior of sliding step is controlled by Step Control Unit (SCU) as a control unit by sensing motor current. The figure 8 shows the configuration of sliding step. [5]

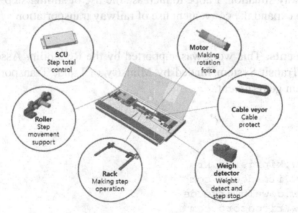

Fig. 9. Sliding step

5   Test Results

The sliding step has been passed all required test. The figures below represent all test results. Nowadays each step is attached below related each door in the advanced EMU and tested to demonstrate reliability factor. [6]

<table>
<tr><td>(a)Water prove</td><td>(b)Step motor</td><td>(c)Characteristics</td><td>(d)TCMS I/F test</td></tr>
</table>

Fig. 10. Test results of sliding step

6   Conclusions

The sliding step has been developed to ensure the passengers' safety including the disabled and the weak by eliminating gap between vehicle and platform. The types of sliding step are divided according to the position that the sliding step is installed. The type of sliding step attached platform is the rubber type that is previously attached to related platform. The installed rubber reduces the gap between vehicle and platform. If the sliding step is installed on the vehicle, it is possible to respond to the various platform typed such as straight or curved form. It also flexible to the height of riding depends on number of passenger and platform conditions and does not require crew's additional operation. The vehicle attached sliding step has been developed adopting the Korean railway situation. I hope to increase the use of sliding step for the disabled and the weak to expand the convenient use of railway transportation system.

Acknowledgements. This work was supported by the Reliability Assessment of Advanced Urban Transit System funded by Ministry of Land, Transport and Maritime Affairs of Korean government.

References

1. http://www.kipris.or.kr
2. http://www.ife-doors.com
3. http://www.dowaldwerke.de
4. http://www.riconcorp.com
5. Joung, E.J.: Development of Sliding Step System for Electric Multiple Unit. In: ICEE 2010, Korea (2010)
6. Kim, G.D.: Development of next-generation advanced urban railway transit. Final Report, KRRI (2010)

The Study on the Effect of Neuro-feedback Trainings on the Brain Waves of Baduk Players

Sang-Kyun Ahn

Dept. of Baduk Myungji University
askyhk@hanmail.net

Abstract. This study has been focused on grasping the possibilities of the change of brain waves and baduk skills, whose data were obtained both before and after the neuro-feedback from 1th July, 2010 to 30th September, 2010. Brain wave activities were measured by performing the linear-analysis of the data obtained on the frontal lobe of research subjects (the experimental group of 10 baduk players, and the control group of 10) after the neuro-feedback training. The data show that the experimental group has the higher mean difference than the control group, and there were statistically significant differences in Attention Quotient (right) (P=0.049), emotional quotient (P=0.025), and Stress Resistance Quotient (left) (P–0.004) and (right) (P=0.003). This means that the improved brain function quotient can lead to improved baduk skills through efficiency optimization training.

Keywords: neuro-feedback, brain wave, brain quotient, baduk players.

1 Introduction

One of the ways to scientifically study the brain and functional states in regard to human thinking is to measure brain waves. Brain waves can be continuously measured as time passes, and used to evaluate the activities of the brain while the subject is performing a long and complicated task. Researches on brain waves started with the early neurophysiology on the basis of the electrical attributes of the nerves, and have been developing in various ways while reflecting the interests of the times. In recent years interest in the brain is very high in the field of sports psychology as a method of psychological skills training through control of brain waves.

As objective research methodologies for psychological skills training within the research scope of applied sports psychology and approaches to find out whether it is possible to utilize brain wave control devices for quantification of research results are attempted, diverse researches on brain waves are conducted. Understanding the brain waves revealed during exercise does not simply mean understanding the wake pattern, but becomes an important information source for training necessary for formulating and applying a personalized and situation-contingent bio-feedback program. In Korea Kim Jin-Gu (2002) reported that alpha self-regulation training for high school shooting players improved athletic performance, and Jeong Cheong-Hee (2001) also

T.-h. Kim et al. (Eds.): SIP/WSE/ICHCI 2012, CCIS 342, pp. 267–271, 2012.
© Springer-Verlag Berlin Heidelberg 2012

reported that the brain wave control training for college tennis players improved concentration and reduced play errors, and thus had positive influence on athletic performance as well. In addition, after alpha self-regulation training was administered to college golf learners, they performed golf putting, and the result was that the group with the alpha self-regulation training was much more consistent in golf performance than the control group (Kim Jae-Hun, 2002). These detailed researches differ slightly from one another in terms of main topics and research methodologies, but they had one thing in common: the purpose of creating positive brain waves of one's own will to improve cognitive ability.

In actuality, even though many baduk players have outstanding capabilities, they often fail to show their real ability in important matches owing to anxiety caused by various reasons, lack of attention, and poor health. Accordingly, it is a very important task for sport psychologists to analyze, explain and predict various factors so as to formulate appropriate strategies and provide baduk players with the psychological conditions in which they can display their abilities to the fullest.

This study attempts to take advantage of neuro-feedback devices to identify the changes in the brain waves before and after training, and gauge the possibility of using neuro-feedback training to improve baduk skills.

2   Research Methodology

2.1   Research Design

After a pre-study conducted from July 1, 2010 to September 30, 2010, this study tries to analyze the difference in brain waves before and after the neuro-feedback training by examining the brain waves of research subjects. The subjects participating in the training were the research students of the Huh Jang-Hee Baduk Research Center located in Dobong-gu, Seoul (KBA members, with a high level of baduk skills and more than 3 years of baduk experience, Jeong Su-Hyeon, 1999), and there were 10 subjects in the experimental group, and 10 in the control group. The subjects did not have any history of mental diseases, never abused drugs, and mostly healthy. The training utilized the coloring analysis program contained in the BQ Test to measure rest, attention, and concentration for a minute respectively, and the lowest score was chosen as the training mode. The mobile neuro-feedback was done more than 3 times a week, and each training session was between 15 minutes and 20 minutes in length.

2.2   Measurement of Brain Waves

The brain wave measurement system used in this study is the neuro-feedback system developed by the Korea Research Institute of Jungshin Science (Neuro-feedback System, Braintech Corp., Korea). Its correlation coefficient with a well-known brain wave measurement system, Grass System (USA), in regard to the alpha, beta, and theta values of the left/right brain waves, was .916(p<.001). Its reliability is proven (Kim Yong-Jin, 2000). It measures the left brain (Fp1) and the right brain (Fp2) in the prefrontal part at the same time, and uses both the unipolar lead and the bipolar lead.

2.3   Analysis of Brain Waves

Objectively speaking, a brain function analysis <table 1>, based on the neuro-feedback technology, is available. Unlike the indirect analysis based on surveys and problem-solving, such as existing IQ tests or aptitude tests, the brain function analysis measures brain waves to directly and quantitatively analyze the developmental state, activity state, balance, attention capabilities, resting and learning capabilities of the brain.

As the brain waves (δ wave, θ wave, α wave, β wave, etc.) are adjusted by frequency range, the brain function quotients can reflect the functional states of the brain. The variability of the brain waves is the standard deviation of the brain waves (Park Byeong-Wun. 2005).

Table 1. The Characteristics of Brain Quotient by Brain Wave Measurement

Analysis quotient	Meaning
Attention quotient (ATQ)	The level of awakening of the brain
Emotional quotient (EQ)	Emotional balance
Stress quotient (SQ)	Level of physical and mental stress resistance
Brain function quotient (BQ)	General judgment of brain functions

2.4   Data Processing

SPSS, a statistical analysis program, was used to process the data obtained from the BQ Test. To understand the difference in the brain waves between baduk players and ordinary people, T-Tests were conducted. Means and standard deviations were calculated for all data, and the significance level was P<.05.

3   Results

The results of the tests before and after the training are shown in <Table 2>.

The attention quotient (right) (P=0.049), the emotional quotient (P=0.025), the stress quotient (left) (P=0.004), the stress quotient (right) (P=0.003), and the brain quotient (P=0.035) showed a statistically significant difference.

Table 2. Brain function quotient before and after the training

		Experimental group			Control group		
		Mean±standard deviation	Delta (mean difference)	P-Value	Mean±standard deviation	Delta (mean difference)	P-Value
Attention quotient (left)	before	65.21±14.65			55.39±15.7		
			8.03	0.201		-4.01	0.588
	after	73.24±7.79			52.38±17.44		

Table 2. (*continued*)

Attention quotient (right)	before	56.57±15.79			58.54±8.87		
			16.1	0.049		1.96	0.688
	after	72.67±8.17			60.50±13.22		
Emotional quotient	before	67.46±5.03			65.33±18.01		
			7.11	0.025		0.94	0.796
	after	74.57±3.73			66.27±9.34		
Stress quotient (left)	before	80.03±5.41			75.10±12.69		
			6.44	0.004		1.86	0.631
	after	86.47±4.61			76.96±9.25		
Stress quotient (right)	before	73.10±11.1			72.71±11.6		
			11.98	0.003		2.92	0.475
	after	85.08±5.43			75.63±7.31		
Brain quotient	before	68.5±4.55			65.94±5.96		
			6.56	0.035		2.75	0.260
	after	75.06±3.46			68.69±6.14		

($P<.05$)

4   Discussion

The training method for the subjects of this study is the 'efficiency optimization training method' which enables them to show their abilities to the fullest. It is intended to induce mental activities, and applied in many fields, such as sports, management and artistic activities. The fact that baduk has positive effects on children's intelligence and emotion, and the mental health of adults is reflected in the statement that "the brain waves of baduk playes may be different from those of ordinary people." There was a statistically significant difference in terms of the attention quotient (Baik Ki-Ja, 2007), and the means of the emotional quotient, the stress resistance quotient, and the brain quotient were higher. Despite the increasing relationship between baduk and human psychology, there is almost no research on how baduk affects brain functions. The possibility of further development of baduk, a mind sport, by improving the skills through efficiency-optimization training based on neuro-feedback for improved brain functions, and the possibility of increasing interest in Korea, the strongest country in baduk, will be examined.

The conclusions of this study are as follows:

Brain waves of the experimental group who went through the neuro-feedback training were changed, and the improvement of the brain function quotient hints at the possibility of using the efficiency optimization training to improve baduk skills.

First, the experimental group who went through the neuro-feedback training showed greater mean differences in all quotients than the control group.

Second, there was a statistically significant difference in the attention quotient (right). The lefthand-side attention quotient of baduk players were significantly different from that of the ordinary people, and their right-side attention quotient was lower. It was confirmed that the neuro-feedback training improves the righthand-side attention quotient.

Third, there was a statistically significant difference in the emotional quotient. It was confirmed that baduk brings emotional stability.

Fourth, there was a statistically significant difference in the stress resistance quotient (left & right). The stress resistance quotient indicates the resistance to physical and mental fatigue caused by internal and external environmental factors. It was confirmed that the neuro-feedback training reduces the physical and mental stress, anxiety and excitement caused by baduk.

Fifth, the brain quotient comprehensively evaluates brain functions on the basis of all the quotients mentioned above. The brain function quotient can be said to be in proportion to IQ, and closely related to the mental and physical health.

The limitation of this study was that the experimental group and the control group were limited to KBA members, and it was difficult to expect improvement of baduk skills in such a short time as 3 months due to the characteristics of baduk as a training for brain development, emotional stabilization, and improvement of attention and thinking power.

References

1. Kimjin-Gu: Motor learning through brain wave self-regulation bio-feedback and EEG change. Korean Society of Sport Psychology 12(1), 1–13 (2002)
2. Jeong, C.-H.: The effects of concentration training utilizing brain waves bio-feedback devices on the performance of archery players. Journal of Korean Society of Sport Psychology 15, 37 (2001)
3. Kim, J.-H.: The effect that concentration and mental image through control of brain waves have on golf putting. Master's thesis, Graduate School of Joongang University (2002)
4. Jeon, S.-H.: A study on the correlation between the baduk problem-solving ability of children learning baduk and their intelligence. Master's thesis, Graduate School of Korea University (1999)
5. Kim, Y.-J.: Evaluation of brain functions based on measurement of brain waves during problem-solving activities. The Journal of the Korea Association of Biological Education 28(3), 291–301 (2000)
6. Park, B.-W.: Introduction to neuro-feedback. The Korean Research Institute for Jungshin Science (2005)
7. Baik, K.-J.: A study on the effect of meurofeedback Training on the Improvement of Brain Function & Baduk Strength for baduk players. Unpublished Doctoral Dissertation, Seoul University of Venture & Imformation (2007)

Weight Assignment Method for Interpolation

Gwanggil Jeon, SeokHoon Kang, and Young-Sup Lee[*]

Department of Embedded Systems Engineering, University of Incheon,
12-1 Songdo-dong, Yeonsu-gu, Incheon 406-772, Korea
{gjeon,hana,ysl}@incheon.ac.kr

Abstract. The bilateral filter is studied in this paper. We implemented bilateral filtering for image and video reconstruction. The bilateral filter consists of domain filter and range filter, and we assign different weights to each filter. The performance of bilateral filter depends on their parameters, and we added another parameter α. To obtain ideal performance with least MSE, parameters should be trained and well assigned. The presented approach reconstructed image and video with significantly reduced artifacts and improved details.

Keywords: Bilateral filter, domain filter, range filter, weight assignment, image reconstruction.

1   Introduction

To remove image denoising, Tomasi and Manduchi presented bilateral filter, which is for noise reducing and smoothing while maintaining image details [1]. The luminance at each pixel in an image is replaced by a weighted average of luminance values from neighbor pixels. The bilateral filter is a non-linear approach which considers local image data to create a kernel which smoothes images without smoothing across edge details. Some literature proved that there is an evidence of straight connection between bilateral filtering and robust estimation of anisotropic diffusion [2].

The traditional bilateral filter employs the Gaussian kernel for filtering. This implies the weight is based on a Gaussian distribution. Note that the weights depend not only on Euclidean distance but also on the radiometric differences such as Andrew's wave, El Fallah Ford, Huber's mini-max, Lorentzian, Tukey bi-weight, Cosine, and Flat [3]. In other words, the weights of domain filtering and range filtering depend on those kernels. In this paper, we implemented bilateral filtering for image and video reconstruction. As the bilateral filter consists of domain filter and range filter, and since the performance of bilateral filter depends on their parameters, we assign different weights to each filter and evaluate the performance and determine the ideal weight. To obtain the ideal performance, the parameters should be trained and well assigned. The presented approach reconstructed image and video with significantly reduced artifacts and improved details.

This paper is organized as follows. Section 2 introduces previous works that based on bilateral filter. Section 3 explains the original bilateral filter and its modification

---

[*] Corresponding author.

T.-h. Kim et al. (Eds.): SIP/WSE/ICHCI 2012, CCIS 342, pp. 272–278, 2012.

by different weight assignment. Section 4 shows the performance results on image and video sequences. Finally, conclusions are presented in Section 5.

2 Review of Previous Work

The bilateral filter was firstly proposed in [1] for color and gray images, which smoothes image and video sequences while preserving edge details based on nonlinear combination of adjacent image values. This has been studied by many researchers. For instance, in [4], authors proposed multi-resolution bilateral filter, where the filter is utilized to the low-frequency subbands of signal decomposition. In [5], authors presented a novel model which is based on bilateral filters and wavelet hybridization for image denoising of diversity of corrupted images. The adaptive bilateral filter for edge sharpness and enhancement with noise removal was presented in [6], where the adaptive bilateral filter enhanced an image by increasing the slope of the edge details without giving overshoot and undershoot. In [3], authors proposed a modification of the bilateral filter, where the filter is a weighted median filter which adaptively calculates the weights in a similar manner to that of the bilateral filter. In [7], authors proposed a new method of image denoising while keeping edge information. To discover edge details of the noisy images during the denoising process, the image is separated into two regions by threshold, i.e., edge region and smooth region. In [8], authors proposed an adaptive bilateral filtering of image signals using local phase characteristics and in [9], authors proposed a method named context bilateral filter. In [10], authors used bilateral filter for medical image denoising.

3 Bilateral Filter

Bilateral filter is a method to smooth noisy images while preserving edge details. The usage of bilateral filter increases swiftly, and now is utilized in several image processing applications such as image denoising and image enhancement [9-10]. There are three main advantages of bilateral filter. Firstly, bilateral filter is simple to use. From bilateral filter, each pixel is replaced by a weighted average of its adjacent pixels. Secondly, bilateral filter has only two parameters which determine the contrast and size of features to maintain. Thirdly, bilateral filter is not an iterative approach. This implies the parameters are simple to be set because their effect is not propagated over iterations. The bilateral filter is achieved by the combinations of two Gaussian kernels, each of them are domain and range filtering. One of them operates in spatial domain and the other one works in intensity domain. The bilateral filter concurrently weights pixels based on spatial distance from the centre pixel as well as intensity difference. Thus, the domain filter weights pixels based on their distance from the centre pixel:

$$w_D(p_c - p_o) = \frac{1}{2}\exp\left(-\frac{(p_c - p_o)^2}{2\sigma_D^2}\right) \tag{1}$$

where p_c and p_o stand for spatial positions of center pixel and other pixel, respectively, and this filter is called domain (D) filter. On the other hand, the range (R) filter is based on photometric difference:

$$w_R\left(y(p_c)-y(p_o)\right)=\frac{1}{2}\exp\left(-\frac{\left(y(p_c)-y(p_o)\right)^2}{2\sigma_R^2}\right)$$

(2)

where $y(\cdot)$ denotes image intensity. Then the bilateral filter is formulated as:

$$\frac{\int y(p_c)\,w_D(p_c-p_o)\,w_R\left(y(p_c)-y(p_o)\right)dp}{\int w_D(p_c-p_o)\,w_R\left(y(p_c)-y(p_o)\right)dp}$$

(3)

In this paper, we modified Eq. (3) as Eq. (4) by adding parameter α. The σ values each domain (σ_D) and range (σ_R) filters are different. We assume both filters use the same $\sigma_S(=1)$, and its function w is w_S.

$$\frac{\int y(p_c)\left(w_S(p_c-p_o)\right)^{\alpha}\left(w_S\left(y(p_c)-y(p_o)\right)\right)^{1/\alpha}dp}{\int \left(w_S(p_c-p_o)\right)^{\alpha}\left(w_S\left(y(p_c)-y(p_o)\right)\right)^{1/\alpha}dp}$$

(4)

4   Experimental Results

The experiments are conducted to determine the best parameter, α. We conduct this experiments in deinterlacing case. All of the test images are converted from the original size into the vertically interlaced size based on the system shown in Fig. 1, and then the reconstructed images, img_{rec}, are compared to the original image, img_{org}.

$$MSE\left(img_{org},img_{rec}\right)=\sum_{i=1}^{width}\sum_{j=1}^{height}\frac{\left(img_{org}(i,j)-img_{rec}(i,j)\right)^2}{width\times height}$$

(5)

Figure 2 shows the employed image and video sequences. They are Airplane, Akiyo, Barbara, Boat, Finger, Girl, Lena, Man, Milkdrop, Peppers, Toys, Zelda, Bus, Football, Mobile, and News.

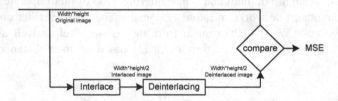

Fig. 1. Performance measurement method

Fig. 2. Test image and video sequences: Airplane, Akiyo, Barbara, Boat, Finger, Girl, Lena, Man, Milkdrop, Peppers, Toys, Zelda, Bus, Football, Mobile, and News

Figures 3, 4, 5, and 6 show the MSE results of Airplane, Boat, Lena, and Mobile. Also, Fig. 7 shows the MSE result of 16 image and video sequences. As we can see, $\alpha=0.11$ gives the best performance throughout 16 images.

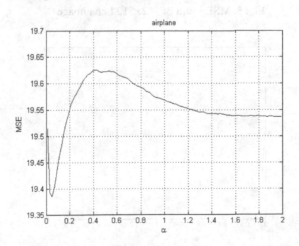

Fig. 3. MSE result of 512×512 Airplane image

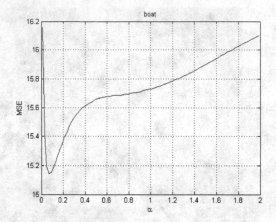

Fig. 4. MSE result of 512×512 Boat image

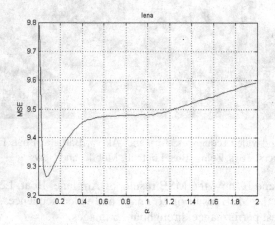

Fig. 5. MSE result of 512×512 Lena image

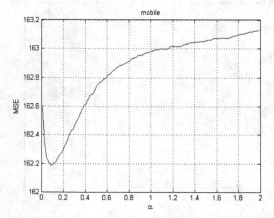

Fig. 6. MSE result of 352×288 Mobile image

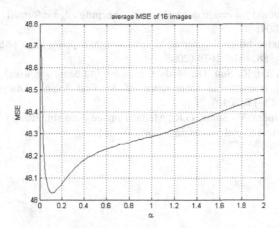

Fig. 7. MSE result of 16 images

5   Conclusions

The modified bilateral filter was introduced in this paper. The bilateral filter consists of domain filter and range filter, and we assign different weights to each filter. The filter performance is depend on the proposed parameter α, and we found α=0.11 gives the least MSE. The presented technique reconstructed image and video with significantly reduced artifacts and improved details.

Acknowledgment. This work was supported by the University of Incheon Research Grant in 2012.

References

1. Tomasi, C., Manduchi, R.: Bilateral filtering for gray and color images. In: Proceedings of the IEEE International Conference on Computer Vision, pp. 839–846 (January 1998)
2. van Boomgaard, R., van de Weijer, J.: On the equivalence of local-mode finding, robust estimation and mean-shift analysis as used in early vision tasks. In: Proc. 16th International Conference on Pattern Recognition, Quebec City, Quebec, Canada, August 11-15, vol. 3, pp. 927–930 (2002)
3. Francis, J.J., de Jager, G.: The bilateral median filter. In: Proc. 14th Symposium of the Pattern Recognition Association of South Africa (2003)
4. Zhang, M., Gunturk, B.K.: Multiresolution bilateral filtering for image denoising. IEEE Trans. Image Processing 17(12), 2324–2333 (2008)
5. Roy, S., Sinha, N., Sen, A.K.: A new hybrid image denoising method. International Journal of Information Technology and Knowledge Management 2(2), 491–497 (2010)
6. Zhang, B.: Adaptive bilateral filter for sharpness enhancement and noise removal. IEEE Trans. Image Processing 17(5), 664–678 (2008)

7. Wei, L.: New method for image denoising while keeping edge information. In: Proc. CISP 2009, pp. 1–5 (2009)
8. Wong, A.: Adaptive bilateral filtering of image signals using local phase characteristic. Signal Processing 88, 1615–1619 (2008)
9. Liao, Z., Hu, S., Yu, Z., Sun, D.: Medical image blind denoising using context bilteteral filter. In: Proc. International Conference of Medical Image Analysis and Clinical Application, pp. 12–17 (2010)
10. Bhonsle, D., Chandra, V., Sinha, G.R.: Medical image denoising using bilateral filter. I. J. Image, Graphics and Signal Processing 6, 36–43 (2012)

Applications of Boryeong Mud Korea's Marketing through SNS Marketing

Moon-Hee Choi

Boryeongmud RIS
Chungwoon University, Korea
moon3713@hanmail.net

Abstract. In this study, Boryeong Mud korea, a local business promotion project initiated by the Ministry of Knowledge Economy, has conducted marketing which was led by a specialized marketing firm Informaster, a participant in 2011. A domestic brand WeMakePrice among SNS marketing firms home and abroad was selected and the new media marketing corresponding to new trend was conducted as Xmas Special Event. The performance achieved through the aggressive marketing on the basis of the new media include 12,741,540 exposures, 3,691 clicks, 0.62% exposure-purchase conversion rate. The findings of this study are expected to be used as important diagnostic tools for Boryeong Mud korea's marketing.

Keywords: SNS Marketing, Boryeong Mud, SNS PR and Marketing Strategy.

1   Introduction

Selected as an excellent task of the local business promotion project initiated by the Ministry of Knowledge in 2009, Boryeong Mud korea pursues the development and the promotion of a leading brand. SNS marketing led by a specialized marketing firm Informaster, a participant in 2011, was conducted in a project where municipalities, universities, research institutes, and private companies participated. A Korean native brand WeMakePrice among SNS marketing firms home and abroad was selected and the new media marketing corresponding to new trend was conducted as Xmas Special Event. This study aims to define the design creative strategies and the marketing management strategies accomplished by Boryeong Mud korea during its SNS marketing and to utilize them as diagnostic tools for further tasks.

2   Paper Preparation

2.1   Birth of SNS Social Media and Its Evolution of SNS

SNS refers to an immediate exchange of ideas through the use of social digital media such as smartphone, smart TV, and to a variety of services based upon that.

T.-h. Kim et al. (Eds.): SIP/WSE/ICHCI 2012, CCIS 342, pp. 279–286, 2012.
© Springer-Verlag Berlin Heidelberg 2012

Table 1. Value of social media from the perspective of marketing

Provenience : Marketing Excutives Networking Group(MENG), Social Media in Marketing, 2008.11.6.

Values	Contents
Quick and easy delivery of messages	SNS Marketing can deliver message quickly and easily. Traditional media conveys information in a top-down manner, whereas social media facilitates horizontal and pyramidal spread through a network of acquaintance.
Low cost	As repeatedly emphasized, social media is less expensive to operate. For example, well-created corporate blogs and Twitters have the power equivalent to popular media, yet the investment cost is on the low side.
Anytime, anywhere	Social media facilitates the delivery of messages anytime and anywhere, because people access popular social media through laptops, mobile phones, and various mobile devices as well as PCs.
Building confidence	Based on interest and friendship, SNS marketing can give customers confidence. Thus, companies can approach customers with more friendly and human images, not formal corporate images.
Gaining new customers	Through SNS marketing, new customers or fans can be secured. A company can gain PR effects through participating in social media. Social media interact with potential customers as well as support the existing customers; and implant positive images of companies and products in customers.

KT Institute of Economics and Business Administration (2010) defined the characteristics of SNS in the categories of participation, disclosure, conversation, community, and connection.

National Internet Development Agency of Korea (2009) categorized cafe · club · Internet cafes, blog · Mini homepage, instant message, human network management services, and virtual reality services. Domestic and international major SNS includes Facebook, Twitter, Cyworld, and me2day. As shown in Table 1.

Marketing Executives Networking Group (2008) suggest 5 social media' marketing values – fast message delivery, low cost, anytime and anywhere, building trust, and gaining new customers.

2.2   Reality of SNS Marketing

Web sites where group purchase based on the word of mouth through SNS is available include Citydeal in Europe, Qpod in Japan, Daberry in Russia, 5 companies(Kupang, Groupon, and WeMakePrice, etc) in Korea, where WeMakePrice is native Korean company. Due to the business models connected through a variety of platforms generate new media and customers with new concept who use those media; and companies carry out aggressive marketing in this new market.

Fig. 1. A Native Korean SNS Marketing Group WeMakePrice

WeMakePrice is forming a social shopping market in Korea under the slogan: "1.5 million WeMakePrice shopahoilics: They are the real prepared consumers who access to shop everyday! "

3   Survey Research and Analysis

3.1   Boryeong Mud Korea's SNS PR Strategy

Boryeong Mud Korea carried out Xmas special event through WeMakePrice SNS channel from Dec 18 2011 till Dec 25 2011. Next is Boryeong Mud Korea's SNS PR strategy through WeMakePrice. First is a customized e-mail service. As shown in Figure 2, Boryeong Mud Korea sent optimized private email DM such as sending cosmetics planned event main banner on Dec 20 2011 Figure 3 and sending mail title on Dec 23 1011 Figure 4.

Fig. 2. Sending email DM with premium zone banner

Fig. 3. Sending email DM with cosmetics planned event main banner

Fig. 4. Sending email DM with email title

Second is the payment DM page configuration. Payment DM page was configured as shown in Figure 5 and it was possible to move to the deal page as shown in Figure 6 through links.

3.2   Boryeong Mud Korea's SNS Marketing Strategy

Next is Boryeong Mud Korea's SNS marketing strategy through WeMakePrice. Banner advertisement also appeared due to the characteristics of internet media.

First is Login Banner. As shown in Figure 7, it was exposed in login and 500,000 ~1.2 million exposures per day were made.

Fig. 5. Payment DM

Fig. 6. Deal page, the result of Payment DM page link

Fig. 7. Login banner

Fig. 8. Premium Zone Fixed Banner

Fig. 9. Left-side top banner

Second is Fixed Banner. As shown in Figure 8, it was fixed on the left and the right zone and 500,000 ~1.2million exposures per day were made.

Third is a left-side top banner. As shown in Figure 9, it was positioned on start page and in internal advertising zone. 690,000 exposures were downloaded (340,000 exposures through iPhone, 350,000 exposures through Android).

3.3   Findings from the Study

As a result of WeMakePrice SNS marketing as above, the results have been derived as shown in Table2. A total of 12,741,540 exposures and a total of 3,691 clicks by customers were made through customized DM, Payment DM, Login Banner, Premium Zone Banner, and Left-side top banner.

Table 2. Summary of PR Results

Item	WeMakePrice exposure	clicks
customized DM	3,824,253	-
payment DM	26,925	-
login banner	105,060	299
premium zone banner	5,169,840	2,948
left-side top banner	7,466,640	444
total	12,741,540	3,691

The results of Boryeong Mud Korea's SNS marketings can be summarized as follows;

As shown in Figure 10, the gender ratio between women and men purchasers is 73%:27%, indicating the main customers of Boryeong Mud Korea are women, Furthermore, men customers which was increased by 30% compared to the prediction indicated the aggressive marketing for men's cosmetics was worth trying.

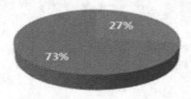

Fig. 10. Gender ratio of purchasers (Female73% ,male27%)

As for the purchasing trend by age group, as shown in Figure 11, the purchase was concentrated on the consumers above 30s, indicating there was a confliction with the fact that Boryeong Mud Korea's festival, a powerful association tool, was exuding youthful energy. Considering that the fact that the cosmetics appeal to the customers above 30s despite its symbolizing youth, there is a need to develop the products through the survey of the contact point with customers.

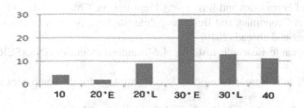

Fig. 11. Number of consumers by age

As for the purchasing trend by region, the purchasing was concentrated in Gyoenggi, Gwanak-gu, and Gangnam-gu. In particular, the purchasing in Gangnam-gu has a great implication because Gangnam-gu's involvement in purchasing is estimated to be high. The results imply that the advancement into metropolitan areas through upgrading and segmentation strategy can be more efficient than the marketing across the nation.

Furthermore, there were a total of 12,741,540 exposures, 5,934 deal page views, and 5,326 visits to page. To maximize the advertisement effect, sending emails two times was added and the position of banner exposure was rearranged to induce additional clicks(The order of left-side top banner exposure and login banner was changed on 21) Exposure-purchase conversion rate was 0.62%, 37 purchases per 5,934 exposures.

4   Conclusion

Boryeong Mud Korea, a project propelled by the Ministry of Knowledge Economy as a local business promotion project, carried out Xmas special event through WeMakePrice, a new media SNS marketing channel, corresponding to a new era. Design marketing was accomplished through SNS PR and Marketing strategy, and the results were: 12,741,540 exposures, 3,691, click, and 0.62% exposure-purchase conversion rate. Thus, the gender ratio of purchasers, age, and regions are expected to be used as important marketing diagnostic tools for Boryeong Mud Korea in the future.

Acknowledgment. This study was made possible by the support from the Ministry of Knowledge Economy for "The Active Marketing through Integrated Brand of Boryeong Mud Industry" in 2012.

References

[1] Marketing Excutives Networking Group (MENG). Social Media in Marketing (November 6, 2008)

[2] Lee, S.H.: Factors affecting the continue use intention of SNS users and their purchase intention: From the perspective of social marketing. Electronic Commerce Study, Graduate School of Chonnam National University, 4–18 (2012)

[3] KT Institute of Economics and Business Administration. Characteristics of SNS (2010)

[4] KT Institute of Economics and Business Administration. Number of subscribers to major SNS both home and abroad (2010)

[5] Samsung Economic Research Institute. 4 Misunderstanding of SNS, SERI Management Notes (2011)

[6] Samsung Economic Research Institute. Success strategy for the companies leveraging SNS (2011)

[7] Choi, M.-H.: Research on Utilization of Boryeongmud Marketing through SNS (Social Network Service) Marketing. In: Proceedings of the KAIS Fall Conference. The Korea Academia-Industrial Cooperation Society, pp. 169–172 (2012)

Multi-modal Interaction System for Enhanced User Experience

Yong Mu Jeong[1], Soo Young Min[1], and Seung Eun Lee[2,*]

[1] SW Device Research Center, Korea Electronics Technology Institute
Seongnam-si, Gyeonggi-do, Korea
{ymjeong,minsy}@keti.re.kr
[2] Dept. of Electronic Engineering
Seoul National University of Science and Technology, Seoul, Korea
seung.lee@seoultech.ac.kr

Abstract. In this paper, we propose a gesture recognition platform for a realistic game. Our Platform provides more effective experience compare to a conventional devices such as a keyboard and a mouse. It consists of one haptic glove (mGlove), four advanced sensing devices (ASD), Gaze tracking module and communication module (zigbee). The communication module establishes the communication channels among the game server, ASD, and mGlove. We demonstrated that a game player can gain full control of an avatar in the realistic game by using the body gestures, enhancing the user experience in the game platform.

Keywords: Gesture Recognition, Realistic Interaction, User Interface.

1 Introduction

Over the last decade, smart interface becomes a major issue that is how to support more natural and immersive user interface. The user interface has evolved from a simple controller such as a pointing device or a button, to a tangible input device. The tangible interface could be able to interact with the virtual space through a physical behavior. Emerging smart interface applications such as gesture recognition, motion tracking, and speech recognition are quickly entering the mobile domain and realistic game systems.

Gesture recognition technology is applied to the game controller such as Nintendo Wii [1] or Microsoft Kinect [2]. Nintendo Wii controller, wiimote, could perceive the user's gesture with infrared emitter in monitor and infrared camera in it. And wii remote plus controller is possible to track the location of controller with acceleration sensor. Microsoft's Kinect consists of the infrared projector and infrared camera. Kinect is able to track user's body based on vision processing.

In order to applicable to realist game systems, a gesture recognition system requires fast response time with adequate accuracy. Previous studies on hand gesture

---

* Corresponding author.

T.-h. Kim et al. (Eds.): SIP/WSE/ICHCI 2012, CCIS 342, pp. 287–294, 2012.

recognition are classified into two categories: 1) optical method based on image processing with a camera, and 2) mechanical method based on measuring joint motion with a data glove. Due to the accurate classification capability and fast response time of data glove based gesture recognition compared to the vision based recognition, it has been adopted by games, simulators or BR systems.

In this paper, we propose a gesture recognition platform for a realistic game. The realist game experience is realized by using acceleration sensors and data glove interacting with a game server. We demonstrate the efficiency of the propose system by controlling an avatar in the game with gestures only.

The rest of paper is organized as following: section 2 explains backgrounds on gesture recognition. Section 3 describes the architecture of proposed platform including description of each module in detail. Section 4 demonstrates the experimental result when applying the proposed system to a game and we conclude in section 5 by outlining the direction for the future work on this topic.

2   Backgrounds

Many researches based on vision[3] or acceleration sensors[4] or gloves[5] have been reported for gesture recognition. Each sensing technology, there are differences in accuracy, detection range, resolution, latency, comfort and cost. Recognition techniques based a on glove typically require the user to wear a cumbersome device. Using vision-based techniques, user should have a limited range of activity. Tracking devices can detect subtle movements of the fingers when the user's hand is moving, but a vision-based system will at best get a general sense of motion.

In addition, many studies on gesture recognition technology were grafted into the game. The data-glove based gesture recognition method can be usefully adopted by games because it can quickly recognize various gestures compared to base on vision. D. Baricevic *et al.* proposed the first person shooter (FPS) game system by using hand gesture recognition with a data-glove [6].

3   The Proposed Multi-modal Interaction System

The proposed system for the realist interaction environment consists of one haptic glove (mGlove)[7], four advanced sensing devices (ASDs)[8], 4 LED illuminator modules, 1 webcam, and communication module (see Fig. 1). Zigbee module establishes the communication channels among the game server, ASD, and mGlove. The gesture recognition and management of interaction between recognized gesture and game server are realized in software. The gesture recognition module consists of aggregator, signal classifier, sequence tracker and gesture recognizer. The interaction manager controls the game server' I/O.

3.1   ASD (Advanced Sensing Device)

In proposed system, motion recognition is made by obtaining the accelerator values of user's motion with the advanced sensing device. We use Em357 [7] as a main

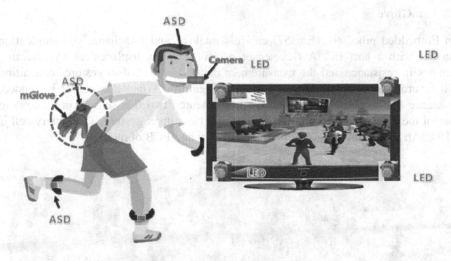

Fig. 1. Overview of the proposed system

processor of ASD. The Em357 combines a 2.4GHz IEEE 802.15.4 radio transceiver with 32-bit microprocessor, flash memory and RAM. In order to obtain acceleration value, we embedded the MMA7260QT [10] in ASD. The MMA7260QT is a low cost capacitive micromachined accelerometer that features signal conditioning, a 1-pole low pass filter, and temperature compensation. PCB antenna is used for cost-effectiveness (see Fig. 2). It operates with 160mAh Li-polymer battery.

Fig. 2. PCB board and mockup case of the proposed ASD

For the communication with the host PC, we used our own packet format as shown in Fig. 3. In order to reduce the communication overhead, the packet transmits 4 consecutive sensor data in x-, y-, and z-axis.

1byte	1byte	1byte	1byte	2byte	8byte	8byte	8byte	1byte
STX	Len	Node ID	Type	SEQ	X ACC / FLX1	Y ACC / FLX2	Z ACC	ETX

Fig. 3. The packet format for our system

3.2   mGlove

An Embedded processor (Em357) controls mGlove and establishes communication channel with a host PC. A flex sensor measures angle displacement by detecting changes in resistance and the measurement data is forwarded to gesture recognition unit in order to complete a hand gesture recognition. When flex sensor is bended, resistance of flex sensor increases. We implemented two flex sensors in mGlove to control the avatar in game through recognizing two-finger gesture. The battery cell is a 160mAh Li-polymer. Fig.4 shows mockup case and PCB of mGlove.

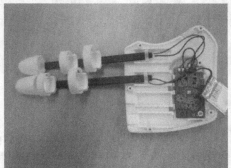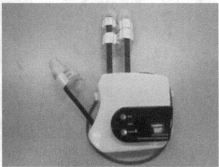

Fig. 4. PCB board and mockup case of the proposed mGlove

3.3   Gesture Recognition Module

Gesture Recognition module classifies user's gesture based on collected sensor data and transmits the result to the interaction manager. The classification is completed by comparing feature vector with predefined DB. In order to match input feature vectors, we use a brute force match algorithm that exhaustively compares a pair of feature vectors from each gesture based on the Manhattan (a.k.a. L1) distance. It should be noted that several other match algorithms are available, but the brute force match is simple to implement and has sufficient accuracy for the usage model of interest. The gesture recognition module requires the following blocks as shown in Fig. 5:

Windowing Unit: The continuous signals from the sensors should be divided into smaller granularity for the recognition purpose. This module extracts feature vectors from the acquired sensor signals in the predefined time window which is dynamically adjusted for the efficient gesture recognition.

Classification Unit: Classification unit requires computation of the Manhattan distance between each pair of feature vectors (one vector from query data and one form the data base) for the brute force matching. For each feature vector of the query data, performing the distance function on all feature vectors of a data based image give us the rank of candidate gestures for the query data within the time-window. We have multiple classification units corresponding to each sensor.

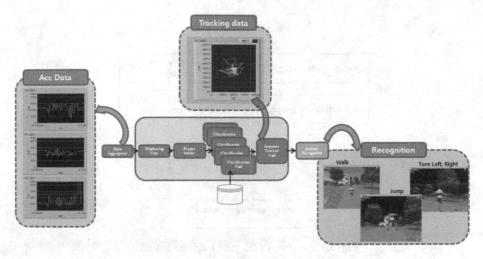

Fig. 5. Diagram of gesture recognition module

Sequence Tracker Unit: The sequence and combination of motions from the sensors form the gesture. The sequence tracker unit keeps track the ranked results of the classification units and completes the gesture recognition.

3.4   Gaze Tracking Module

Gaze tracking module consists of one camera, four Ir LED illuminators, and monitor, as shown in Fig.6. The resolution of captured images with eye camera is 640x480 pixels and images capture rate is 30 frame/s. We remove infrared rejection filter in eye camera and replace near IR passing filter. Four Ir LED illuminators are mounted on the corner of monitor.

Fig. 7 shows the flow chart of the gaze tracking modules. An image is captured by the eye camera on face. Our system localizes the center of gaze using labeling. Four LEDs attached on a monitor (See Fig. 8) are used to extract the location of reflection of the gaze. The movement of the gaze is recognized by using the position of the gaze and reflection, enabling the gaze tracking to control of the game system.

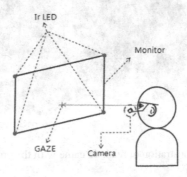

Fig. 6. Diagram of gesture recognition module

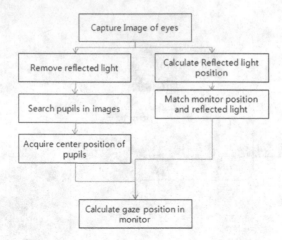

Fig. 7. Flow chart of the gaze tracking modules

4   Experimental Results

4.1   Experimental Setup

We set up FPS game in order to evaluate the proposed interaction system. Gesture recognition with interaction manager is used for sending events to the game system and the game server. We implemented that mGlove can control the avatar movement and gun shooting by finger recognition and ASD can control the position of gun target by hand position recognition and Gaze tracking module can control the sight of avatar by user's gaze recognition.

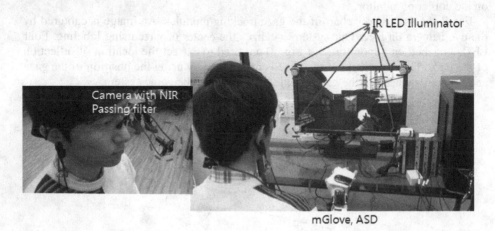

Fig. 8. A demonstration of realistic game with the proposed system

4.2   Results

In order to demonstrate the performance and enhanced user experience, we built a realistic game environment adopting the proposed ASD, mGlove and Gaze tracking module (see Fig. 8). The recognized gesture information is translated to the command for the FPS game client through the interaction manger, realizing the control of the avatar in the realist game only using the gestures. The accuracy of the gesture recognition is suitable to experience the realistic game. The sensor data is sampled in 25 msec interval and transmitted to the host PC after packing 4 consecutive data into a packet. The response time of the gesture recognition time was less than 150msec which is sufficient latency to enjoy the game. The maximum power consumption including the LED light for debug purpose was 35mAh.

5   Conclusions

In this paper, we proposed the gesture recognition platform for the realistic game. We accomplished to gain full control of the avatar in the realistic game by using the body gestures, enhancing the user experience in the game platform. The future work in this area is as follows. We plan to improve the gesture recognition time for the real-time synchronization between a user and a avatar. We also plan to establish bi-direction communication channel to feedback the experience of the avatar to the game player. We expect that enhancing the user experience on virtual world such as realist game will bring forth a new spectrum of novel usage models for smart devices, bio-medical equipments, entertainment system for automobile and robotics.

Acknowledgement. This research was supported by R&D Program of MKE (Ministry of Knowledge Economy) in Korea, [10033356, Development of driver and driving state sensing technology].

References

1. Nintendo Wii, http://www.nintendo.com/wii
2. Microsoft Xbox Kinect, http://www.xbox.com/en-US/Xbox360/Accessories/Kinect/kinectfo-rxbox360
3. Roh, M.C., Christmas, B., Kittler, J., Lee, S.W.: Gesture spotting for low-resolution sports video annotation. Pattern Recognition 41(3), 1124–1137 (2008)
4. Hofmann, F.G., Heyer, P., Hommel, G.: Velocity Profile Based Recognition of Dynamic Gestures with Discrete Hidden Markov Models. In: Wachsmuth, I., Fröhlich, M. (eds.) GW 1997. LNCS (LNAI), vol. 1371, pp. 81–95. Springer, Heidelberg (1998)
5. Belmontea, O., Castanedab, M., Fernándeza, D., Gila, J.: Federate resource management in a distributed virtual environment. Future Generation Computer Systems 26, 308–317 (2010)
6. Baricevic, D., Dujmic, H., Saric, M., Dapic, I.: Optical tracking for QAVE, a CAVE-like virtual reality system. In: International Conference on Software, pp. 25–27 (2008)

7. Jeong, Y.M., Lim, K.-T., Lee, S.E.: mGlove: Enhancing User Experience through Hand Gesture Recognition. In: Jin, D., Lin, S. (eds.) Advances in EECM Vol. 1. LNEE, vol. 139, pp. 383–386. Springer, Heidelberg (2012)
8. Jeong, Y.M., Lim, K.-T., Lee, S.E.: Advanced Sensing Device for Gesture Recognition. In: Jin, D., Lin, S. (eds.) Advances in EECM Vol.2. LNEE, vol. 140, pp. 63–66. Springer, Heidelberg (2012)
9. Ember em357, http://www.ember.com/products_zigbee_chips_e300series.html
10. Freescale MMA7260QT, http://www.freescale.com/webapp/sps/site/prod_summary.jsp?co-de=MMA7260QT

A Study on the Pre-elderly Consumers' ICT Service Needs of Planning Elements for Aging Friendly Ubiquitous Home Based on Lifestyle

Hyeji Ryu

Dept. of Space Design, Chungwoon University, Hongseong, Chungnam, South Korea
hjryu@chungwoon.ac.kr

Abstract. Korea is progressing towards a Super Aged Society. ICT services as an applicable element to ubiquitous home are the significant part to enhance Quality of Life of the elderly. Therefore, the purpose of this study is to seek the ICT service development direction and planning elements that can be applied to aging friendly ubiquitous home by exploring the pre-elderly consumers' ICT service needs based on lifestyle. The literature survey and web-surveyed were used for this study. The results of this study are as follows. First, it was found sixth lifestyles according to physically healthy, economically stable and socially active of respondent's people. Type 5 was found to have the highest percentage in sixth lifestyle types. Second, the level of preferences on ICT services used in ubiquitous home deferred depending on their lifestyle. Third, invasion & theft protection was preferred the most of all lifestyle types. Forth, ICT service needs were significantly varied on the kitchen in ubiquitous home. Finally, suggesting ICT services in consideration of resident's lifestyle as well as characters is vital in designing ubiquitous home.

Keywords: Ubiquitous Home, Aging Friendly, Pre-Elderly Consumers, ICT Service Needs, Lifestyle.

1 Introduction

As Korea has already faced an Aging Society and been substantially progressing towards an Aged & Super-Aged Society, various social and economic problems on the elderly are expected to be emerged more. Due to physical deterioration of the elderly, home environment should be designed to be supportive in order to solve this matter [1]. There is a limit to resolve this by only human resources, thus a digital technology requires to be utilized which would enhance Quality of Life (QOL) of the elderly. In response to this, ubiquitous home has appeared which provides Information & Communication Technology (ICT) and has potential to make the elderly physically healthy, economically stable and socially active as it is future-oriented home environment where all electronic devices are connected via wired & wireless home network system using various ICT [2]. Although many ubiquitous experimental home cases exist worldwide at present, they have been mainly for patients and the disabled, not for the elderly. Thus, more ubiquitous homes for them

T.-h. Kim et al. (Eds.): SIP/WSE/ICHCI 2012, CCIS 342, pp. 295–303, 2012.

are necessary and investigating the needs of a pre-elderly group between 30s and 50s on ubiquitous home's ICT service is vital in designing elderly housing for the future as they are an actual end users.

Lifestyle is a means of forging a sense of self and to create cultural symbols that resonate with personal identity. Since the importance of residential living behavior and lifestyle have been recognizing, house and furniture design and can be perceived as a lifestyle.

Thereby, the purpose of this study is to seek the ICT service development direction and planning elements that can be applied to aging friendly ubiquitous home by exploring the pre-elderly consumers' ICT service needs based on lifestyle.

2   Literature Review

2.1   Current Ubiquitous Home and ICT Development Situation

Ubiquitous home provides housing environment 'information-oriented factor, convenience, comfort, entertainment and others' and contains 'automation, unmanned and superhighway networks features' due to its internet use friendly environment and home automation system installation. In addition, it offers security system, indoor environment adjustment system, housework support system, control system, and others which are for culture, health and life. As digitalized electronic goods production has been accelerated and communication, broadcasting sector etc tend to be digitally converged, home digitalization is becoming a new housing trend [3].

ICT that is applied on ubiquitous home assists residents to live better life by supplying   computing environment with network, multi-media, automation and sensor techniques. It also helps to overcome time and place limitation and offers optimized service to individuals [4].

At present, ICT items of ubiquitous home are developed and applied in experimental houses i.e. Adaptive House, Place Lab, Aware Home in USA, Europe and Japan and apartment model houses i.e. Hillstate pavilion, U-Style pavilion and 14 ubiquitous cities in Korea. However, none of these were developed by user based design, thus building up user based aging friendly home is an imperative matter.

2.2   Current Aging Situation

As the ratio of people 65 years and over reached 10.4% in 2008, Korea has already faced an Aging Society and Korea would enter an Aged Society with 14.3% in 2018 and a Super-Aged Society with 20.8% in 2026 [Figure 1] [5].

Current middle-aged people in Korea who would face the Aged and Super-Aged Society by the time they are 65 years and over are expected to have higher education level than the current 65 years and over population. They would have longer life expectancy, higher academic level-health-economic power and would be manifested via increased welfare demand, expanded economic activity participation and senior power performance as a political force [6].

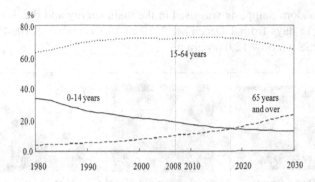

Fig. 1. The ratio of population composition transition on each age group

2.3   Characteristics of Lifestyle

Lifestyle is the way a person lives [7]. A lifestyle typically reflects an individual's attitudes, values or world view. Therefore, a lifestyle is a means of forging a sense of self and to create cultural symbols that resonate with personal identity. Not all aspects of a lifestyle are voluntary. Surrounding social and technical systems can constrain the lifestyle choices available to the individual and the symbols she/he is able to project to others and the self [8].

Social Environment includes and individuals living and working conditions, income level, educational background, community and religious believe if they have one. Technology and diversity have greatly changed the lives of people in society. Technology has positive and negative effects on our daily lives. However, the positivity and negativity of technology depends on how much we use it and how much we are exposed to it. In other words, our lifestyle controls our use of technology, while technology influences our lifestyles. Technology has also made it easier for other factors to affect our lifestyles, such as the house and furniture. All in all, technology has made our lives much easier in our house living [9].

3   Methodology

Surveyed people in this study were aged between 30 and 59. For accuracy of the study, a preliminary survey and a main survey were carried out. The preliminary survey was a Small Group Workshop on the Panel that consisted of 4 teams of 5 people each, 20 people all together and it was to find in-depth needs of the pre-elderly on ICT services of ubiquitous home. The workshop was progressed for 2 hours and the main 66 ICT of ubiquitous home related questions were constructed from Aware Home, Adaptive House, Hillstate Pavilion, U-Style Pavilion, and Ubiquitous Dream Pavilion [10][11]. To help the Panel's understanding, ICT images [Figure 2] were provided and explained and their 32 preferred ICT service items in ubiquitous home were extracted.

Clustered Random Sampling was used in the main survey and the web-survey was carried out for 15 days from 1 December 2010 to 15 December 2010. 450 data were analyzed by SPSS window 12.0 program.

Fig. 2. Ubiquitous home ICT Images [12][13][14]

4   Data Analysis and Results

4.1   Socio-demographical Characteristics

Surveyed people's general characteristics are shown in Table 1. The ratio of male was 54.o% and the ratio of female was 46.6%. The age ratio is nearly equal. 91.4% of surveyed people were graduated from a high school. Over 92% of surveyed people's monthly income was over 2 million won. In December 2010, national monthly labouring income was around 2.17 million won, therefore the surveyed people's monthly income was generally high. Overall, the majority of surveyed people were above high school graduates and monthly income was higher than 2 million won.

4.2   Types of Lifestyle

Table 2 shows surveyed people's lifestyle types based on physically healthy, economically stable and socially active of respondent's people.

First, it was found eighth lifestyles. But, type 6, 7 and 8 were below 10%. Then type 6, 7 and 8 were combined one type. Finally, it was found sixth lifestyles.

Type 5 which was the highest physical, economy and social state people was found to have the highest percentage in sixth lifestyle types. Type 1 which was the lowest physical, economy and social state people was found to have the second percentage.

Table 1. Socio-demographical Characteristics of Surveyed People

Section	Clarification	f	%
Gender	Male	243	54.0
	Female	207	45.0
	Total	450	100.0
Age	30-39yrs	150	33.3
	40-49yrs	150	33.3
	50-59yrs	150	33.3
	Total	450	100.0
Educational Background	Under Middle School	39	8.6
	High School	162	35.9
	2yrs Course University	40	8.7
	University	187	41.5
	Graduate Studies	22	5.3
	Total	450	100.0
Monthly Income	Under 1milionWon	16	3.5
	1million-2 million Won	19	4.3
	2million-3 million Won	93	20.7
	3million-4 million Won	114	25.4
	4million-5 million Won	122	26.9
	Above 5milionWon	102	22.7
	Total	450	100.0

Table 2. Sixth Types of Lifestyle

Type 1			Type 2		
	Physically healthy	low		physically healthy	low
	socially active	low		socially active	high
	economically stable	low		economically stable	low
	f	83		f	46
	%	18.2		%	10.3

Type 3			Type 4		
	Physically healthy	low		Physically healthy	high
	socially active	high		socially active	high
	economically stable	high		economically stable	low
	f	58		f	70
	%	12.7		%	15.5

Table 2. (*continued*)

Type 5			Type 6		
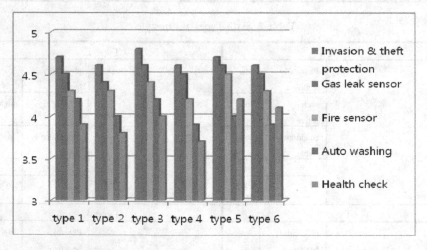	Physically healthy	high		Physically healthy	High, low
	socially active	high		socially active	low
	economically stable	high		economically stable	low, high
	f	126		f	67
	%	27.7		%	14.6

4.3   Needs on ICT Services Based on Lifestyle

Figure 3 shows surveyed people's needs on ICT services based on lifestyle of them. Type 1, 2, 3 and 4 preferred ICT services in order of 'Invasion & theft protection, Gas leak sensor, Fire sensor, Auto washing and Health check'. But, type 5 and 6 preferred ICT services in order of 'Invasion & theft protection, Gas leak sensor, Fire sensor, Health check and Auto washing'. On the whole, invasion & theft protection was preferred the most of lifestyle types.

Fig. 3. Preferred top 5 ICT Services based on Lifestyle

4.4   Needs on ICT Services in Ubiquitous Home Based on Lifestyle

Figure 4, 5 and 6 show surveyed people's needs on ICT services in Ubiquitous Home based on lifestyle of them.

Figure 4 shows preferred top 3 ICT services in the living room based on lifestyle. All types preferred ICT services in the living room in order of 'Ventilation control, Heat control and Digital TV'.

Figure 5 shows preferred top 3 ICT services in the bedroom based on lifestyle. All types preferred ICT services in the bedroom in order of 'Heat control, Light control and Ventilation control'.

Figure 6 shows preferred top 3 ICT services in the kitchen based on lifestyle. Type 1 and 4 preferred ICT services in the kitchen in order of 'Gas leak sensor, Food waste managing and Cooking support'.

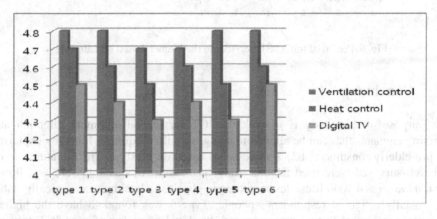

Fig. 4. Preferred top 3 ICT Services in the living room based on Lifestyle

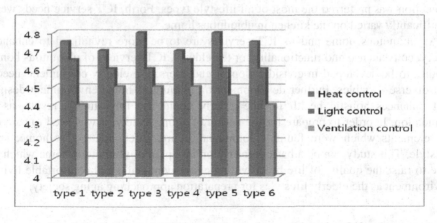

Fig. 5. Preferred top 3 ICT Services in the bedroom based on Lifestyle

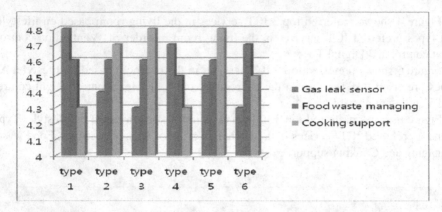

Fig. 6. Preferred top 3 ICT Services in the kitchen based on Lifestyle

5   Conclusion

The purpose of this study is to seek the ICT service development direction and planning elements that can be applied to aging friendly ubiquitous home by exploring the pre-elderly consumers' ICT service needs based on lifestyle. The literature survey and web-surveyed were used for this study. The results of this study are as follows. First, it was found sixth lifestyles according to physically healthy, economically stable and socially active of respondent's people. Type 5 was found to have the highest percentage in sixth lifestyle types. Second, the level of preferences on ICT services used in ubiquitous home deferred depending on their lifestyle. Third, invasion & theft protection was preferred the most of all lifestyle types. Forth, ICT service needs were significantly varied on the kitchen in ubiquitous home.

As ubiquitous home and its ICT services are to be more revitalized to enhance safety, convenience and functionality for the elderly, ICT services of ubiquitous home require to be developed in consideration of end users: pre-elderly consumers' needs and diverse variables. Further development on ubiquitous home environment design that enhances holistic health for the elderly could use this study's results as a foundation. In order to prepare for the period of aging society, it was need to care of the elements which were family's communal living, safety matters at home, and lifestyle. This study can be a basic information in a plan of ubiquitous home which is able to raise the quality of life by providing convenient, safe, and comfortable living environment as the elderly lifestyles for preparation approaching aging society.

References

1. Yoon, J.: Adult-Aged Psychology, Korea, 114–122 (1985)
2. Choi, J.: Digital Home Converged Appliances Policy for Actualization of Digital Life. Korea Information and Communications Society 20(6), 14–24 (2003)
3. Byeun, J.: A Study on the Human Interface Design Application under the Ubiquitous Environment: Focused on Living Space. Sookmyung Women's University, Korea (2005)

4. Kim, C.: Computing Service Development Methodology, Korea (2004)
5. Korean Statistical Information Service (KOSIS), Statistics on the Elderly (2008)
6. Kim, J.: Life Innovation Plan for the Elderly in Ubiquitous Society, Korea, 12 (2005)
7. Online Etymology Dictionary (2012)
8. Spaargaren, G., VanVliet, B.: Lifestyle, Consumption and the Environment: The Ecological Modernisation of Domestic Consumption. Environmental Politics 9(1), 50–75 (2000)
9. http://ec.europa.eu/health-eu (2012)
10. Ryu, H.: A Case Study of Ubiquitous Home Service for Future House Design. Korean Society of Basic Design and Art 9(2), 331–339 (2008)
11. Lee, Y., Kim, M., Lee, J.: Preferred Living Arrangement of the Elderly referring to the possible provision of Housing services. Korea Institute of Ecological Architecture and Environment 7(5), 99–106 (2007)
12. http://www.awarehome.gatech.edu (2012)
13. http://www.hillstate.co.kr (2012)
14. http://www.ubiquitousdream.or.kr (2011)

Development of Electric Plug Door and Test Results

Euijin Joung

Korea Railroad Research Institute
ejjoung@krri.re.kr

Abstract. The noise coming from outer side of EMU has been an important issue for the passenger comfort because high speed operation has been required.

The main cause of increased noise is the imperfect air tightness of passenger
doors. The plug-in door system has advantages for the noise reduction in the
high speed area. Recently, many types of plug-in door along to driving type are
introduced to reduce noise and enhance reliability. Electric plug-in door has
been developed to correspond to performance in actual operation circumstances. In this paper, I will deal with the role of several units of plug-in door,
development process and the test results.

Keywords: Electric plug-in door, Advanced EMU, Modularized door, Water-
proof, Sound-proof, Wind-proof.

1 Introduction

The plug-in door has advantages for the noise reduction characteristic in the high
speed area. So the plug-in door can reduce the noise coming from outer side of vehicle. Air driven type plug-in door has been already developed and operated in several
railway lines. Some years ago critical element including motor and Door Control Unit
(DCU) were not developed in Korea and imported from other countries. Also the
electric plug-in door was not developed. So a number of electric plug-in door were
imported by the operating authority to insure reliability of the door system. To solve
these problems, electric plug-in door has been developed with adopting the Korean
operating condition, and serving economic and dramatically improved performance.
In this paper, we will deal with the role of several units of plug-in door, development
process and the test results.[1]- [2]

2 Various Types of Door System

Usually three types of Door system, Pocket-sliding type, Out-sliding type, and Plug-in
type are used in Korea. The former two sliding doors have same driving principle.
The figure 1 shows the sliding door and plug-in door system.[3]

Pocket-sliding type door system is operated in the pocket in the car body. This type
is widely used in the EMU in the world. Out-sliding type door system is equipped
outside of vehicle. A number of out-sliding door system are used after development of

T.-h. Kim et al. (Eds.): SIP/WSE/ICHCI 2012, CCIS 342, pp. 304–310, 2012.

the pocket-sliding door system and is widely used in the Malaysia, Hong Kong, and Australia, etc. The Plug-in door is opened after the door is extruded outside. This type door system has several advantages due to full-sealed structure.

(a)Sliding door   (b)Plug-in door

Fig. 1. Types of Door in EMU

Nowadays train requires higher operating speed than before and passenger comfort is a main factor to make a new EMU. Noise is a main factor because more speed up makes more noise. Air tightness technology has to be applied to reduce noise in the door system. Several types of sliding and plug-in door system are developed in Korea. The below describes the door system currently developed by manufacturer in Korea.

— Air driven pocket out-sliding door: Design and production is possible in Korea itself and is operating now.
— Electric pocket out-sliding door: Design and production is possible in Korea itself and is operating now.
— Air driven plug-in door: Design and production is possible in Korea itself and is operating now.
— Electric plug-in door system: Developed in this project.

3   Development of Plug-in Door

Electric plug-in door is typically composed of door operator, hanging device, and door panel. Door operator is organized in DCU, motor, screw gear, ball nut, rail, limit switches and electrical devices. (Terminal blocks, connectors, ports, and cable), Hanging device linked with motor has connectors to connect door panel to linear bush and shaft. Door panel is composed of panel (left/right), windows and sealing. It also includes internal and external emergency manual opening device and coordination bar.

The main concept of developed plug-in door is modularization. The developed plug-in door is modularized and it is easily installed by bolting 4 points. The figure 2 describes the modular type electric plug-in door. [4]- [5]

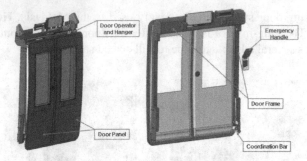

Fig. 2. Modular type Electric Plug-in Door

3.1   Door Panel

Passenger door is composed of aluminum sheet, aluminum honeycomb core and liquid adhesive. These materials are so excellent for the stiffness and strength that it is possible to reduce the weight of advance electric multiple unit (EMU). The door panel is bonded to form a sandwich structure by pasting together between aluminum sheet and aluminum honeycomb cores.

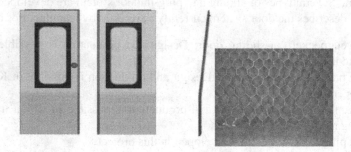

Fig. 3. Door panel and honeycomb core in plug-in door

— Door window: Laminated glass mounted by using adhesive sealant is applied to the door panel to minimize air resistance during vehicle operation. Door window is significantly large to give more visibility effect to passenger.
— Door rubber: Door rubber applied to door panels is made of neoprene to meet the specifications of the flame retardant regulation of urban railway law in Korea.

3.2   Emergency Handle

Sliding door is usually moved to both sides (left and right), but plug-in door is pushed a little and moved to both sides to open the door. The door engine of plug-in door changes movement direction complicated together to the X, Y axis. So the locking force is two times stronger than general sliding type door. Emergency handle is easily operated even though the weak can deal with it. We replace the handle type from existing rotary emergency handle to the lever type emergency handle to give more sufficient torque to it. Figure 4 shows the type of emergency handle adopted in advanced EMU.

Fig. 4. Emergency handle

3.3   Individual Door Open Switch

In the advanced EMU, individual door open switch is applied inside and outside of vehicle for passengers to open door directly to get on and off the vehicle. The switch is useful in case the number of passenger is small, such as in the station located in a suburban area or in the time period that get off rush hour. If the number of passenger is small, we don't need to open and close all the vehicle doors. The equipment has energy saving effect. The figure 5 shows the shape of individual door open switch installed on door.

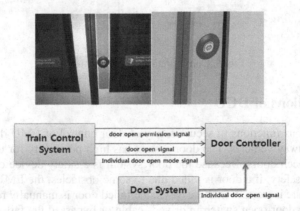

Fig. 5. Operation of Individual door open switch

Usually train control system gives door open signals to door controller to open all the doors in vehicles. When the situation that the passenger is small is occurred, the driver gives individual door open mode signal to door controller, then the passenger can use the individual door open switch.

— Wiring of door system and internal logic control of DCU are designed.
— Onboard signaling device is reviewed to control doors.

3.4   Door Control Unit

Door control unit has been designed and developed for the purpose of control of sliding plug-in door system. Figure 6 describes the configuration of door control unit. Door control unit has three parts such as power module, motor driving module and input/output module, control module and communication module. Control and communication between DCUs are performed by RS232C and RS485. DCU is operated by receiving several data coming from Door Closing Switch (DCS), Door Locking Switch (DLS), Emergency handle, and individual door open switch. Train Control and Monitoring System (TCMS) gives an order to DCU to control motor drive of electric plug in door and also check the status of doors in advanced EMU.

— Basic model is developed based on external interface.
— Functions are standardized in Korea.
— Door control unit is designed to accept functions applied to the advanced EMU.
— Door control unit is designed to observe environmental conditions and test criteria of subway vehicle.

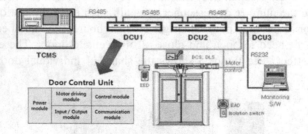

Fig. 6. Configuration of door control unit

4   Functions of DCU

DCU has various functions to secure safety of door control of EMU due to the unique features of railway vehicles. The door system has high possibility for the failure due to obstacles between doors. Because the door system is a safety device closely related to the passenger safety, if a door is failed due to some obstacles, the EMU cannot operate before the failure is treated. In these cases, the failed door is manually re-opened several times by using door open switch in driver's cabin or bypassed the failed door units. All the function is treated by DCU. The following list describes the functions of DCU.

— Automatic door open and close control by train control signal
— Error detection of door control by measuring driving motor current
— Door control by predetermined pattern
— Logical processing of inputs from train operating signal and door operating switch
— State control of door

— High/Low   voltage monitoring
— Self-detection of DCU fault
— Storage of fault data
— Parameter setting and storage of door control status and operating status
— Correspondence for internal/external power status
— Data transmission of self-state and fault via RS485 through TCMS-DCU
— DCU address setting by external jumper
— Self-diagnostics and firmware downloads though RS232
— Calculation of counter electromotive force measuring and filtering driving motor current and voltage
— Protection of electrical Disturbance
— Real-time self-monitoring.

5   Test Results of DCU

The electric plug-in door has been passed all required test. The figures below represent all test results. Nowadays the door is attached to the advanced EMU and tested to demonstrate reliability factor. [6]

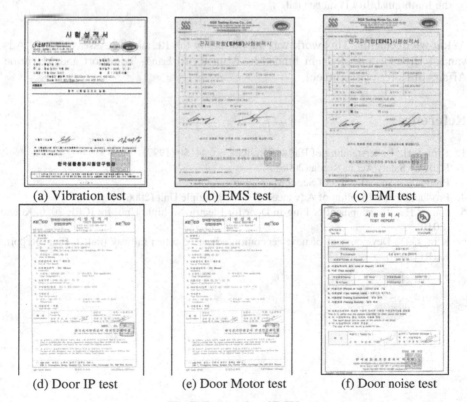

| (a) Vibration test | (b) EMS test | (c) EMI test |
| (d) Door IP test | (e) Door Motor test | (f) Door noise test |

Fig. 7. Test results of DCU

6   Conclusions

Electric plug-in door system is selected as a door system in the advanced EMU and has been developed. The door system has many advantages in many areas as reviewed above. Especially there are many improvements in noise reduction of vehicle, elegance design, durability and high reliability improvements compare to the existing door system. We also reflect the following differentiation in this study.

— The lifecycle of door engine is almost semi-permanent. If the dominant factor of lifecycle in door engine is depend on the media that transmit power generated from door engine. In the developed plug-in door, ball screw structure is adopted to guarantee the semi-permanent lifecycle of door engine. Because the screw type transmission system gives advantage of low power for transmission and quick operation.
— Plug-in door reduces the amount of leakage and ensures air-tightness.
— The applied wide window increases the passenger's visibility.
— Hanging Devices reduces operation noise and it is easy to adjust variables by installing coordination bar vertically.
— Modularized plug-in door give us the effect of simplicity and reliability and also the maintainability is increased.

Acknowledgements. This work was supported by the Reliability Assessment of Advanced Urban Transit System funded by Ministry of Land, Transport and Maritime Affairs of Korean government.

References

1. Kim, S.H.: Understanding of Railway system, pp. 44–50 (1997)
2. Railway Safety Act in Korea (2006)
3. Production Specification of Seoul Metro line 1,2,3,4
4. Production Specification of Advanced Electric Multiple Unit (2006)
5. Joung, E.J.: Development of Plug-in Door for Electric Multiple Unit. In: ICEE 2010, Korea (2010)
6. Kim, G.D.: Development of next-generation advanced urban railway transit. Final Report, KRRI (2010)

Human Stimulation Threshold of Interferential Current Type Low Frequency Stimulator for Electric Shock Experience Education System

Jeong Chay Jeon[1], Jae Hyun Kim[1], Jae Geun Yoo[1], and Hyun Seob Cho[2,*]

[1] Korea Electrical Safety Corporation
#27 Sangcheon-ri, Cheongpyeoung-myeon, Gapyeong-gun, Gyeonggi-do, 477-814,
Rep. of Korea
[2] Department of Electronic Engineering, ChungWoon University
#San29, Namjang-ri, Hongseong-eup Hongseong-gun, Chungnam, Rep. of Korea
{Hyun Seob Cho,kescoin}@naver.com

Abstract. To prevent electric shock accidents, an experience education is more effective than indoctrination education. But an electric shock experience education system required a proper physical stimulation on human body to experience electric shock. This paper experiment threshold values of a human body by using Interferential Current Type Low Frequency Stimulator in order to apply to an electric shock experience education system. And the proper stimulation values are calculated according to age (divided child and adult) and gender. Results of this study could be applied to an electric shock experience education system.

Keywords: Electric shock, accident, experience, education, stimulation.

1 Introduction

In spite of a wide variety of activities to prevent electrical safety accidents, electric shock accidents had not decreased in Korea as shown in table 1 [1, 2]. The most of electrical safety accidents happen because of human error. In order to prevent these accidents by human error, a systematic and long-term education is required. It is very important that people are aware of electrical hazards and the proper preventative actions including education to reduce electrical shock [3].

Table 1. Electric shock accident statistics for the recent three years in Korea

Year	Death	Injury	Sum
2008	68	497	565
2009	46	533	579
2010	46	535	581

---

* Corresponding author.

T.-h. Kim et al. (Eds.): SIP/WSE/ICHCI 2012, CCIS 342, pp. 311–316, 2012.
© Springer-Verlag Berlin Heidelberg 2012

So far, education to prevent electrical safety accidents was indoctrination using text and image. Since the passive methods of education that are currently used by using audio-visual education are not the most effective. It is unsuitable except adult who concern about electrical safety. Especially, introduction of various education method for child and infants who concentration and understanding are lack than adult is needed.

The advancement of virtual reality (VR) technology and medical device enable to develop a system to experience electric fire and electric shock. An experience education system to prevent electrical safety accidents, which must use the proper stimulation values on a human body to experience electric shock accident.

In this paper, Interferential Current Type Low Frequency Stimulator was considered as the method to experience electric shock. Generally, Physiological therapy using Interferential Current Stimulator (IFS) has been in use for many years and its effectiveness is well documented. The basic principle of IF) is to utilize the strong physiological effects of the low frequency electrical stimulation of muscle and nerve tissues at sufficient depth, without the associated painful and somewhat unpleasant side effects of such stimulation.

Although IFS is useful for experiencing electric shock in the electrical safety education system, there are many problems that must be considered. If stimulation on a human body is too strong to heighten learning effect, motive level could fall down because displeasure or trauma in severe cases can happen. On the other hand, if stimulation is too weak, there is no learning effect because arousal status to detect danger of electric shock can be dropped. But there is no literature on the intensity of stimulation according to age, gender, education content and so on.

Therefore, in order to maximize learning effect, it is need to determine threshold values of electric shock stimulation according to age, gender and experience education contents. This paper calculated threshold values of a human body according age and gender in using Interferential Current Type Low Frequency Stimulator in order to apply to an electric shock experience education system.

2   Method

Interferential Current Type Low Frequency Stimulator STI-300, which can adjust current stimulation from 1 mA to 50mA, was used to calculate electric stimulation values on the human body that can be applied to an electric shock experience system.

66 healthy volunteers participated in the experiment. They consist of 38 male (child 11, adult 27) and 28 female (child 13, adult 15). Before the experiment, data to have an influence on current stimulation values like as height, weight, age and gender was collected. Interferential currents two independent kilohertz frequency alternated currents (ACs) of constant intensity that are applied by two pairs of electrodes placed diagonally. The interference of the two ACs at the intersectional area produces sinusoidal current modulation at a frequency equal to the difference between the two ACs [4]. $3 \sim 20$mA current stimulation provided in right palm and the forearm (adult 12 cm and child 10 cm) for 4 seconds in order to remove tiredness effect as shown in Fig. 1 and 2. And self-report 5-point scale about displeasure, awakeness and pain was reported by experiment participants.

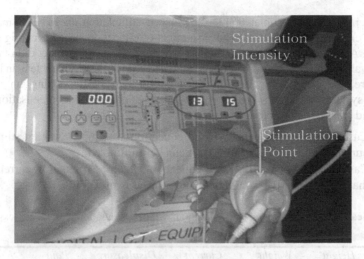

Fig. 1. Stimulation point and intensity control

Fig. 2. Test scene using Low Frequency Stimulator STI-300

3   Results

Table 2 shows the mean, maximum and minimum intensity of Interferential Current (IFC) stimulation of total 66 experiment participants. The mean intensity was 14mA and mean of displeasure, pain and arousal was under 3-level (normal level). And there is no pain, inconvenience and displeasure in experiment. Table 3 shows experiment results according to gender (male and female) and age (child and adult). In case of child, there is no gender difference but In case of adult, there is the male and female interaction. But displeasure, arousal and pain on mean stimulation are low and if stimulation exceeds the maximum value, it is expected that there is an adverse effect of education because of big pain on stimulation. And maximum stimulation values according to age and gender didn't result in maximum value of arousal because of displeasure and pain as shown in table 3 and 4.

Therefore, the criteria for selecting stimulation current depending on whether education system has a powerful penalty-based contents or compensation-based contents and can be made as follows:

- Case of a powerful penalty-based education system: Maximum stimulation current (mA) that body side effect can be minimized.
- Case of a compensation-based education system: Stimulation current (mA) that which negative is minimum and arousal is maximum.

Table 2. Mean, Maximum (max), and Minimum (min) stimulation current of experiment participants

	Height [cm]	Weight [kg]	Current [mA]	Displeasure Mean	Pain Mean	Arousal Mean
Mean	164.00	56.92	14.30	2.68	2.67	2.63
max	189	85	20	3.83	4.00	4.19
min	104	18	8	1	1	1

Table 3. Mean, Maximum (max), and Minimum (min) stimulation current according to age and gender

Male child	Height [cm]	Weight [kg]	Current [mA]	Displeasure Mean	Pain Mean	Arousal Mean
Mean	148.91	42.64	8.91	1.90	2.18	1.87
Max	171.00	63.00	10.00	3.00	3.00	3.00
Min	104.00	18.00	8.00	1.00	1.29	1.00
Male adult	Height [cm]	Weight [kg]	Current [mA]	Displeasure Mean	Pain Mean	Arousal Mean
Mean	177.04	71.89	18.26	2.91	2.76	2.91
Max	189.00	85.00	20.00	3.64	3.61	3.78
Min	168.00	58.00	12.00	1.39	1.56	1.00
Female child	Height [cm]	Weight [kg]	Current [mA]	Displeasure Mean	Pain Mean	Arousal Mean
Mean	151.00	41.92	8.92	2.24	2.36	1.88
Max	165.00	58.00	10.00	3.83	3.50	3.29
Min	122.00	22.00	8.00	1.00	1.00	1.00
Female adult	Height [cm]	Weight [kg]	Current [mA]	Displeasure Mean	Pain Mean	Arousal Mean
Mean	162.87	53.47	15.80	3.24	3.16	3.32
Max	174.00	59.00	20.00	3.81	4.00	4.19
Min	155.00	45.00	9.00	2.00	2.38	1.85

Table 4. Stimulation current and education effect

Male child	Max arousal, Min Current[mA]	Negative-Max arousal	The most negative stimulus
Mean	8.00	3.57	3.71
Max	9.00	5.00	5.00
Min	6.00	1.50	1.50
Male adult	Max arousal, Min Current[mA]	Negative-Max arousal	The most negative stimulus
Mean	13.78	4.42	4.86
Max	19.00	5.00	5.00
Min	7.00	2.50	3.50
Female child	Max arousal, Min Current[mA]	Negative-Max arousal	The most negative stimulus
Mean	7.63	3.44	4.19
Max	9.00	5.00	5.00
Min	6.00	2.00	3.00
Female adult	Max arousal, Min Current[mA]	Negative-Max arousal	The most negative stimulus
Mean	11.77	4.54	4.92
Max	18.00	5.00	5.00
Min	8.00	3.50	4.00

4   Discussions

In this paper, stimulation of IFC applied to human body was gradually increased. Also, in case that critical pain and displeasure of participants by large stimulation current was reported, the intensity of stimulation was adjusted to smaller level than the intensity which they can endure because of dangerousness of human body and psychological Trauma. And, in case of child, the reliability problem of the self-report 5-point scale by child's uncertain concept about displeasure, pain and arousal was minimized by securing statistically stable participants.

5   Conclusions

This paper calculated threshold values of a human body by using Interferential Current Type Low Frequency Stimulator in order to apply to an electric shock experience education system. And the proper stimulation values are calculated according to age (divided child and adult) and gender. In future, results of this study could be applied to the determination of the proper stimulation values of an electric shock experience education system according to a variable such as electric shock education contents and age, gender, weight and height of user.

Acknowledgement. This work was supported by the Power Generation & Electricity Delivery of the Korea Institute of Energy Technology Evaluation and Planning (KETEP) grant funded by the Korea Government Ministry of Knowledge Economy (*No. 2011T1001215*).

References

1. National Emergency Management Agency, Fire Statistics Year Book (2008-2011)
2. Korea Electrical Safety Corporation, Electrical Disaster Statistics Analysis Report (2009-2011)
3. Lucas, Zhao, Thabet: Using Virtual Environments to Support Electrical Safety Awareness in Construction. In: Proceedings of the 2009 Winter Simulation Conference, Austin, TX (2009)
4. Furuta, T., Takemura, M., Tsujita, J., Oku, Y.: Interferential Electric Stimulation Applied to the Neck Increases Swallowing Frequency. Springer Science Business Media, LLC (2011)

The Formation of Space Diagram and Its Application to the Architectural Design Education

Hyoungjun Kim

School of Architecture, Jeju National University
102 Jejudaehakno, Jeju-si, Jeju Special Self-Governing Province
690-756, Republic of Korea
kimhj@jejunu.ac.kr

Abstract. The architectural design methodology had been changed under control of Modern life. At that time, architectural design education was formed directly by modern life and its characteristics. Therefore it is important to observe the original form of architectural design education in the point of finding origin of present architectural design education. Under this critical mind, this research examined the timeline, from the diagram that was made for maximization of factory efficiency in 1910's, to the space diagram that shows the relations space and function in 1920's. This research also analyzed the application of space diagram into architectural design education. In 1930's, this space diagram applied to architectural design education, emphasizing the efficiency and rationality. For this, looking for the formation of space diagram and rationalization of architectural design education has a meaning in the basis of architectural design education.

Keywords: Diagram, Space diagram, Architectural design, Rationality.

1 Introduction

This study aims to grasp the formation of diagram which was developed to maximize the productivity of factories in the 1910's. It also examines changes in the diagram from the 1920's on. In addition, it analyzes how the diagram changed into a space diagram that represents the relation between space and functions. How the space diagram has been applied to architectural design education after 1930's is examined as well. All the achievements above will contribute to clarifying the process that reasonableness in machinery production is applied to architectural design and education through a space diagram. The subjects of this study include the machinery production system of factories in the 1910's, the diagram in the 1920's, and the space diagram in the 1930's. The study method is to trace and analyze the changes in such study subjects.

2 Arrangement of Production and Time

Machinery production in the Industrial Revolution advanced as it maximized production efficiency over time. Shortly after the Industrial Revolution, the initial

T.-h. Kim et al. (Eds.): SIP/WSE/ICHCI 2012, CCIS 342, pp. 317–322, 2012.
© Springer-Verlag Berlin Heidelberg 2012

production system that maximized the efficiency of machinery production was the assembly line. At the beginning point was the automated flour milling designed by Oliver Evans, the U.S., in 1783, which removed the needs for human labor in all of the process of milling including corn washing, powdering, selecting, and so forth. The way of transferring grains without stop with no need for human labor was a technical innovation. This assembly line continued to advance through the successors. As this assembly line was applied to the meat industry in the U.S., in the 1860 to 70's, the modern assembly line finally showed up. About this assembly line, Giedion says this:

"There is only one way if you want to increase the production. That is to reduce the time wasted between lines and to minimize the efforts of the laborers carrying heavy chunks of meat. Wrapped with chains at the intervals of 24 inches, chunks of meat move in line as if they flow in front of laborers. The origin of the modern assembly line appears here[1]"

The time and work in the assembly line at factories are segmented. The segmented time and work are arranged in the space as part of a layout. The assembly line segmented a series of works, divided them to many individuals, and then arranged them. The intervals of each segmented work were, not merely for segmentation but for indication of the works to do and the allotted time. As this was in line with space, the space of factories had to be structured in accord with rationality of time and work. Such segmented works and time corresponded to a certain space of workers.

The assembly line, originated from Oliver Evans, changed the machinery production system, and again this was designed as a separate system by Frederick Winslow Taylor. This methodology, known as the Taylor's System, was known to the world through his work, <The Principles of Scientific Management> in 1911. The book pointed out that the operation without any clear plans was the biggest cause of waste of the production capacity. He insisted that the effective solution would be scientific management, making it a subject of his research. In Taylor's methodology, work and motion were regarded as one element. The time taken for this element was measured quantitatively. Scientific management meant to arrange the measured work and time in the most efficiency manner. The goal of the Taylor's System, focusing on enhancing the machinery productivity and reducing the working hours, was to arrange production and time. The Taylor's System, which attempted to make the most efficient production process by arranging work and time became the very foundation of diagrams thereafter.

3   Formation of a Diagram

Taylor's methodology was handed down to his student, Frank Bunker Gilbreth. Just as Daylor did, Gilbreth studied time, but he went further by analyzing time within the area of space. While Taylor focused on time analysis by means of a stopwatch, Gilbreth focused on space rather than time. Besides, Gilbreth did not regard the stopwatch-based method as accurate. Gilbreth stressed out that a stopwatch was just a mute that could not indicate in what form motions were represented. Instead, Gilbreth made use of a projector that emerged in France to visualize the work and time within a certain space[2].

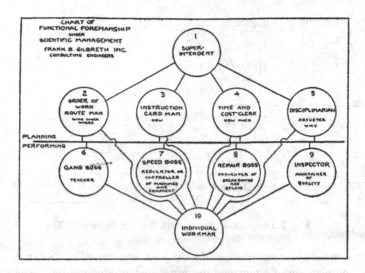

Fig. 1. Frank Bunker Gilbreth's Diagram, 1917

As a result, he successfully analyzed time in a space, and found out that working hours could be adjusted by adjusting the working space itself. There appeared the becoming-time of space. As the assembly line introduced the becoming-space of time, Gilbreth introduced the becoming-time of space. This way, Gilbreth presented as a methodology to create a streamlined production line the diagram that visually schematized time, work, and space. In 1917, Gilbreth He described his study subjects – work, time, and space – in a diagram, which was widely known thereafter as it was applied to plant systems. Having sought to maximize a production system, experts finally could design a schematized, visualized, optimal production process through Gilbreth's diagram. As the production system of a plant was recognized as a reasonable method to achieve the max efficiency, the diagram was applied even to space arrangement for production lines.

As Gilbreth verified that the arrangement of working space had a direct influence on productivity, space became a subject to be handled most reasonably. Since 1910, the recognition became common that the less working motion, the more efficient, and the shorter traffic line, the more streamlined. When it comes to space arrangement, an arrangement that removed unnecessary motions and traffic lines were regarded as the most efficient and streamlined. In other words, the space of max efficiency was considered as reasonable.

In Gilbreth's diagram, a circle indicates a space, and contents in it indicate the details. The line connecting circles indicates time. This diagram excludes social regulations, values, and objective judgment. Such visual forms as circle to circle, circle to line, and so forth represent the optimal space and time that is measured, not based on one's objective judgment but quantitatively and reasonably. Thus, anyone who observes this diagram could objectively grasp the contents and time and the size of the space of each work. The reasonableness of the optimization of a production line is visualized through the diagram. This shows that a space diagram functions as a methodology that represents reasonableness.

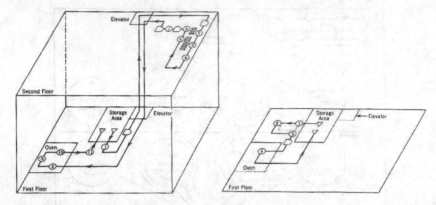

Fig. 2. Diagram of proper work flow in factory. 1920's

The awareness of reasonableness of a diagram was raised further in the 1920's. In time, the optimization of automated machines and production lines was accelerated, and as a result, labor time was reduced while production and incomes increased. Consumption and expenditure of laborers increased accordingly, and this consumption became the dynamic force of production again. Thus, plant facilities had to adopt the optimal production system for mass production. The methodology applied to this end was a diagram, through which plant owners would optimize their factories since plant owners recognized a diagram as a reasonable methodology to optimize a plant. In this process, a diagram and reasonableness were regarded as the same, and the use of diagrams was rapidly spread as plant development was accelerated in the 1920's.

4   Space Diagram and Its Application to Architectural Design

The diagram designed by Gilbreth started to be applied to architectural design in the 1930's[3]. Although the exact timing and reason are unknown, diagrams were widely adopted in various areas as a methodology for objective and reasonable plans at factories, and as a result, the area of architecture was also influenced.

In examination of <the Architectural Record>, published in the U.S in the 1930's, various schematic symbols appeared in relation to diagrams. In the early 1930's, a circulation was drawn on a plan, or the space was described as a circle to distinguish the function of space. In the mid 30's, a space was schematized as a circle, and circles were connected as a circulation, which led to the formation of a diagram. In the late 30's, a diagram included various forms of figures to describe a space separately from the plant. These diagrams were different from those for the max efficiency and optimization of factories. Diagrams used for architectural design aimed mainly at classifying space based on functions and connecting them systematically.

Diagrams were adopted to visually systematize the spatial composition and objectify the decision-making and judgment process on the space. In this regard, the use of diagrams was different from that of Gilbreth, and this could be defined as space diagrams. In other words, space diagrams are the very results of applying diagrams to architectural design that emerged in the 1920's at factories.

Diagrams and space diagrams are in common in that the products in use of them are recognized as objective and reasonable. As various conditions are visualized into space diagrams, architects can decide the space composition in an easier manner than before. In addition, since space diagrams produce simulations for a variety of situations, the decision-making process become more objective and reasonable[4]. The fact that reasonableness was secured in the decision-making process of architectural design was the most outstanding advantage of space diagrams. For this reason, space diagrams started to be widely used in the area of architectural design since the 1930's.

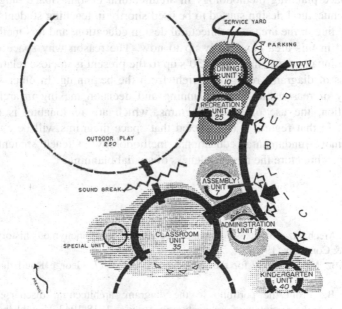

Fig. 3. Space diagram for teaching, 1941

As space diagrams became a recognized methodology of spatial planning in the area of architectural design, they were applied to architectural design education. The important factors in modern-day architectural design education were reasonable positioning and arrangement of space in spatial planning. The use of space diagrams was an easy method for the professor to deliver the ideas of spatial planning to students in an easy, understandable fashion. For this reason, space diagrams became an essential education means for education of reasonable spatial planning from then on[5]. In addition, space diagrams became a fundamental learning element in almost every corner of architectural design since the 60's and 70's. Even up to now, these are adopted in lectures as an essential design methodology in architectural design education. The reason why space diagrams became a key element in architectural design education was in close relation to the reasonableness of diagrams recognized right from the beginning. Utilization of space diagrams in education contributed to teaching students the reasonableness of architectural design in an effective manner.

5   Conclusions

Having been developed to maximize the production efficiency at factories in the 1910's, diagrams were used to describe the relation between space and functions and space and traffic lines in the 1920's. In the 1930's, they appeared in architectural magazines, being utilized specifically in the area of architectural design. While going through such a process, diagrams turned to space diagrams, which became a reasonable space planning methodology in architectural design. Space diagrams for reasonable architectural design started to be used shortly in teaching students the way of spatial planning in the area of architectural design education, and this methodology has been used in this area continually up to now. The reason why space diagrams have been continually used since the 1930's up to the present is in close relation to the reasonableness of diagrams recognized right from the beginning. In other words, to teach the way of reasonable spatial planning and decision making in architectural design education, the use of space diagrams, which are reasonable, is the most effective way. In that regard, it is expected that space diagrams will be continually used as the most fundamental educational methodology to teach students in the department of architecture the reasonableness of spatial planning.

References

1. Giedion, S.: Mechanization takes command: A contribution to anonymous history, pp. 55–67. Norton & Company (1969)
2. Gilbreth, F.B.: Motion study for the handicapped, pp. 5–17. George Routledge & Sons (1920)
3. Hyungmin, B.: From the portfolio to the diagram: architectural discourse and the transformation of the discipline of architecture in America 1918-1943. Unpublished Ph.D.'s thesis. MIT University, U.S.A. (1993)
4. Palmer, M.A.: The architect's guide to facility programming, pp. 198–205. The American Institute of Architects (1981)
5. Ilbum, B.: Program Diagram. Spacetime, 34–54 (2005)

Application Effect of Information Education Using Computer for the Prevention and Early Detection of Breast Cancer

Seong-Ran Lee

Department of Medical Information, Kongju National University, 56 Gongjudaehak-ro,
Kongju, Chungnam, Korea
lsr2626@naver.com

Abstract. This paper is focused on application effect of information education using computer for the prevention and early detection of breast cancer. The subjects of this paper were 291 patients who had been visited a general hospital which located in the area of metropolitan. The pairwise t-test was done to compare the changes of practice rates for the breast cancer prevention before and after information education using computer. The present research showed that practice rate for breast cancer prevention can be increased to 57.4-82.6% by the education. In order to maintain the education effect well, it is very important to determine adequate education period and perform various programs in consideration of their circumstances.

Keywords: Application effect, Information education, Computer, Prevention, Early detection, Breast cancer.

1 Introduction

Breast cancer has a high prevalence especially among women in Korea and is a leading cause of cancer death[1],[2]. Incidence rate of female breast cancer to the Korean population was estimated to be 11.7(95% Cl : 9.2-13.6) per 100,000 persons in 2010. Age-standardized rate to the world population was 10.3 persons, and the truncated rate for ages 35-64 was 31.7 per 100,000 persons[2],[3]. Validity of these estimates is discussing in comparison with previous methods of incidence estimation in Korea. Epidemics show that the incidence and mortality of breast cancer increasing due to rapidly changes of women's life style and Westernized food, and so on. The risk factors for breast cancer included hormone-related factors such as early menarche, menopause, late birth, hormone replacement therapy and genetic background[4].

The strategies for the prevention and early detection of breast cancer are best for decreasing the mortality rate with a relatively low incidence of breast cancer. Early detection of breast cancer can be achieved by performing mammography or sonography, and so on. Many researches indicated that this could be detection of early breast cancer as well as decreasing the rate of death from breast cancer among

T.-h. Kim et al. (Eds.): SIP/WSE/ICHCI 2012, CCIS 342, pp. 323–330, 2012.

women[5],[6]. Previous research have on one-time screening rather repeat adherence so far and most people are not having the regular screening at recommend intervals. We also don't have any national program at all about it. In order to solve the urgent problem, we should look for the practical plans. There were few studies to deal with effect of information education using computer for the prevention and early detection of breast cancer patients until present in Korea. To overcome this situation, this paper performed effective information education using computer.

This paper sought to apply the effect of it on the change of practice behavior of subjects for the prevention and early detection of breast cancer. The series of information education for the prevention and early detection of breast cancer were performed to subjects and the evaluation survey was conducted at the end of this trial to compare the change before and after information education using computer for the practice behavior of breast cancer prevention.

Thus, this paper is designed to develop the short-term information education using computer for the prevention and early detection of breast cancer and ultimately to analyze the educational effect through its application. This will take advantage of basic data for researcher and indicate the direction of their education using computer in the future.

2   Materials and Methods

2.1   Materials

The subjects of this paper were 291 patients who had been visited health examination center of a general hospital which located in the area of metropolitan hospital from October 10, 2011 to February 10, 2012. Training researchers performed to find out the effectiveness of information education using computer on practice behavior of subjects for breast cancer prevention. The education was performed four times for four months using Video, CD-ROM, case study, discussion, and others[Fig. 1].

And then the education effect was estimated by the practice rates for the breast cancer prevention after education compared with that before education. In this work, the practice rates after education were plotted as a function of time elapsed after education : 10 days, 40 days, 70 days, and 120 days. The evaluation was performed for the examination of differences in the satisfaction of subjects after information education using computer between two aged groups.

2.2   Methods

Basic information of study subjects was analyzed with descriptive statistics. The pairwise t-test was done to compare the changes of practice rates for the breast cancer prevention before and after information education using computer. Average and standard deviate were obtained. On the other hand, the chi-square test was used for the examination of differences in the satisfaction of subjects after information education using computer between two aged groups.

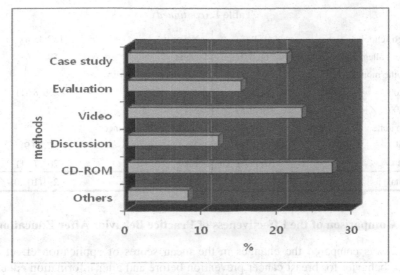

Fig. 1. Assign of Information Education Using Computer

3   Results

3.1   Basic Information of Study Subjects

Table 1 presents basic information of study subjects. In a marital status, it showed that 83.8% married women higher than 16.2% single women. In the classification of religion, 76.6% subjects who have a religion are higher than 23.4% subjects who do not have religion. In the examination of job, 72.9% subjects who do not a job are higher than 27.1% subjects who have a job. In the examination of experience of delivery. 82.1% subjects who have delivery experience are higher than 17.9% subjects who do not have delivery experience.

Table 1. Basic Information of Study Subjects

Variables	N(%)	Variables	N(%)
Age/yrs.		Religion	
⬜40	48(16.5)	Has a religion	223(76.6)
40-49	136(46.7)	No religion	68(23.4)
50-59	75(25.8)	Job	
≥60	32(11.0)	Has a job	79(27.1)
Marital status		Jobless	212(72.9)
Married	244(83.8)	Menopause	
Single	47(16.2)	Yes	164(56.4)
Education level		No	127(43.6)
Under middle school	54(18.6)	Cancer screening	

Table 1. (*continued*)

High school	141(48.5)	Never	132(45.4)
Over college	96(33.0)	Done	159(54.6)
Income/month.		Experience of delivery	
∠200	83(28.5)	Yes	239(82.1)
≥200	208(71.5)	No	52(17.9)
Menarche		History of breast cancer	
☐14	259(89.0)	Yes	87(29.9)
≥ 14	32(11.0)	No	204(70.1)
Total	291(100.0)	Total	291(100.0)

3.2   Comparison of the Effectiveness of Practice Behavior After Education

Table 2 was compared the changes in the mean scores of application effect about practice behavior for breast cancer prevention before and after information education. As a result, the mean score of the concerns about breast cancer prevention was 11.46 point before education and the mean score of that after education was 14.71 point. There was a statistically significant difference between the two groups(t=-2.95, p<.05). After receiving education(18.59 point), there were significant changes for the body weight than before education(13.74 point) in the mean score of body weight control(t=-15.72, p<.01).

Table 2. Comparison of the Effectiveness of Practice Behavior After Education

Variables	Before Mean±SD	After Mean±SD	T
Concerns about breast cancer prevention	11.46±3.82	14.71±3.62.	-2.95*
Practicing breast self-examination	4.72±1.49	6.96±0.95	-7.03*
Attitude towards breast cancer screening	5.63±1.27	8.24±1.19	-5.27*
Exercise	10.28±3.51	11.47±3.57	-2.49
Stress control	5.95±0.83	4.62±0.84	6.81
Body weight control	13.74±5.06	18.59±4.50	-15.72**
Participation of education program	4.86±0.79	5.19±0.81	-6.24
Control of food intake	4.69±0.45	9.12±0.52	-7.06**
Control of favorite food intake‡	8.25±1.62	9.74±0.79	-5.87
Importance of cancer education	4.91±0.71	5.34±0.61	-6.39

* p<.05   ** p<.01

‡Cigarette smoking, alcohol drinking, etc.

3.3   Durability of Education Effect of Two Aged Groups

Fig. 2 was done to compare the durability of education effect as a function of time elapsed after information education using computer for two groups of women aged under 50s and over 50s. The education effect was estimated to be higher at the women aged under 50s old than women aged over 50s for the breast cancer prevention, regardless of time elapsed of 40 days after the education. In particular, the education effect was estimated to decrease more rapidly with time elapsed of 70 days after the education at the women aged over 50s compared to the women aged under 50s.

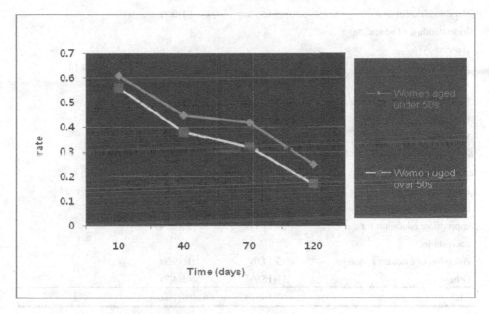

*Slope=$\dfrac{\Delta Y}{\Delta X}$ Where ΔX : time interval
    ΔY : variation of education effect
*Ratio=$\dfrac{\Delta Ya}{\Delta Yb}$ Where ΔYb : practice rate before education
    ΔYa : practice rate after education

Fig. 2. Durability of Education Effect of Two Aged Groups

3.4   Evaluation of the Satisfaction After Education

Table 3 presents the evaluation of the satisfaction after information education using computer by two aged groups. 33.6% of women aged under 50s and 42.1% of women aged over 50s answered that they was very sufficient for time assigned for education. On the other hand, 43.0% of women aged under 50s and 63.6% women aged over 50s answered the most the emphasis on practice of breast cancer screening as methods for the breast cancer prevention. There was a significant difference between two aged groups(X^2=10.72, p<.05).

Table 3. Evaluation of the Satisfaction After Education

Variables	Under 50s† N(%)	Over 50s‡ N(%)	X^2
Time assigned for education			
Very sufficient	36(33.6)	45(42.1)	14.09
Sufficient	48(44.9)	34(31.8)	
Fair	14(13.1)	19(17.8)	
Insufficient	7(6.5)	8(7.5)	
Very insufficient	2(1.9)	1(0.9)	
Understanding of education			
Contents			
Very high	51(47.7)	49(45.8)	9.14
High	36(33.6)	34(31.8)	
Fair	12(11.2)	11(10.3)	
Low	5(4.7)	8(7.5)	
Very low	3(2.8)	5(4.7)	
Methods for the breast			
cancer prevention			
Emphasis on practice of	46(43.0)	68(63.6)	10.72*
breast cancer screening			
Appropriate education for	29(27.1)	24(22.4)	
each subject			
Adoption of evaluation system	15(14.0)	10(9.3)	
Others	17(15.9)	5(4.7)	
Total	107(100.0)	107(100.0)	

* p<.05
† Women aged under 50 years old   ‡aged over 50 years old

4   Discussion

This paper was to evaluate the effect of information education using computer for the prevention and early detection of breast cancer. To evaluate the impacts of the practice behavior before and after education, the target subjects were allocated randomly to experimental groups. They were divided into two groups which were women aged under and over 50s.

The information education through computer for the breast cancer prevention was more effective in encouraging the practice of breast cancer screening. This intervention did not increase smoking, alcohol drinking rate significantly, and then multi-displinary approach is required to reduce the smoking prevalence. Based on the results obtained by the study, it is anticipated that this paper may be used as basic data for developing and intervening for the breast cancer prevention with integration of individual and contextual associated factors.

The result of this paper, after receiving education, there were significant changes for the body weight than before education in the mean score of body weight control. The finding was consistent with the result of earlier research[7]. Therefore, it needs to perform systematic information education. There is a need for a separate program to be implemented on the groups who characterize having lower levels of health knowledge and health promotion behavior. The education effect was estimated to be higher in the group under the age of fifty than group over the age of fifty in the rate of practice for the breast cancer prevention, regardless of time elapsed of 40 days after the education. In particular, the education effect was estimated to decrease more rapidly with time elapsed of 70 days after the education at the women over the age of fifty as compared to the women under age of fifty. Thus, year-based education should be performed more often women over the age of fifty than women under the age of fifty. The present research showed that practice rate for the breast cancer prevention can be increased to 57.4-82.6% by the education, which is similar to data reported in the previous studies[8],[9]. However, it should be noted that the education effect does not maintain for so long. Therefore, in order to maintain the education effect well, it is very important to determine adequate education period and perform various programs in consideration of their circumstances.

The present work elucidated throughout the statistical analysis how effectively the synthetic and systematic education contributes to practice behavior for the prevention and early detection of breast cancer. The future work should focus on the study of the education effect as a classification of patient throughout more prolonged research based on a larger data base. Methods for the breast cancer prevention on the evaluation in information education revealed the significantly the highest at the emphasis on breast cancer screening practice. This is similar with previous studies on the clinical education[10],[11]. This paper presented the satisfaction over 80.0% in evaluation after information education, the result of this would be the enhancement of practice behavior for the prevention and early detection of breast cancer.

Concerning the education methods, most of the domestic programs imposed the knowledge on the life habit through the lecture or through watching video so far. In order to get out such a stagnant reality, however, this paper was performed the advanced methods which consist of information education using computer, discussion, and evaluation.

The objective measurement on the changes of the behaviors of the subjects would be more valuable than mere abstract testimonies that are only responses to the questions provided by the programs. Therefore, this paper was proposed important data such as information education using computer. These may also be used for the planning report for the prevention and early detection of breast cancer in the future. Thus, this paper indicated that the implemented systematic information education using computer showed significant positive effects on the life of subjects and health behavior.

5   Conclusion

This paper identified positive effects of information education using computer for the prevention and early detection of breast cancer. The information education using computer can be used as an effective method to improve the knowledge of breast cancer information and to enhance the practice rate of breast cancer screening. This paper, therefore, resulted in significant improvement in the quality of life of women and its implications could be used as the basic data for developing further systematic materials on computer-aided health education of breast cancer patients.

References

1. Ministry of Health and Welfare, Annual Report of Cancer Registry Programmes, pp. 23–24 (2011)
2. Statistics Korea, Annual Report on the Cause of Death Statistics, pp. 13–15 (2011)
3. American Cancer Society, The American Cancer Society Guidelines for the Cancer Related Checkup, Cancer, pp. 42–43 (2003)
4. Kyrkejebo, J.M., Hage, I.: What We Know and What They Do: Nursing Students' Experiences of Improvement Knowledge in Clinical Practice. Nurse Education Today 25(3), 168–170 (2005)
5. Montano, D.E., Thompson, B., Tayler, V., Mahloch, J.: Understanding Mammography Intention and Utilization Among Women in An Inner City Public Hospital Clinic. Preventive Medicine 26(4), 818–820 (2007)
6. Suarez, L., Lloyd, L., Weiss, N., Rainbolt, T., Pulley, L.V.: Effect of Social Networks on Cancer-Screening Behavior of Older Mexican-American Women. Journal of the National Cancer Institute 86(10), 776–778 (2004)
7. Moran, W.P., Nelson, K., Wofford, J.I., Velez, R.: Computer-Generated Physician and Patient Reminder Tools to Improve Population Adherence to Selected Preventive Services. J. Fam. Pract. 5(2), 534–536 (2002)
8. Omstein, S.M., Garr, D.R., Jenkins, R.G., Rust, P.F., Amon, A.: Computer-Generated Physician and Patient Reminder Tools to Improve Population Adherence to Selected Preventive Services. J. Fam. Pract. 32(2), 83–85 (2008)
9. Litzelman, D.K., Dittus, R.S., Miller, M.E., Tiene, W.M.: Requiring Physicians to Respond to Computerized Reminders Improves Their Compliance with Preventive care Protocols. J. Gen. Intern. Med. 8(6), 315–316 (2003)
10. Surra, K.A.: The Influence of the Interactive Network on Developing Relations Families and Social Networks. Stage, Beverly Hills (2009)
11. Rosenstock, I.M., Strecher, V.J., Becker, M.H.: Social Learning Theory and the Health Belief Model. Health Education Quarterly 15(2), 176–178 (2006)

A Study on the Development of a Course Evaluation Tool for Cyber University Consortium in Korea

Seung Lock Han

Kongju National University, South Korea
hsrcom@kongju.ac.kr

Abstract. The purpose of this research was to investigate criteria of course evaluation which are proper for cyber university consortium in Korea. For the purpose of this study, two research problems were examined. First, what should be the sub-categories of the course evaluation criteria for the cyber university consortium? Second, what items should be developed for each sub-category of the criteria in the evaluation tool? The results of this study were as follows: First, professors as well as students agree the cyber university course evaluation should include 3 areas : (1) infra for course management in its nature, (2) student satisfaction, and (3) relevance of class management. And their weights should be reflected respectively. Second, the research suggested the sub-categories of the evaluation criteria as the following 5 areas: 'class design', 'communication', ' quality of learning contents', 'participation activities of students' and 'passion of lecturers'. Third, the areas and contents of questions should be properly revised and supplemented by considering the relevance and weight levels of the questions as for 15 evaluation questions of the current student survey and measures to evaluate scores of each question at different weights by the weigh level of each question are required to be considered.

Keywords: cyber course evaluation, cyber university course evaluation, cyber course evaluation criteria.

1 Necessity of Research

This study was conducted as a way of improving the quality of courses, which were provided through the Open Cyber University(OCU) Consortium in Korea. The OCU consortium is the largest academic exchange campus in Korea as of 2012 since its first establishment in 1997. Currently it is operated with more than 35 participating universities and mainly provides the online courses of liberal arts and advanced major courses.

The OCU consortium carried out "Study on Improving Course Evaluation System" in 2010 to improve course quality in consideration of cyber university characteristics, which suggested researches including "researches on course evaluation program improvements of OCU consortium", "researches on how course evaluation results contribute to academic achievement improvement as a result by feedback to course quality improvements", "researches on what are demands of member universities

T.-h. Kim et al. (Eds.): SIP/WSE/ICHCI 2012, CCIS 342, pp. 331–337, 2012.
© Springer-Verlag Berlin Heidelberg 2012

concerned, professors in charge of lectures and students concerning a OCU course evaluation program and how they should be reflected in course evaluation program improvements", etc. are required.

This study was done in order to fulfill the suggestions of the previous research to improve the quality of the courses offered by the OCU consortium. The two research questions were investigated for this study as follows:

Research Question 1: What should be the sub-categories of the course evaluation criteria for the cyber university consortium?
Research Question 2: What items should be developed for each sub-category of the criteria in the evaluation tool?

To investigate research question 1, newly improved OCU course evaluation rubrics were intended to be devised by reviewing relevancy based on precedent researches about OCU consortium course evaluation criteria. Specific research methods for this are as followings.

   a.   Collection and analysis of precedent study results on key professor behaviors related with university lecture effects and key criteria of university course evaluation.
   b.   Development, survey and analysis of a questionnaire for developing cyber university course evaluation criteria in consideration of cyber lectures.

To investigate research question 2, implications to develop evaluation questions which fit in course evaluation rubrics by analyzing the current OCU consortium course evaluation criteria and relevance of evaluation questions through survey were drawn up.

   a.   Derive sub-areas of OCU consortium course evaluation by reviewing developed course evaluation criteria.
   b.   Drawing implications of subsequent specific course evaluation question development by analyzing and reviewing the current OCU consortium course evaluation sub-areas and relevance of specific evaluation questions by such area based on sub-areas derived.

2 Literature Review

2.1 Purpose and Usages of Course Evaluation

The university course evaluation system was introduced in late 1980' in Korea and actually has been implemented from mid 1990's. The purpose of course evaluation lies in improving quality of lecture. Although various approaches are required to enhance quality of lecture, few approaches but course evaluation have been utilized. In respect of a current university education policy trend where university education is converted from lecturer oriented paradigms to consumer oriented paradigms and quality improvements of universities are attempted by introducing competitive programs such as incentive programs based on professors' academic achievements. The course evaluation system has been used quite successfully to control professors and implement the policies related to the course management.

The usage of course evaluation program in Korea are generally summarized as follows : ① the securement of materials for professor personnel administration such as promotion of individual professors, retirement age guarantee, etc. ② the securement for quality improvements of professor-student learning ③ the information for students' course and professor selection ④ diverse class studies related with lectures, etc.

Research issues which have been discussed in several studies on university course evaluation of Korea in the past are as followings. First, Jong-Seung, L. [1] asserted results of course evaluation should bring in certain changes of professors' lecture behaviors to contribute to quality enhancement and improvements of lectures and reasonable for criteria which shows professor effectiveness. In this respect, he suggested questions such as "The criteria of high quality lectures are recognized equally by professors who get evaluation and students who evaluate? Are lecturing capabilities are proportional to course evaluation scores by students? Can it be said qualities of education activities including professors' lectures are high when professors' course evaluation scores are high?" should be reviewed. For this, Mi-Gyeong, Y. [2] insisted effects or characteristics which professor expected can be recognized in completely different appearances as there are structural differences of recognition systems for university lectures between professors and students. According to a study of Suk-yeol, L. and Young-ju, H. [3], they pointed out course evaluation take more than 40% in professor achievement evaluation although there are various aspects such as development of new courses, development of lecture contents, student guidance, research activities, etc. besides lectures in education activities of professors.

Also Yeon-Wook, C. [4] categorized the criteria of course evaluation into 9 areas such as 'course organization and preparation', 'learning materials', 'homework', 'tests and grades'. 'lecture skills', 'interaction between lecturers and students', 'effects on achievements and development of students', "general review on lecture', etc. concerning course evaluations and evaluation areas.

Sung-Mi, P. [5] developed the five categories of the criteria for the course evaluation as follows: 'organization of lecture', 'interest level of a professor in students', 'communication channel', 'use of education media' and "feedback on homework and tests through the examination of the previous studies related to course evaluation in Korean universities.

2.2   Criteria of Cyber University Course Evaluation

Characteristics of web-based cyber university lectures may be summarized by 3 characteristics such as a technology/ system factor, an interactional factor and a self-directional learning factor. The technology/ system factor means that expansion of infrastructures such as information telecommunication networks, use of computers, modems, advanced high-speed internet networks and multimedia materials, and support of IT experts which are proper for web-based on-line education are required. The interactional factor means bi-directional communications between a lecturer and a student or a learner through computer networks. These bi-directional interactions in cyber lectures are mainly made in a discussion room, bulletin board, material room, electronic mail, etc. and various social networks such as Twitter, Wikipedia, Blog, Facebook, Cacao Talk, etc. Those various learning and technology tools maximize knowledge and experience of students, maintain interest of students and promote problem-solving abilities, critical thinking, creativity, etc. Also, the self-directional learning factor means a learning situation in which students are more assigned of responsibilities and authorities of planning, implementation and evaluation for voluntary learning. The course evaluation of cyber lecture may be classified into 3 factors such as the program evaluation, class evaluation and academic achievement evaluation considering 3 characteristics of the cyber education like these [6]. Also Dae-Joon, H. [7] implied cyber lecture areas to divide technological bases of remote universities into 4 classes such as 'academic management class', 'contents creation class', 'education service class' and 'service access class' and asserted remote universities were operated focusing on these 4 classes. Junghoon Lim and Insung Jeong [8] classified the evaluation areas of cyber lectures into ① environmental factor (psychological and physical support environment) ② academic achievement and course satisfaction factor (awareness of education effects, course satisfaction, awareness of general information communication capability improvement and positive attitude on computer media telecommunication) ③ learning contents and professor design factor (contents variable cause, contents indication strategy, screen design, interface strategy and learning management strategy) ④ operation factor (operator, online teaching assistant and online discussion), etc. Also, Jae-Young, P. [9] classified into ① learning contents ② learning ③ teaching design ④ screen suggestion strategy ⑤ lecturer, teacher and promoter ⑥ evaluation ⑦ learning activities ⑧ technology support ⑨ administrative support ⑩ academic achievement ⑪ overall evaluation ⑫ suggestion for improvements, etc.

3   Current Situations of OCU Course Evaluation

3.1   Criteria of OCU Consortium Course Evaluation

The current criteria of course evaluation utilized in the OCU consortium are: ① evaluation of lecture operation (25% of total question items) ② subject student survey evaluation (70% of total question items) and ③ class management relevancy (5% of total question items).

As shown in Table 1, the student questionnaire is composed of 15 questions. The question 15 is an open-ended item that asks students to describe some suggestions for the improvement of lectures. These 15 items are categorized into several criteria as follows: class design (items of 1, 2, 3 and 6), professors' passion on lectures (item of 4), education contents area (item of 7), education media area (item of 8), education evaluation area (items of 9,10,11,14), motivation area (item of 5), communication area (items of 6 and 12), and learning activity support area (item of 13).

Table 1. The current questionnaire items of course evaluation

Question	Contents	Score	Question	Contents	Score
1	Advance information	5	9	Assignment and evaluation management	5
2	Syllabus (proceeding)	5	10	Use of evaluation factors	5
3	Subject notice (introduction)	5	11	Achievement evaluation	5
4	Lecturing attitude	5	12	Communication evaluation	5
5	Motivation	5	13	Student guidance	5
6	Relevancy of teaching plan composition	5	14	Overall evaluation	5
7	Quality of teaching plan (quality)	5	15	Subjective opinions	
8	Use of teaching media	5	Total		70

In the current OCU course evaluation tool, the criteria of 'class design' and 'education evaluation' were more frequently asked than the other categories of 'passion for lecture'. 'quality of education contents', 'education media', 'motivation', 'communication' and 'learning support activities'. The relevance of the current criteria composition should be examined by students as well as lecturers.

4   OCU Course Evaluation Criteria Development

4.1   Survey Tool and Survey Objects

To review criteria of OCU consortium course evaluation and relevancy of questions, a questionnaire asking 'course evaluation method', 'course evaluation sub-areas', 'relevancy of course evaluation criteria', was developed. The responses of 3,386 subjects (3,326 students attending OCU consortium lectures, 50 professors in charge of lectures, and 10 staffs who manages lectures) have been collected. However, only a professor group and a student group were chosen as comparative objects because the number of staff was too small for the analysis of response results.

4.2   Response Analysis of Course Evaluation Method

As for questions of OCU consortium course evaluation methods, questions such as 'What do you think of evaluation time and collection?, 'Do you think criteria or questions of course evaluation should vary on lecture types?', 'Which should be considered at course evaluation to enhance reliability of course evaluation by students?', etc. were made and analyzed.

As a result of analysis, one time performance at the end of each semester took 77.7% as for the time and number of course evaluation and respondents does not show much response to providing feedback materials for lecture improvements to applicable professors after taking LV on the start or in the middle of lecture to improve quality of lecture. As for lecture types of which evaluation methods should be changed by lecture type in the course evaluation, lecture-oriented class, discussion type class, practice-oriented class, etc. took high responses. To improve reliability of course evaluation by students, the assertion course evaluation results by students under top 5 % and low 5% academic achievements should be excluded in the analysis was positively answered by 47.9 and negatively answered by 17.6% while 72% answered positively in a professor group and only 47.5% answered positively in a student group. Also, as one of measure to improve reliability of students' course evaluation, the assertion students in very low academic achievements should be excluded in the evaluation was responded positively by 72% in a professor group while only 47.5% positively answered in a student group. As for the assertion students who are very unfaithful to lectures such as students with much absence or with various obstacles should be excluded in the evaluation, 54.3% responded positively while 92% in a professor group and 53.7% in a student group responded positively.

4.3   Response Analysis of Course Evaluation Criteria Relevance

As for relevance of course evaluation factors, 10 evaluation factors were suggested in precedents studies related with a course evaluation program and priorities on these evaluation factors were asked to select. The derived priority was analyzed to be in the order of 'class design', 'communication', 'quality of learning contents', and 'passion of lecturer'. As for weights of course evaluation factors, the current composition of 25% class operation, 70% student survey evaluation and 5% class operation relevance was demanded to 30% class operation, 55% student survey evaluation and 15% class operation relevance. As for course evaluation questions, about 7 through 10 questions were preferred most by 70% while a professor group preferred 10~15 questions and a student group preferred 7 ~ 10 questions.

4.4   Response Analysis on Course Evaluation Contents Relevance

If Student survey questions of the current OCU consortium course evaluation factors are proper as course evaluation factors and how each weight level of evaluation questions should be were analyzed. As a result of analysis, 'advance providence of information for course registration', 'providence of lecture according to a syllabus', 'sincere and passionate lecture', 'relevance of understanding textbook contents', etc. showed high relevance. As for weight levels, 'advance providence of information for course registration', 'providence of lecture according to a syllabus', 'sincere and passionate lecture', and 'course notice which are helpful to class attendance', etc. showed high weight levels.

5   Conclusion and Suggestions

This study aims at developing course evaluation criteria which are appropriate for the cyber university and questionnaire items in order to enhance the quality of the OCU consortium lecture.

The results of this research are as follows.

First, professors as well as students agree that the cyber university course evaluation should include 3 criteria such as infra for course management in its nature, student satisfaction and, relevance of class management and that their weights should be reflected by 25%~30%, 55%~70% and 5%~15% successively.

Second, the current OCU consortium course evaluation put high weights mainly on the criteria of 'class design' area and 'education evaluation'. However, the result of this study suggested that the evaluation should include 5 categories of criteria such as 'class design', ' communication', ' quality of learning contents', 'participating activities of students' and 'passion of lecturers'.

Third, the questionnaire items should be revised considering the relevance of each question and giving different weights on each question when analyzing the survey results.

References

1. Jong-Seung, L.: A study on course evaluation of professor. CNU Journal of Educational Studies 14(1), 83–95 (1992)
2. Mi-Gyeong, Y.: Significance and limitation of university course evaluation based on students' rating. Educational Principle Research 13(1), 93–122 (2008)
3. Suk-Yeol, L., Young-Ju, H.: Problems and improvements of university course evaluation. The Journal of Namseoul University 16(1), 287–309 (2010)
4. Yeon-Wook, C.: Constructing items for course evaluation. Master's thesis. Graduate School of Ewha Woman University (1995)
5. Sung-Mi, P.: A study for development and validation of the 'course evaluation' scale of learner centered. Fishers and Marine Science Education 23(1), 13–22 (2011)
6. Wan-Young, Y.: Web-based education – evaluation on web-based education. Kyoyook Book Publishing Co., Seoul (1999)
7. Dae-Joon, H.: Special contribution: The current operation situation and development plan of Cyber Universities (1999),
   http://www.dpc.or.kr/dbworld/document/9911/gigo.html
8. Lim, J., Jeong, I.: A study on the student satisfaction of web-based instruction. Journal of Educational Broadcasting 5(2), 151–175 (1999)
9. Jae-Young, P.: A study on the students' evaluation of online courses at the university level. Master's thesis, Graduate School of Hanyang University (2000)

The Study of the Relationship between Young Children's Decision Making Ability and Self-esteem

Jiyoung Park[1,*] and Junghwan Park[2,**]

[1] Chonnam National University, South Korea
jy9332@hanmail.net
[2] Jeju National University, South Korea
edu114@jejunu.ac.kr

Abstract. The purpose of this study was to analyze the relationship between young children's decision making ability and their self-esteem. In order to achieve the purpose, questionnaires were conducted with 360 young children in area D and J, and the collected data is analyzed with regression analysis and the product-moment correlation of Pearson. Results of the study are follows: first, young children's decision making ability and self-esteem had significantly positive correlations. Also, decision making ability is an important variant to be able to estimate their self-esteem level. This result suggests that efficient educational approach may need to be introduced to increase young children's decision making ability for improving self-esteem of young children.

Keywords: Decision Making Ability, Self-control Ability, Situation analysis Ability, Emotion-application Ability, Problem-coping Ability, Referential Communication Ability, Self-esteem.

1 Introduction

Young children experience their own discerning and decisions making process when being provided with many choices during not only play, but learning process and other different problematic circumstances. Young children's decision making ability is the ability to select and decide a most appropriate alternative through the process of rationalization, with awareness of self-responsibility, in order to effectively achieve the goal of the young children himself/herself or the group [1]. This is an important and necessary ability when conflicts and problems among different groups should be resolved, thus, it is required to understand that the young children should be provided the chances to voluntarily and actively participates in decision making processes from the early ages and that this experience would be stepping stone and continue to affect adolescence and adulthood [2, 3].

Until recently, efforts has been made to devise methods to measure and improve decision making ability, in the researches[4, 5, 6] that developed programs for young

---

[*] First author.
[**] Corresponding author.

T.-h. Kim et al. (Eds.): SIP/WSE/ICHCI 2012, CCIS 342, pp. 338–346, 2012.

children's decision making ability. In other researches about with young children [7, 8, 9, 10], decision making of young children was analyzed, and the importance and necessity of the decision making ability were claimed, but they were insufficient to define related concepts or suggest related variables of the young children. Hence, Park [1, 11] introduced the elements related to the ability of young children, developed a testing tool, analyzed relative differences in factors, such as sex, age, and disposition, that well present individual tendencies in relation to the ability, and suggested developmental qualities. With this consideration and acceptance of the diversity of variables of each young children, it is necessary to identify how young children's decision making ability is related to the other variables, if proper education is intended to set and implemented with objectives to encourage a young children to grow to a holistic being.

Furthermore, young children's self-esteem is a positive view toward the existence of oneself, and it is a vital element to have good relations with others and to consider oneself to be happy and to live a satisfying life. Self-esteem is as sense of worthiness recognized by oneself, and is a tendency to think that he/she deserves to have happiness, physical and mental stability, respect, friendship, love, achievement, and success [12]. Self-esteem is germinated from the age of about two based on human interaction that oneself is regarded as important being by others. Self-esteem is built on trust and reliability by experiencing small achievements, compliments, or success through everyday tasks [13, 14]. Young children with high self-esteem are independent, have responsibility for one's own business, have generous attitude toward every aspect and have sense of accomplishment [15]. Therefore, in order for them to have desirable self-esteem, young children has to be encouraged to have positive results in self-evaluation through comparisons to peer group with one's own appearance, property, family background, and peer acceptance, and in view of expected standards of his/her own.

The correlation with young children's variables and the necessity of self-esteem are identified by several researches [16, 17, 18, 19, 20, 21, 22]. Individual variables, such as sex, society, and emotion, and social environment variables, such as parents and social comparison, are important factors that have effect on development of self-esteem. Among individual variables, emotional and social intelligences had stronger influences than sex and physical ability on self-esteem [19]. Among environmental variables, on the other hand, child-rearing attitude, such as compliment, encouragement, and words and behaviors with respect from parents [18], and relationship with the parents and the level of harmony [20] had influences on building up positive self-esteem. In this way, it is self-esteem that builds up with positive thinking, regard for others, and the sense of one's own worth and confidence and positive and active attitude toward life.

In spite of this necessity suggested, researched was conducted insufficiently to identify the relationship between young children's decision making ability and self-esteem until a recent date, and only some researches proved the correlation between the decision making ability and emotional intelligence [19, 23], and communication [24, 25]. Jang [26] suggested that the improvement in self-regard is an element that reinforces the practice of decision making, and self-worth is a driving force of autonomy that keeps decision making and actions maintain consistently. This implies that voluntary making decisions, not by practices under coercion, may be the influence factor of self-worth. In addition, the process of making one's own decision and judgment may help acquiring the ability the ability to explore problem solving skills, cognitive ability, self-control ability, self-regard and autonomy, learning-application ability etc. [10, 27, 26].

From the grounds above, self-esteem may improve confidence of oneself through the processes of strategically expressing one's emotions and controlling one's desire or behavior with the young children's own judgment and thinking skills in situations of decision making, and regarding oneself valuable. Therefore, the process of clear understanding young children's decision making ability and determining its correlation with individual variables are needed. Also, the detail steps to help growth and development accordingly should be suggested. Hence, this study attempts to identify what the correlation between young children's decision making ability and self-esteem are, and how the decision making ability influences self-esteem for the purpose of realizing the ultimate education goal. Hence, two research questions are as follows to analyze the relationship between young children's decision making ability and self-esteem;

1.1. What is the relationship between young children's decision making ability and self-esteem?
1.2. What is the influence of young children's decision making ability on self-esteem?

2   Research Method

2.1   Subjects of the Research

For the selecting subjects of this researcher, 360 young children of 3-5 years old in 6 private six kindergartens located in D, J zones were sampled. Subjects were 179 males and 181 females, and made a total of 360 young children. 120 children for 3 different age ranges, respectively and ages are evenly distributed with 3 years-old (M = 50.72, SD = 3.54), 4 years-old (M = 61.35, SD = 3.62), 5years-old (M = 70.81, SD = 3.87).

2.2   Research Tools

2.2.1   Young Children's Decision Making Ability Test
In this study, young children's decision making ability Test developed by Park [1] was used to test young children's decision making ability. This test consists of 5 sections. Each question consists of a four-point rating scale and the total score of the test with 32 questions has 32-128 point distribution. In this study, Cronbach's α, reliability level of the tools showed: the self-control ability as .80, Situation analysis Ability as .78, emotional information utilization ability as .78, Problem-coping ability as .72, referential communication ability as .76, and overall as .86, which is good because it

exceeds .60 in Cronbach α which acknowledges reliability of test in the social science [28].

2.2.2. Young Children Self-esteem Test

In this study, the test tool developed by Dan & Lee [29] is used to test Young children self-esteem. This test consists of 4 sections. Each question consists of a five-point rating scale and the total score of the test with 31 questions has 31-155 point distribution. In this study, Cronbach's α reliability of the tool is: the competence as .70, the sense of belonging as .72, self-worthy as 0.78, controllability as 0.78, the overall as 0.67. Likewise above, this is good since it exceeds .60 at nominal value of Cronbach α.

2.3   Consistency in Researchers and Raters

This study conducted a preliminary examination to figure out usability of test tools and consistency among researchers. From June 18th, 2012 to June 22th, 2012, preliminary examination was conducted with 11 of the homeroom teachers, who are the subjects of this study and 11 full time care children who is not related with this study. The result showed no difficulties of understanding the test tool, understanding the test, consistency between researchers in young children's decision making ability consistency as 0.90 and self-esteem as 0.87. The examination was rated by homeroom teacher of 360 children, who are the subjects of this study, at the kindergarten located in D and J zone and conducted for 2 weeks from July 2th to July 13th, 2012.

2.4   Data Analysis

Examination data about young children's decision making ability and Self-esteem were calculated average of each section, and ratios against overall, standard deviation, skewness, kurtosis in order to figure out the general tendency of these two factors. Also, Pearson's product-moment correlation coefficient was calculated, and multiple regression analysis was conducted by setting decision making ability as independent variable and self-esteem as dependent variable in order to figure out how decision making ability effects to self-esteem.

3   Result and Analysis

3.1   General Tendency of Young Children's Decision Making Ability and Self-esteem

Before examining the relationship and effect of young children's decision making ability and self-esteem, general tendency of these two were reviewed. Average score for each sub-sections under decision making ability is 14.23~24.00, the standard deviation is 2.13~4.33, skewness is -.73~.21, kurtosis is .35~1.07, respectively.

When absolute value of skewness is over 3, and the one of kurtosis is over 8, it is considered as violations of the normal assumption (Kline, 2005). Therefore, the data of this study is seen as satisfied with assumption of normality. Also, average score for each sub-sections under self esteem is 16.60~37.57, standard deviation is standard deviation is 2.13~4.33, skewness is -.73~.21, kurtosis is .35~1.07, respectively. skewness is -.44~.09, kurtosis is -.61~.31, respectively, which is also seen as satisfied with assumption of normality.

3.2   Analysis of Relationship between Young Children's Decision Making Ability and Self-esteem

Overall, it is found that young children's decision making ability and self-esteem have a statistically significant positive correlation(r=.588, p<.01). for each subsection, self-control ability was r=.558(p<.01); Situation analysis Ability was r=.476(p<.01); emotion-application ability was r=.554(p<.01); Problem-coping ability was r=.375(p<.01); referential communication ability was r=.492(p<.01), and again, it showed significant positive correlation with self-esteem. In other words, the higher young children's decision making ability is, the higher self-esteem goes.

Table 1. Analysis of Relationship between Young Children's Decision making ability and Self-esteem

Self-esteem Decision Making Ability	Competence	Sense of belonging	Sense of feeling valuable	Controllability	Total
Self-control Ability	.321**	.644**	.329**	.262**	.558**
Situation analysis Ability	.474**	.348**	.222**	.274**	.476**
Emotion-application Ability	.537**	.470**	.212**	.313**	.554**
Problem-coping Ability	.492**	.341**	-.012	.167**	.375**
Referential Communication Ability	.528**	.458**	.074	.293**	.492**
Total	.595**	.538**	.166**	.312**	.588**

**p<.01

3.3   Analysis of How Young Children's Decision Making Ability Effects to their Self-esteem

For the relationship between young children's decision making ability and self-esteem, decision making ability took 45% of the total variance to explain self-esteem (R^2= .45, F=60.03,p<.001), which shows statistically significant level. To sum up, young children's decision making ability is a significant variable in explaining self-esteem.

Table 2. Analysis of how young children's decision making ability affects to their self-esteem

depéndent váriable	independent variable	B	S.E.	β	t	R²	adj.R²	F
Self-esteem	(constant)	29.96	4.61		6.48***			
	Self-control Ability	2.35	.31	.35	7.57***			
	Situation analysis Ability	.50	.32	.08	1.55			
	Emotion-application Ability	1.78	.30	.30	-2.23*	.45	.45	60.03***
	Problem-coping Ability	-.43	.19	-.13	3.45**			
	Referential Communication Ability	.90	.26	.20	3.406**			

$p<.05$, ** $p<.01$, *** $p<.001$

4   Discussion and Conclusion Research Method

This study has analyzed the relationship between young children's decision making ability and self-esteem level. Based on previous researches, the followings are the summary of the discussions and conclusion.

First, Young children's decision making ability and self-esteem have significant correlation. As a result, the higher decision making ability young children have, the more self-esteem can be improved. It is worthy of note that above research findings partially corresponds to the research of Park, Choi, & Park [23], which showed a meaningful correlation between young children's self-esteem and self-emotion-regulation, self-emotion-practice, emotion-regulation and emotion-practice of others. In addition, it's partially in line with the research of Choi & Park [31] which suggested that a young children may be confident in his/her linguistic ability and reasoning skill through the process of problem solving in play situation, and that process of sharing toys or resolving conflicts within the rules of continuum of play may influence confidence in performing given tasks, sense of ability, satisfaction, and independence. Furthermore, this study shows that referent communication skill that provides and impresses the other party the information of one's choice as well, is highly related to self-esteem, as communication skill which improved through communication training had positive influence on self-esteem [24].

When examining relative influence of young children's decision making ability on self-esteem, it was proved that young children's decision making ability was an significant variable to explain self-esteem 45%. Among the sub factors of self-esteem, the sense of belonging was critical. This finding supports the result of Choi & Shin's research [19] that social and emotional intelligence is individual variables influencing self-esteem of a young children. Besides, the result of this research showed the ability of emotion-application ability is a significant variable that has effects on every sub factors of self-esteem, is rooted on the researches of Kahn & Isen [33] and Isen [32] that suggested that positive emotion might influence decision making by promoting self-regulated thinking and additional information exploration. In other words, the result shows that a young children with outstanding ability to use emotional knowledge and information, and to effectively approach emotional problem solving, is good at appreciating the value of himself/herself, and effectively performing tasks voluntarily will to solve tasks and problems, through adjustments with others.

As stated above, self-respect has relationship with young children's ability of decision making, and this research points out the necessity of educational attempt to improve this ability. In other words, the result implies that the process to improve the ability is required in our education, that is, a young children feels his/her own value and the sense of belonging can be improved when the chances for young children to actively participate, and to express his/her opinions are provided by educational institutions. It also implies that young children are expected to improve qualitatively self-esteem in open environment and they are encouraged to freely participate in decision making. Thus, it is worthwhile to note the value and importance of the ability of decision making. In order to promote the ability, it is urgent to develop a program that reflects demand and reality through practical research and interviews with parents and teachers. Following studies are also required to provide evidences and to raise the significance of the effects of programs to promote young children's ability of decision making. It is also necessary to identify the process what young children's decision making ability are also affected and correlated by various social environment variables such as relationship with parents and peer as well as individual variables of young children. Moreover, additional study is required how young children's decision making ability is differentiated based on specialty of teachers, which is raised as one of important factors in educational programs.

References

1. Park, J.Y.: Development and Validation of Decision Making Ability Test for Young Children. Department of Early Childhood Education Graduate School of Chonnam National University (2012)
2. Kim, S.S.: Creative problem solving & decision making. Myungkyungsa, Seoul (2005)
3. Park, H.J., Go, E.H.: Development of the Brainwriting Decision-Making Model. Theory and Research in Citizenship Education 34(20), 123–148 (2002)
4. Kim, Y.J.: The influence of parents' child rearing attitudes and the child's decision making style on the self-efficacy. Department of Early Childhood Education Graduate School of Hanyang University (2010)
5. Bai, J.S.: A Qualitative Study on the Decision Making Processes of the Elementary Students. Department of Early Childhood Education Graduate School of Korea National University of Education (2009)
6. Son, K.W.: A Study on the implications of moral education from moral autonomy. Department of Early Childhood Education Graduate School of Seoul National University (2005)

7. Kang, J.J.: A Study on the Relationship between the Verbal Communication Style of Mothers and the Decision Making Behavior of Children. Department of Early Childhood Education Graduate School of Kyounggi University (1995)
8. Lee, S.H.: The Decision-Making and Response in Free-choice Activity of 5-year-old Class. The Korean Association for Early Childhood Education & Educate Administration 13(2), 277–298 (2009)
9. Choi, H.R.: The study on Decision Making of Young Children. Department of Early Childhood Education Graduate School of Chung-Ang University (1984)
10. Johnson, J.E., Christie, J.F., Wardle, F.: Play and early childhood development. Allyn & Bacon, Boston (2005)
11. Choi, M.S., Park, J.Y.: A study on the influence of young children's temperament on their decision making ability. The Journal of Korea Open Association for Early Childhood Education 17(3), 133–156 (2012)
12. Bettie, B.Y.: How to develop self-esteem in your child: 6 vital ingredients. Fawcett Columbine; Ballantine Books, New York (1990)
13. Song, M.J.: Developmental psychology. Hakjisa, Seoul (2008)
14. Jung, O.B.: Child development. Hakjisa, Seoul (2010)
15. Thompson, R.A.: The development of emotion regulation: A theme in search of definition. Monographs of the society for Research in Child Development 59, 25–52 (1994)
16. Kim, S.H.: The Effect of Mother's Early object Relation for Mother Rearing Attitude and Young Children's Self-esteem. Department of Early Childhood Education Graduate School of Sungkyunkwan University (2007)
17. Park, E.K.: The relationship between children's self-esteem and mothers' reactions to children's negative emotion. Department of Early Childhood Education Graduate School of Silla University (2007)
18. Yoon, S.Y., Jung, H.S.: An Inquiry into the Impact of Fostering Behavior by their Parents on Young Children's Self-esteem. Childhood Education Research & Review 14(5), 27–54 (2010)
19. Choi, H.M., Shin, D.J.: Development and Validation Study for Young Children's Self-Esteem Rating Scale. Korean Jounal of Early Childhood Education 32(1), 133–158 (2012)
20. Han, M.Y., Lee, H.S.: Effects of Self-Esteem, Relationships with Parents and Peer Relationships on Adolescents' Internet Addiction. Journal of Korean Home Economics Education Association 18(4), 55–66 (2006)
21. Kemple, K.M.: Shyness and self-esteem in early childhood. Journal of Humanistic Education and Development 33(4), 173–182 (1995)
22. Nelson, L.J., Rubin, K.H., Fox, N.A.: Social withdrawal, observed peer acceptance, and the development of self-perceptions in children ages 4 to 7 years. Early Childhood Research Quarterly 20, 185–200 (2005)
23. Park, Y.A., Choi, Y.H., Park, I.J.: Characteristics and Relationships of Emotional Intelligence and Self - Esteem in Children. Korean Journal of Child Studies, 5–23 (2000)
24. Seo, J.E., Lee, Y.N.: The Effects of Communication Training on Improving kindergartner's Self-esteem and Prosocial Behavior. Educational Research 31, 1–24 (2008)
25. Jang, H.S., Kang, T.W.: The Effects of Parent-Adolescent Communication on Their Self-Esteem and Self-Efficacy. Journal of Human Communication 13(2), 104–130 (2005)
26. Jang, Y.H.: A Study on the Elements to strengthen the Practice of Decision-Making. Theory and Research in Citizenship Education 39(4), 91–113 (2007)
27. Yang, O.S.: The Significance of Choice in Free-Choice Activities. Korean Journal of Early Childhood Education 23(3), 131–152 (2003)
28. Song, J.J.: Statistical analysis by SPSS/Amos. 21cbook, Paju (2010)

29. Dan, H.K., Lee, M.S.: The Preliminary Study of Young Children's Self-esteem Rating Scale by Teacher. The journal of Korea Early Childhood Education 13(4), 81–104 (2006)
30. Kline, R.B.: Principles and practice of structural equation modeling, 2nd edn. Guilford, New York (2005)
31. Choi, J.Y., Park, Y.Y.: A Study of the Relations among Young Children's Play Characteristics, Peer Competence, and Self-Esteem. Childhood Education Research & Review 16(3), 229–244 (2012)
32. Isen, A.M.: Positive affect and decision making. In: Lewis, M., Haviland, J.M. (eds.) Handbook of Emotions, 2nd edn. The Guilford Press, New York (2000)
33. Kahn, B.E., Isen, A.M.: The influence of positive affect on variety seeking among safe, enjoyable products. Journal of Consumer Research 20, 257–270 (1993)

The Physical Thermal Environment
for a Learner-Centered Comfort Learning Environment
in Summer: The Comparison of PMV- and CSV-Based
Thermal Comfort Conditions

Boseong Kim[1], Yoon-Ki Min[2,*], and Jin-Ho Kim[3,*]

[1] 275 Budaedong, Cheonan, Chungnam, 330-717, Korea
navyk439@kongju.ac.kr
[2] 99 Daehak-ro, Yuseong-gu, Daejeon, 305-764, Korea
ykmin@cnu.ac.kr
[3] 182 Sinkwandong, Kongju, Chungnam, 314-701, Korea
kjh@kongju.ac.kr

Abstract. This research examined it would be appropriate how to control physical thermal environment elements in order to make up a comfort learning environment. To do this, we compared physical thermal environment elements based on the predicted mean vote (PMV) with those based on the comfort sensation vote (CSV). As a result, in the condition of not-using air conditioning systems, an air temperature, relative humidity, and mean radiant temperature were higher on the CSV-based thermal comfort condition than on the PMV-based thermal comfort condition. While in the condition of using air conditioning systems, an air temperature and relative humidity were higher, and a air velocity was lower on the CSV-based thermal comfort condition than on the PMV-based thermal comfort condition. It suggest that it should be needed the correction controlling of physical thermal environment elements rather than controlling the physical thermal environment elements based on the PMV to make up a learner-centered comfort learning environment.

Keywords: Comfort Learning Environment, Thermal Comfort Condition, CSV, PMV.

1   Introduction

Why do people want to make up a comfort learning environment? It is the reason that people expect a comfort learning environment would improve their performance of a learning task. So many studies looked out how a comfort learning environment would be configured [1~2, 7]. Lee and Lee (1986) suggested the range of comfort temperatures on a learning environment in summer and winter. They said the range from 22 ℃ to 25.2 ℃ was a comfort temperature range in summer, and the range from 14.7 ℃ to

---

* Corresponding authors.

T.-h. Kim et al. (Eds.): SIP/WSE/ICHCI 2012, CCIS 342, pp. 347–353, 2012.
© Springer-Verlag Berlin Heidelberg 2012

18.1 ℃ was a comfort temperature range in winter. Meanwhile, Ahn et al. (2003) proposed that it should be better in terms of learners ℃ comfort using a radiant floor heating system than a convection heater system. A comfort learning environment could be configured by the proper ventilation through ventilation systems by checking indoor air quality as well as the appropriate control of humidity in winter [2]. Abovementioned studies used a comfort value with a well-known PMV (predicted mean vote) index which published in 1970 by Fanger [3] and established in 1984 as ISO-7730 [4].

However, Kim et al. (2011) showed that the correlation between a subjective comfort sensation of occupants and the PMV value was low. It suggested that the configured environment based on the PMV value should not provided occupants to optimal comfort sensation in an indoor environment, and the same results would also appeared in a configured learning environment based on the PMV value [6].

Therefore, this study examined the difference of physical thermal environment elements between on the comfort condition based on learners' subjective thermal comfort sensation with CSV (comfort sensation vote) and on the comfort condition based on the PMV value in the learning environment. And then, this study also examined how much those difference would be changed depending on whether the air conditioning system operated in summer or not.

2   Method

2.1   Participants

Twelve female high school students participated in the experiment. The average age was 17.83(SD=0.58), and they had normal or corrected to normal eyesight. They had no difficulty perceiving the stimulus presented on a LCD monitor. They waited in the waiting room, the air temperature of which was same as the initial temperature of the experimental room for 10 minutes before the experiment. In addition, their clothing was set to 0.7 clo (based on ISO 7730 Annex C of the typical combinations of garments). Their activity was set to 1.0 met, because they sat in a chair watching a computer screen and simply pressed two keys as specified in the task.

2.2   Experimental Apparatus and Learning Task

The air temperature, relative humidity, mean radiant temperature, air velocity and the PMV were measured for every 1 minute at a height of 1.2m with the KEM's AM-101. The Learning task was conducted with E-Prime 1.2 program. The stimulus of learning task was presented on a 19-inch LCD monitor with a resolution of 1024*768 and a refresh rate of 75Hz. The 70cm distance between the participants and the screen was maintained, and all stimuli were presented with black color on a gray background color. A stimulus was a square (visual angle 1.2*1.2 degree) with a gap of 0.6 degree size in one of the four sides. The target stimulus had a gap to the left or right side, and the distracter stimulus had a gap to the upper line or the bottom line.

2.3   Procedures

The experiments were conducted twice by the participants for 50 minutes. One session of the experiments was the environmental condition of not-using air conditioning system, and the other session was that of cooling with a air conditioning system. The presented order of conditions was counter balanced, and a resting time was included for approximately 5 minutes between sessions. In addition, eight blocks were included in a session, and a brief recess was included for 30 seconds between blocks. Participants checked their comfort sensation with the comfort sensation vote (CSV) at the beginning of every block, and then they performed the learning task. The CSV was made up as the 7-pointed Likert scale (1 : very uncomfortable, 4: neutral, 7 : very comfortable). In the learning task session, participants pressed '1' key when the presented target stimulus has a gap to the left side, while they pressed '2' key when it had a gap to the right sided.

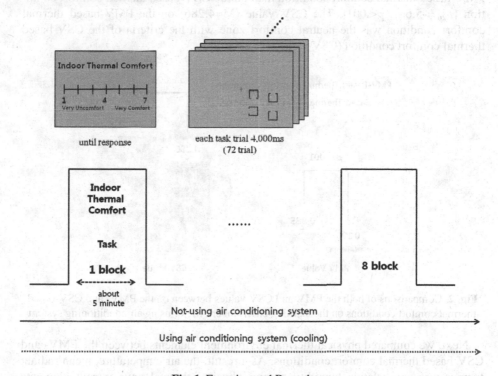

Fig. 1. Experimental Procedures

2.4   Design and Analysis

Among the data collected by participants, all block data (included physical thermal environment elements (air temperature, relative humidity, mean radiant temperature, and air velocity)) within PMV- (-0.5 < PMV value < +0.5) and CSV-based comfort condition (CSV value > 4) were extracted respectively. And then we compare the measured data of the PMV-based thermal comfort condition with those of the CSV-based thermal comfort condition used the independent sample t-test [8].

3   Results

3.1   The Learning Environment of Not-Using Air Conditioning System

First, we compared both the PMV and CSV value between the PMV- and CSV-based thermal comfort conditions. As a result, the PMV value was higher on the CSV-based thermal comfort condition than on the PMV-based thermal comfort condition [$t_{(19.08)}$=-6.176, $p<.001$]. The PMV value (M=0.88) on the CSV-based thermal comfort condition was not included a comfort zone with the criteria of the PMV-based comfort condition (-0.5 < PMV value < +0.5). And then, the CSV value was lower on the PMV-based thermal comfort condition than on the CSV-based thermal comfort condition [$t_{(26)}$=-5.667, $p<.001$]. The CSV value (M=4.286) on the PMV-based thermal comfort condition was the neutral comfort zone with the criteria of the CSV-based thermal comfort condition (CSV value = 4: neutral).

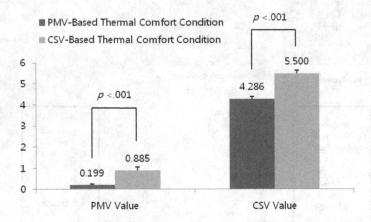

Fig. 2. Comparisons of both the PMV and CSV values between on the PMV- and CSV-based thermal comfort conditions on the learning environment of not-using air conditioning system

Next, we compared physical thermal environment elements between the PMV- and CSV based thermal comfort conditions. As a result, the air temperature, mean radiant temperature and relative humidity among physical thermal environment elements were higher on the CSV-based thermal comfort condition than on the PMV-based thermal comfort condition [air temperature: $t_{(26)}$=-6.196, $p<.001$; mean radiant temperature: $t_{(16.971)}$=-5.761, $p<.001$; relative humidity: $t_{(26)}$=-4.659, $p<.001$]. Whereas the air velocity was not significantly different between on the PMV- and CSV-based thermal comfort conditions [$t_{(20.022)}$=.483, $n.s.$].

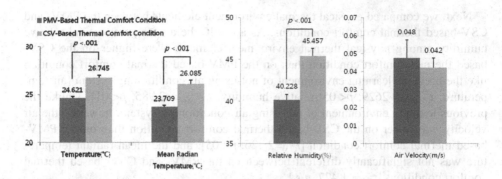

Fig. 3. Comparisons of the physical thermal environment elements between on the PMV- and CSV-based thermal comfort conditions on the learning environment of not-using air conditioning system

3.2 The Learning Environment of Using Air Conditioning System (Cooling)

First, we compared both the PMV and CSV value between the PMV- and CSV-based thermal comfort conditions. As a result, the PMV value was higher on the CSV-based thermal comfort condition than on the PMV-based thermal comfort condition [$t_{(37.460)}$=-2.734, $p<.05$]. Unlike the previous learning environment of not-using air conditioning system, however, the PMV value (M=0.43) on the CSV-based thermal comfort condition was included a comfort zone with the criteria of the PMV-based comfort condition. And then, the CSV value was lower on the PMV-based thermal comfort condition than on the CSV-based thermal comfort condition [$t_{(73)}$=-7.019, $p<.001$]. This result was same as previous learning environment of not-using air conditioning system. The CSV value (M=4.130) on the PMV-based thermal comfort condition was the neutral comfort zone with the criteria of the CSV-based thermal comfort condition.

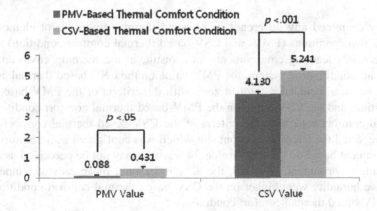

Fig. 4. Comparisons of both the PMV and CSV values between on the PMV- and CSV-based thermal comfort conditions on the learning environment of using air conditioning system (cooling)

Next, we compared physical thermal environment elements between the PMV- and CSV-based thermal comfort conditions. As a result, the air temperature and relative humidity among physical thermal environment elements were higher on the CSV-based thermal comfort condition than on the PMV-based thermal comfort condition like the previous learning environment of not-using air conditioning system [air temperature: $t_{(37.153)}$=-2629, p<.05; relative humidity: $t_{(35.467)}$=-2.985, p<.01]. Unlike the previous learning environment of not-using air conditioning system, however, the air velocity was lower on the CSV-based thermal comfort condition than on the PMV-based thermal comfort condition [$t_{(73)}$=2.426, p<.05], and the mean radiant temperature was not significantly different between on the PMV- and CSV- based thermal comfort conditions [$t_{(73)}$=-1.427, $n.s.$].

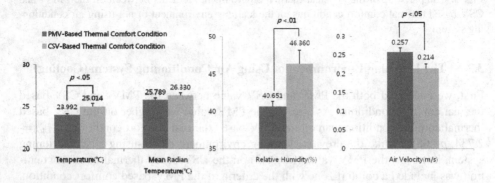

Fig. 5. Comparisons of the physical thermal environment elements between on the PMV- and CSV-based thermal comfort conditions on the learning environment of using air conditioning system (cooling)

4   Conclusion and Discussion

This study examined any difference of physical thermal environment elements according to two conditions (PMV- and CSV-based thermal comfort condition) to configure a comfort learning environment. As a result, in the learning environment of not-using air conditioning system, the PMV value on the CSV-based thermal comfort condition was not included a comfort zone with the criteria of the PMV-based comfort condition, and the CSV value on the PMV-based thermal comfort condition was the neutral comfort zone with the criteria of the CSV-based thermal comfort condition. It suggested the learning environment which was configured as a comfort learning environment based on the PMV value for learners may not be perceived as a comfort learning environment. In detail, the air temperature, mean radiant temperature, and relative humidity were higher on the CSV-based thermal comfort condition than on the PMV-based thermal comfort condition.

And then, in the cooling air conditioning environment, we examined whether the above-mentioned differences of two conditions change or not. As a result, the PMV value on the CSV-based thermal comfort condition was not included a comfort zone with the criteria of the PMV-based comfort condition, and the CSV value on the PMV-based thermal comfort condition was the neutral comfort zone with the criteria of the CSV-based thermal comfort condition. These results were the same as the above results in the learning environment of not-using air conditioning system. In detail, although there were some differences with the previous detailed results, the air temperature and relative humidity were higher on the CSV-based thermal comfort condition than on the PMV-based thermal comfort condition, and the air velocity was lower on the CSV-based thermal comfort condition than on the PMV-based thermal comfort condition. It supported the findings of Kim et al. (2011) which there is a problem to utilize the PMV value as an indoor thermal comfort indicator.

Accordingly, for configuration of a learner-centered comfort learning environment in summer, it is necessary to correct the physical thermal environment elements which control with the PMV value.

Acknowledgement. This work was supported by Priority Research Centers Program through the National Research Foundation of Korea (NRF) funded by the Ministry of Education, Science and Technology (2009-0093825) and by the Human Resources Development of the Korea Institute of Energy Technology Evaluation and Planning (KETEP) grant funded by the Korea government Ministry of Knowledge Economy (20114010203040).

References

1. Ahn, C.L., Kim, J.J., Shin, B.H., Kum, J.S.: Characteristics of thermal environment and evaluation of thermal comfort in classrooms in winter. J. Korean. Soc. Living. Environ. Sys. 10(4), 251–256 (2003)
2. Cheong, S., Sheng, N., Kim, D., Lee, J., Hwang, Y., Park, J., Seo, S.: Analysis of comfortable environment in the classroom with humidification and ventilation in winter. Korea Journal of Air-Conditioning and Refrigeration Engineering 21(7), 402–408 (2009)
3. Fanger, P.O.: Analysis and Application in Environmental Engineering: Thermal Comfort. Danish Technical Press, Copenhagen (1970)
4. ISO 7730: Ergonomics of the thermal environment: Analytical determination and interpretation of thermal comfort using calculation of the PMV and PPD indices and local thermal comfort criteria (2005)
5. Kim, B., Jeon, Y.C., Lim, D.H., Shin, J.W., Min, Y.K., Min, B.C., Kim, J.H.: Effects of indoor environmental variables on human thermal comfort sensation. The Japanese Journal of Ergonomics 47, 374–377 (2011)
6. Kim, J.H., Min, Y.K., Kim, B.: Is the PMV index an indicator of human thermal comfort sensation. International Journal of Smart Home (in press)
7. Lee, J.Y., Lee, K.H.: A study on the model setting of thermal comfort zone in elementary school classroom. Proceedings of the Architectural Institute of Korea 6(1), 279–282 (1986)
8. Min, Y.K., Kim, B.: The Basis of Scientific Data Analysis. CNU Press, Daejeon (2011)

Development of Haptic Interface for Representing Tactile Sense of Electric Shock

Tae-Sub Chung[1] and Keun-Wang Lee[2,*]

[1] Dept. of Broadcasting & Digital Media, Chungwoon University
San29, Namjang-ri, Hongsung, Chungnam 350-701, South Korea
[2] Dept. of Multimedia Science, Chungwoon University
San29, Namjang-ri, Hongsung, Chungnam 350-701, South Korea
{ggam98,kwlee}@chungwoon.ac.kr

Abstract. Because haptic technology exchanges two-way energy among users by the electrical stimulation, its unstable motion could be a harmful factor for the users. Thus, the matter of the safety is the most important concern for the movement and operation of the haptic. In this paper, we examined the electrical stimulation so that the users can make the most of more accurate, stable and safe haptic controller through the safety of the immersive simulation controller haptic and safety of electric stimulation through haptic.

Keywords: Haptic Interface, Electric Shock, Electric Power, Tactile Sense.

1 Introduction

Haptic is whole hardware, software and cognitive psychological scientific technology required to provide various information in virtual or augmented or real environment through touch [1]. Especially the word 'haptic' is also used as the meaning of all devices that can be controlled through all touches and it is the research of all methods that transfers tactile information as a study. Haptic technology has been recognized as the technology that has much potentials of development after 2006 and began to be known as a name of a mobile phone widely. It is possible to be forecasted to play the important role between new media and interface through the development of interface. If the case of current remote control is also regarded as the newly-appeared interface, haptic technology can be regarded as the technology that can be highlighted newly.

Virtual reality got to be known widely as Jaron Lanier described 'immersive visual experience produced by computer' as the work 'virtual reality (VR). It is the created thing that is most similar to real environment and means another world in computer. It is something that can experience safety education in real life or simulation by five senses through new environment especially by representing the space in real life like that. Virtual reality can be regarded as real one only if following three factors are arranged. First, sensible immersion should be accomplished into virtual space,

---

* Corresponding author.

T.-h. Kim et al. (Eds.): SIP/WSE/ICHCI 2012, CCIS 342, pp. 354–361, 2012.
© Springer-Verlag Berlin Heidelberg 2012

second, the user should be capable of sailing into virtual space, third, and the interaction should be available. And, the kind of virtual reality is divided into immersive type, projection type, augment type and desktop type.

Because haptic technology uses two-way energy exchanges among users by the electrical stimulation, its unstable motion could be a harmful factor for the users. Thus, the matter of the safety is the most important part for the movement and operation of the haptic. Thus, in this research, we focused on the response of human body against haptic electrical stimulation and the matter of the safety. Haptic technology can be largely divided into haptic mechanism, the design of actuator and haptic machine, haptic rendering that can contact and detect virtual object and calculate the contact force and the response of human body, that is, human haptics which enable to feel tactile sense or power. In this research, we studied the response of the human haptics and the development of haptic machine based on the electrical stipulation.

Haptic takes the important part in such virtual environment and the method that can feel stereo-scopic image by cognition and touch and touch by tactile sense and various methods is under research in the image through that. Currently, such researches are being studied focusing on simulator-type virtual reality. Regarding controlling method in virtual reality, it is controlled by using keyboard, mouse, haptic and joystick. Therefore, this study is willing to discuss the development of interface for the tactile sense of electric shock by applying electric shock to haptic technology that is the control device required for virtual environment and the standard of brain recognition stimulation value against electrical or physical simulation value through that.

2   Research Trends

Haptic technology is defined as three types in large [1]. First is divided into machine haptics, computer haptics and human haptics. Machine haptics means mechanical technology that deals with mechanical design and control of haptic device, and computer haptics is the calculation of tactile sense information such as contact with virtual object and power, etc. and the calculation of such information is called haptic rendering. Human haptics means the technology of psychophysical research, measuring variables and user assessment that human feels [1].

Development of haptic technology is expected in next generation of computer or personal devices. Especially, next generation of haptic technology is used through the expansion of distribution of smart phone and the development of smart devices that is not PC-based brightens the outlook of using haptic [2]. And, haptic technology can be used as the device for physically-challenged person beyond the stage of using tactile sense and it can be used in virtual game and navigation with the response through haptic in smart phone base. Haptic technology can be used in museum or exhibition hall, but it is not installed at many places due to price matter and repair matter for multiple users. But, the extension to virtual-type haptic can be the matter of time through transferring technology of tactile sense. It is because a lot haptic researchers proceed with it as the most interesting field and it has the merit that it can be processed like real user through simulation by virtual experience [3]. Especially, now that virtual medical simulation that uses haptic technology can produce each environment without operation patient or dummy and get it proficient through the reaction along that and training of operation, a lot of studies are under progress and haptic technology can be used as the method of saving cost through virtual war and training for military purpose. Haptic is being used in the researches of simulator that can practice operation technology in more delicate and realistic environment by putting corneal surgery together with spinal surgery in the United States. And, the part of representing reality by safety and intuition of driver is currently considered by attaching rotation controller in car through haptic technology. It is for raising the driving effect of changing driver or inexperienced driving by handling of the hands and operating level.

The linkage of educational simulation through haptic device should always make sure safety and accuracy. In operating haptic, the accuracy between educational simulation and the game and the haptic device should improve the immersion of the users and allow them to focus on the game at the short time through exact motion. Securing safety plays an important role in order to satisfy the five senses as well as to improve the accurate factor of information delivery at the passive motion.

3   Development of Haptic Interface for Representing Tactile Sense of Electric Shock

3.1   Composition of Simulator

Haptic interface that this study developed is the simulator for use and safety of electricity [4]. The composition of basic devices of simulator developed in this study is largely basic hardware, monitor and haptic device as shown in Fig. 1. The most important part in this study is the generation of electrical stimulation to load kinesthetic stimulation to simulator for education through haptic [5]. That is because electrical stimulation consumes less energy, the response is prompt against human body, volume gets smaller and the educate can raise learning ability of electrical safety through electrical stimulation.

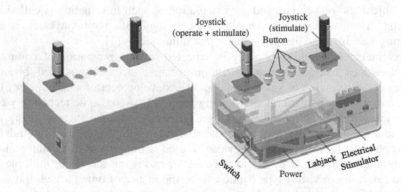

Fig. 1. Haptic production and composition for test

3.2   Development Process of Simulation

Now that haptic interface-based simulator developed in this study is the simulator for use and safety of electricity, it focused on the brief usability rather than professional contents [5]. Whole development process consists of planning & environment configuration, collection of related information, drawing up scenario, drawing up storyboard, modeling, applying program and linkage with haptic in sequential order. Adjustment is raised as the important matter through linkage with haptic that is capable of electrical simulation during development process of simulation. The standard of electrical stimulation is required absolutely through the experiment because electrical stimulation that stimulates haptic is the important part for stimulation value. Especially, when considering the users whose age group is low, strength of electrical stimulation can be raised as the important matter. So, the standard of stimulation value against safety matter and physical stimulation value through this experiment is willing to be proposed.

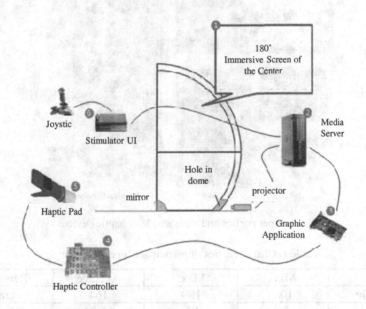

Fig. 2. System composition of a trial product

The parts which are necessary for the haptic stimulation considering the features of the electrical safety accident are composed of electrical stimulation by electrical shock, electrical impulse by the shock and vibration by the physical stimulation. We can design a haptic interface suitable for realization electrical safety accident.

3.3   Experimental Standard

This study is the proper calculation that is suitable for being used in simulator along sex, age, weight and height against electrical stimulation that is similar to stimulation of electrical impulse and stimulation of low frequency at 1~20mA in wireless way by using STI-300 targeting 66 persons whose ages are 3~39 and discomfort, degree of wake-up and degree of pain were measured by using 5-point Likert scale. It is important to let them experience the actual situation to increase learning effect, but it has the allowing limit against electrical stimulation against the situation that can threaten like electrical impulse, etc. and it took finding physically-safe critical value simulating actual situation to solve such limit as the standard. Total 66 persons that consist of 28 females (13 children & 15 adults) and 39 males (11 children & 28 adults) who have normal hearing & sight and don't have psychopathological disorder whose ages are 3~12 for child and considered as substantial beneficiary and 19~39 for adult participated in the experiment as the object of study. They are divided into child and adult each other and the average & minimum/maximum values are as Table 1.

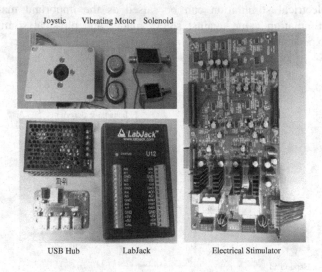

Fig. 3. Inner control and parts inside of haptic device

Table 1. Characteristics of participants in experiment

	Min.	Max.	Average	Remark
Height	104	189	164	cm
Weight	18	85	56.91	kg
Age	6	39	21.2	years old

Interferential current-type low frequency stimulator was used as the research equipment required for the experiment, it is capable of adjusting IFC mode to 2p, maximum output current to 50mA/500Ω, interferential frequency to 50Hz and current to 1~50mA and wet type and dry type were used at contact point with human body. Demographic information that can influence on current stimulation such as height, weight, age and sex were collected prior to the experiment and the stimulus of 3mA~20mA was applied for 4 seconds in wireless way to remove fatigue effect and the results were classified into three items such as discomfort, wake-up and pain by 5-point scale. In case of reporting pain in the middle, the maximum value was calculated by raising it up to maximum stimulus by themselves after finishing stimulus that is composed of pseudorandom and right palm and forearm were fixed as the stimulating points with compression bandage by wet-type 12cm for adult and 10cm for child.

The independent variables are electrical impulse(mA), child(3~13 years old), adult(19~39 years old), sex(male & female), height and weight and the dependent variables are 5-point Likert scale reported as discomfort, pain and wake-up. Analysis of variance between each independent variables and correlation between maximum values of each discomfort, pain & wake-up and mA value were analyzed by using SPSS 12.0.

4   Results of Experiment

Mean and deviation of each statistics from the experiment are as Table 2 and Fig. 4. In case of max ampere through mean and standard deviation against total 66 persons, mean 14ma of 66 persons was mean value as max ma from the implemented experiment, and mean value of discomfort, pain & wake-up divided into under 3 points (normal) and electrical stimulation did not cause much pain or inconvenience or discomfort for long time during experiment.

Table 2. Max value & mean value of total participants

Total	Height	Weight	Max ampere	Discomfort M	Pain M	Wake-up M
Mean	164.00	56.92	14.30	2.68	2.67	2.63
SD	15.47	15.60	4.80	0.80	0.68	0.88
Case	66	66	66	66	66	66
max	189	85	20	3.83	4.00	4.19
min	104	18	8	1	1	1

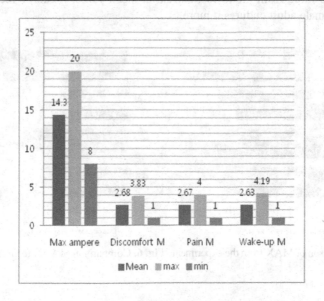

Fig. 4. Mean values of whole participants in experiment

The current of 14.3A appeared as maximum value of common current in general. But, the feel of discomfort appeared at 3.83A, pain at 4A and wake-up at 4.19A. It consists of mean value of all values of adults, children and females and the difference occurred at current value through mean value. In case of lowest value, it showed the value of 1A, but it showed the value of 8A through current value of maximum A.

When divided maximum ampere with the independent variables such as sex and age based on the mean, all were significant statistically. So, when divided it with sex (male & female) and age (child & adult), the statistics were as the same as shown in Fig. 5 and 6.

In case of child, there was no difference between sexes, but in case of adult, the interaction that generates difference between sexes happened and discomfort, pain and wake-up were low against mean stimulus and it is expected that the reverse effect of learning occurs because pain stimulus is huge if it exceeds max. In case of child, it should be adjusted according to the measure of wake-up. It means that the values of discomfort or pain should be adjusted close to maximum value. It means that the stimulus of pain is required according to the importance.

In case of male adult, the experiment was performed targeting total 27 persons. If looking at the values of this experiment, it could be recognized that the value of wake-up differed along height and weight. It showed the range of 12~20A. It can be recognized that there were big differences among discomfort, pain and wake-up along this value. And, it did not show big difference from male children regarding wake-up. It can be recognized that there was nearly no difference among male, female and child as shown in following Fig. 5 and 6.

The value that should take most attention showed the biggest difference at discomfort. In case of female adult, it can be recognized that the value is higher. If looking at the value from the lowest current at mean value, it can be recognized that the case of female adult endures it more.

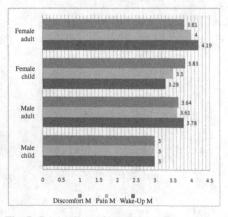
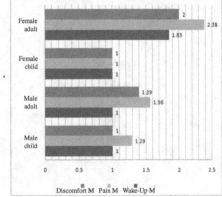

Fig. 5. Comparison of MAX from the experiment **Fig. 6.** Comparison of MIN from the experiment

Further stimulus did not make wake-up be the highest value due to burn injury, discomfort and pain. So, there was a possibility that the optimization of learning can take place because the current stimulus that the difference between the score of wake-up and negative feeling (discomfort & pain) becomes the maximum value raises wake-up and it contains less negative feeling. The selection of them needs to set the criteria regarding if actually-developing scenario of contents is strong punishment-centered or reward-centered, and the results appeared that max ampere value that minimizes physical side effect is effective in case it is strong punishment-centered and the best learning effect can appear at ampere value that negative feeling is minimized and wake-up is maximized if it is reward-centered. The standard of haptic interface technology can be arranged through that.

5   Conclusion

Haptic technology has been developing from existing vibrating haptic to something that is effective for provoking users' alert by electrical stimulation. The haptic caused electrical stimulation can maximize the stimulation of human tactile perception ability. Currently, it has passed the safety test so that all age groups can use it now. It shows that there is no significant difference of simulative electric current between adults and children. If we combine several tactile devices with accurate data through haptic technology, we can use them effectively for the various educational purposes and it would be possible to achieve accuracy in operation, high level of immersion, educational effectiveness and realistic control of the real environmental factors. The result of this research is useful enough for the educational simulations in haptic technology that needs electrical stimulation. In the further researches, we are going to study the adjustment and interaction of more educationally effective haptic through the linkage of immersive display.

Acknowledgment. This work was supported by the Power Generation and Electricity Delivery of the Korea Institute of Energy Technology Evaluation and Planning (KETEP) grant funded by the Korea government Ministry of Knowledge Economy (No. 2011T100100215).

References

1. Ryu, J., Kim, J., Seo, C., Lim, Y., Kim, J.: A survey of haptic control technology. Journal of the Korea Society of Mechanical Engineers 33(4), 283–295 (2009)
2. Massie, T.: Design of a three degree of freedom force-reflecting haptic interface. BS Thesis. MIT (1993)
3. SensAble Technologies, http://www.sensable.com
4. VR Lab. at Univ. of Tsukuba,
   http://intron.kz.tsukuba.ac.jp/index_e.html
5. CHAI3D.org, http://robot.kaist.ac.kr/haptics

Exploring the Role of Perceived Interactivity in Establishing Behavioral Intention in Micro-blog Environments

Wang Tao[1], Chul-Ho Jung[2,*], Young-Soo Chung[1], and Kang Ming-Hui[1]

[1] Dept of Business Administration, Chungnam National University, Daejeon, 305-764 Korea
{ccnuwt,kmhui66}@naver.com, ychung@cnu.ac.kr
[2] Dept. of Business Administration, Mokwon University, Daejeon, 302-729 Korea
cjung@mokwon.ac.kr

Abstract. The growing prevalence of the Web2.0 is promoting micro-blog as one of the most promising innovations in the past few years. This study develops a model aims at investigating the effects of perceived interactivity in establishing behavioral intention within micro-blog environments. We also categorized micro-blog users into extroverts and introverts to examine whether differences exist in the role of perceived interactivity in predicting behavioral intention. The results suggest that behavioral intention is determined by perceived interactivity, performance expectancy, sense of belonging, and hedonic expectancy which together provide a strong explanation. The results of this study provide directions for service providers to achieve higher levels of micro-blog usage by developing multi-faceted strategies.

Keywords: motivational model, micro-blog, interactivity, behavioral intention.

1 Introduction

Micro-blogs are widely used to expand friendship, facilitate information sharing and information seeking [3, 4, 5]. It's a new form of communication channel in which users can present their opinion in short posts distributed by instant messages, mobile phones, email limited to 140-text characters in length [4]. This issue calls for an increasing attention by researchers. Although there are a number of studies exploring the factors underlying popular micro-blogs [4, 5], none of research has been reported from the perspective of interactivity [4, 7, 9]. The research objectives of this paper are to provide a review of interactivity and investigate whether perceived interactivity can influence user's behavioral intention of micro-blog services through performance expectancy, sense of belonging and hedonic expectancy. Besides, we classified all respondents into extroverts and introverts to examine whether differences exist in the role of interactivity in predicting behavioral intention of micro-blog services.

---

* Corresponding author.

T.-h. Kim et al. (Eds.): SIP/WSE/ICHCI 2012, CCIS 342, pp. 362–368, 2012.
© Springer-Verlag Berlin Heidelberg 2012

2 Theoretical Background

2.1 Interactivity

Micro-blog is identified as an informal communication technology which comprises the feature of interactivity [4, 7]. Interactivity is a vital concept in computer-mediated communication system as it is usually considered as a major advantage of computer-mediated communication medium. Authors [4] confirmed that improved interactivity can enhance effectiveness, efficiency and enjoyment of an information technology; Authers [7] further reconfirmed authors [4]'s findings; A later study by author [8] confirmed the effects of perceived interactivity on connectedness and intentions to use IPTV services.

2.2 Motivational Model

Motivational model posits that behavior can be both extrinsically and intrinsically motivated [6, 7]. Extrinsic motivation is defined as the performance of an activity because it is perceived to be instrumental in achieving valued outcomes. Performance expectancy is a form of extrinsic motivation [2]. Intrinsic motivation refers to the fact of doing an activity for its own sake: the activity itself is fun, ideology, etc. Hedonic expectancy is described as a form of intrinsic motivation [1]. Several studies have confirmed that both intrinsic and extrinsic motives are significant outcomes of interactivity and predictors of behavioral intention [2, 6]. However, motivational theory may have limited ability to explain the mediating effects between interactivity and behavioral intention. For example, some individuals may participate in a micro-blog service, while others may not, even if their expectancies in terms of usefulness and enjoyment are similar. Specifically, this study focuses on sense of belonging as a mediation factor [9]. Sense of belonging is identified as a factor peculiar to computer mediated communication tool and visual community [9]. Users' sense of belonging to the micro-blogs also makes a significant impact on taking part in micro-blog activities.

3 Research Design

This study focused on the interactivity perception resulted from communication through micro-blogs [4, 7, 8]. This research conceptualizes variance in the perceived interactivity as being caused by changes in the levels of active control, interactive communication and synchronicity: 1) active control concerns the extent to which users are provided choices of available information, such as content, timing and sequence of a communication [4, 8]; 2) interactive communication captures the bi-directional flow of information [7, 8]; 3) synchronicity concerns with the messages received both from individuals and the computer, a key element is time [4, 8]. Author [8] examined interactivity related to purchase intention and intention to return to the website; Authors [8] tested the relationship of perceived interactivity to enjoyment, effectiveness, efficiency, they also noted that the higher the interactivity level of a web, the more

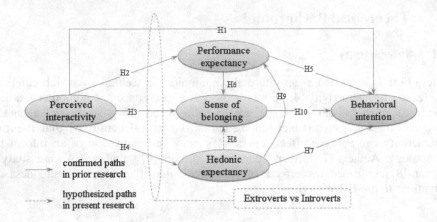

Fig. 1. Conceptual research framework

connectedness and attractive it is. Since perceived effectiveness and efficiency is similar to performance expectation, connectedness is similar to sense of belonging, and enjoyment is similar to hedonic expectation. We hypothesize that:

- Perceived Interactivity is positively related to behavioral intention, performance expectancy, sense of belonging and hedonic expectancy.

According to diffusion theory, individuals are willing to accept innovations if those innovations provide a unique advantage compared to existing solutions [1, 6, 8]. In addition, hedonic expectancy suggests a type of intrinsic value from using the IT in everyday social life [6, 7]. Hedonic expectancy was also an inseparable part of one's use of communication technologies in the social context [1]. Based on various theoretical and empirical studies about the effects of perceived usefulness and enjoyment on IT adoption intention [1, 7], this paper hypothesizes:

- Performance & hedonic expectancy is positively related to behavioral intention.

Hedonic expectancy is argued to increase the deliberation and thoroughness of cognitive processing and lead to enhanced perceptions of an extrinsic motivation variable [1, 6]. Authors [6] confirmed that the pleasure and enjoyment derived from using IM positively affected an individual's perception of the usefulness in supporting the interaction process. Thus, this research hypothesizes:

- Hedonic expectancy is positively related to performance expectancy.

A high sense of belonging is expected to lead to greater intention to be further involved in the community [9]. So in order to make the member to visit the site, the members' sense of belonging should be established. Thus we hypothesize:

- Sense of belonging is positively related to behavioral intention.

The effect of usefulness on sense of belonging has been confirmed in previous studies [9], although the effect of hedonic expectancy on sense of belonging has not been supported in previous studies, it's our belief that hedonic expectancy should also enhance sense of belonging because an enjoyable experience would enhance one's interest in the activities of the virtual community. Thus, the sense of belonging can be built up through the usefulness and hedonic of a technology.

- Performance & hedonic expectancy is positively related to sense of belonging.

4   Hypothesis Testing and Data Analysis

4.1   Survey Procedure and Measurement Model Validation

A Total of 620 questionnaires were distributed in the survey between March-June, 2012. The survey was conducted through the mail, personal visits to people who were working in diverse industries and social institutions that were drawn at random in the city of Fuzhou, Wuhan and Xi'an of China. Altogether, 338 questionnaires were collected. After reviewing, 42 questionnaires were eliminated due to invalid answers, leaving 296 questionnaires for the empirical analysis. Our sample comprised 43.2% male and 56.8% female respondents. In terms of age, A majority of 45.3% respondents are between 20 and 29 years old.

Both of validity and reliability were determined to evaluate the measurement model. The Cronbach's α value of each construct in our research model is over 0.7, which represents good reliability. The variables in this study were derived from existing literature, thus exhibiting strong content validity. The CFA results indicated that all the factor loadings for all items exceed the acceptable level of 0.6, and all factor loadings are significantly related, via t-tests at $p<0.001$, to their respective constructs, thus exhibiting convergent validity. The composite reliability of the constructs ranged from 0.77 to 0.86, and thus all exceeded the generally accepted value of 0.70. In addition, the AVE ranged from 0.53 to 0.67. Hence, all three conditions for convergent validity were met. The shared variance between each pair of constructs was less than the average variances extracted, providing evidence of discriminant validity.

4.2   Test of Structural Model for All Respondents

Most of the paths are significant in the expected directions. Exceptions are two paths connecting perceived interactivity with sense of belonging as well as path connecting performance expectancy with hedonic expectancy. The effects of perceived interactivity on performance expectancy, hedonic expectancy and behavioral intention are significant ($\beta_{PI-BI}=0.322$, $t=3.712$, $p<0.001$; $\beta_{PI-PE}=0.336$, $t=4.224$, $p<0.001$ and $\beta_{PI-HE}=0.187$, $t=1.034$, $p<0.005$). These results indicate that when users perceive micro-blog to be interactive, they will be more likely to form favorable beliefs of usefulness and enjoyment and will adopt micro-blog services

In contrast, the effects of perceived interactivity on sense of belonging is non-significant ($\beta_{PI-SB}=0.134$, $t=2.321$, $p=0.063$). Since micro-blog is a new emerging technology, not all of users have experiences of taking full advantage of interactivity, some of them are purely passive receiver of information. Thus, a sense of belonging can only be formed indirectly by an enhanced interactivity through performance or hedonic expectancy.

In addition, performance expectancy has substantial effects on behavioral intention and sense of belonging (β_{PE-BI}=0.358, t=4.756, p<0.001; β_{PE-SB}=0.415, t=5.078, p<0.001). The results indicate that when individuals perceive the service to be useful, they are more likely to form a sense of belonging. This research also confirmed that hedonic expectancy has a substantial effect on sense of belonging (β_{HE-SB}=0.386, t=4.465, p<0.005), while has no influence on performance expectancy (β_{HE-PB}=0.086, t=1.042, p=0.241). The results indicate that individuals' perception of usefulness will not be enhanced no matter how they perceive the service to be interesting. A possible explanation may be that the chief aim of micro-blogs in not to generate enjoyment or playfulness, micro-blogs are mainly employed as an effective tool to expand friendship, facilitate information sharing and seeking. Finally, the impacts of hedonic expectancy and sense of belonging are positively associated (β_{HE-BI}= 0.299, t=4.302, p<0.001; β_{SB-BI}= 0.318, t=4.374, p<0.001) with behavioral intention. This is an important finding because sense of belonging is not an original construct in IS adoption model and thus is often not considered.

4.3   Separate Tests of Structural Model for Extroverts and Introverts

In this paper, we conducted an analysis between extroverted and introverted respondents based on their responses to the questionnaire items. The results of our classifications showed that a majority of 59.4% respondents considered themselves as extroverts while 40.6% referred themselves as introverts.

Table 1. The classification of extroverts and introverts

Questionnaire items	Type
I'm motivated from "without" and my attention is directed outward. When I feel low in energy, or stressed, I'm likely to look outside myself for relief.	Extroverts
I'm motivated from "within" and I'm oriented towards the inner world of ideas, reflection. When I'm tired or stressed, I'm likely to engage in reflective activity.	Introverts

The separate results of hypothesis testing also generated highly consistent results with the results for the all respondents. Exception is a relationship between interactivity and hedonic expectancy. This difference is most likely observed because interactivity is mainly perceived by extroverts through their interpersonal behaviors via micro-blogs such as interactive communication, discussion and so on, while interactivity is mainly perceived by introverts through the human-to-computer interaction via micro-blog services.

5   Implications and Limitations

This study makes several contributions to the research literature. This study is among the first to test empirically the role of perceived interactivity on behavioral intentions in the context of micro-blog services. We confirmed the significant effects of perceived interactivity on performance, hedonic expectancy, sense of belonging and behavioral intention. The findings contribute to theoretical development of interactivity and behavior formation regarding IT adoption in the context of micro-blogs. From the perspective of theory advancement, this study contributes to the Motivational model by adding sense of belonging into the model. The empirical findings demonstrate that employing sense of belonging construct would be a worthwhile extension in the micro-blog context.

Inspired by these findings, service providers can increase the adoption of micro-blogs by providing more interactive functions. Specifically, service providers should make full use of the rich media capability of the Internet to include pictures, videos and vote and etc. in a micro-blog service to facilitate user experience. Service providers should provide more intuitive functions in their micro-blog products, they can build a search window on the webpage through which users can easily find the people they want to follow or the information they want to see. Individuals may be inherently motivated to feel connected to communities or others within a virtual environment. Creating a virtual community such as microgroup is therefore likely to improve motivation towards using micro-blog services. In addition, they can facilitate interactivity by adding intuitive communication tools, feedback spaces or enhancing the responsiveness of information, such efforts can help enhance user's perceived interactivity.

This study has several inherent limitations due to the sampling methods and measurement instruments used. First, a convenience sampling method was used to select the sample. There is no evidence that the sample is representative of the whole population of Chinese micro-blog users. Future studies should investigate and compare different samples to increase representativeness. Second, the survey data used in this research were gathered at a single time point and the survey process was not longitudinal. A longitudinal investigation would be more convincing in explaining how user adoption behavior changes over time.

References

1. Agrifoglio, R., Black, S., Metallo, C.: Twitter Acceptance: The Role of Intrinsic Motivation. In: Proceedings of ALPIS itAIS, vol. 10, pp. 2–5 (2010)
2. Davis, F.D., Bagozzi, R.P., Warshaw, P.R.: Extrinsic and Intrinsic Motivation to Use Computers in the Workplace. Journal of Applied Social Psychology 22, 1111–1132 (1992)
3. Ebner, M., Lienhardt, C., Rohs, M., Meyer, I.: Microblogs in Higher Education - A Chance to Facilitate Informal and Process-oriented Learning. Computers & Education 55, 92–100 (2010)

4. Gerlach, L., Hauptmann, S.: Microblogging as s Tool for Networked Learning in Production Networks. In: Proceedings of the 7th International Conference on Networked Learning, pp. 176–182 (2010)
5. Hughes, A., Palen, L.: Twitter Adoption and Use in Mass Convergence and Emergency Events. In: Proceedings of the 6th International ISCRAM Conference, Gothenburg (2009)
6. Lin, K.Y., Lu, H.P.: Why People Use Social Networking Sites: An Empirical Study Integrating Network Externalities and Motivation Theory. Computers in Human Behavior 27, 1152–1161 (2011)
7. Ryan, R.M., Deci, E.L.: Self-determination Theory and the Facilitation of Intrinsic Motivation, Social Development, and Well-being. American Psychologist 55, 68–78 (2000)
8. Shin, D.H.: An Empirical Investigation of a Modified Technology Acceptance Model of IPTV. Behaviour & Information Technology 28, 361–372 (2010)
9. Teo, H.H., Chan, H.C., Wei, K.K.: Evaluating Information Accessibility and Community Adaptivity Features for Sustaining Virtual Learning Communities. International Journal of Human-Computer Studies 59, 671–697 (2003)

Embodied Cognition, Human Computer Interaction, and Application Areas

Anant Bhaskar Garg

Centre for Information Technology
University of Petroleum & Energy Studies, Dehradun
anantgg@yahoo.com

Abstract. The paper intends to discuss two main approaches (symbolic and connectionist) to study cognition as prevalent in cognitive science. But as we live in the world, environment and interaction with others play an important role. This thinking leads to theories of embodied and situated cognition, where cognition is seen as taking place not only in the brain, but also in interaction with the world supported by the body. This paradigm finds applications in various research projects notably robotics, autonomous agents, and interactive interfaces. These research directions will also be central for developments in Human Computer Interaction (HCI). Better interaction between human and computer, enhance our capacities or augment cognition as facilitated by technology. Finally, the paper would attempt to explore methods to analyze the relation between brain and action such as neuro-ethology, robotics, and computer simulation approach to model the behavior of interacting agents.

Keywords: Embodied Cognition, Interfaces, Agents, Cognitive Style, Situated Cognition, environment interaction.

1 Introduction

The development of computers also gives rise to a new model for human thinking. The cognitive science initially was driven by the analogy that the brain functions like a computer that result in thinking which is popularly known as symbols processing and manipulation. All meaning arose via correspondences between symbols (words, mental representations) and things in the external world. The mind was seen as a mirror of nature, and human thought as abstract and disembodied. Another paradigm is parallel distributed processing approach and connectionism, where thinking is modeled as associations in artificial neuron networks. Some connectionist models are directly based on the developments in the neuroscience, while others are more general models of cognitive processes such as concept formation. The computational aspect of cognitive science explores understanding, hypotheses, and axioms of the nature and limits our cognitive and information processing system, as well as to emphasize principles for designing effective systems to support individuals, groups, and organizations. But intelligent behavior is not just symbolic manipulation and deductive reasoning, but also interaction with others. This requires awareness of the relationship

T.-h. Kim et al. (Eds.): SIP/WSE/ICHCI 2012, CCIS 342, pp. 369–374, 2012.

with the world, physical coordination, intelligent action, creativity, and other affective behavior responses. Everyday human intelligence includes all of above states and many more that we can understand through embodied and situated cognition – which is emerging as an alternative paradigm in cognitive science.

2   Situated and Embodied Cognition

This paradigm finds applications in various research projects and areas, notably are modern studies of robotics, autonomous agents, and interactive interfaces. The situated view on cognition is linked to distributed and augmented cognition approaches. These research directions stress on enhancing the limits of information processing capacities of human and machine. In this regard, present research explores the complex work environment to study the cognition that may result in computational model of particular task or some general framework for information handling. How do we explore mental processes and physical embodiment together? Situatedness and embodiment have become important concepts in practically all areas of cognitive science since the late 80s. Many researchers have emphasized the importance of studying cognition in the context of agent-environment interaction and sensorimotor activity [1], [2], [3], [4], [5], [6], [7], [8], [9], [10], [11], [12]. The viewpoint known as embodied or situated cognition treats cognition as an activity that is structured by the body and its situatedness in its environment - which result in an embodied action. In this view, cognition is due to experiences through a body with sensorimotor capacities. These capacities are embedded in an encompassing biological, psychological, and cultural context.

Perception is understood as perceptually guided action. Such behavior is facilitated through elaborate feedback mechanisms among sensory and motor apparatus as shown in figure 1. Hence, cognitive structures emerge from the recurrent sensorimotor patterns that enable the perceiver to guide his or her actions in the local situation. That is, the emergent reinforced neural connections between the senses and the motor system form the basis for cognition. The mind's embodiment provides natural biases for inductive models and representations, and thus automatically ground cognitive processes that might normally be considered disembodied. This view provides a sharp contrast from the standard information-processing viewpoint, in which cognition is seen as a problem of recovering details of the pre-given outer world [6].

In this light, the mind is no longer seen as passively reflecting the outside world, but rather as an active constructor of its own reality. In this perspective, the fundamental building blocks of cognitive processes are control schemata for motor patterns that arise from perceptual interaction with the body's environment. The motivation for the cognitive system for such interaction comes from within the system in the form of needs and goals. This can also be linked to an organization. We can make more sense of our brains and bodies if we view the nervous system as a system for producing motor output. The cerebellum is connected almost directly to all areas of the brain - sensory transmissions, reticular (arousal/attention) systems, hippocampus (episodic memories), limbic system (emotions, behavior). It is largely accepted in AI that embodiment has strong implications on the control strategies for generating purposive and intelligent behavior in the world.

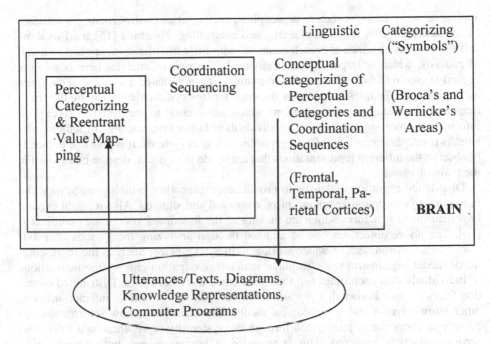

Fig. 1. Situated action view of sensorimotor coordination. The nesting of boxes explain how "reentrancy" or feedforward aspect of past organizations (categories and sequential coordinations of multimodal sensory and motor systems) biases the present, ongoing activation [adapted from [13].

Cognition as described in practice was found to be not at all in the same realm as cognition in an abstract, unsituated setting of first two paradigms in cognitive science. Similarly, Clark discusses the ambiguity of the boundary between "mind" and "world," along the lines of a distinction between "user" and "tool." When a bird drops a nut from a great height to crack it open, does the ground become a tool? [1] Rather, the bird is exploiting an aspect of its environment to extend its physical capabilities; the concept of a tool dissolves. In tune with this, Brian Smith's explanation of registration of various activities by a Frog through connect and disconnect activities also shows dissolving of boundaries [14]. He provides a different explanation for the notion of representation. In this regard, Brooks works on behaviour based robotics is crucial [2]. In sum, the theory of embodiness encompasses both neuropsychological and socio-environmental views of cognition. Embodied cognition stresses physical, temporal, and functional situatedness, and enforces interaction between the agent's body and its environment.

3   Research Directions in Embodied Cognition

In this regard, the present work will explore the different studies undertaken to know about cognition and cognitive capacities in terms of memory, leaning, and attention. This approach is also known as distributed cognition and we can relate it to the "Augmented Cognition" project of DARPA. Further, it discusses the computational models to explain the sensory system. Finally, it discusses work on "Cognitive Interfaces" applied to many domains such as power plant, nuclear plant control room, car interfaces for better decision making, planning and controlling. Hutchins [15] tried to show that the cognitive science approach could be, with little modification, applied to a unit of analysis, which is larger than an individual. The unit of analysis here is a larger cognitive (socio-technical) system, for example, an automated industrial setting and airline cockpit. The question remains the same for this system also: what are the structures and processing of representations which are internal to the system? To explain information-processing properties of individuals or larger systems, it is difficult to infer what is inside their mind. But for larger socio-technical systems, it is possible to directly observe the different representations that are inside the system, despite being outside the brain of agents.

Distributed cognition endeavor to provide an explanation, which goes beyond the individual to conceptualize cognition as, embodied and situated. Also it might explain how distributed structures which are making up the functional system are coordinated [16]. The above objectives can be attained through analyzing the various contributions of the environment in which work activities take place. Such as the representational media (e.g. instruments, displays, manuals, navigation charts), the interactions of individuals with each other and their interactive use of artifacts. Distributed cognition focus on how knowledge is transmitted between agents and its interactions with other human agents and technological media. Simultaneously, how information necessary to cooperate is propagated through the system by representational states and across artifacts is analyzed. This is regarded as computational, but concepts from other social sciences are borrowed to explain socially distributed cognitive phenomenon, such as organizational learning. At the brain level of analysis, interactions between different processing units at the neural level are important [17]. Another approach to understand the way cognitive leaning is implemented in the brain is interactivist-constructivist (I-C) approach to modeling intelligence and learning as a dynamical embodied form of adaptiveness [18].

Besides this, study of basic cognitive style (the characteristic ways in which individuals conceptually organize or structure the environment) helps in identifying the filtering and processing mechanisms of information of individuals. This in turn helps to know how we give psychological meaning to things. In other words, cognitive style acts as a mediator structure that modifies the relationships between stimulus and response. Moreover, differences among people may effect the optimum design and usability of human-computer interfaces [19]. This knowledge imparts the understanding of basic information processing strategies that people employ in their interaction with the artifacts (computer systems). Further, by analyzing the cognitive processing in terms of information processing, visualization in multimodal way and cognitive load we can enhance human capacities and learning. The distribution cognition theory identifies a set of core principles that widely apply to study such diverse situation and environment [20].

4   Embodied Cognition, HCI, and Application Areas

4.1   Educational and Online System

Web-based Educational Systems (WBES) that are intelligent and adaptive to satisfy the learner's state of understanding are now under development. In this regards, concept based or ontology oriented models are promising methods in the development of such systems. Conceptual structures based model assist learner in retrieving, evaluating, and comprehending information through the use of semantic associations (maps). This helps in knowing, how we discover and learn regularities in the environment from the consequences of our actions. How information, communication and technologies (ICT) can best be used for effective and efficient transmission of information to all irrespective of socio-cultural background and abilities [21].

4.2   Cognitive Design and Robotics

In the research we aim at understanding the cognition underlying human interactions with artifacts, and applying that knowledge for the improvement of design of both artifacts and work situations [22]. Research is currently being carried out on a number of ways of adapting technology, computer interfaces tailored to individual differences in cognitive style, educational uses of technology, design that reduces error, design that enhance cognitive capacities, and navigation of robots in real environment.

4.3   Autonomous Agents

An autonomous agent can be seen as a system capable of interacting independently and effectively with its environment via its own sensors and effectors in order to accomplish some given or self-generated tasks. Therefore, in various situations autonomous agents can be used to study the phenomenon that will improve the know-how of the dynamics of real problem [23].

4.4   Cognitive Interfaces

By analyzing work settings with the help of cognitive work analysis and human work interaction design approaches we can improve the design of user interfaces. For example, in power plant control room by studying the context of human system interactions, work and task analysis interfaces are improved using ecological interface design principles [24]. This approach helps in reducing cognitive workload on operator which can result in reduction in errors in managing the control room of the power plant. Another example is to improve car interfaces using the above approach which lessen the amount of short term memory required.

5   Conclusion

How we could design machines so that they help human in every aspect and they act as efficient and effective assistants. This problem is not simply programming but it involves cognition, our spatio-temporal movements, and our awareness of the environment in which we work. Therefore this problem includes representation of the world and relation with the world. This understanding of the interaction especially between human, objects (artifacts) helps in enhancing knowledge base about the objects, properties, and their relations between themselves and with the world.

References

1. Clark, A.: Being There: Putting Brain, Body and World Together Again. MIT Press, Cambridge (1997)
2. Brooks, A.R.: Intelligence Without Representation. Artificial Intelligence Journal (47), 139–159 (1991)
3. Brooks, A.R.: Building Brains for Bodies. Autonomous Robots 1(1), 7–25 (1994)
4. Rutkowska, J.C.: An Infant's-Eye View of Adaptive Behaviour and Change in Situated Embodied Systems (1992)
5. Rutkowska, J.C.: Can Development Be Designed? What We Learn from the Cog Project. In: ECAL, pp. 383–395 (1995)
6. Varela, F.J., Thompson, E., Rosch, E.: The Embodied Mind. MIT Press, Cambridge (1992)
7. Dennett, D.C.: Consciousness in Human and Robot Minds. In: Ito, M., Miyashita, Y., Rolls, E.T. (eds.) Cognition, Computation, and Consciousness, pp. 17–29. Oxford University Press, New York (1997)
8. Damasio, A.R.: Descartes' Error: Emotion, Reason, and the Human Brain. Putnam (1995)
9. Damasio, A.R.: The Feeling of What Happens: Body and Emotion in the Making of Consciousness. Harcourt (1999)
10. Dautenhahn, K.: Embodiment in Animals and Artifacts. In: AAAI Symposium on Embodied Action and Cognition. AAAI Press (1996)
11. Dautenhahn, K.: Embodiment and Interaction in Socially Intelligent Life-Like Agents. In: Nehaniv, C.L. (ed.) CMAA 1998. LNCS (LNAI), vol. 1562, pp. 102–142. Springer, Heidelberg (1999)
12. Lakoff, G., Nunez, R.: Where Mathematics Comes From: How the Embodied Mind Brings Mathematics into Being. Basic Books, New York (2001)
13. Clancey, W.J.: Situated Action: A Neuropsychological Interpretation Response to Vera and Simon. Cognitive Science 17, 87–117 (1993)
14. Smith, B.C.: On the Origin of Objects. MIT Press, Cambridge (1996)
15. Hutchins, E.: Cognition in the Wild. MIT Press (1995)
16. Rogers, Y., Ellis, J.: Distributed Cognition: an alternative framework for analysing and explaining collaborative working. Journal of Information Technology 9(2), 119–128 (1994)
17. Scaife, M., Rogers, Y.: How do graphical representations work? International Journal of Human-Computer Studies (1996)
18. Christensen, W.D., Hooker, C.A.: An Interactivist-Constructivist Approach to Intelligence: Self-Directed Anticipative Learning. Philosophical Psychology 13(1), 5–45 (2000)
19. Ambardar, A.: Human-Computer Interaction and Individual Differences. In: Singh, I., Parasuraman, R. (eds.) Human Cognition: A Multidisciplinary Perspective. Sage Publications, New Delhi (1998)
20. Hollan, J., Hutchins, E., Kirsh, D.: Distributed Cognition: Toward a New Foundation for Human-Computer Interaction Research. In: Carroll, J.M. (ed.) Human-Computer Interaction: In the New Millennium. Pearson Education Asia, New Delhi (2002)
21. Clancey, W.J.: Representations of Knowing: In defense of Cognitive Apprenticeship. Journal of Artificial Intelligence in Education 3(2), 139–168 (1992)
22. Garg, A.B.: Can Vision Provide Answers to Consciousness. In: International Conf. on Theoretical Neurobiology, National Brain Research Centre, Manesar, Haryana, February 24-26 (2003)
23. Jonker, D., Catholijn, M., Jan, T.: Agent-Based Analysis of Dynamics in Biological. In: Cognitive and Organisational Domains, tutorial at AAMAS 2002, Bologna (2002)
24. Garg, A.B.: Design of Information System Interfaces: Using Human Computer Interaction and Cognitive System Engineering Paradigm. In: 2nd Uttarakhand Science Congress, Nainital, November 15-17 (2007)

Author Index